DATE DUE

DEMCO 38-296

In a comparative and historical study of the interplay between democratic politics and authoritarian states in post-colonial South Asia, Ayesha Jalal explains how a common British colonial legacy led to apparently contrasting patterns of political development – democracy in India and military authoritarianism in Pakistan and Bangladesh. The analysis shows how, despite differences in form, central political authority in each state came to confront broadly comparable threats from regional and linguistic dissidence, religious and sectarian strife, as well as class and caste conflicts. By comparing and contrasting state structures and political processes, the author evaluates and redefines democracy, citizenship, sovereignty and the nation-state, arguing for a more decentralized governmental structure better able to arbitrate between ethnic and regional movements. This original and provocative study will challenge students and scholars in the field to rethink traditional concepts of democracy and authoritarianism in South Asia.

Contemporary South Asia

Democracy and authoritarianism in South Asia

Contemporary South Asia 1

Contemporary South Asia has been established to publish books on the politics, society and culture of South Asia since 1947. In accessible and comprehensive studies, authors who are already engaged in researching specific aspects of South Asian society explore a wide variety of broad-ranging and topical themes. The series will be of interest to anyone who is concerned with the study of South Asia and with the legacy of its colonial past.

Democracy and authoritarianism in South Asia

A comparative and historical perspective

Ayesha Jalal

Columbia University

CAMBRIDGE
UNIVERSITY PRESS

Published by the Press Syndicate of the University of Cambridge
The Pitt Building, Trumpington Street, Cambridge CB2 IRP
40 West 20th Street, New York, NY 10011-4211, USA
10 Stamford Road, Oakleigh, Melbourne 3166, Australia

                                        versity Press, Cambridge

                                  ailable from the British Library

                                  ublication data

                                n South Asia: a comparative and historical per-
spective / Ayesha Jalal.
    p.   cm. – (Cambridge South Asian studies.)
Includes bibliographical references.
ISBN 0 521 47271 7 (HC). – ISBN 0 521 47862 6 (PB)
1. South Asia – Politics and government. I. Title. II. Series.
DS341.J34 1995
320.954–dc20 94-17045 CIP

ISBN 0 521 47271 7 hardback
ISBN 0 521 47862 6 paperback

CE

Contents

Maps

Map 1 is based on Joseph E. Schwartzberg (ed.), *A Historical Atlas of South Asia* (Chicago and London, 1978), p. 76.

Preface

This volume has taken shape during my sojourns at various academic institutions in the United States since 1987, all of which share the credits in different measure. Intellectually it forms a bridge between my earlier monographs and current research on multiple identities and theories of sovereignty in South Asia. The inspiration for it was provided by my students at Wisconsin-Madison, Tufts and, above all, Columbia and it is largely for them that I decided to undertake a work of this level of generality and, hopefully, accessibility.

While teaching South Asian politics at the University of Wisconsin-Madison, I was struck by the absence of any historical and comparative analysis of states and political processes in India, Pakistan and Bangladesh. The arbitrary lines drawn at the time of India's partition in 1947 – the subject of my doctoral research – appeared to have become a mental barrier to a comparative and thematic treatment of post-independence developments in the subcontinent. After completing a study of the first decade of Pakistan's independence, I turned to culling material on post-independence India available in British and American archives. The findings convinced me that the immediate post-independence period in both countries was not only comparable but a key to understanding the divergences in their post-independence history. After the 'transition' to democracy in Pakistan and Bangladesh, any comparative exercise had to try and explain why political, social and economic developments in the subcontinent were apparently showing signs of converging. With the chronological scope of the project defined, I set about tackling the main conceptual and contextual issues.

Between 1988 and 1990 a research fellowship at the Harvard Academy for International and Area Studies gave me an opportunity to flesh out my conceptual approach and conduct further research on India, Pakistan and Bangladesh. I am grateful to the senior scholars at the Harvard Academy for their enthusiastic support of my project. During 1990–1 I was able to test my arguments with a group of students at Tufts University. Since joining Columbia in 1991 I have benefited enormously from the engaging and stimulating questions asked by students, both graduate and undergraduate, taking my course on South Asia in the Twentieth Century. I owe them a debt which many of them may not have seen reflected in their final grades. This book is a tribute to their diligence and tireless efforts to keep up with the extensive readings and my demanding lectures.

I have gained much from exchanges with a number of colleagues and friends. One individual who deserves a very special mention for her friendship and support is the late Professor Barbara Stoler Miller. A leading scholar of Sanskrit, Barbara Miller took a keen interest in contemporary developments in the region. She had a vision of the field rare among scholars of South Asia. I dearly cherish our conversations during the summer of 1992, Barbara's last with us, when I was writing the manuscript for publication.

Over the years, Professor Chris Bayly of Cambridge University and Dr David Washbrook of Oxford University offered me many constructive comments which have helped clarify and improve the argument. Dharma Kumar's trenchant criticisms came as an unexpected bonus, particularly since she disagreed with the general drift of the analysis while at the same time conceding its importance. I have also received much encouragement from Professor Amartya Sen at Harvard University and Emma Rothschild at Cambridge University. Many colleagues at Columbia have responded approvingly to aspects of my central argument. I would like to thank Marigold Acland of the Cambridge University Press for her efforts in preparing the groundwork for the publication of this book.

My family as ever has offered me unflagging support. Without the sensitivity and understanding of my mother, whose confidence in me is a constant source of reassurance, it would be difficult to justify bearing the burdens of an academic career. Friends in London, New York and Lahore have been indulgent of my scholarly pursuits while reminding me of the lighter side of things. At Columbia a challenging group of graduate students, including Ritu Birla, Farhad Karim, Farina Mir, Mridu Rai and Shabnum Tejani, have kept me intellectually alert and in good humour.

Sugata Bose has seen this work from its very inception to the end. If not for his firm conviction in the pressing need for a study of this nature, this book may never have materialized. He has scrutinized the manuscript at different stages and made invaluable suggestions. I am indebted to him for spurring me on with probing questions, being gracious enough to lose more than an occasional debate and helping restore morale when pessimism began outstripping plausibility.

Throughout the years of research and writing, an array of people, young and old, from different walks of life have expressed an interest in the project. It has been gratifying to know that I am not alone in believing that the prospects for a better South Asia lie in scholars and students shunning

the insular agendas of the nation-state and exploring the myriad inter-
linkages and common dilemmas that bind subcontinental states and societies long after the chilling blow of the partitioners' axe. If the results of the
endeavour fail to warm many hearts, the blame is entirely my own.

Columbia University   AYESHA JALAL

Introduction

Among the more fascinating themes in contemporary South Asia has been the 'success' of democracy in India and its 'failure' in neighbouring Pakistan and Bangladesh. Yet studies of democratic politics in India and military dominated authoritarian states in Pakistan and Bangladesh have rarely addressed, far less explained, why a common British colonial legacy led to apparently contrasting patterns of political development in post-independence South Asia. The lacuna in the literature is surprising given the oft-heard scholarly laments about the artificial demarcation of the subcontinent's political frontiers at the time of the British withdrawal. Many historians are coming to question the inclusionary and exclusionary claims of both Indian and Muslim nationalisms and, more guardedly, the appropriateness of the concept of the 'nation-state' in subcontinental conditions. The spatial and temporal artifact that has been the modern nation-state in post-1947 South Asia nevertheless remains inextricably stitched on to the scholarly canvas.

Analyses premised on historical disjunctions, even when acknowledged as arbitrary, tend to emphasize differences rather more than similarities. The loss of a subcontinental vision has not only compartmentalized South Asian historiography but deflected from any sort of comparative understanding of the common dilemmas of the region's present and the interlocking trajectories of its future. While most historians see the dividing line of 1947 as the outer periphery of their scholarly terrain, politicial scientists take it as an obvious point of entry from where to begin analysing the state–society nexus in India, Pakistan or Bangladesh. But the writing of a history of post-colonial South Asian states and polities cannot await the opening of official secrets stored away in ministerial and archival buildings. The orthodoxies of the political science discipline on the other hand have demanded a high degree of conceptualization in attempts to make the inimitable complexities and specificities of the region easily accessible. Yet a conceptualization of contemporary South Asia cannot be so transfigured by ideas of nationalism, the nation-state and territorial sovereignty as to obscure a five-millennia-old history in which processes of social and cultural fusions vied with and frequently overlaid those of political fissions.

This study straddles the realm of the empirical and the conceptual in an attempt to bridge the gap between the domains of the historian and the political scientist. An interpretative synthesis, it seeks to historicize and conceptualize the defining moment of partition as it has impinged upon and moulded the course of political, economic and social developments in the states which replaced the British raj in the subcontinent. Instead of being a point of departure for ferreting out the 'national' histories of India, Pakistan and, after 1971, Bangladesh, partition and the colonial legacy of which it was a product are key ingredients in the enterprise of comparing and contrasting states and societies in the region. A comparative analysis of the processes of state construction, consolidation as well as the imperative of and resistance to their reconstitution in post-colonial India, Pakistan and Bangladesh is a long overdue exercise. It promises to provide a welter of insights into as well as restore a better balance of perspective on the distinctive and common features of the socio-economic and political problems currently facing South Asian states and societies.

The closing decades of the twentieth century have seen central political authority in each state grappling uncertainly with regional and linguistic dissidence, religious and sectarian strife, class and caste conflicts and a bewildering permutation and combination of all of these. Many of these expressions of discontent are traceable to the pre-independence period, underscoring the lack of convergence between social identities and the frontiers of the post-1947 modern state. Though not unique to South Asia, the assertion of distinctive identities by variously defined social groupings has come to pose the biggest challenge to the dominant idioms deployed to sustain and legitimize post-colonial state structures in the subcontinent. In certain regions where clashes between dissenting social currents and state authority are especially acute, a key defining feature of the modern state has been seriously undermined – its monopoly over the instruments of coercion. With identities spilling across porous frontiers, the acquisition of sophisticated weapons technologies by disgruntled segments of civil society are resulting in stronger linkages between domestic dilemmas and international tensions than ever before.

These developments make the need for a comparative framework capable of analytically breaching exclusive interpretations of modern states and politics in the subcontinent more urgent than ever. The recurrence of the twin dialectics of centralism and regionalism as well as nationalism and religious communalism in the pre- and post-independence eras can help restore a subcontinental perspective. Insofar as the modern 'nation-state' has played a decisive role in shaping these dialectics in the post-colonial era, its structural and ideational postures must necessarily inform the contours of any comparative framework. In other words, the comparative approach cannot dispense with the construct of the modern nation-state at the analytical level if there is to be a systematic critique of its defining idioms or the structural mechanisms of its relations with diverse social groupings differentiated along regional, linguistic, caste, class and religious lines.

The principal concern of this study, the interplay between democratic politics and authoritarian states, lends itself well to comparative analysis. Given the loose and varied meanings attached to 'democracy' and 'authoritarianism', leaving them undefined might be analytically imprudent and invite a wail of misconstrued readings of the argument. An analytical distinction between a formal and substantive democracy, as well as overt and covert authoritarianism is intended to avoid conflating the empirical and normative aspects of two very broad terms deployed for purposes of historical interpretation. A formal democracy is a genuine democracy insofar as it guarantees, among other things, the right to vote and the freedom of expression. Yet it may not evince all the features of its normative ideal, thus the notion of a substantive democracy. A compound of its formal and substantive meanings, democracy here refers to more than the exercise of citizens' voting rights in elections or even the right to free speech. Though an important feature of democratic processes, elections are only the political manifestation of democratization in the wider social sphere. Democratization's normative or substantive appeal derives from the empowerment of the people, not as abstract legal citizens but as concrete and active agents capable of pursuing their interests with a measure of autonomy from entrenched structures of dominance and privilege. Insofar as dominance underpins any social formation, democratization entails the capacity to resist and renegotiate relations of power and privilege. Authoritarianism is defined as organized power embedded in the institutional structure of the state. It is seen as distinguishable, though not insulated, from the myriad structures of dominance lining the larger body politic. So while an element of covert authoritarianism inheres in any state structure, the degree of its overt manifestation is contingent upon the existence or the absence of formal, much less substantive, democracy.

Far from representing a neat and sharp dichotomy, democracy and authoritarianism are reflective of ongoing struggles between dominance and resistance. Without blurring the distinction between them it is important to acknowledge that they may frequently overlap irrespective of the formal designation of polities and states as democratic or authoritarian. It seems more apt to view democracy and authoritarianism as both antithetical and interdependent historical processes, co-existing in tension while at the same time each informing and transforming the other. The pairing of two concepts, commonly regarded as polar opposites, aims at a more probing historical analysis of the structures of dominance and resistance in sub-continental South Asia. This in turn should allow for a more nuanced appreciation of citizenship rights, not merely political but also economic and social, paving the way for meaningful comparisons between three otherwise distinctive states and societies. The comparative framework for the study rests on an exploration of the intertwined theme of democratic politics and authoritarian states in India, Pakistan and Bangladesh through a periodization of the interactions between political processes and state structures, the former moulded by social and economic dynamics that influence as well as are influenced by the policies, institutional interests and ideological postures of the latter.

Only diehard protagonists of difference as the highest common denominator of the destinies of subcontinental states and polities would deny that democratic representation in India and military dictatorship in Pakistan and Bangladesh have of late beset them with analogous, if not similar, sets of problems and challenges. The end of Congress hegemony in India and eleven years of military dictatorship in Pakistan by the late 1980s saw mainly regionally based political forces challenging and aspiring for, if not actually successfully seizing central state power and, implicitly and explicitly, claiming legitimacy in terms of some variant or other of regionalism or religious majoritarianism. In Bangladesh, an unpopular military regime was forced to pass the mantle to a popularly elected government touting the unifying principles of Islam for the first time in the country's electoral politics to mobilize support amidst growing social conflict and economic crisis. While underlining the need for a major restructuring of relations between state and society, in particular the redefinition of the concept of the centre and the related issues of sovereignty and citizenship, these paradoxically similar results of nearly four decades of democratic and authoritarian rule defy conventional explanations. The overarching question posed by recent developments in India and Pakistan, and in many ways also in Bangladesh, is why – despite the divergent forms taken by their state structures – political and economic developments, and ideological responses to them, are showing ostensible signs of convergence. Any plausible answer would have to investigate the extent to which the divergences were real in the first place and whether the convergences are disguising some qualitative differences. Political, economic and ideological developments in post-independence India and Pakistan, including present-day Bangladesh, are particularly amenable to a comparative analysis. The colonial legacy – institutional, strategic, economic as well as ideological – informed the dialectic between state construction and political processes in critical ways. An assessment of this legacy and its role in articulating relations between state and society in

India and Pakistan, therefore, forms an important pillar of the comparative edifice.

On the face of it, the transition from colonialism was almost as difficult for India as it was for the newly created state of Pakistan. With partition India lost some of its key agricultural tracts and the sources of raw materials for its industries, especially jute and cotton, not to mention a captive market for manufactured products. The division of the assets deprived India of civil and military personnel, as well as of financial resources, complicating the task of resettlement of the millions fleeing East and West Pakistan, to say nothing of the integration of the 562 princely states. Yet India inherited the colonial state's central government apparatus and an industrial infrastructure which, for all its weaknesses, was better developed than in the areas constituting Pakistan. It is true that unlike its counterpart the All-India Muslim League, which had practically no organizational presence in the Muslim-majority provinces, the Indian National Congress had made an impact on the local structures of politics in the Hindu-majority provinces. However, it is an open question whether, in the process of transforming itself from a loosely knit national movement into a political party, the Congress in fact retained its pre-independence advantages over the Muslim League in Pakistan.

A work of this sort has to contend with serious issues of comparability. India's geographical size and an ideal of its unity, albeit largely mythical and symbolic, are often cited as key differences with Pakistan, a fabrication of political necessity split into two parts separated by a thousand miles. Without denying the significance of scale and symbol, it is important not to let the determinisms of political geography and the imaginings of sacred mythology cloud historical analysis. In the absence of an inherited colonial administrative and political structure capable of coordinating its heterogeneous territories, India's size could just as well have been a disadvantage of gigantic proportions. As for the symbols which gave the most explicit expression to the nationalist idiom of Indian unity, these had been so appropriated and altered by autonomous local and regional political economies and cultures as to defy the centralized state's hegemonic project to infuse them with a singular and monolithic meaning.

The intention is not to replace the distinctions of geographic scale and mythic symbol with modern institutional structures, administrative and political, which were colonialism's weightiest imports into India. But the uniquely colonial construct of the centralized state with its institutional underpinnings – an administrative bureaucracy and a standing army in particular – and attendant ideological trappings – ordered unity, indivisible sovereignty and the like – provides common ground for meaningful, if not exhaustive, comparisons and contrasts between political entities of unequal spatial and temporal proportions. On this view the post-independence adaptations of the colonial concept of the centre, both in its institutional and ideological manifestations, is the strongest cement in a comparative analysis of how processes of state construction in India and Pakistan aided the functioning of parliamentary democracy in one and its abortion in the other.

The apparently statist orientation of the analysis is a product of unease with studies of political processes in post-independence South Asia rather than an implicit critique of society centred approaches. Instead of privileging one over the other the study uses the historical method to unravel the points of interaction between state and society. While the prolonged suspension of political processes in Pakistan has resulted in an obsessive concern with the two main non-elected institutions of the state, the civil bureaucracy and the military, the formalization of democracy in India has fixated attention on the fortunes of a single political party. Yet the supremacy of the military and bureaucracy in Pakistan is inexplicable without reference to the complicitous role of certain dominant social groups in eschewing the politics of resistance to gain privileged access to state authority and patronage. By the same token, the practice of democracy in India cannot be attributed to the changing societal moorings of a political party with no mention of its implications for the overall state structure.

Political scientists writing exclusively on India have been so enamoured by the chequered political history of the premier political party, the Indian National Congress, that they have until very recently neglected to assess its symbiotic relationship with the civil bureaucracy, the police and the military. So although much is known about parties and politics, and more still about the constantly shifting sands of factional alignments in different regions, there is at best an inadequate understanding and critique of the nature of the post-colonial state in India. A focus on the Congress, rising or falling, has seen a succession of political scientists of India writing in a manner reminiscent of the old historians of empire. The themes of awakening and decay, institutionalization and deinstitutionalization, consensual and conflictual politics, dominance and decline, not only obscure the state but give only partial glimpses of the polity, whether commanding or demanding. Unresearched and uncritical eulogies of the Nehruvian era have led some analysts to suggest an ahistorical disjuncture in India's political processes during the late 1960s. Righteous indignation at Mrs Gandhi's personalized and plebiscitary politics, and the ensuing erosion of the Congress's organizational foundations, has obfuscated the ways in which her populist politics might at least in the immediacy have deepened and broadened the party's social bases of support. If preoccupations with a party have coloured perceptions of the larger polity, the extent to which relations between elected and non-elected institutions influence democratic and authoritarian tendencies within the state has fallen out of view.

The significance of institutional imbalances in establishing the quantum of democracy and authoritarianism has been further obscured by the civil–military dichotomy employed by scholars working within the liberal–democratic paradigm. This approach lumps the administrative bureaucracy on the same side as elected civil institutions in examining civil–military relations. A partnership of elected politicians and non-elected bureaucrats may imbue a democratic dispensation with elements of authoritarianism rooted in the structures of the state. Moreover, a partnership of civilians does not preclude the potential for a conflict of interest between elected representatives or political institutions and the unelected bureaucratic arms of the state in a formally democratic polity. And finally, the civil–military equation ignores the possibility of a nexus between the civil and military institutions of the state in the enforcement of authoritarian rule. Democracy as expressed in the formalization of regular elections can and often does co-exist with the inherently authoritarian tendencies of the state. Overt authoritarianism is shaped more by institutional imbalances between the elected and non-elected institutions of the state than by changes in civil–military relations alone. The ambiguities, paradoxes and imbrications that hide behind the labels of democracy and authoritarianism can be better exposed to scholarly analysis by concentrating on the unfolding dialectic between state structures and political processes.

This analysis of necessity steers a none-too-easy course between the general and the specific which might ruffle practitioners of grand theory and fastidious detail alike. So certain self-denying ordinances appear to be in order. References to the state are not meant to postulate a notion of institutional coherence which any close empirical study would easily fracture. Neither the administrative bureaucracy nor the military are institutional monoliths immune from internal jockeying for position between their different arms. Nor is the state viewed as omnipotent or completely distinct from society. The domain of the state is seen to be one of accommodation and contest by innumerable and contending sites of power embedded in society at the regional and sub-regional levels. Though not an empirical study of regional or sub-regional political economies and cultures, their dialectical relations with the layered institutional structures of the state are assessed and conceptualized. In attempting to capture the shifting balance between state and society at particular moments in time the argument is pitched at a level of informed generality that aims at facilitating the project of comparative historical interpretation on a subcontinental scale without causing injury to either the realm of fact or precision. Not a research monograph, it is a goad and an invitation to those in the field of

South Asian studies to consider the possibilities and richness of analyses in the comparative vein.

Chapter 1 investigates the impact of partition and the colonial legacy on India and Pakistan and sets the stage for a close analysis of political developments in the two countries during subsequent decades. The following two chapters are linked thematically but divided chronologically. Both address the issue of the emerging balance between elected and non-elected institutions within the state structure in the context of the interplay between domestic, regional and international factors. Chapter 2 looks at the period leading up to the 1967 general elections in India and the ten years of parliamentary democracy and the decade of military rule under General Mohammad Ayub Khan in Pakistan. In chapter 3 the theme is extended to the populist interlude presided over by Indira Gandhi, Zulfikar Ali Bhutto and Sheikh Mujibur Rahman in the seventies and their authoritarian aftermath, overt or covert, in the 1980s and the 1990s. The focus then shifts to a more explicit consideration in chapter 4 of the political economies in India, Pakistan and Bangladesh to give an added edge to a comparative study on a subcontinental scale. A better understanding of the dimension of political economy and the apparent failure of planned development to achieve the goal of national integration allows for a better perspective on centre–province and centre–state relations in Pakistan and India. Chapter 5 addresses the issue of centralized state power and regional dissidence. It provides a critique of the notion of 'ethnicity' and analyses the sub-continent's federal dilemmas in the context of historically changing state–society relations. Chapter 6 weaves together the aspects of state structure and political culture by examining the formulation and projection of mono-lithic ideologies. Social dynamics at the local and regional levels are explored in terms of the dialectic between state structures and political processes as well as relatively autonomous cultural and ideological idioms. The interaction of state ideologies, secular or Islamic, with regional and sub-regional cultures strives for a more measured assessment of relations between states and societies.

The conclusion pulls together the different threads of the argument by way of a finale, explaining the apparent and the real differences and similarities between India, Pakistan and Bangladesh. In highlighting some of the insights gained from trespassing across arbitrarily defined temporal, spatial and disciplinary frontiers it sketches the course of a more comprehensive comparative research agenda for scholars and students of subcontinental South Asia to jointly and severally embark upon.

1   The colonial legacy in India and Pakistan

Few political decisions in the twentieth century have altered the course of history in more dramatic fashion than the partition of India in 1947. To be sure, the end of formal colonialism and the redrawing of national boundaries was a tumultuous event, sending tremors throughout much of Asia and beyond. Yet perhaps nowhere was the shock felt more intensely or more violently than in the Indian subcontinent. Economic and social linkages which over the millennia had survived periods of imperial consolidation, crises and collapse to weld the peoples of the subcontinent into a loosely layered framework of interdependence were rudely severed. Political differences among Indians over the modalities of power sharing once independence had been won sheared apart the closely woven threads of a colonial administrative structure that had institutionally integrated, if never quite unified, the subcontinent. That the culmination of some two hundred years of colonial institution-building should have sapped the subcontinent's capacity for accommodation and adaptation is a telling comment on the ways in which imperialism impressed itself on Indian society, economy and polity.

A rich and complex mosaic of cultural diversities which had evolved creative political mechanisms of compromise and collaboration long before the colonial advent, India through the centuries had managed to retain its geographical unity despite the pressures imposed by military invasion, social division and political conflict. There was little agreement on the basis of this unity or on its precise boundaries. Yet the idea of India as a distinctive geographical entity largely escaped the rigours of searching scepticism. Tracing its origins to the epic period in ancient Indian history, the concept of Bharat or Mahabharat had come to encapsulate a sub-continental expanse of mythical, sacred and political geography. Later the Arab and Persian exogenous definitions of Al-Hind or Hindustan, as the land beyond the river Sindhu or Indus, became readily internalized and identifiable in the geographical lexicon of Indo-Islamic culture and civiliz-ation. By and large the fluidity of the boundaries of geographical India were matched in the pre-colonial era by the flexibilities of political India.

Even in periods of imperial consolidation empire-builders generally aspired to a loose form of hegemony over diverse and autonomous constituent units.

Before the British stepped into the breach, a succession of empire-builders had sought to bring the contours of political India into conformity with those of its vast geographical expanse. Only for fleeting moments in the pre-colonial era did India's geographical unity correspond with its political unity. An overarching geographical identity contrasted sharply with a political unity that had constantly to be negotiated and renegotiated between diverse peoples inhabiting the domains of sovereign or quasi-sovereign regional rulers. What made the colonial period unlike any other in history was the British attempt to turn the bare facts of geographical India, variously and imaginatively construed, into defining principles for a centralized political unity based on the notion of a singular and indivisible sovereignty. This conflation of categories had large implications, not only at the level of the colonial legal system and institutional structures but also of Indian ideology and politics. It is in the dialectical interaction of these two levels that the seeds of partition and, by extension, of the colonial legacy itself can be identified and assessed.

To the extent that the British effort to stretch the ambit of imperial control through rule-bound institutions based on Western concepts of contractual law and impersonalized sovereignty rather than on the personal patronage of rulers was without historical precedence in the subcontinent, so too were the consequences. A political unity conceived and constructed in cold-blooded fashion and frozen in the impersonal rationality of bureaucratic institutions could neither reflect, nor capture, the internal dynamics of a society accustomed to direct, personalized rule. Although the British succeeded in giving a semblance of institutional coherence to much of geographical India, the integrative process never qualified as political unification. The gap between the integrative institutions of the colonial state and the myriad distinctions and divisions within Indian society proved unbridgeable. With the spread of Western education a small elite could work the institutions of the colonial state to their own advantage. But access to these institutions, though competitive, was limited to the select few. For the vast majority of Indians, local bureaucrats such as the district collector – a quintessential creation of the British administrative system – disbursed a personalized form of patronage and judicial arbitration within the overall context of a rule-bound, indirect and impersonalized institutional structure. Except for a brief period in the early nineteenth century, the British avoided assertive interventions in the cultural domain, conceding a measure of autonomy to India's social diversities while exerting control over its politics and economy. Anomalies arising from the co-existence of rationalistic colonial laws and the customs of Indian society afforded some limited scope for a subject people denied individual rights of citizenship to avoid the legal domain and instead seek redress within an attenuating arena of communitarian self-expression. The steady advance over time of a public sphere defined in colonial terms eroded, though never eliminated, the social space which could nurture the reciprocal rights and responsibilities that had characterized pre-colonial community. So while maintaining a distinction between the public and private spheres for its own purposes, the colonial state remained unconcerned about separating the legal aspects of individual subjecthood from its social manifestations in communitarian identity.

Discrepancies between colonial theory and practice were to have grave ramifications for the nationalist struggle whose promise of individual citizenship rights after the winning of independence had to contend with an assortment of communitarian forms of social organization and expression. Although the very character of Indian society forced a dilution of the purely rule-based logic of colonial institutions, constitutional control over them remained a primary objective of nationalist ambitions. The contradiction between a personalized Indian society and, in theory if not always in practice, an impersonalized colonial state apparatus became more acute after the introduction of the elective principle. The prospect of an increasing measure of self-government intensified the scramble for power and resources along religious, caste and regional lines. By the closing decades of the raj the conflicting aspirations of Indians, erroneously viewed in terms of the great religious divide between Hindus and Muslims, appeared to have become irreconcilable. With rival strands in Indian nationalism claiming sovereignty, whether whole or in part, keeping intact the unitary and centralized administrative structure demanded a modicum of compromise and political accommodation over and beyond the dominant idioms of colonial rule.

By collapsing the meaning of geographical and political unity, by insisting on defining unity solely in terms of the centralized institutionalized structures of the British raj, and by scorning the principles of accommodation and compromise that had earlier enabled the subcontinent to sustain itself as a unified if politically disparate geographical entity, Indian leaders demonstrated the extent to which their thinking had been coloured by the ideas and institutions of Western colonialism. Drawing upon India's pre-colonial past and imaginatively devising mechanisms of power sharing capable of accommodating the aspirations of diverse peoples and regions may have seemed impracticable. Yet a notion of unity which was to be preserved through a continuation of the same institutional rigidities and legal niceties that had been the bane of nationalists during the colonial era was hardly a fitting start to the subcontinent's independent future.

Partition then did not destroy a political unity forged by Indians through processes of negotiation, compromise and accommodation; it merely replaced a constitutionally unified centralized institutional framework with two mutually exclusive and independent sovereignties – India and Pakistan. Part epitaph and part antithesis of British rule, partition left an indelible mark on all the legacies of colonialism in India – institutional, strategic, economic as well as ideological. The continuities and discontinuities between the colonial and post-colonial periods in both India and Pakistan are, therefore, best grasped through the refracting prism of the partition process that accompanied the British transfer of power in the subcontinent. Yet insofar as partition itself was a product – albeit unintended – of British rule, the broader historical context is a necessary point of reference in unravelling colonialism's differential legacies for states and societies in subcontinental South Asia.

The historical context of partition

Bringing political India into conformity with geographical India proceeded directly from British perceptions of imperial requirements, both strategic and economic. By contrast with the loosely woven web of suzerainty claimed by pre-colonial empires, the British established an essentially unitary state structure in colonial India. This required a skilful manipulation of two of the key dialectics that have spanned the history of the subcontinent's internal struggle to align its geographical and political frontiers: between centralism and regionalism on the one hand, and between all-India nationalism and communalism on the other. A formidable administrative structure with no formal separation between the bureaucracy and the political executive penetrated the lowest reaches of Indian society. In addition, the British entered into a series of treaty arrangements with a range of princely rulers whose territories they had found convenient not to annex and who were allowed varying degrees of autonomy in their internal affairs. This division of the subcontinent into directly and indirectly ruled territories – British India and princely India respectively – may not have been very tidy but it suited imperial purposes of administrative economy and coordination. While the princely rulers remained loyal compendiums of the British empire until 1947, a gradual process of administrative control brought their domains under closer scrutiny of the centralized colonial state apparatus.

In British India the colonial edifice, despite regional variations, relied on the trappings of bureaucratic authoritarianism and collaborative networks of local rural intermediaries to balance and cancel out pressures emanating from below. A series of constitutional reforms in the early twentieth century, aimed at broadening the colonial state's social bases of support, conceded the principle of elective representation, but only by diverting

Indian political attentions towards safe local and provincial pastures and keeping the unitary centre firmly in British hands. Even the most nominal form of representation at the local and provincial levels was a potential threat to the colonial state. So the Morley–Minto reforms of 1909 took the momentous step of creating communal categories, for instance separate electorates for Muslims, in the arena of limited electoral politics at all levels of representation. The structural contradiction between an emphasis on local and provincial arenas of politics on the one hand and communally compartmentalized electorates on the other was to have large implications for Indian politics. Localizing the spoils of office and state patronage was designed to encourage vertical rather than horizontal aggregation of political demands. With the institutions of representative government striking root in less than propitious soil, the disjunction between India's geographical and political unity was to become even more difficult to square. For now, the institutionalized fragmentation of Indian politics allowed the colonial state to manipulate and administer the affairs of a society differentiated by region, class, caste and community.

Indian nationalists, especially once Mohandas Gandhi nailed his colours to the Indian National Congress, went some way towards circumventing the strategy of the colonial state to alternatively regionalize and communalize Indian politics. Launching all-India agitational campaigns with the help of an imaginatively, if selectively, conceived nationalist pantheon of unifying idioms contested the colonial strategy of emphasizing difference in diversity. The more paradoxical results of British constitutional manoeuvres lay in the heightening of contradictions within Muslim politics. Indian Muslims were not merely a construction of twentieth-century British colonial social engineering. Yet neither did they represent a unified and solid community of interest to justify their compartmentalization into a separate all-India communal category for purposes of political representation. Far from facilitating the construction of an all-India Muslim identity – the logical concomitant of Muslims being a distinct political category with separate representation – the Montagu–Chelmsford reforms of 1919 and the government of India act of 1935 reinforced regional particularisms in the Muslim-majority provinces and intra-Muslim factionalism within the protected walls of specifically Muslim constituencies. While the Congress under Gandhi was partly successful in raising its organizational umbrella over the old factional structures of politics in the Hindu-majority provinces, the local and provincial politics of Muslims continued to operate outside the framework of the All-India Muslim League established in 1906 to promote and safeguard the interests of the 'Muslim' community. Indeed, the politics of those who happened to be Muslim were bounded more by locality and province, and not infrequently led to cooperation with members of other religious communities, than by the specifically communal concerns of the tiny elite directing the Muslim League.

Despite a narrow base of support and a perilously weak organizational structure, particularly in the Muslim-majority provinces, the All-India Muslim League used the fact of Muslims being a separate political category to good advantage in the closing decades of the British raj. Challenging the Congress's claim to represent the whole of India and, therefore, its right to seize power at the unitary centre created by the British, the All-India Muslim League led by Mohammad Ali Jinnah found it convenient to reinstate the distinction between geographical and political unity which had been dropped from the lexicons of colonialists and nationalists alike. Acknowledging the fact of India's geographical unity, Jinnah left it an open question how that unity was to be reflected in a political structure representing the aspirations of not only India's Muslims but also the 562 princely states covering two-fifths of the subcontinent. Asserting that there were two nations in India, Hindu and Muslim, Jinnah demanded the creation of two essentially sovereign states, Pakistan – representing the Muslim-majority provinces – and Hindustan – representing the Hindu-majority provinces. There was force in Jinnah's contention that India was a geographic and, at best, an administrative rather than a political unity. Indian political unity, Jinnah maintained, could not be decreed and enforced by the unitary and centralized administrative structures of the colonial state. It had to be forged through a process of negotiations between the main political contenders to power after the British quit India. Implicit in this line of argument was a notion of Indian sovereignty as divisible and negotiable. Such an idea of sovereignty was at fundamental variance with Congress's notion of an indivisible and non-negotiable sovereignty for independent India. Sensing its ability to lay claim to the whole cake, Congress was understandably in no mood to debate the quality of its ingredients.

Jinnah's argument for keeping Indian geography and politics on separate but parallel tracks was part of a carefully planned strategy to win a large share of power for Muslims at the all-India level on the basis of their combined numerical majorities in the north-west and north-east of the subcontinent. This would give the Muslim League the leverage it needed to negotiate constitutional safeguards for Muslim minorities in the rest of India in exchange for those it would confer on the large non-Muslim populations residing within the territories of the Muslim state. Unfortunately for Jinnah and the Muslim League, the contradictory constraints imposed by the colonial political system on Muslim politics, namely the emphasis on provincial and local arenas of politics on the one hand and communally compartmentalized electorates on the other, worked to thwart the broader objectives for which the demand for Pakistan had been raised. If the demand was to have the support of Indian Muslims, in majority as well as minority provinces, it had to appear to offer something to all Muslims. It could do so only if it was framed in communal terms. Yet the politics of Muslims at the regional level did not pour neatly into communal moulds. The affinities of regional geography were not always consistent with the emotions and aspirations elicited by the ideal of a united all-India Muslim politics. As was true for all of India, there lay a wedge between the unities of geography and the unities of Muslim politics. Consequently, while the Pakistan demand injected strong communal overtones into Indian politics, the Muslim League could not pull the different and frequently conflicting regional strands in Muslim politics into a unified and coherent whole. So even though the oscillation between communalism and regionalism influenced the final showdown between Indian nationalism and British colonialism as a whole, the clash between the communal and regional identities of Muslims had a more decisive bearing on the Muslim League's movement for a Pakistan.

Designed to safeguard the interests of all Indian Muslims, the League's communal demand for a Pakistan carved out of the Muslim-majority areas in the north-west and north-east of the subcontinent failed to contain the regionalisms of the Muslim provinces. These provinces lent support to the Muslim League in the hope of negotiating a constitutional arrangement based on strong provinces and a weak centre. This is why the Pakistan resolution of March 1940 had spoken of 'Independent Muslim states' in which the constituent units would be 'autonomous and sovereign'. Jinnah had taken care to hedge this concession to Muslim-majority province sentiments. An unlikely advocate of provincialism, Jinnah was looking for ways to restrain the regionalisms of the Muslim-majority provinces so as to bring their combined weight to bear at the all-India level. The cabinet mission plan of May 1946 came close to giving Jinnah what he needed by proposing the grouping of Muslim and Hindu provinces at the second tier while restricting the federal centre to only three subjects – defence, foreign affairs and communications. Significantly, on 16 June 1946 the All-India Muslim League rejected the mission's offer of a sovereign Pakistan carved out of the Muslim-majority provinces in the north-west and the Muslim-majority districts of partitioned Punjab and Bengal and accepted the alternative plan for a three-tier federal constitutional arrangement covering the whole of India.

The implicit, if not explicit, assumption of a shared sovereignty between the Hindu-majority and Muslim-majority groups was unacceptable to a Congress advocating a composite nationalism based on an indivisible sovereign central authority. Inheriting the strong central apparatus of the colonial state was Congress's best insurance of quelling movements for autonomy in the Hindu-majority provinces and bringing the princely states firmly into the Indian union. So Congress found it politically expedient to abandon its commitment to India's geographical integrity and allow the division of the subcontinent along ostensibly communal lines rather than weaken the impersonalized institutional structures of the colonial state to accommodate the powerful regionally based aspirations of the Muslim provinces. Such a vision of India's political unity, unbendingly and uncompromisingly captured in the frozen embrace of colonial institutions, was chilling to say the least. Yet here was the rub. Having successfully laid claim to the centralized apparatus of the colonial state, Congress insisted on using the term 'India' to define its polity even while carrying out the vivisection of geographical India. Jinnah and the Muslim League made strong, but ineffectual, protests that there could be no political India bereft of territories inhabited by Muslim majorities. Investing the geographical term 'Hindustan' with new political meaning in opposition to the demand for a Pakistan, Jinnah argued that a federal or confederal union of India could only be based on an equal partnership between Hindustan and Pakistan.

With partition just around the corner, Jinnah's arguments fell on deaf ears. In control of three-quarters of the subcontinent, the Congress leadership required no special pleading to win British approbation in appropriating the international personality of British India. This minimized the psychological impact of partition, allowing the Congress leadership to keep alive the fiction of India's political unity surviving the subcontinental division even after the loss of its geographical integrity had been recognized internationally. But the multiple and complex bonds which through the centuries had locked together the different parts of India had not all been snapped by the sudden and arbitrary drawing of the lines of political division alone. It would require considerable administrative and political effort before the freshly demarcated frontiers could be made to reflect two wholly independent sovereignties in the subcontinent. Before that could happen a way had to be found to dismantle some key features of the colonial administrative structure, in particular those which had served to integrate the rest of India with the north-western and north-eastern extremities of the subcontinent.

The administrative legacy

In the closing months of the British raj in India, the twin dialectics of centralism and regionalism, and nationalism and communalism converged in complex ways, tearing apart the unity but retaining the substance of the very centralized administrative structure which had extended the colonial state's hold over Indian society. A casualty of partition and yet the most

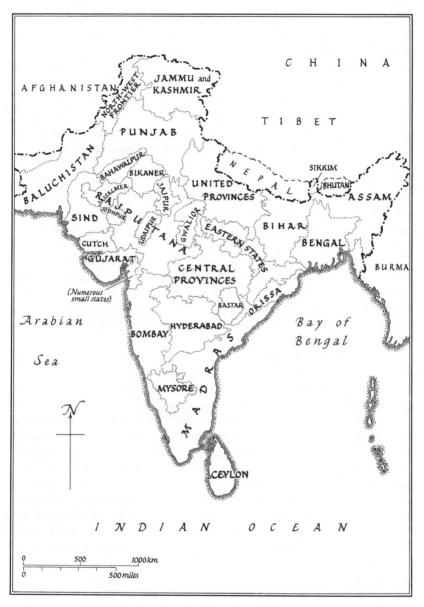

1 The Indian Empire: administrative divisions, 1947

imposing legacy of colonialism, the division of the British Indian administrative structure is a key factor in assessing the differential inheritances of India and Pakistan. While India inherited the colonial state's unitary central apparatus without seriously rupturing its links with the lower rungs of the administration, Pakistan had to construct an entirely new central government before it could begin coordinating the affairs of the provincial, district and local levels of society.

The departure of British and Muslim officials of the Indian civil service undoubtedly complicated India's task of resettling millions of refugees fleeing both the eastern and the western wings of Pakistan, and completing the integration of the princely states which had enjoyed a quasi-autonomous status under the paramount colonial power. Of a total of some 955 ICS officers before partition, excluding Muslims but including British officers, 392 remained in India in the immediate aftermath of partition. Yet despite some personnel problems, India's transition from colonialism was smoothed considerably by the continuities provided by a pre-existing central state apparatus, to say nothing of the advantages of inheriting the domestic and international personality of British India. By contrast, the absence of a basic machinery linking the various tiers of the administration, a grave shortage of competent and experienced personnel and the unenviable status of having seceded from an internationally recognized sovereign and independent state compounded Pakistan's problems in asserting central authority over territories separated by over a thousand miles.

Notwithstanding the differential administrative legacies, both India and Pakistan drew heavily on the colonial state's methods of bureaucratic control and centralization. The government of India act of 1935, strengthening the very bureaucratic 'steel frame' of the British raj that had been the bête noire of Indian nationalists, was adapted to serve as the constitutional framework in both countries. In principle, a commitment to the ideal of democracy based on the Westminster model of parliamentary government ensured a formal separation between the bureaucracy and a representative political executive. But in actual practice the bureaucratic authoritarianism inherent in the colonial state structure remained largely intact. It proved difficult at the very onset to establish the principle of legislative supremacy over the executive. Despite the general scholarly view which traces its origin to a later period of institutional atrophy, the attractions of personalized patronage soon became prevalent in the operations of supposedly rule-bound institutions, elected as well as non-elected. In the words of an observer of the Indian administrative bureaucracy in the immediate aftermath of independence, 'the rule of law was ever bent to subserve either executive action in the administration or the will of dominant elements of society'.[1] A greater propensity for executive action by politicians strengthened the hands of the administrative bureaucracy, the erstwhile non-elected representatives, many of whom openly derided the feasibility of democracy in subcontinental conditions.

Yet the legitimizing force of democracy in the wake of independence was too strong and pervasive to be discarded for the sake of administrative convenience. Instead of undertaking a massive reorganization of the administrative apparatus of the colonial state to guarantee the supremacy of elected institutions, the Indian and Pakistani political leadership alike formed alliances of convenience with members of the civil bureaucracy, the Indian civil service in particular. This was publicly justified on the grounds of pragmatism and the need to maintain some sort of administrative continuity to cope with the massive dislocations and law and order problems that followed in the wake of partition, especially in the northern, north-western and eastern parts of the subcontinent. The co-existence of formal democracy with bureaucratic authoritarianism has been one of the more enduring legacies of colonial rule in the subcontinent.

In keeping with the principles of democracy, the emphasis in the post-independence period was on strengthening the bond between the elected representative and the voter, in contradistinction to that between the local bureaucrat and the common people during the colonial period. But these measured nods in the direction of representative democracy, louder in Congress-dominated India than in Pakistan, scarcely disguised the dependence of both sets of leadership on the colonial bureaucracy. In the absence of a genuine commitment to an ideology of socio-economic development, granted Congress's socialist rhetoric and the Muslim League's placid appeals to Islamic social justice, relations between voters and their representatives were largely limited to elections. Although local bureaucrats were theoretically in a subordinate position to the elected representatives, they remained by virtue of their proximity and accessibility for all practical purposes the main representatives of the common people. Few politicians could expect to muster support in a constituency without at least the tacit support of the local administration. Unfamiliarity with the workings of both the political and administrative institutions of the state was another reason why most politicians had to try and establish a working, and often a dependent, relationship with the local bureaucrat.

So at the local levels of society in both dominions where the majority of the voters were bunched there was little qualitative change in the balance between the elected and non-elected institutions. Consequently, the exten-

[1] B. B. Misra, *Government and Bureaucracy in India: 1947–1976*, Delhi, 1986, p. 90.

sion in India of universal adult franchise did not energize the polity with the spirit of citizens' rights as distinct from the formal periodic exercise of voters' rights. The subservience of democratic politics to authoritarian states coupled with the attraction of caste and communal modes of mobilizing voters prevented the rise of an ethic of representatives' accountability to citizens that would be the hallmark of any substantive democracy. In parts of India where the Congress was relatively better organized, local party bosses could expect to successfully manipulate the administrative machinery to their own advantage in securing the support of a clientele of voters. Yet this merely confirmed the extent to which political success at the locality depended on the cooperation of the administrative bureaucracy. Where the Congress machinery was practically non-existent and riven with factionalism, bureaucrats had much greater leeway in administering the affairs of the locality. This kept alive the old face of bureaucratic despotism tempered by a personalized style in the operations of local administration even as the impersonalized, rule-bound service traditions were lauded and streamlined in both countries.

The persistence of bureaucratic authoritarianism in such marked fashion in the localities serves as a cautionary note against celebrating the boons of the new democratic dispensation which accompanied the transition from colonialism in India and Pakistan. As already alluded to above, even at the higher levels of the political system, the central in particular, the frequency and ease of executive action at legislative expense – often dubbed the 'viceregal' tradition – tended to supplant many of the basic precepts of democracy. While these qualifications are necessary to maintain perspective, it was undoubtedly at the central and provincial levels that the supremacy of the elected institutions – both executive and legislative – over the non-elected could be asserted with a greater or lesser measure of success. And it is here that the main differences between the Indian and Pakistani experiences have to be detected and analysed.

As part of the process of maintaining the greatest possible degree of administrative continuity, the political leaderships in both countries opted to retain the existing all-India services. These were recruited in open competitive examinations held at the all-India level and constituted into separate cadres for each of the provinces. Establishing the origin of recruits was an important feature of the colonial policy of posting members of the all-India services to the provincial and local levels. Generally speaking, members of the all-India services were appointed in provinces other than their own, a policy that was expected to inculcate an all-India outlook and help maintain a better measure of administrative objectivity. The policy was criticized – for instance by Bombay, West Bengal and the United Provinces in India – on the grounds that it was becoming increasingly necessary for officers to be familiar with the language and the customs of the people. But its integrative overtones were attractive for central governments seeking to establish their writs at the different layers of the administration, especially in areas where political institutions were either non-existent or poorly developed. Though the impact of the policy varied from region to region, the overall effect was to deepen the process of administrative integration and fortify centralized state authority. There were more than the occasional hitches since the provinces enjoyed powers granted to them under the government of India act of 1935 and were not prepared to assist in a reversal of their autonomy. To offset provincial resentments at being dictated to by the centre in matters to do with their own administration various concessions were made, but none so great as to alter the essential thrust of the drive towards centralization. Under the terms of an agreement signed on 21 October 1946 between the centre and seven (later nine) provincial governments in India, the latter would approve the appointments of all central recruits. A similar arrangement was made between the Pakistani centre and the provinces. In both dominions quotas were fixed for recruitment to the ICS – renamed the Indian administrative service – and the Indian police service from each provincial civil and police service. For instance, under the emergency recruitment plan in operation in India between August 1947 and 1949, of the 454 new members of the IAS half were recruited from the provincial services.

Later the newly integrated Indian states, with the sole exception of Jammu and Kashmir, also accepted the same IAS and IPS schemes. This enabled the Indian centre to post members of the IAS and the IPS to the princely states, usually with extraordinary powers over the public representatives to expedite the process of administrative integration. Once again it was the institutional continuities at the centre which enabled the Indian states ministry to accomplish the feat of imposing New Delhi's sovereign authority over a bewildering collage of administrative units in erstwhile princely India. Pakistan's north-western provinces, where officials often tended to exercise larger discretionary powers than their counterparts in many British Indian provinces, provided an even more attractive canvas than princely India. With a centrally appointed official combining revenue, executive and magisterial and judicial functions in the districts, there was considerable scope for bureaucratic control and administrative centralization in West Pakistan.

So although both states went through a greater measure of administrative centralization than undivided India, the absence of a central state apparatus gave added impetus to that process in Pakistan. Given the weaknesses of the Muslim League's organizational machinery in the Muslim-majority provinces and the relative strengths of the Congress organization in the

Indian provinces, the Pakistani political leadership had to concede much greater autonomy to the administrative bureaucracy in order to consolidate state authority than its opposite number in India. Differences in their institutional inheritances, administrative as well as political, therefore, played a significant part in determining the degree of centralization in Pakistan and India during the initial years of independence. But the precise ways in which this shaped the dialectic between state construction and the political process depended in large part on the economic and strategic legacies of colonialism and, above all, of partition in the two countries.

The economics of partition and separate defence

Quite apart from the need to impose central authority, the expansion and centralization of the administrative machinery in Pakistan was needed to augment meagre state resources and finance the requirements of the defence establishment. Pakistan started its independent career with 17.5 per cent of the financial assets and 30 per cent of the defence forces of undivided India. With a mere Rs.200 million as its opening cash balances, Pakistan after 1 December 1947 when the division of the military personnel was completed had to cough up an estimated Rs.35 to Rs.50 million a month for the upkeep of its defence forces alone. Assuming responsibility for the defence of the strategically vulnerable north-western and north-eastern marcher regions of the subcontinent was well beyond the capacities of the newly created state. Already in the initial year of independence Pakistan's defence expenditure was higher than that of the undivided government of India.

In subsequent years the annual budgets of the Pakistani central government were essentially defence budgets with practically nothing available for developmental purposes. Such a crushing defence burden called for a drastic change in the financial relationship between the newly established Pakistani centre and the provinces. Very soon after partition the Pakistani provinces were hustled into relinquishing their right to a whole range of taxes by the central government in the interest of establishing the financial stability of the new state. And while India too had to reckon with a considerably weighty defence bill, it could afford to do so without placing the pre-independence financial relationship between the centre and the provinces in jeopardy. In 1950-1 the Pakistani central government for the first time sanctioned a paltry sum of Rs.1 crore for provincial development purposes. By contrast, the central government of India had been allocating between Rs.25 to Rs.30 crores annually as grants-in-aid to the provinces for reconstruction and development programmes. The per capita revenue of the Indian provinces was 40 per cent more than that of the Pakistani provinces. East Bengal had a per capita revenue below that of the poorest Indian provinces such as Assam, Orissa and Bihar. While the Pakistani centre had to syphon off a large proportion of provincial resources to remain solvent, the Indian centre was able to fund 35 per cent of provincial development programmes. Under the circumstances the Pakistani provinces could not even emulate the modest achievements of their Indian counterparts in the financing of basic social services like education, public health and transport and reduce the differentials in the quality of life between the two countries.

So institutionally, strategically, economically and, consequently, politically, Pakistan was left facing a grimmer reality than India. This is not to suggest that things were light and easy for India; it is the balance of difficulties which underlines Pakistan's hapless predicament. With 23 per cent of the land mass of undivided India and 18 per cent of the population, Pakistan had less than 10 per cent of the industrial base in the two states and just a little over 7 per cent of the employment facilities. Mainly a raw material and foodstuff producing area, Pakistan could not expect to meet the expenditure for its strategic defence without expanding the state's administrative machinery and taking the politically precarious path of digging deeply and widely into provincial resources. Alternatively, Pakistan had to solicit foreign aid and, in this way, increase its dependence on the centres of the international capitalist system. The outbreak of military hostilities with India over the north Indian princely state of Kashmir within months of independence narrowed Pakistan's already restricted options.

Although predominantly agricultural, India was relatively better placed than Pakistan since the bulk of the industries in undivided India were situated in its territories. While possessing a considerably more diversified economy with the potential to tackle the problems of both unemployment and underemployment, the loss of some of the best irrigated land in the subcontinent to Pakistan increased India's food shortage by 0.5 to 0.7 million tons per annum. Despite centrally directed 'grow more food' campaigns and a concerted procurement drive, New Delhi had perforce to go in for large-scale food imports which in 1948–9 accounted for as much as 60 per cent of India's balance of payments deficit on current account. The deficit had to be financed by periodic releases from India's sterling balance account with the Bank of England and the purchase of $100 million from the International Monetary Fund in 1949. Before partition India had been a net earner of dollars with a healthy balance of payments position. By mid-1949, as a result of continuous annual trade deficits, transfers to Pakistan of its share of the sterling balances and remittances to Britain for the capitalized value of military stores and pensions, India had managed to reduce its inherited sterling balances by half, from Rs.1750 crores to Rs.825 crores. Increases in taxation, generally at the expense of the urban middle classes, failed to ease the financial crisis by improving the level of productivity.

Evidence of business confidence in the stability of the government in India did not translate into greater investment activity or help reduce levels of unemployment. Most of the revenue from the new taxes was used to pay for top heavy government expenditure which rose from some Rs.200 crores for united India to about Rs.600 crores for partitioned India. Government extravagance and rising food prices contributed to a post-war inflationary spiral made worse by the severe after-effects of partition.

Yet India's financial woes were more manageable than those enveloping Pakistan where efforts to stave off an imminent bankruptcy had been afoot since November 1947. While sharing most of the worst features of India's post-independence financial difficulties, Pakistan's exclusive reliance on the export of agricultural commodities magnified the problems fourfold. Only in relation to India did Pakistan initially enjoy some trading advantages. Its surplus foodstuffs as well as jute, cotton, hides, tanning materials, dyestuffs were exported to factories located in India. Indian industry and trade were dependent on these items, especially Pakistani raw jute and raw cotton which constituted 70 per cent and 40 per cent respectively of the total production in the subcontinent. But in return Pakistan was dependent on a number of Indian manufactured commodities and energy resources: cotton piece goods, iron and steel products, soap, coal, cement, petroleum, sugar and alkalis, as well as chemicals. Admittedly, these could be purchased from anywhere in the world. Yet under a standstill agreement currency, exchange, customs imports and export control and other matters of mutual concern were administered on an all-India basis until 31 March 1948. These arrangements, necessitated by the interdependence of the Indian and the Pakistani economies, soon crumbled under the strain of congenital rivalry between the two states.

The interdependence of the two economies in the initial years of partition is in part reflected by the foreign trade figures. In 1948–9, Indo-Pakistan trade accounted for just under 20 per cent of India's total foreign trade or 18 per cent of its imports and 16 per cent of its exports. By comparison, inter-dominion trade accounted for as much as 41.2 per cent of Pakistan's total foreign trade or 37 per cent of the imports and 61 per cent of the exports. Clearly, Pakistan was far more dependent in aggregate terms on trade with India. Yet the trade figures underplay the extent to which Indian jute mills in Calcutta and cotton mills in Bombay, Ahmedabad and Cawnpore depended on imports of Pakistani raw materials. The inelasticity of demand for raw jute and raw cotton gave Pakistan far more bargaining power with the government of India than the statistical evidence suggests. This was exemplified by the nonchalance with which Pakistan refused to devalue its rupee following the devaluation decisions taken by Britain and India in September 1949. Yet Pakistan's search for alternative sources and markets for its imports and exports was a long and arduous one and, not infrequently, entailed policy decisions that were economically and politically more damaging than the existing arrangements with India. And while the Indian economy showed remarkable resilience by increasing the production of raw jute and raw cotton, the disruption of free internal trade between the different regions in the subcontinent did extract considerable costs in human, financial and infrastructural terms from both dominions.

The ideological dimension

If the institutional legacy provided critical elements of continuity between the colonial and the post-colonial periods, reversing the economic interdependence of the subcontinent together with the altered strategic imperatives of the two states underline the main points of discontinuity. The ideological legacies of colonialism are in many ways a reflection of and a reaction to these continuities and discontinuities. Ostensibly, the secularism of the Congress and the communalism of the Muslim League are the main ideological legacies of the colonial era in India and Pakistan. But it is only by scaling the gap between rhetoric and reality that the ideological impact of colonialism in the subcontinent can be meaningfully assessed. Both creeds were formulated as a response to colonialism in a bid to win the allegiance of large segments of Indian society. As the most likely inheritor of the British colonial mantle, Congress's secularism derived from pragmatic quite as much as ethical and moral considerations. Congress's claim to be the only representative organization in a society divided along community and caste lines demanded the conscious projection of a secular ideology.

The translation of a secular ideology into secular politics, however, proved to be fraught with contradictions. In one of the typical paradoxes of Indian society the very factors necessitating the politics of secular nationalism laid the basis for particularistic religious communalism. Despite the official creed of secularism, a succession of Congress leaders both before and after Gandhi had grasped the expediency of resorting to popular Hindu religious symbols. An assertion of cultural confidence against alien rule as well as a strategy for political mobilization, the use of the Hindu idiom did much to narrow the gap separating India's localized public arenas from the larger purposes of the nationalist leadership. Yet what was intended to paper over the innumerable cracks within the majority community had the unwitting effect of appearing to set Hindus apart from non-Hindus, Muslims in particular.

The manipulation of religious symbolism in a secular nationalist garb had deeper intellectual moorings. Since the late nineteenth century leading voices in the anti-colonial struggle repeatedly equated their conception of the Indian people as a collectivity or a 'nation' with *Bharatvarsha*, the land of the mythological Vedic ruler Bharat. A definition of the Indian nation fashioned on ideas of territoriality found in ancient Hindu texts and popular mythology was not seen to compromise Congress's secularism. Presaging Gandhi's political philosophy in the twentieth century, Bipin Chandra Pal – by no means the most strident proponent of a religiously or racially based nationalism – had nevertheless argued forcefully along with many others that Hinduism was not simply a religion but an all-encompassing social system subsuming the diverse peoples and cultures inhabiting the geographical space that was India. On this view, it was 'unpardonable ignorance' to suggest that India was no more than a mere geographical entity consisting of 'a chaotic congregation . . . of tribes and races, families and castes, but not 'in any sense a nation'.[2] Despite its multifarious diversities, social and political, India was united by an overarching cultural ideal based on shared spiritual meanings and the disciplines of *dharma*. The main contribution of the Muslims was to lend a greater measure of political and administrative unity to a country already possessing a strong sense of its common spiritual and emotional roots. This was the India which the British came to and conquered, not 'an unorganised, unconscious, and undeveloped chaos' devoid of any sense of its collective identity.[3]

Insofar as nations are the constructions of educated imaginings, there is nothing extraordinary about this convenient substitution of history with mythology. Much the same tendency is discernable in the writings of Indian nationalist luminaries as far apart ideologically as a B. G. Tilak, an Aurobindo Ghosh and even a Subhas Chandra Bose. Arguing the prior existence of an Indian nation was intrinsic to the nationalist struggle against colonialism. It was a claim made by ideologically disparate nationalists to contest the attempt by the colonial masters to emphasize India's manifold social divisions even while establishing administrative centralization. But the claim came to dominate nationalist discourse only after the 1920s when Gandhi successfully began translating ideology into the politics of mass action. Yet ironically enough it was in the domain of politics that the notion of a singular Indian nation, albeit one containing many divergent strands, was most effectively contested. Intended to buttress the nationalist cause, the claim of Indian nationhood closely associated with such explicitly Hindu concepts as *varnashramadharma* and *Ram Rajya* gave impetus to the very diverse forces it intended to harness against the colonial state.

Pejoratively dubbed communal, these forces were not quite the artifacts of colonialism which the nationalists mistakenly believed. Unable to

---

[2] Bipin Chandra Pal, *The Soul of India: A Constructive Study of Indian Thoughts and Ideals* (fourth edition), Calcutta, 1958, p. 93 [first published in 1911].
[3] Ibid.

identify with many of the symbols deployed by the Congress, especially after the Gandhian takeover, many Muslims given their minority status were susceptible to anyone offering an alternative cultural construct for their politics. As the clash of cultural symbols, Hindu and Muslim, played itself out on the various levels of the Indian political stage, the lines dividing the vision of an inclusionary Indian nationalism from that of an exclusionary communalism became more clearly defined. The alienation of a growing number of Muslims and the British perception of them as a separate communal category was capitalized upon by the All-India Muslim League, not as a first step towards the attainment of an Islamic state but as a political ploy to win the support of a constituency divided by class, region and language in order to counter the Congress's unchallenged ascent to power in an independent India. In other words, the League's recourse to an exclusionary, religious communalism was in response to Congress's inclusionary, secular nationalism which borrowed heavily from Hindu ethical ideals and mythology. This is not to deny the possibility that some Muslim League leaders were genuinely attached to Islamic cultural symbols. Yet one does not have to plough the depths of cynicism to view the League's communal stance as a matter of political necessity on the part of a party purportedly representing an ideologically and organizationally divided minority.

Instead of representing two sharply divergent or mutually exclusive world views, secularism and communalism in the subcontinental context in fact reveal themselves as alternative strategies of political mobilization. As such they appear less as polar opposites than competing and interacting political forces. Just as the Congress's secularism was frequently overwrought with evocations of Hindu symbolism, the League's communalism was shot through with concerns that were other than purely religious. The paradox of Mohammad Ali Jinnah with his secular leanings advocating the League's communal demand for a Pakistan, and Gandhi with his strong Hindu beliefs propounding the doctrine of communal unity, rapidly appropriated as one of the central pillars of Congress's secular post-colonial ideology, is a comment on the ambiguities surrounding the uses made of religion in South Asian politics.

Contradictions between the rhetoric and reality of Congress's secularism and the League's religious communalism were not confined to the top leadership alone. A powerful group of Hindu ideologues took the cover of Congress's secularism to advance their cause while an array of Islamic ideologues stayed outside the Muslim League's corral to protest its lack of Islamic commitment. What is more, Congress's acceptance of partition along communal lines for the sake of a strong centralized state power was a complete reversal of its policy of acquiring power over a secular and united

India. That a movement claiming higher moral ground over its rivals and long guided by Gandhi, for whom the very notion of centralized state authority was the organized annihilation of individual spirituality and freedom, should in the end have sacrificed all at the instance of Congress's machine politicians – Jawaharlal Nehru and Sardar Vallabhbhai Patel in particular – for control over the colonial masters' satanic institutions of oppression is one of the more profound ironies of recent subcontinental history. And as for the Muslim League which at least had been consistently confused ideologically, the goal of Pakistan was attained by dividing the very Muslim community whose interests it supposedly wanted to represent and safeguard.

If partition deflected, even distorted, the ideological positions of the Congress and the Muslim League, the institutional, strategic and economic legacies of colonialism contorted many of the objectives for which independence had been won. The commitment to democracy was compromised by the attractions of governance through the bureaucratic instruments of the state. A communal holocaust following partition and the onset of military hostilities between India and Pakistan made a mockery of Gandhian notions of non-violence. The assumption of the centralized power of the raj by the Congress professing an ideology of reformist class conciliation but in fact representing the interests of specific privileged groups postponed the goals of socio-economic reform aimed at eliminating poverty, discrimination and exploitation. In Pakistan, the unifying bonds of Islam could not prevent the imperatives of constructing a central apparatus and raising a viable shield of defence against India from exacerbating the sense of alienation and socio-economic deprivation in the various regions.

So the dominant idioms of nationalism, secularism and communalism of the late colonial era left rather contradictory and confusing legacies. It was the Western colonial ideology of an indivisible sovereignty as underwritten by a centralized state structure that held the more unambiguous attraction for the managers of the subcontinent's post-colonial states. This was an ideology of sovereignty that, ironically enough, survived the agonizing political division of the subcontinent and was sought to be replicated at the central apexes of two independent sovereign states. The ideological inheritance has had a powerful bearing on the centre–region dialectic and the authoritarian strains within state structures in post-colonial South Asia. Analysed in interaction with the contrasting institutional legacies of the colonial state it provides a critical ingredient to a comparative study of the relationship between state structures and political processes in post-independence India and Pakistan.

2 State formation and political processes in India and Pakistan, 1947 to c.1971

A compelling yet under-investigated question in contemporary South Asian history is why the partitioned inheritance of the British raj resulted in a different balance between state structures and political processes in post-independence India and Pakistan. A matter of wide and often imaginative speculation, it has invited explanations owing more to the predilections of specific schools of thought than to an actual examination of the historical factors that have contributed to making India a democratic polity and Pakistan a military dominated state.

Those steeped in the liberal democratic tradition have stressed the unique organizational phenomenon of the Indian National Congress. This is seen to have provided India's founding fathers, generally regarded as men of considerable political acumen and vision, with the institutional support necessary to lay the foundations of a stable, liberal democratic state. Marxist theorists for their part have sought explanations in the 'overdeveloped' institutional legacies of the colonial state and the corresponding weaknesses of dominant classes in civil society. Shades of determinism have clouded both interpretations. Long experience of working together in the anti-imperialist struggle had been more conducive to understandings among the top leaders of the Indian National Congress than was the case with the Muslim League, a communal party with no real organizational existence in Muslim India before the final decade of the British raj. Yet placed in identical circumstances after independence it is debatable whether the Indian leadership would have done much better at institutionalizing representative democracy than their supposedly less able counterparts in Pakistan. Stressing personal leadership qualities without reference to contextual difference makes for more interesting narrative exposition than insightful analytical history. By the same token, an exaggerated sense of the Congress's strength in linking and mediating politics at the central, provincial and local levels and the Muslim League's relative organizational weaknesses conveys the impression that the success of political processes in India and their collapse in Pakistan was unavoidable.

The Marxist focus on weak class structures and the 'overdeveloped'

29

nature of the post-colonial states is even less able to explain the contrasting evolution of political processes in India and Pakistan. Marxist writings on post-independence South Asian politics have maintained a tantalizing silence on why, if colonial institutional legacies were broadly similar and the underlying class structures only marginally different, one country success-fully established a political democracy while the other ended up under military dictatorship. Political cultural interpretations have fared no better in arguing that differences between India and Pakistan stem from the peculiar traits of authoritarianism and tolerance intrinsic to Muslim and Hindu cultures – facts plainly contradicted by the egalitarian and hier-archical tendencies within both social orders. Contrasting the Congress leadership's ideological leaning towards Western liberal democracy with the Muslim League's moorings in conservative reaction is a simplistic claim that does scant justice to the complexity of the historical evidence. If theoretical determinism has triumphed over history, culture abstracted from its structural underpinnings has tended to grossly oversimplify reality.

More celebrated variants of the cultural approach to politics, notably that of Ashis Nandy, avoid some of the pitfalls. His emphasis on the tradition–modernity dichotomy may be open to methodological questioning. Yet it offers interesting insights, implicit as well as explicit, into the changing relationship between society and politics in colonial and post-colonial India. According to Nandy, politics in 'traditional' India were often corrupting, instrumental and amoral, but in the absence of an 'authoritative centre' the impact was localized and compartmentalized by the *dharmic* codes guiding social life. Unlike in Western societies, politics in India never made the transition from the private to the public domain. For all the rhetoric about 'public interest' and 'public policy', politics in modern India has remained highly personalized. It was Gandhi who in giving primacy to politics as a vehicle against the centralized colonial state unintentionally laid the basis for corruption, cynicism and dishonesty in post-independence Indian poli-tics. The ensuing disenchantment with the sheer banality of a politics driven by the self-interested pursuit of power and the ineffectiveness of state action fostered increasing support for the amoral authoritarianism that had always been deeply embedded in Indian culture. The search for secur-ity in authority gave rise to a new civic consciousness which eventually found expression in Indira Gandhi's emergency in 1975.[1]

What this otherwise intriguing explanation of the cultural basis of authoritarianism in India does not reveal is why the formally democratic façade took as long as it did to crumble or for that matter why when it did crumble it stopped short of complete collapse. By looking only at the

---

[1] Ashis Nandy, *At the Edge of Psychology: Essays in Politics and Culture*, New Delhi, 1980.

cultural underpinnings of politics, Nandy misses the opportunity of assessing the qualitative historical changes that accompanied the expansion of the colonial public sphere and the strains of authoritarianism, more covert than overt, rooted in the post-colonial Indian state structure. Analysing the dialectic between an implicit amoral authoritarianism in Indian political culture and a no less implicit structural authoritarianism within the state would appear to be the more promising approach. Moreover, given Nandy's exclusive focus on India, the comparative explanatory value of his political cultural analysis for military dominance in predominantly Muslim Pakistan remains open to conjecture.

Recourse to the drawing board of history and a comparative analysis of state formation and political processes in the two countries seems the best way of addressing the issue of democracy in India and military dictatorship in Pakistan. The legacies of colonialism – institutional, strategic, economic and ideological – provide the broad analytical framework in which to tease out the reasons for the apparently divergent political developments in India and Pakistan. In evaluating the dialectic of state formation and political processes three inter-related points need underlining at the very outset. First, the concept of the centre, or more precisely the differential inheritances of India and Pakistan in this regard, is critical in understanding the contexts in which state formation proceeded in the two countries. Second, the fact of a pre-existing and a non-existing central state apparatus has to serve as the main point of reference in assessing the roles of the Congress and the Muslim League in shaping political processes in India and Pakistan during the initial years of independence. And finally, it will be necessary to consider how the strategic and economic consequences of partition combined to influence state construction and political processes in both countries.

Contrasting inheritances and outcomes, 1947–1951

Partitioning India and seizing control of the colonial state's unitary central apparatus in New Delhi was the Congress high command's response to the twin imperatives of keeping its own followers in line and integrating the princely states into the Indian union. From the Congress's angle of vision, the League's demand for a Pakistan based on the Muslim-majority provinces represented a mere fraction of a larger problem: the potential for a balkanization of post-colonial India. It was convenient that in 1947 the communal question had shoved the potentially more explosive issue of provincial autonomy into the background. Cutting the Gordian knot and conceding the principle of Pakistan had a sobering effect on provincial autonomists in the Hindu-majority provinces and generated the psychological pressure needed to temper princely ambitions. Congress's ability to turn partition into an advantage in state formation is highlighted by the successful integration of the princely states and the rapidity with which the process of constitution-making was completed.

A transfer of power entailing the lapse of British paramountcy over the princes raised the alarming prospect of some of the states jointly or severally asserting their right to opt out of the Indian union. It was only by foregoing full independence and accepting dominion status within the British commonwealth that the Congress was able to use the good offices of Britain's last viceroy, Lord Mountbatten, to dispel any illusions of independence nurtured by the princely states which accounted for nearly 45 per cent of Indian territory. As governor-general of independent India, Mountbatten, carrying the colours of imperialism on one brow and of royalty on the other, did a splendid job for the Congress in cajoling and coaxing Britain's erstwhile princely clients to accede to the union. But the ultimate credit for the integration of the princely states goes to Sardar Vallabhbhai Patel, Congress's foremost machine politician, and V. P. Menon, the agile secretary of the states' ministry. Together Patel and Menon masterminded a plan based on the classic bait and switch technique. The original instruments of accession offered the bait – the princely states had only to delegate defence, foreign affairs and communications to the centre. Once the princes had acceded on this basis to the union it was time for the switch: the instruments of accession were gradually amended to give the union centre increasing sway over the states.

Adjusting the constitutional relationship between the centre and the princely rulers was relatively simple compared with the problems of co-ordinating the affairs of state administrations at vastly different levels of development. Under the watchful eye of the states' ministry, whose powers were greatly extended for the purpose, an elaborate process of administrative integration was carried out within a short period of time. Some 216 princely states were merged into existing contiguous provincial administrations; 310 were consolidated into six states' unions and a half-dozen or so were converted into chief commissioners' provinces and ruled directly by the centre. At the end of the integrative process, the 554 quasi-autonomous princely states that acceded to India had been replaced by fourteen administrative units. With help from members of the IAS and the IPS these were subsequently tailored to fit the larger all-India-administrative structure, thus providing organizational coherence to the sprawling edifice of the post-independence Indian state. The fiscal integration of the states took appreciably longer to accomplish as did the process of merging the different armed forces of the princely states into the Indian military establishment. Problems arising from discrepancies in the centre's relations with the states and the provinces during the transition were met by giving the president powers to directly monitor the affairs of the states for a ten-year period. This was reminiscent of the constitutional position prior to the 1935 act when provincial governments were partly responsible to their legislatures and partly subjected to the directives of the central government. The justification for phasing the process of democratization in the states was that neither their administrative services nor the political parties operating within them were in a position to assume full unaided responsibility for their administrations.

Anomalies in its practice, however, were carefully balanced with the maintenance of democratic form. Except for the delay involved in bringing the state administrations on a par with the provinces, the process of constitution-making was breathtakingly swift. The need for a new election to the constituent assembly was summarily dispensed with on pragmatic grounds. The central assembly elected in 1945–6 on an indirect basis served as the constitution-making body. Partition increased the share of Congress's seats in the assembly from a formidable 69 per cent to an overpowering 82 per cent. Yet it was not simply the Congress's commanding majority which determined the pace and the direction of constitution-making. Congress's inheritance of the centralized state apparatus of the raj facilitated its task of shaping independent India's constitution. Pandering to the values of consensus and accommodation as well as speech-making by a large number of members notwithstanding, the substance of the constitution was decided upon by a coterie of about a dozen individuals led by Jawaharlal Nehru and Sardar Patel. Informal promises and gentle arm twisting by the central high command ensured that provincial bosses accepted a strong union centre capable of stamping out the disorders accompanying partition and undertaking a range of social and economic reforms. As Patel emphatically stated: 'the first requirement of any progressive country is internal and external security . . . It is impossible to make progress unless you first restore order in the country.'[2] Giving short shrift to Gandhian ideas of self-governing village republics, other than a purely cosmetic gesture to *panchayati raj*, the constitution-makers opted for a strong central government of the parliamentary form. There were to be two houses, the lower house or the Lok Sabha with representatives directly elected on the basis of population and the upper house or the Rajya Sabha with members elected indirectly by state assemblies. Majority support in the Lok Sabha would form the basis of the executive branch of government, consisting of a prime minister and a cabinet whose advice would be binding on the president.

---

[2] Speech to Congress planning conference, 26 May 1950, cited in Granville Austin, *The Indian Constitution: Cornerstone of a Nation*, London, 1966, p. 45.

Where did these arrangements among the rulers leave all those who were to be ruled? The will of the people was sought to be given expression in the constitution's enunciation of fundamental rights and the directive principles of state policy. Seven fundamental rights were listed: the right to equality, the right to freedom, the right against exploitation, the right to freedom of religion, the right to education, the right to property and the right to constitutional remedies. Yet the constitution authorized the state to qualify or curtail several of these rights. For instance, the state could confiscate property after providing compensation. Far more serious was the dilution of the right to due process of law. In its quest for security the constitution permitted the state to hold its citizens in preventive detention without trial for at least three months. The Congress's justification that these powers were necessitated by the extraordinary times facing India was countered by the argument that constitutions were for the most part meant to be in force during ordinary times. Congress of course had its way, which led at least one critic to charge that the Indian constitution was an unacceptable patchwork of 'myths and denials'.

If qualifications to fundamental rights left the way open for the establishment of a 'police state', the directive principles were expressions of the state's bona fides in eventually turning India into a welfare state. The state according to these principles committed itself to raise the level of nutrition and standard of living, promote international peace and just dealings among nations, provide a uniform civil code and a *panchayat* system of local government, promote cottage industries, agriculture and animal husbandry and prohibit the use of liquor and harmful drugs. However, the constitution carefully avoided making any mention of socialism. In any case, none of the high-flying objectives of the directive principles of the state were justiciable in a court of law. The grand declaration of lofty principles sufficed to reaffirm the democratic promises of the nationalist struggle. Yet there was no certainty that the bulk of the citizenry could unproblematically lay claim to their democratic right to economic and social justice.

Although the constitution created three lists of legislative subjects – federal, state and concurrent – the centre was equipped with all the requisite powers to govern India as a unitary state. The all-India services – the IAS and the IPS – were to serve as the kingpin of unitarianism in a system that was supposedly federal in form. To appease provincial autonomists a moderate concession was made: the proportion of posts in the IAS cadre to be filled by promotion from the provincial services was raised from 20 per cent to 25 per cent. But most of the financial powers, and certainly the more lucrative categories of taxation, were given to the union centre. The president upon the advice of the prime minister and the cabinet had the power to proclaim a state of emergency if the union was threatened by external aggression, internal disturbance or financial crisis. During the period of emergency union powers extended to giving states direction concerning executive government and to legislate on items not on the union list. Direct rule by the centre could be imposed on being advised by a centrally appointed governor that a state could not be governed in accordance with the constitution. It was this constitution, federal in its protestations but unitary in its shape and structure, which was adopted by the constituent assembly on 26 November 1949. Two months later, on 26 January 1950, India was proclaimed a sovereign republic, albeit within the British commonwealth. Membership in the commonwealth was deemed to be consistent with the republic adopting a strictly non-aligned policy under Nehru's direction.

Shunning association with the major power blocs and stolidly supporting anti-colonial movements the world over was to remain the governing principle of India's foreign and defence policies. While it would be plainly naive to take the policy of non-alignment at face value, there can be no question that Nehru played a key role in guiding India away from the power blocs whose strategic imperatives bore so heavily on the emerging state structures in the developing world during the cold war era. Non-alignment in Nehruvian parlance did not preclude associating with the Anglo-American bloc in circumstances favourable for Indian national interests. The British at any rate were quite sanguine that 'Nehru's great aversion from any entanglements' notwithstanding, the dangers of isolationism and the impossibility of joining the Communist camp made sure that India had 'no real alternative to ... inclining more and more towards the West'.[3] Non-alignment certainly did not prevent India from becoming one of the major recipients of US aid, well ahead in aggregate if not per capita terms of the decidedly more pliant client America found in Pakistan. Indeed, long before the border war with China in 1962 forced open the doors to Washington's largesse in the form of military assistance, India was one of the main beneficiaries of American economic aid and advice. The total US programmed economic assistance to India until financial year 1961 amounted to 3,270 million dollars by comparison with 1,474 million dollars to Pakistan.

If reliance on external assistance is taken as the sole criterion, India was no less aligned than Pakistan. What gave India comparative advantage in negotiating better terms with the centres of the international capitalist system was not simply a result of Nehru formulating a more circumspect foreign policy than his opposite number in Pakistan. That in itself would have been difficult if not for India's geographical size, its undeniable

---

[3] Archibald Nye to the Secretary of State for Commonwealth Relations, 17 May 1951, FO 371/92870, PRO.

military importance as a regional power and the political stature which came with the historical continuities evoked by its international nomenclature. So without being dismissive of Nehru's role in placing India on a non-aligned path in a world where alignment seemed the most opportune way of forging ahead in the international arena, it is important to account for the fortuitous conditions which made his foreign and defence policies conceivable in the first instance. Nehru's contribution in minimizing the impact of the international environment of the cold war on India's domestic politics and economy is less open to question. Yet to attribute this wholly to his superior intellectual and moral qualities, as some have argued ad nauseam, is to discount the significance of his privileged position as head of an essentially unchallenged government and party.

It was for all these reasons, more contextual than personal, that the interplay of domestic, regional and international factors moulded the dialectic between state formation and political processes in India and Pakistan in substantially different ways. Such a perspective makes it more feasible to assess the precise manner in which the balance beween democratic and authoritarian tendencies was struck in the two countries.

When it came to choosing a domestic political system the Indian constitution clearly laid the foundations for representative government elected on the basis of universal adult franchise. But apart from removing the limits on the franchise, almost two-thirds of the 1950 document reproduced clauses in the 1935 act and replicated its overall structure. With the all-India administrative and police services providing continuities with the colonial era, the rules of democracy laid down in the constitution were not the only pillars on which the edifice of the new state was built. The dialectic between state formation and political processes in India was at each step shaped by a symbiosis between the agenda of the premier nationalist party and the administrative legacies of colonialism. In neighbouring Pakistan the absence of a central state apparatus placed the dialectic between state formation and political processes on an altogether different footing. In the initial months of independence Jinnah's powers as governor-general were the only basis for the exercise of central authority over the Pakistani provinces. In due course the imperative of constructing an entirely new central authority over territories which for so long had been governed from New Delhi, together with the weaknesses of the Muslim League's organizational machinery, saw the administrative bureaucracy gaining an edge over the political arms of the state. The provinces continued to be the main arenas of political activity in Pakistan. Those engaged in constructing and then managing the new central government apparatus were politicians with little or no social bases of support in the provinces and were, consequently, unable to stand their ground against civil servants trained in the best traditions of colonial bureaucratic authoritarianism. Already handicapped by a meagre share of the spoils of partition, the new Pakistani centre faced the challenge of severe socio-economic dislocations and a threat to its newly demarcated frontiers from India. The outbreak of armed hostilities over Kashmir gave added impetus to the consolidation of central authority in Pakistan, but at the same time sharpened the contradictions between state formation and political processes and, by extension, between the newly constructed centre and the provinces. In the early days of independence fears of the reincorporation of areas within Pakistan into the Indian union served to blur the differences between external and internal threats to security and central authority. The dilemma was compounded by the sorely insufficient resource endowment Pakistan possessed to finance its external defence and internal security needs. So the early outbreak of belligerence with India entailed the diversion of scarce resources extracted from the provinces into a defence effort before political processes could become clearly defined.

In the international context of the cold war and a subtle but significant British–American rivalry, officers at the top echelons of the non-elective institutions – the military and the bureaucracy – began to skilfully manipulate their international connections with London and Washington. The manner of the insertion of Pakistan into the post-world war II international system played a critical role in combination with regional and domestic factors to create a lasting institutional imbalance within the Pakistani state structure. Members of the Pakistan constituent assembly fumbled uncertainly with the constitution-making process complicated by the demographic fact of a Bengali majority under-represented in the non-elective institutions and a fierce debate on whether Pakistan should adopt an Islamic or a secular form of government. Dominant trends in public opinion in the political arenas were swayed by the populist nationalisms of Iran, Palestine and Egypt. While Pakistan's first prime minister, Liaquat Ali Khan, had a feel for the popular pulse, the structural constraints informing state formation in Pakistan were too severe to prevent a shift in the institutional balance of power in favour of the bureaucracy and the military. The mandarins and the praetorian guards were prepared to be hard-headed about the business of proceeding with state formation in a difficult regional and international environment without let or hindrance from the complex social dynamics underlying political processes in the two wings of Pakistan. By early 1951 American policy makers had made up their minds that the Persian–Iraq sector could not be defended without help from Pakistan. They were by now also ready to bypass the British and make direct approaches to the Pakistani establishment. The early managers of the Pakistani state were prepared to deal with the Americans even though their motives in forging a special relationship with the United States had more to do with a desire to acquire a better military balance in relation to India than from fears of communist inroads into the Islamic heartlands of the Middle East. By the fall of 1951, the military and the civil bureaucracy had registered their dominance within the emerging structure of the Pakistani state.

The different colonial inheritances of a central state apparatus, the relatively milder impact of the strategic and economic consequences of partition on India than on Pakistan and the nature of their international links were the most important factors leading to alternative outcomes in the two countries. In October 1951 Pakistan's first prime minister, Liaquat Ali Khan, fell victim to an assassin's bullet. At that very moment India's first prime minister, who by then had established himself as the main architect of the country's foreign and defence policy, was preparing to lead the Congress party to the first of its many victories in a general election. The reasons for Nehru's success and the very long shadow it has cast on interpretations of India's tryst with democracy call for a closer analysis of not only the man and the context but also the nature of Indian politics.

Party politics and structural authoritarianism in India, 1947–1967

Some twenty days before he was assassinated, Gandhi called for the dissolution of the Congress party which he believed was in 'decay and decline' and a hot-bed of 'corruption and power politics'. But the Mahatma was a stretch removed from reality – now that independence had been won politics was more about power than ever before. The more so since Congress emerged from the anti-imperialist struggle committed to two potentially contradictory objectives: (1) the social transformation of India and (2) the projection of a single unified nation. Needing to minimize social conflict to achieve the second objective, the Congress was awkwardly poised to preside over the magnitude of changes needed for the effective attainment of the first. Despite the inherent tension between the two, both objectives required the establishment of a political system dominated by the Congress – one whose legitimacy would be assured by a conscious accommodation of dissent from an array of social groups occupying strategic positions mainly within but also outside the movement. The dual roles of authoritative spokesman of the entire nation and an instrument of social change could be performed in the post-independence period only by transforming the movement – containing disparate elements – into an effective ruling party.

Ignoring the Mahatma's last will and testament, the Congress leaders began establishing the structures of political dominance, while taking care not to wholly undermine the existing patterns of dissent. Possessing the self-confidence of a nationalist organization whose unchallenged dominance had been confirmed further by its inheritance of the colonial state's unitary centre, Congress was careful not to damage its legitimacy by muzzling such isolated pockets of dissent as existed. This did not mean that Congress critics, both within and outside the party, could operate with impunity. Communists and proponents of autonomy for linguistic states were put down with a heavy hand in the initial years of independence even as the Congress strove to exercise dominance within a multi-party system. In 1948, Sardar Vallabhbhai Patel began the reorganization of the party with a view to making it an even more effective instrument of dominance. He persuaded the working committee to amend the Congress constitution forbidding the existence within the organization of parties which had a 'separate membership, constitution and programme'. Although Patel succeeded in his objective of turfing out the Congress Socialist party, he was less successful in turning Congress into a well-knit party. Nehru, unlike Patel, was less apprehensive of ideological differences within the Congress and seemed to have a better understanding of the Congress's dual role as a governing party as well as a continuing political movement. Yet Nehru's perception of the Congress was far from perfect. He was ready to see it play an autonomous role vis-à-vis the government at the state level but was unwilling to tolerate a separation of government and party at the national level. When Patel with the support of the Congress right wing managed to get Purushottamdas Tandon, an arch conservative from UP, elected as Congress president, Nehru threatened to resign as prime minister. A well-rehearsed Nehruvian posture, it did have the intended effect. In 1951 he eventually forced Tandon's resignation and took over as president of the Congress. Throughout his long tenure as prime minister Nehru kept a tight grip on the party at the centre while exploiting divisions between Congress ministries and the party organization at the state level to his own political advantage.

The dominance of a single party in an essentially multi-party system of parliamentary democracy worked reasonably well. Here the momentum of the nationalist movement, the Congress's organizational structure and the similarity in the social background of the top leadership and their shared experiences in the anti-imperialist struggle proved invaluable. Yet political stability is rarely achieved without a price. On the face of it, the creeping sense of disillusionment with what Nandy has dubbed India's 'banal politics' appeared in better harness during the initial years. But just beneath the surface calm of single-party dominance, the politics of patronage were widening the scope for corruption and the self-interested pursuit of power by privileged social groups both within and outside the state apparatus. The dichotomy between inherited rule-bound colonial institutions and a personalized Indian society became more accentuated under democratic dispensation. Shortly after independence, Congress ministers and state governors began jockeying for monetary and other privileges well beyond their due and, invariably, without reference to the appropriate legislative authority. The whimsical flouting of rules and laws was infectious, especially in the states where Congress politicians preferred to act in their executive capacities. This left members of the higher bureaucracy in the awkward role of trying to enforce old rules in a dramatically different game. The process of adaptation proved relatively effortless for state and local level bureaucrats, accustomed to a more personalized style of governance in which rules could be bent without being broken.

Complicity between bureaucrats and public representatives reduced tensions between the administrative and political arms of the state, unlike Pakistan where members of the superior and the provincial services did not have to reckon with central and provincial governments capable of asserting their will through organized and autonomous party machines. The qualitatively different balance of power between bureaucrats and politicians in the two states helps explain the relative success of formal democracy in the one and its apparent failure in the other. While the holding of elections at regular intervals in India underlined the primacy of politics and increased the politician's stature relative to that of the civil servant, the virtual denial of the people's voting right in Pakistan and the generally low status accorded to a political career saw a corresponding rise in bureaucratic prestige and power. Yet what was auspicious for the future of formal democracy in India was ominous for its substance. The attractions of Congress's patronage system, together with the policy of open membership, brought droves of lesser mortals into the organizational fold. Weakened in calibre and fired more and more by the politics of opportunism, the Congress was slowly but subtly becoming even more of an organizational mainspring for corruption and self-interest than Gandhi may have feared. For every one who wrested a piece of the pie there were many more whose disappointments lent added fury to the politics of competition and social conflict festering under the Nehruvian veil of stability.

In the absence of any national alternative, however, Congress had little difficulty romping home to victory in the first three general elections, further confirming its dominance at the national as well as the state levels. Refining the art of electoral manipulation, the Congress distributed tickets in the rural constituencies on the basis of caste, community and religious considerations. Lack of adherence to the party's socio-economic programmes or service in the nationalist movement was no barrier to the selection of candidates capable of mustering electoral support. The triumph of expediency bore handsome results. During 1952 and 1957 Congress won between 74 and 75 per cent of the central parliamentary seats and between 61 and 68 per cent of the seats in the state assemblies. But it did so with only 45 to 47.5 per cent of the electoral vote, hinting both at the success of opposition parties and their failure to fully capitalize on the advantage by cobbling together a united front against the Congress. An electoral system based on territorial constituencies meant that Congress candidates could get elected even if they polled a mere 30 per cent of the total popular vote cast. Except for a few fringe groups, opposition parties in the early years of independence saw their task as a corrective rather than a competitive or confrontational one and spent the better part of their energies trying to influence factions within the Congress. In other words, opposition parties which were highly fragmented to begin with played a major part in lending legitimacy to the Congress dominated political system, preferring to work within it or, alternatively, trying to gain control over it.

There were of course challenges from parties like the Jan Sangh, which was opposed to the Congress's secular creed. But the Jan Sangh became tarred by its association with the Rashtriya Swayamsevak Sangh, a para-military organization, one of whose members – Nathuram Godse – assassinated Gandhi in January 1948. The Jan Sangh's support base in any case was mainly limited to north Indian urban Hindu small trading groups. Yet here state Congress leaders were 'more resourceful and less liberal' and had few compunctions about appropriating the Jan Sangh's communal demands. For instance, the Jan Sangh's campaign in the immediate aftermath of partition against Urdu being granted the status of a second official language in UP was preempted by the state Congress government's adoption of a Hindi-only policy.[4] The Praja Socialist Party, an offshoot from the Congress Socialist party, considered Nehru's socialism to be a sham. Although it did well in the 1957 elections, polling the second highest number of popular votes, the PSP was unable to make a significant dent on the Congress's hold over north India. Congress under Nehru relied on the personalized and caste-based networks of local bosses to deliver the support of the lower social orders in the rural areas. Despite a spread of support in UP, the PSP was unable to attract a majority of the voters with its radical socialist rhetoric. The Communist Party of India was constrained by its pre-independence support for the British war effort and the demand for Pakistan. Its main bases of support were in Kerala where it won the 1957 state elections and in Andhra Pradesh and West Bengal. In 1964 the CPI, reeling from the dismissal of its government in Kerala by the centre in 1959, split into pro-Moscow and pro-Beijing factions. Among the more

[4] Bruce Graham, *Hindu Nationalisim and Indian Politics: the Origins and Development of the Bharatiya Jana Sangh*, Cambridge, 1990, pp. 111–28 and 156–7.

important regional opposition parties was the Dravida Munnetra Kazhagam (DMK). It emerged from the anti-Brahmin Dravida Kazhagam established by E. V. Ramaswami Naicker, known as Periyar or Mahatma among his Tamil-speaking followers. In 1949, a faction led by C. N. Annadurai parted company with the Dravida Kazhagam to form the Dravida Munnetra Kazhagam (literally, the Dravidian Progressive Federation) to push for the creation of a separate Tamil state in Madras. Congress, however, managed to hold its ground against the DMK until the mid-1960s.

But the survival of India's parliamentary system in the long run is inexplicable without reference to the symbiotic relationship between the Congress high command and the non-elected institutions of the state – the civil bureaucracy, the police, and the army. Without the IAS, the IPS and when necessary, as during the insurgencies in the north-east, the Indian army, the Congress party alone could not have assured the political centre's authority throughout the length and breadth of the country. The subtler and less visible role of the Indian army in securing central authority flowed in part from the existence of para-military forces such as the border security force and a centrally armed instrument like the central reserve police. These could be called upon to smoothe New Delhi's little local troubles without creating an undue reliance on the army command. With a choice of coercive instruments other than the army at their disposal, the political arms of the state were also able to maintain an edge over the administrative machinery at the all-India level. However, members of the IAS and the IPS in their capacity as agents of the centre could often overrule the political leadership at the state and local levels of society. Yet according to the terms of the understanding, instances where they actually curbed the activities of state and local politicians were restricted to matters vital to the imperatives of the state and the party high command. Politicians and bureaucrats, especially at the district level, more often than not worked hand in glove at all levels of the political system with complicitous ease. The growth of public sector enterprises and licensing controls over the private sector created new spheres of state patronage, giving the central political leadership ample scope for rewarding loyal and cooperative non-elected officials. Contemporary observers could discern that the all-India centre while leaning heavily on the non-elected institutions of the state 'disguise[d] a tendency to authoritarian rule' through a 'conscious and studied observance ... of parliamentary forms' as a 'convenient substitute for democratic practices'.[5] Even in these early years there were loud whispers in support of some sort of a socially non-interventionary and politically benevolent authoritarian rule for India.

[5] Christie's report no. 23 for September 1949, DO 133/108, PRO.

Yet the degree of support for authoritarian rule among influential segments of society, while important at the level of elite discourse, in itself is not sufficient in decoding the contrasting political developments in India and Pakistan. This in turn serves notice against giving credence to specificities of a political culture without relating them to the structures of state and political economy. The singular focus on parties and politics by some scholars and on political culture by others has deflected from the fact that the practice of formal democracy in India, expressed in the holding of elections at regular intervals, has always co-existed with a covert authoritarianism inherent in the state structure. One reason why this has been less conducive to detection and dissection is that the structural authoritarianism of a state made tolerable by a formally democratic political system tends to be more enduring and diffuse than one based on direct military rule.

This is not to discount the very real differences between covert and overt authoritarianism. India's success in forestalling military rule is no small feat. But once again the credit cannot be given to its politicians without noting the propitious circumstances which made the neutralization of the military institution possible. These included the fact of a pre-existing unitary central apparatus, a formidable defence establishment sustained by a modest but adequate resource base and a geographical expanse so vast as to make the coordination of a military takeover highly improbable, if not altogether impossible. There can be no doubt that unlike the Muslim League in Pakistan the Congress leadership took concerted steps to downgrade the army's social and political profile and establish civilian control over the military as a whole. In 1955 the office of commander-in-chief of the defence forces was abolished. Instead there was a chief of army staff who was on an equal footing with the other two service chiefs. As if to add insult to injury, the Indian state's warrant of precedence put the chief of army staff in twenty-fifth place, trailing behind state court chief justices, members of the planning commission and even state cabinet ministers. Initially the chief of army staff had a four-year term. After 1966 the tenure of all the three service chiefs was reduced to three years with no possibility of extension. The service chiefs were subordinate to a civilian minister of defence and their budgets placed under the scrutiny of non-elected officials in the defence ministry. Modelled on the British practice of parliamentary government, civilian control over the defence services in India did not mean elective supremacy. The close monitoring of defence budgets by civil servants is not the same as military accountability to a representative parliament.

From the point of view of the Indian military there may not have been much to choose between civil or elective supremacy. And indeed, there was more than one military voice bemoaning the shabby treatment meted out to the Indian defence services during the years 1947 to 1955, incidentally the very years that sowed the seeds of military dominance in Pakistan. The induction of Krishna Menon as minister of defence in May 1957 proved to be a mixed bag of treats for Indian military personnel. Defence production was stepped up but so too were Menon's jibes at the service chiefs as well as the Indian army which in his view was simply a 'parade-ground army'.[6] Menon's ambitious plans to modernize the army led to frequent clashes with members of the defence establishment and also with the private sector which wanted a larger cut of the ensuing boons. Until the Indo-China war in 1962 forced a major review of New Delhi's military policy, Menon, who could be as irascible as he could be ingenious, rivetted public attention on matters to do with defence as never before. Apart from politicizing the ministry of defence, Menon contravened the military's tradition of seniority as the basis for promotion on the grounds that merit was a requisite for efficiency. He had a point which was rammed home to parliament with strong backing from Nehru despite howls of protest against his summary treatment of military precedent.

Menon's tenure as minister of defence is usually regarded as one under-scoring the supremacy of the elected over the non-elected institutions of the state. But it seems more apt to describe it as one which exposed the liberal democratic theory's myth of the neutrality of non-elected institutions. Civil bureaucrats and military officers alike reacted to Menon's decisions by furnishing evidence to members of parliament and actively canvassing their support. If the spectacle of men in uniform in the visitor's gallery of the Lok Sabha avidly following the debate on their respective cases was a rarity for India, so too would it have been for military dominated Pakistan. That said, it is undoubtedly true that Menon-type interventions in military matters would have been inconceivable in a country where the defence estab-lishment enjoyed a vantage position in the political configuration by virtue of the state's grossly inflated strategic requirements. By the time the border skirmish with China forced New Delhi to press down on the pedal of military expansion, civilian control of the defence services as well as the state itself had been well established.

As for the partnership between the premier political party and the civilian bureaucracy, this in contrast to that in Pakistan was made possible in the context of a pre-existing and essentially unitary structure of the Indian state. Admittedly, the Congress party possessed something of a federal structure in the first two decades of independence. Nehru made accommo-dations with Congress party bosses at the state level who were permitted a certain degree of autonomy. Such a policy of the central leadership only

[6] Cited in C. P. Bhambhri, *Bureaucracy and Politics in India*, New Delhi, 1971, p. 178.

worked so long as the rural under-classes remained relatively quiescent and patron–client relations in the states remained substantially intact. With the expanding sphere of democratic politics, the limitations of this policy became evident; in the 1967 elections the Congress party was swept out of power in as many as eight states. It is necessary therefore to address the political dividends as well as costs of the strategy of class conciliation rather than class conflict pursued during the Nehru years.

Throughout the pre-independence period provincial and district Congress committees were in the hands of dominant landowning castes allied with urban middle-class intelligentsia, businessmen and merchants. During the 1930s, nearly half of the new Congress recruits were drawn from prosperous proprietor classes with holdings of between 21 and 100 acres. After independence, conservative coalitions built up by dominant land-owning castes in alliance with urban businessmen gained effective control of district and state Congress committees. In mobilizing the rural under-privileged for electoral purposes, the Congress encouraged alliances along caste, community and regional rather than class lines. During the first two decades after independence the Congress party remained an instrument of largely upper caste and class interests. Access to state power enabled the Congress to foil all attempts that might have assisted the organization of the underprivileged cutting across the divisions of caste, community as well as region and, in this way, stretching the parameters of an economically based national politics to allow for some measure of self-assertion by the sub-ordinate classes. For all the hue and cry about Nehru's 'socialist' leanings, his government's policies catered to the interests of the propertied groups. Socialism, in Nehru's parlance, was not inconsistent with a mixed economy. The aim was not to create an egalitarian society so much as encourage the rapid growth of productive forces in society. India's first three development plans were characterized by state supported public sector industrialization and the promotion of the private sector. Nehru's policy of class conciliation and accommodation lent a semblance of cohesion to the Congress party and helped consolidate state power. But by the same token, this policy under-mined its representative capacity and, by extension, the Indian state's ability to carry out redistributive reforms.

For instance, legislation abolishing *zamindari* during 1953–5 took away the rent collecting rights of absentee landlords but, in most instances, allowed resident landlords to retain vast tracts of their land. The policy was a gift to the Congress's rich farmer supporters. There was no effective social programme of redistributive justice for the subordinate castes and classes. Yet even these nominal land reforms were unacceptable to the Congress's provincial bosses. Since the ceiling legislation in the early decades was on an individual basis, landlords opted for retrospective registration of land in the name of family members or, failing that, bribing the administrative bureaucracy to block the effective implementation of the reforms.

By the end of the second decade of independence Congress's limited social bases of support and its dependence on an oligarchical coterie of party bosses began to backfire seriously. Between 1962 and 1966 and around the time of the general elections of 1967 there were mass defections from the Congress. In Bihar and UP, Charan Singh broke from the Congress to form the Bharatiya Kranti Dal which later became the Bharatiya Lok Dal. In West Bengal a United Front consisting of the Communist Party of India – Marxist (CPI-M) and thirteen other parties defeated the Congress. In Bihar socialists did well at the Congress's expense. The DMK routed Congress in Tamil Nadu. The results of the 1967 elections marked the end of the first phase of Congress dominance in India and the emergence of a number of regionally based opposition parties.

The most dramatic instances of opposition to the ruling Congress party have invariably come from regional forces. This tendency is partly explained by the fact that the Congress was the only party with nation-wide bases of support. But more importantly, it had much to do with the initial reluctance of Nehru and other leaders to implement Congress's commitment to a linguistic reorganization of the states. Violent agitations following a fast unto death by a prominent Gandhian leader forced the government in December 1952 to concede the principle of a Telugu-speaking state of Andhra. The recommendation of a states' reorganization commission to form fourteen linguistic states in 1955 did not extend to the provinces of Bombay and Punjab. Major language riots in Bombay in 1960 forced the centre to create the states of Maharashtra and Gujarat and the long-standing demand for a Punjabi subah or province was conceded only as late as 1966. The most serious regional threat in the late 1950s and early 1960s came from the southern states, Tamil Nadu in particular, which were virulently opposed to the imposition of Hindi as the national language. It was simply that the limits of Nehruvian policy of working with the Congress party's regional bosses were not fully registered until the setback suffered in the fourth general election of 1967.

Contrary to the common view that dynasticism within the Congress party and the Indian state structure was started by Nehru's daughter, Indira Gandhi, the dynamics of centre–state relations had already begun swinging the pendulum away from parliament and the party leadership towards executive authority concentrated in the prime minister's hands long before Nehru's death in 1964. Centralization of authority in Nehru's hands was a result of the Congress organization at the state and the district levels being weak, loose and riven with inter- and intra-group factionalism. The changing balance of power within the elected institutions was reflected in their relationship with the non-elective institutions of the state, the civil bureaucracy in particular. So there is reason to pause and consider before joining the scholarly chorus to celebrate Nehru's achievements in putting India on the road to democracy. Whether as government, party or state manager, Nehru was more of a juggler than an architect of democratic institutions. For instance, he used a formula known as the 'Kamaraj plan' of 1963 to replace most of the central ministers and state chief ministers and bring confirmed loyalists into positions of power. Nehru showed both imagination and ability to use his political stature to mask the actual processes of organizational disintegration within the Congress. The bureaucrats had no reason to be uncomfortable with the statist socialism propounded by Nehru. India's first and most celebrated prime minister deployed his socialist rhetoric with telling effect to placate the paragons of social justice while at the same time succouring the appetite of state officials as well as the bigbags of Indian capitalism who financed the Congress party's election campaigns.

The Congress party's descent into state party bossism and an oligarchical form of politics became complete during the brief prime ministership of Lal Bahadur Shastri between May 1964 and January 1966. Unable to withstand pressures from party bosses, euphemistically known as the 'syndicate', Shastri clutched at the arms of the higher civil service in India. This seemed to be the only way to prevent an increasingly unrepresentative gang of regional bosses from exploiting the Congress party and, in the process, seriously undermining the centre's capacity to promote the interests of its main beneficiaries both within and outside the state structure. After Shastri's sudden death, the syndicate believed that they had a malleable prime ministerial candidate in Indira Gandhi. They could not have been wider of the mark. In an attempt to neutralize the party bosses and restore the Congress's sagging electoral fortunes, Indira Gandhi turned not only to elements within the bureaucracy but decided to deliver to the party and the country a potent dose of populism.

The legacy of the Nehru era of Indian politics had both positive and negative aspects. On the positive side, the practice of formal democracy had become an established routine as the four general elections of 1952, 1957, 1962 and 1967 exemplified. On the negative side, the symbiotic relationship of the ruling party with the civil bureaucracy gave a fresh lease of life to the strand of authoritarianism that had been inherent in the Indian state structure. Despite the formal separation of the legislature and the executive, rule by ordinance was by no means a thing of the past. According to one estimate, during the first two decades of independence in addition to 1,600 statutes, including twenty-one constitutional amendments, more than 100 regulations, 100 presidential acts and 150 ordinances were enacted. As if this riot of executive regulations was not enough, various government departments are believed to have been issuing about 5,000 rules annually. Together with the vastly increased scope of bureaucratic discretion, these rules and regulations far from systematizing relations between state and society provided opportunities galore for patronage, corruption and extortion. Two decades after independence India possessed a unitary state resting equally on elected and non-elected institutions, neither of which were above twisting and turning the rules to accommodate a personalized style of politics and government, and a federal ruling party that was becoming increasingly hamstrung by factionalism and a narrowing regional and class basis of support.

Qualifying the successes of Indian democracy is not to slight the Nehruvian Congress's very significant achievement in institutionalizing the phenomena of general elections at five-year intervals. Elections at least give the ruled the priceless power to periodically hold rulers accountable, even if they cannot be seen as a sufficient basis to gauge the substance of democracy. Unless capable of extending their voting rights beyond the confines of institutionalized electoral arenas to an effective struggle against social and economic exploitation, legal citizens are more likely to be the handmaids of powerful political manipulators than autonomous agents deriving concrete rewards from democratic processes. Granted the small mercies voters extract from politicians during the time of electoral mobilization, these fall well short of the rights of equal citizenship that dignify democracy over all other forms of governance. To equate the right to vote with the full rights of citizenship is to lose sight of the ongoing struggle between dominance and resistance which informs and can potentially transform the nexus between democratic politics and authoritarian states in post-independence South Asia.

Party politics and military dominance in Pakistan, 1947–1971

Pakistan's abject failure to institute even a formal democracy with regular elections at the national and provincial levels provides the obverse side of the British colonial legacy in the subcontinent. It took no less than twenty-four years to hold the first general election on the basis of universal adult franchise in 1970. Some of the reasons for Pakistan's singular inability to evolve a democratic political system have been sketched out earlier. Fleshing these out further should make the comparisons and contrasts of the dialectic between state formation and political processes in the two countries more vivid and accessible.

As already suggested, Congress's inheritance of the colonial state's unitary centre and its assumption of British India's international personality placed Pakistan at a severe disadvantage. Cast in the role of a 'seceding state', and with Muslim provincial particularisms providing a major driving force for its creation, Pakistan had somehow to confirm its independent existence by creating a viable central authority over territories which apart from being separated by over a thousand miles of Indian territory had until August 1947 been governed directly from New Delhi. The imperative of constructing a central government from scratch wholly outweighed the resources and capacities of the newly founded state. For one thing the Muslim League was not a patch on the Indian National Congress; indeed the League's organizational machinery was weakest precisely in the areas which became part of Pakistan. With the onset of military disputes with India over the north Indian princely state of Kashmir, it became particularly urgent for the Pakistani leadership to assert central authority over the provinces.

The need to firm the state's defences against India and establish central authority over the provinces, however, turned out to be contradictory requirements. They were contradictory because Pakistan's share of the assets of undivided India was hopelessly meagre; it inherited an army which possessed the manpower but no matching firepower. The initiation of hostilities with India so soon after independence saw the centre extracting financial resources from the provinces and diverting them into the defence procurement effort before political processes in Pakistan had become more clearly defined. In the event, the requirements of the defence establishment served to distort relations between the new central government and the provinces. Facing massive socio-economic dislocations as a result of the demographic changes and communal carnage that accompanied partition, the provinces were averse to surrendering their limited financial resources to beef up the Pakistani military. In India during the first years of independence some of the larger states like Bombay and Madras successfully resisted the centre's attempts at reducing their financial powers. While the matter was eventually settled in accordance with the centre's wishes, efforts were made to accommodate provincial demands through negotiation and compromise. Ironically, in Pakistan where the newly formed centre had to tread particularly carefully to win the allegiance of the constituent units, all caution was set aside in chipping away at the financial autonomy enjoyed by the provinces under the 1935 act. Executive ordinances replaced the process of long and hard political bargaining while coercion substituted consensus in relations between the Pakistani centre and the provinces.

Since the provincial arenas remained the hub of political activity, the steady etiolation of provincial powers did not auger well for the political process. This made the position of an essentially migrant political leadership at the centre even more precarious, forcing it to rely on the administrative bureaucracy to counter the mounting resentments in the provincial and local Leagues, such as they existed. Enhanced powers for the administrative arms of the state were good for the proponents of bureaucratic authoritarianism but bad for relations between a newly formed centre and provinces deeply attached to their autonomy. The initial high profiled presence of Urdu speakers from north India in the upper echelons of the administrative bureaucracy was soon supplanted by a profusion of Punjabis, giving the Pakistani brand of centralization strong provincial overtones. Bengalis, Sindhis, Pathans and Baluch alike resented the part played by the centre's appointees, both Punjabis and Muhajirs, in the extraction of their already very limited provincial revenues to bolster a defence establishment dominated by Punjabis. Yet although predominantly Punjabi, the two main non-elected institutions of the Pakistani state were by no means working exclusively to promote the interests of Punjabi politicians. Despite a common socio-economic background there were plenty of contradictions between state bureaucrats and the primarily landlord politicians of the Punjab. On the rare occasions when there was no conflict between class and occupational interests it was possible to detect a loosely based alliance between Punjabi politicians, bureaucrats and military officials. But instances of conflict more than balanced those of collaboration and even intrigue, as many non-Punjabis were wont to believe. Punjab's rural bosses, like their counterparts in other provinces and also in India, were not minded to play second fiddle to state bureaucrats unless the force of circumstances demanded otherwise.

This is where the different inheritances of the two states proved critical. The imperative of consolidating central authority outweighed all others since separation from India achieved on paper was not matched by the hard realities on the ground. In dire financial straits within months of its creation, the Pakistani centre found it difficult to meet its own requirements without undermining provincial powers. Strained relations with the provinces were hardly conducive for the smooth functioning of political processes given that the main national party had barely scratched the surface in the vast majority of the constituencies. This is where reliance on civil bureaucrats seemed the only option for a central leadership sensing not only its own but, possibly, the state's rapid demise. So it was not merely the absence of democratic ideals that spurred Pakistan's political leaders from Jinnah onwards into seeking comfort in bureaucratic authoritarianism.

The consolidation of central authority under mainly bureaucratic auspices was to place state formation on a collision course with the dynamics informing political processes in the constituent units. What confounded the problems plaguing Pakistan during the initial years of independence were the vexing implications of its demographic arithmetic. While power was concentrated in the western wing, Bengalis in the eastern wing had an overall majority in the country. In any system of representative democracy, the Bengalis would be in a position to use their majority in parliament to dominate the central government. This was anathema to the civil and defence officials and their allies among important West Pakistani landed and business families. So although landlord politicians in the western wing had no intention of becoming junior partners to the non-elected institutions, the need to prevent Bengali domination of the state led them into an uneasy alliance with civil bureaucrats and military officials who were increasingly coming to define state imperatives in terms of their own more narrowly focused institutional interests.

Together this alliance of mixed conveniences worked to undermine the role of parliament in the evolving structure of the state. No national elections were held. Constitution-making was delayed on account of fierce disagreements on how political and financial powers were to be apportioned between the centre and the provinces and whether Pakistan was to have an Islamic or a secular form of government. A parliament elected in 1945–6 on the basis of a restricted franchise under the government of India act of 1935 acted as both legislature and constitution-making body. Its unrepresentative character, its inability to draft a constitutional document and the tendency of the executive to bypass it and rule by ordinance ensured that Pakistan's first parliament lost all credibility with disastrous consequences for the future of the representative system. To this day the national assembly in Pakistan is a pale reflection of the Indian Lok Sabha. Without an effective legislative organ it is particularly difficult for a political party system to strike roots.

The supremacy of the executive over not only the legislative but also the judicial organs of the state was established fairly early on in Pakistan's history. Without judicial autonomy from the executive there was no effective way to seek redressal for the state's infringement of fundamental rights. This was in contrast to India where a series of judicial rulings upholding the right to property put the brakes on land reform legislation in a number of states. While some of the decisions taken by the Indian courts can be challenged for being ultra conservative in their interpretation of private property rights, and consequently a drag on progressive social and economic legislation, these judicial interventions at least served to create the semblance of institutional checks and balances that was so sorely lacking in Pakistan. It is not without significance that the relative stature of the judiciary in the two countries until recently has been in direct proportion to the democratic and authoritarian tendencies in their respective political systems.

Undermining the legislative and judicial institutions of the state was intrinsic to the process of strengthening central authority. Apart from heightening the coercive aspects of governance, this hastened the decay of an already perilously weak political party system. This suited the bureaucratic–military combine and its allies among the dominant classes in West Pakistan. Needing and wanting to hold on to power at the centre without seeking a mandate from the people, there was every reason for this opportunistic alliance to stonewall the framing of the constitution. And indeed it took nine long years, during which India went to the polls twice, before a constitution could be framed in Pakistan.

Some seven years before the first military takeover, the political process had slipped off the rails. After the assassination of Liaquat Ali Khan in October 1951 a succession of unelected civil bureaucrats assumed elective office. Pakistan's third governor-general, Ghulam Mohammad, was a hardened bureaucrat who had no appetite for democratic practices. In April 1953 Ghulam Mohammad in close concert with the military and bureaucratic establishment dismissed the Bengali prime minister, Khwaja Nazimuddin, who enjoyed the confidence of a majority in parliament and slotted in Mohammad Ali Bogra, a political nonentity from Bengal who seemed more concerned about promoting American interests than those of his own province. In October 1954, Ghulam Mohammad dismissed the first constituent assembly when it tried curbing some of his powers and brought in a so-called 'cabinet of talents' remarkable only for its utterly unrepresentative character.

This was to set a pernicious precedent for future relations between the executive and legislative arms of the state. Justifying his action, the governor-general lambasted the constituent assembly for being unrepresentative and accused its members of delaying constitution-making in order to avoid facing the electorate. The fact that some of the assembly members were facing corruption charges under the public representatives disqualification order lent substance to this line of argument. Yet it was judicial complicity with the executive rather than force of popular opinion that determined the outcome of Pakistan's first and most decisive constitutional crisis. Significantly, the Sind high court upheld the appeal of the president of the constituent assembly, Maulvi Tamizuddin Ahmed, when it declared the governor-general's action to be unconstitutional. Assured of support from the Punjabi chief justice of Pakistan, Muhammad Munir, the government took the matter to the supreme court. Backed by the civil bureaucracy and the government controlled media, the governor-general and his associates succeeded in getting a favourable hearing from the supreme court and winning popular compliance with the final verdict. Stretching the law of necessity to its outer limits and spuriously equating revolutionary legality with legitimacy, the chief justice deftly steered the bench into giving a ruling which was to have far-reaching effects on the already uneasy balance between state formation and political processes in Pakistan.

The principles which guided the supreme court's verdict in 1955 were later used to lend legitimacy to the first direct military intervention in Pakistan. For now, judicial sanction gave legal cover to the military–bureaucratic axis's plans for a constitutional structure unimpaired by the fact of a Bengal majority. After forcibly imposing the one unit system in West Pakistan – which abolished provincial boundaries and practically placed the smaller provinces of Sind, Baluchistan and the North West Frontier Province under Punjabi dominance – and ensuring parity of representation between the two wings, the bureaucratic–military combine and their political allies felt relatively certain about their ability to keep the Bengali majority at bay.

As in India, Pakistan's constitutional framework was federal in form but unitary in substance. The centre had all the necessary powers, legislative, administrative and financial, to overwhelm the quantum of autonomy granted to the provinces. In India, Congress's federal structure and Nehru's policy of making accommodations with regional party bosses kept the unitarianism of the state structure in harness during the first two decades of independence. But by the time the first Pakistani constitution was ratified in March 1956, the Muslim League had disintegrated – a victim of deliberate neglect and rivalries along personal and provincial lines. In the absence of a federally based political party the 1956 constitution merely served to further embitter relations between the centre and the provinces. The inauguration of the new constitution saw a bureaucrat with a military background, Iskander Mirza, manoeuvring himself into presidential office while yet another bureaucrat, Chaudhri Mohammad Ali, became the prime minister. As bureaucrats and generals called the shots, politicians willing to do their bidding were shunted in and out of office.

All this should not lead to the simplistic conclusion that the weaknesses inherent in the political process were the main reason for military dominance in Pakistan. The example of India makes it equally difficult to view rampant corruption and political divisiveness, pervasive for many of the same reasons at all levels of Pakistani society during the first decade, as anything more than subsidiary factors leading to direct military rule. It is equally unconvincing to argue that the Pakistani military's superior institutional coherence in relation to ill-organized political parties pushed it into assuming the reins of governance in a divided society. Endorsed by modernization theorists explicitly and by Marxists implicitly, such an interpretation does not stand the test of the available historical evidence. The immediate aftermath of partition underlines the brittleness of both elected and non-elected institutions. Far from being the 'agents of modernization' or the 'overdeveloped' pillars of the state, both the civil bureaucracy and the military were desperately short of skilled manpower and the requisite institutional infrastructure. It was the interplay of domestic, regional and international factors during the late forties and fifties – in particular, the links forged with the USA – that served to erode the position of parties and politicians within the evolving structure of the Pakistani state by tipping the institutional balance towards the civil bureaucracy and the military.

The dominance of the non-elected institutions was a result of a concerted strategy by the higher echelons of the bureaucracy and the military to exploit rivalries among Pakistani politicians and systematically weaken the political process by manipulating their connections with the centres of the international system in London and Washington. In the final analysis the responsibility for Pakistan's inability to work a parliamentary system of government must be shared by its civil bureaucrats, military officials, chief justices and politicians, both secular and religious. Yet the reasons why they succeeded as well as they did in emasculating the people's democractic rights are only partly located in their seemingly inordinate appetite for political intrigue. Without exonerating them, the collective roles of its leading lights in undermining the political process has to be set against the awesome structural constraints Pakistan inherited at the time of its creation. Most of these were further exacerbated or distorted by a rivalry with India which because it led to a futile quest for military parity distorted the internal political equation and forced Pakistan into compromising its sovereignty and autonomy vis-à-vis the centres of the international system.

One of the lingering questions about Pakistan's first decade of independence is why a military institution that had already established dominance by 1951 deemed it necessary to maintain the façade of parliamentary government with all its inconveniences until 1958. As long as elections could be postponed with impunity, there was no reason to abandon an arrangement in which non-elected officials called the shots and politicians bore the responsibility. But once the process of constitution-making had been completed, a reference to the people was inescapable. Successful in discrediting parties and politicians, the civil bureaucracy and the army were unsure of maintaining their dominance within the state structure after the general elections scheduled for 1959. Fearing a major realignment of political forces after the elections, the army high command in combination with select civil bureaucrats decided in October 1958 to take direct control over the state apparatus and, in this way, deter all potential challenges to a position of privilege they had for long enjoyed. So it cannot be argued that the failure of the 'parliamentary system' in Pakistan flowed from the 'power vacuum' created by politicians at the helm of parties with no real bases of popular support.

Realizing that dominance over the state apparatus did not guarantee control over the political process, the military–bureaucratic axis chose to tear down the façade of parliamentary democracy. This removed the only existing hindrance, and a highly compromised one at that, to the promotion of state imperatives defined by the institutional concerns of the civil bureaucracy and the army. While tensions with India and international pressures imposed serious limitations on available options, the criteria used to make policy choices served to distort relations between the centre and the provinces in particular and the dialectic between state construction and political processes in general. The links which the top echelons of the military and the civil bureaucracy in Pakistan enjoyed with the centres of the international system in London and Washington during the height of the cold war were of vital importance in this respect. Instead of filling a 'power vacuum', senior civil and military officials, alarmed by the severe resource crunch facing the state on the eve of general elections in 1959, sought the blessings of their international patrons for a policy aimed at depoliticizing Pakistani society before it slipped into the era of mass mobilization. It was a momentous decision. The institutional shift from elected to non-elected institutions in the first decade, which the military intervention of 1958 sought to confirm, was to endure all variety of experiments in governance, some more desperately authoritarian than others.

For now Pakistani society settled to the uncertain treats of governance by a socially liberal and politically benevolent authoritarian regime led by General Mohammad Ayub Khan, the commander-in-chief of the army. The regime continues to be hailed in some quarters as the most stable in Pakistan's chequered history. If statistical evidence alone could enlighten, the regime did appear to have scored some important successes in jolting the national economy out of stagnation. Yet upon closer examination the Ayub regime's main political legacy was in centralizing state authority by confirming many of the latent and manifestly distorting tendencies of the first decade. Its achievements on the economic front have to be set against the low base line in both the agricultural and the industrial sectors and, in any case, were muted by a policy emphasis on growth rather than distribution. Whether seen from the political or the economic angle, the Ayub era stands out as a watershed in defining relations between state and society in Pakistan.

A product of martial law, the Ayub regime survived on coercion, mixed with adroit political engineering, only to perish at the hands of the very forces it assiduously sought to curb and contain. Until 1962 the regime governed under martial law with Ayub as unchallenged dictator, who was commander-in-chief, chief martial law administrator and president of Pakistan at the same time. Banning parties and instituting a purge of politicians under the elective bodies disqualification order, Ayub began his tenure confidently promising to restore dignity and integrity to public life. But such noble intentions apart, Ayub knew better than anyone that both his survival and success depended upon the continued support of Pakistan's essentially, if not exclusively, Punjabi federal bureaucracy and, above all, its predominantly Punjabi army.

Even military dictators need a way of legitimizing their rule and so have to try and win the support of at least a section of the people. So in 1962 Ayub formally lifted martial law, presented the country with a fait accompli in the form of a constitution and allowed certain parties to function within the restricted domain of his new political order. Both phases are instructive for the unseemly effects of bureaucratization of a polity and economy differentiated by region, class and the rural–urban divide. The Ayub regime turned to the well-worn colonial policy of co-option and collaboration. Selected social and economic groups with localized instead of provincial or national political appeal were extended state patronage and offered other nostrums in return for their tacit support of military and quasi-military rule. Ayub Khan had long ago come to the conclusion that parliamentary government based on the Westminster model was unsuited for a highly personalized society like Pakistan where patron-client and clan-based ties determined the nature of politics. What Pakistanis needed was some form of 'controlled democracy', the emphasis being on control rather than democracy.

Immediately upon assuming power Ayub with the help of senior members of the civil service of Pakistan, the CSP, began considering ways of taking the sting out of the political process through a selective mobilization of the rural areas under the supervision of the administrative bureaucracy. Proclaimed in 1959 in the form of a basic democracies order, Ayub's idea of representative government was candidly undemocratic in letter as well as in spirit. Its main purpose was to cultivate a new rural constituency for the regime that would endorse rather than set its political and economic agendas. The politically least pliable elements in society – industrial labour and the urban intelligentsia – were denied any real stake in the new dispensation. Heavily weighted in favour of the rural areas, the system allowed for 80,000 so-called basic democrats, later increased to 120,000, who were equally divided between the two wings of the country. They were to be elected on the basis of adult franchise to union councils and union committees in the rural and urban areas respectively. These would then indirectly elect members to the higher level local bodies, the tehsil/ thana councils in the rural areas and the municipal committees and cantonment boards in the urban areas as well as the district and the divisional councils. The basic democrats were also to serve as the electoral college for the election of the president and the provincial and national assemblies. All four tiers of the system were controlled by the bureaucracy which nominated as many as half of the members to the district and divisional councils. Extending the scope of bureaucratic and police patronage to rural localities was intended to release the exercise of central authority from constraints imposed by parties and politicians with provincial bases of support. Preserving the one-unit administration in West Pakistan and giving a cold shoulder to the rising aspirations for provincial autonomy in East Pakistan, the strategy of placing local political processes under centrally directed bureaucratic control was laden with dangers for the state's essentially federal configuration. Poorly represented in the senior echelons of the civil bureaucracy, non-Punjabis both within and outside the state apparatus resented their marginal role in the processes of decision-making. Despite the resumption of political party activity, the confining logic of the basic democracy system and stringent press censorship precluded the effective ventilation of mounting provincial and class-based grievances. After 1962, the judiciary which had earlier legitimized the military takeover was given nominal scope to try and check the unbridled exercise of executive authority. But the judiciary's abject dependence on an all-powerful executive meant that its rulings merely kept alive the citizenry's hopes of legal redress without substantively altering the inequitable equation between state and civil society.

The denial of fundamental political rights in practice, if not in theory, was paralleled by economic policies designed to bolster privileged segments of rural and urban society. During the 1960s the Ayub regime orchestrated a process of social class formation by linking policies of differential economic patronage with its overall goal of depoliticization. Encouraged by its international patrons and their main vehicles of economic control, the World Bank and the International Monetary Fund, the regime unabashedly accepted the logical consequences of 'functional inequality' in an attempt to achieve rapid growth. Betting on the strong to expand its economic base in the shortest possible time, the regime unfurled a spate of policies that assisted the transformation of landlords into capitalists and merchants into industrialists. By turning Pakistan into a veritable haven for the bigwigs of commercialized agriculture and business interests, the Ayub regime presided over an economic boom that contained all the explosive ingredients for a massive political bust.

The regime's palpable lack of interest in policies of redistribution has been attributed to its need for support among Pakistan's dominant social groups, especially the landed elite and nascent industrialists in the western wing. Mindful of their continued clout in the rural areas, the regime took care to offset the political losses of the larger landlords by conferring favours in the economic domain. Its much vaunted land reforms in 1959 avoided denting Pakistan's skewed agrarian structure. No agricultural income tax was imposed even as the terms of trade were kept tilted against the agrarian sector by overvaluing the rupee by as much as 50 per cent. Yet currying support among vested economic interests in the rural areas, many of whom enjoyed direct or indirect influence within the bureaucracy and the military, was ultimately less significant than the regime's innovative policies of locating state functionaries at strategic points in key economic sectors. In what was to be repeated with even greater alacrity in the 1980s, the Ayub regime gave senior military and civilian officials privileged access to agricultural land, urban property, business and industrial licences and top posts in public corporations. Much of the land resumed by the state under the 1959 reforms was handed out to government functionaries, Punjabis in the main. This helped create a class of middling landlords whose dependence on the state apparatus guaranteed solid support for the regime.

This brand of socio-economic engineering was not simply a highly controlled method of institution building as some Western observers were mistakenly led to believe. It depended on a closed personalized network involving some 15,000 senior civil servants, 500 or so top military officers, less than two dozen wealthy urban families controlling the bulk of the industrial, banking and insurance assets of the country and, finally, a somewhat more sprawling bunch of basic democrats drawn mostly from among middle-sized landlords in the rural areas.

With a limited social basis of support, the Ayub regime perpetuated itself under the thick protective covering provided by the basic democracies system and a maze of controls on a demoralized, if not entirely strangulated, journalistic community. The system of press advice and the establishment of a national press trust in 1963 was the handiwork of one of the most controversial CSP officers of the period, Altaf Gauhar, who later became secretary of the ministry of information. Intended to insulate the president from all unpleasant societal developments, it bound Ayub to a small coterie of bureaucratic flatterers and self-servers – an imprudent style of governing even for a military ruler. There were early indications of the regime's lack of touch with popular opinion. When the 1962 constitution dropped Islam from the nomenclature of the state there were loud growls from the bearded men of religion. Within a year Pakistan had reverted to the 1956 constitution's definition of the state as an Islamic republic. And while it remained firmly in support of the family law ordinance of 1961 which safeguarded the rights of women and children in instances of divorce and custody, the regime slumped into hobnobbing with the forces of religious orthodoxy despite its formally liberal and secular orientation. Such vacillation on matters to do with Islam did not assure the support of religious leaders, among the harshest critics of the Ayub regime, and further alienated the intelligentsia.

On the international front the Ayub regime continued the policy of courting the United States of America. But in the changed circumstances following the Indo-China war, the resulting economic and military assistance from Washington disappointed the authors of Pakistan's foreign policy and infuriated those who had always believed in the merits of non-alignment. Under fire for mortgaging Pakistan's sovereignty to an unreliable ally, Ayub turned to China without entirely shaking off the stigma of alignment with the USA. An unwieldy posture, which together with the capitalist orientation of the regime's economic development policies prepared the ground for a major swing to the left in the political arenas, both formal and informal.

Oblivious of the growing opposition to the entire gamut of government's policies, Ayub continued to depend on his bureaucratically controlled basic democracies system to parry challenges from the political opposition. In a development loaded with extra irony, the man on horseback had changed into civilian attire mid-way in his tenure to become the self-appointed leader of a government-sponsored political party, the Convention Muslim League. With a party to legitimize his claim and the state bureaucracy to manipulate the electoral process, the general turned politician fancying his chances called for the first presidential elections under the 1962 constitution. Held in January 1965, Ayub had an easy walkover against Fatima Jinnah, the sister of the Quaid-i-Azam, who had the support of a rag-tag coalition of opposition parties united only in their intense dislike of the man who had denied them so much for so long.

The elections unveiled all the impediments to dislodging Ayub from within the controlled parameters of the basic democracies system. Dependent on bureaucratic and police support, candidates for political office were not likely to bite the hand that fed them. Yet the growing frustration and anger in a society undergoing a painful process of urbanization and experiencing heightened regional and class disparities in rural and urban areas alike offered plenty of opportunities for Ayub's opponents, not only outside but increasingly within the state apparatus. It is known that Ayub was wheedled into fighting the 1965 war with India by a group of fawning bureaucrats, cabinet ministers and military men, some of whom saw it as Pakistan's last opportunity to snatch Kashmir out of New Delhi's sharpening military jaw while others, more on the mark, hoped it would spell the end of the general's rule. Whatever the precise motivations of Ayub and his principal advisers, the inconclusive Indo-Pakistan war and the Tashkent peace accord which followed it proved to be the swansong of a regime slouching under the combined weight of Pakistan's multiple political and economic woes. The prompt suspension of American military assistance advertised the hollowness of the regime's foreign and defence policies, emboldening its critics within the military and bureaucratic institutions, just what the political opposition needed to deal the fatal blow.

After the mid-sixties the politics of exclusion and the economics of inequality were coming to haunt Ayub's regime with a vengeance. Labour militancy at industrial sites and rampant student radicalism in campuses around the country provided the background for the opposition's renewed efforts to settle old scores. In May 1967, four political parties – the East Pakistani based Awami League, the Council Muslim League, the Jamat-i-Islami and the Nizam-i-Islam – formed the Pakistan Democratic Movement. Among its demands were the reintroduction of the parliamentary system, direct elections, a federal structure with the devolution of all powers to the constituent units except defence, foreign affairs, currency, communication and trade, separate foreign exchange accounts for the two wings based on their export earnings, the shift of the naval headquarters to East Pakistan and regional parity in the services within ten years. The regime responded by extending the defence of Pakistan rules, enacted during the 1965 war, and declaring virtually all forms of political activity as anti-state.

Yet the resort to draconian powers no longer disguised the regime's growing nervousness. In a desperate measure to retrieve lost ground, the central government accused Sheikh Mujibur Rahman – the leader of the Awami League – and a number of his associates of conspiring with India and, more incredulously with the United States, to force the breakaway of East Pakistan. Known as the Agartala conspiracy case, Mujib's imprisonment and subsequent trial only served further to enrage the Bengali majority. The Awami League's six-point programme for provincial autonomy, justified on account of wide economic disparities between the two wings and inadequate representation of Bengalis in the services, became a formidable rallying cry for the opposition to Ayub in the eastern wing. Defiance of state authority in the east was paralleled by labour and student strikes in West Pakistan, creating an atmosphere more akin to social anarchy than controlled politics. It was just desert for the regime's handling of Pakistani society, politics and economy.

An ailing man whose personal reputation had been marred by his immediate family's well advertised nepotism and corruption, Ayub was not up to the task of salvaging something out of the wreckage. In his final days in office Ayub no doubt felt betrayed by the very men whom he had invested with unprecedented powers and let down at a critical moment by his main international patron. Yet in perhaps the biggest irony of all, his regime was caving in to the very forces it had successfully preempted a decade earlier. Lulled into complacency by the top echelons of the bureaucracy officiating over the personalized ties of power and privilege, Ayub had erred gravely in overestimating the loyalty of the military in clamping down on the urban protestors bent upon turfing him out of office.

Between November 1968 and March 1969, students, industrial labour, professional groups, low-ranking government employees and the ulema all took to the streets in massive anti-government demonstrations in key urban centres. Some 250 people died in the ensuing clashes with the police and the army. What these street scenes demonstrated to Ayub and his bureaucratic associates was that confusing the rules of selection with those of election cannot satisfy the sentiments that fire political processes. Pressed from all sides, Ayub had no choice but to comply with the military high command's unequivocal demand that he immediately hand over power to General Yahya Khan, the commander-in-chief of the Pakistan army.

The Ayub era in Pakistan provides a cautionary tale of the very grave consequences which controlled and very highly selective representative institutions can have on culturally and linguistically diverse societies like Pakistan. This is why such a controlled system had to be abandoned by the military regime of Yahya Khan. In November 1969 Yahya announced general elections to be held on the basis of adult franchise in October of 1970. To allay the criticism of the regionalists Yahya declared the abolition of the one-unit system in West Pakistan, but avoided any specific reference to Bengali demands for provincial autonomy. In March 1970 the regime announced a legal framework order which gave Yahya the power to veto any constitutional document produced by the national assembly. The military high command clearly had no intention of handing over power to political groupings, whether from the eastern or the western wings, which aimed at restructuring the state and overturning the dominance of the military and the bureaucracy.

In the elections which were eventually held in December 1970 the Awami League secured an absolute majority, winning as many as 160 out of 162 seats from East Pakistan. The Pakistan People's Party led by Zulfikar Ali Bhutto, who had served his political apprenticeship in Ayub's cabinet, saw its support base confined to the Punjab and Sind but managed to bag 81 of the 138 seats from West Pakistan in the national assembly. The Awami League's six-point programme for maximum provincial autonomy with its confederal overtones was anathema to the West Pakistani dominated establishment, but it won the enthusiastic support of Bengali middle-class professionals, students, small and medium scale businessmen and industrial labourers. A poverty-stricken peasantry also responded to the Awami League's clarion call, having been the main victims of inter-regional economic disparity and neglect during a catastrophic cyclone in the fall of 1970. The PPP's support base included middle-sized Punjabi farmers, landed notables from Sind and the Multan districts of the Punjab, Punjabi urban middle-class professionals, the newly organized industrial labour in Karachi and the Punjab, rural–urban migrants and the Punjabi rural under-privileged strata.

Although the Awami League and the Pakistan People's Party won the 1970 elections in the eastern and the western wings respectively, their exclusively regional bases of support gave Yahya Khan the opening he needed to delay the transfer of power in the hope of extracting terms which could perpetuate the existing state structure and, with it, the embedded dominance of the military and bureaucratic establishment. The dogged resistance of these two non-elected institutions to accepting the verdict of the people seriously limited the politicians' room to manoeuvre. Zulfikar Ali Bhutto, the West Pakistani politician commonly accredited with the break up of the country, was in a precarious negotiating position. And while his cavalier political style led to some astounding excesses in public speaking at quite the wrong moment in history, these were the utterances of a man whose sense of his own vulnerability combined with the natural ambition of a politician forced him into a position of intransigence in a manner remi-niscent of Pakistan's creator. That Bhutto is for some segments of Pakistani society what Mohammad Ali Jinnah has been for many in India is not altogether surprising. Yet a history focusing on the posturings of 'great men' frequently misses the real point. True of Jinnah's role in the partition of India, it is equally so in the case of Bhutto, the supposed destroyer of Pakistan's national integrity.

Defying the entrenched non-elected institutions of the state and striking a bargain with the Awami League required much more than acts of personal political generosity. The stakes were as high as the power of the individual politician was low. Both Bhutto and Mujib represented a melange of political forces which were not above tossing them to the winds if their interests failed to be accommodated. Yet it would be no less erroneous to maintain that irreconcilable differences between East and West Pakistani electorates doomed the search for a political formula that could prevent the disintegration of the country. Over a decade of military and quasi-military dictatorship had denied the people of both wings the luxury of an open national politics where views could be exchanged, misunderstandings removed and vital interests accommodated. This is why the electorate neatly divided along regional lines in the first ever general elections to be held on the basis of universal adult franchise. And this was also why politicians tried covering their tracks by establishing contacts with the military high command, creating that ambience of distrust which made fruitful political negotiations impossible.

Until the availability of critical official papers in Pakistan and Bangladesh the precise point at which political negotiations broke down, if they did so irreversibly, will remain shrouded in mystery. What is known is that on 25 March 1971 Yahya's regime ordered a military crackdown in East Pakistan. Excluded from their rightful place in the governance of the country, the Bengali majority decided to part company with West Pakistan and declared the formation of a sovereign independent state of Bangladesh. The Pakistan army's campaign against Bengali resistance left thousands dead and an exodus of millions into India. This prompted the Indian government in December 1971 to deploy troops on the side of the Bangladeshi rebels to expedite the disintegration of Pakistan.

Conclusion

On the face of it in 1971 a military dominant within the state structure for two decades suffered defeat at the hands of a counterpart subjected to civilian political control. But more importantly, the débâcle in East Pakistan was the cumulative result of the Pakistani defence establishment's political rather than military failures. The military action in East Pakistan followed the inability of a manifestly authoritarian regime to preside over a transfer of power in the aftermath of the country's first general elections held on the basis of universal adult franchise. Underscoring the consequences of the different balance between elected and non-elected institutions in the two countries, on 10 March 1971 India had successfully concluded its fifth general elections to the Lok Sabha. So if the authoritarian features within their state structures are roughly comparable, the absence of even the most nominal democratic practices in Pakistan makes for a glaring contrast with India.

The success of formal democracy in India is generally attributed to the organizational strengths of the Congress and the political skills of its leaders. Yet India's inheritance of the British raj's unitary centre and the forging of very different sorts of international links in the first decade of independence appear to be the more important variables. It is common knowledge that the Congress leadership lost no time embracing and extolling the very same Indian civil service which had been a consistent target of their attack under colonialism. But it is less well-known that the IAS and the IPS played a decisive role in ensuring the centre's writ in many areas where the Congress machinery was unable to deliver the goods. The disarray within the Congress, especially at the provincial and local levels, was no less than dissension within the Muslim League. In the initial years of independence the similarities and weaknesses of a single party state in both India and Pakistan were striking. However, the Indian polity was better able to preserve parliamentary forms, if not wholly democratic practices.

A pre-existing unitary central government and the relatively lighter, though by no means insignificant, impact of defence expenditure on the national economy are important clues to why political processes in India were not subjected to the same pressures as in Pakistan. First, the Indian central apparatus was institutionally, economically and militarily viable enough to avoid impinging on the autonomy of the constituent units in the same measure as its Pakistani counterpart which, apart from being in the process of construction, began confirming its authority by poaching on provincial powers and resources very early on in the day. Secondly, relatively lower levels of tension in centre–state relations had salutary effects on the political process in India, foreclosing the possibility of the Indian civil bureaucracy and military developing international connections independently of the political leadership at the centre.

If the parallels with Pakistan were merely implicit in the Nehru era, they become quite explicit in the heyday of the 'syndicate', a euphemism for Congress's descent into state party bossism and an oligarchical form of politics. Lal Bahadur Shastri may not have been of the same calibre as his illustrious predecessor, but his political fate had more to do with the structural changes set in motion by Jawaharlal himself. Nehru's reluctance to mobilize the underprivileged strata in society through a bold radical socio-economic agenda or to countenance organizational reforms within the Congress left the grand old party with a limited social base of support and increasing factionalism at both the state and local levels. Saddled with a decaying party and pressed by unrepresentative party bosses, Shastri decided to strengthen the higher civil service in his effort to exercise centralized political authority. But before there could be a decisive shift in the balance of power between the political and administrative arms of the Indian state, Indira Gandhi chose a slightly different way of addressing the problems facing her party and the continued assertion of central authority. The path of populism which she attempted to take did not mean simply relying on elements within the civil bureaucracy, but also a widening and deepening of the social bases of support of the Congress party.

The location and role of the civil bureaucracy are of key significance in unravelling the actual workings of political democracy in India and military dictatorship in Pakistan. Placing the administrative bureaucracy on the same side as the elected 'civil' institutions in examining civil–military relations ignores the more important question of balance and potential contradictions between elected and non-elected institutions. As the case of Pakistan indicates, the balance between the elected and non-elected institutions of the state has a far greater bearing on the prospects for democracy than is captured by the civil–military dichotomy. At the same time, as India's experience during the first two decades of independence suggests, democracy expressed in the formalization of regular elections can, and often does, co-exist with the inherently authoritarian tendencies of the state. The milder impact of regional tensions with Pakistan and international pressures on domestic politics and economy in India were advantageous for the functioning of a formal democracy. Critical in this regard was the emerging role of the military institution within the two state structures. In Pakistan the civil bureaucracy became junior partner to the military to keep the East Bengali majority at bay and push for a political economy of defence whereas the more acceptable logic of the electoral arithmetic in India saw the civil bureaucracy and the police allying with a national political party committed, however tenuously, to a political economy of development.

3 The 'populist' era and its aftermath in India, Pakistan and Bangladesh, 1971 to c.1993

The 1970s witnessed the crystallization of significant changes in the state-society dialectic in South Asia. During the 1960s state interventions in the economy had contributed to important alterations in social structures and in the process broadened the arena of mass politics. In the absence of any perceptible movement towards the strengthening of equal citizenship rights for the many who remained outside the charmed circle of a small elite, largely unorganized resistance to established structures of dominance assumed new levels of potency. The expansion and radicalization of the social bases of politics posed challenges to oligarchical democracy and military authoritarianism alike. These were sought to be met by comparable experiments in what widely came to be termed 'populist politics' during the late sixties and the seventies.

Populism by its very nature is an elusive concept. Open to varied interpretations, populist politics in the South Asian subcontinent have escaped the exactitudes of a searching or rigorous historical analysis. To the extent that populism has been defined at all the emphasis lies on the personal aspects of the phenomenon. Yet a focus on the role of charismatic leaders has produced a somewhat shadowy, if not distorted, view of the populist drama. The appeal of populism lay in its claim to give voice to the frustrations of the dispossessed and downtrodden and in its declared aim to dent the existing structures of domination and privilege. It was really more a matter of temperament than ideology. Slogans such as *garibi hatao* (abolish poverty) or *roti, kapra aur makaan* (bread, clothing and shelter) encapsulated the spirit of the political changes being attempted, but did not rest on any systematic class analysis of social inequities. Often couched in the legitimizing idioms of the nationalist discourse, populism was more emotionally charged than organizationally cohesive. It promised to improve the wretched lot of subordinated classes, castes and communities without encouraging their empowerment through well-knit political organization. Falling short of ideological integrity but rising above the dismal cynicism of existing power equations, those who articulated the populist dream raised hopes of a better future among millions and instilled fears among privileged coteries. It is the politics of this dialectic of hopes and fears which lend the terms populism and anti-populist reaction a measure of both substance and meaning. Many populist leaders emerged from within structures of state power, whose institutional efficacy and legitimacy was either eroded or eroding, to satisfy the manifold demands being raised in the expanding mass arenas of politics. Populism, therefore, can be only profitably analysed in the specific historical context of the interplay between state structures and political processes.

In India attempts were made to correct the Congress's descent into an oligarchical form of politics resting on regional party bosses through a populist mobilization of those occupying the lower rungs of the social order. Pakistan emerged from over a decade of depoliticization under military rule and a bloody civil war which marked the breakaway of its eastern wing and the establishment of Bangladesh. The Pakistan People's Party and the Awami League in Bangladesh were faced with the task of channelling populist expectations which had played such a key part in the dismantling of the military regimes of Generals Ayub and Yahya.

This chapter examines the factors that powered the populist currents in India, Pakistan and Bangladesh and the reasons why before the end of the decade they not only ran out of steam but exacerbated the authoritarian strains which had always bedeviled their state structures. One of its main premises is that the failure of populism is inexplicable without reference to the structural imperatives, both internal and external, of existing states and political economies in the South Asian subcontinent. Analysts of populism in the region have concentrated on teasing out the personal motivations and choices of key politicians like Indira Gandhi, Zulfikar Ali Bhutto and Sheikh Mujibur Rahman. The emphasis on the role of the individual has something to do with the very nature of populism – devoid as it is of a coherent class-based ideology or organization – but at best gives a partial view of the conjuncture in which populist politics were attempted, amended and ultimately abandoned. Populism's moment in subcontinental history has also been attributed to its inherent limitations as a political strategy. Couched in generalities aimed at appealing to the 'poor' and disempowered citizenry across regional and linguistic divisions, populist programmes have tended to lack the specificity of purpose and solidity of organized support necessary to force the pace of redistributive reforms. Yet as the preceding analysis has suggested, recourse to populism in each of the three countries was resorted to by elements already situated within the cloisters of power in the face of wide socio-economic developments that had given rise to new and insistent political demands and challenges from below. Moreover, it is one thing to point to the tactical errors of populist politics and quite another to fault its strategic goal of redistributive reforms. The practical difficulties

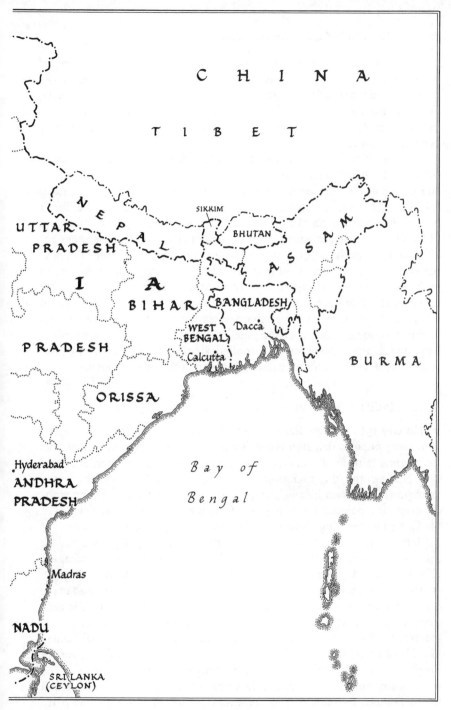

2   Political divisions of South Asia, 1972

of effectively mobilizing a disparate cross-section of society, consisting of some ensconced as well as newly mobilized groups, against existing structures of dominance and privilege is far greater than has been given credence. So it might be more meaningful to examine the limited potential of populism as a historical phenomenon at the contextual rather than the purely personal or conceptual level.

Assessing how the imperatives of existing states and political economies served to constrain the manoeuvrability of self-professedly populist parties and politicians is a necessary antidote to the overemphasis on individual leaders. This is not to deny the role of human motivation and choice. But it is only by focusing on the interstices of human agency and structural possibility that one can gain a sense of the opportunities, real or apparent, afforded by populist politics. It is perhaps the exaggerated sense of opportunity presented by populism that has made it such a difficult process to evaluate and tainted interpretations of its authoritarian aftermath, mostly covert in India and overt in Pakistan and Bangladesh. A reconsideration of populism followed by a comparative assessment of the qualitative changes in the state-society dialectic from the late seventies to the present might help explain the reasons for the paradoxically analogous results of democratic processes and military authoritarianism in the three countries.

Indira Gandhi and Indian 'populism'

In January 1966 the 'syndicate' bosses who had come to control the Congress party organization after Nehru's death in 1964 selected Mrs Gandhi as their prime ministerial candidate, certain of keeping her at their beck and call. But against the backdrop of soaring prices, food shortages and unemployment, lower income groups in the various regions had been withdrawing their political loyalties to the Congress. The main beneficiaries of the Congress's eroding social base of support were political parties, both to the left and the right, that were able to fuse the appeal of populism with regionalism. Although the two wings of the Communist Party of India, the CPI and the CPI(Marxist), as well as the Jan Sangh claimed all-India status, their support was essentially regional in nature. All three had made considerable organizational strides at the Congress's expense since the 1962 elections. In addition, there was a flood of defections from the Congress just before and after the 1967 elections, including that of key regional leaders like Charan Singh in UP, Ajoy Mukherjee in West Bengal, Rao Birendra Singh in Haryana and Govind Narain Singh in Madhya Pradesh. The formation of united fronts against the Congress served to reduce opposition fragmentation, the single most important factor in ensuring one-party dominance in an effectively multi-party system. In a dramatically changing political arena, big business too appeared to be hedging its bets. Between 1961 and 1964 the Congress's share of political donations by business interests was approximately 85 per cent; by the time of the 1967 elections it had dropped to 73.7 per cent. The right-wing Swatantra party was the second major recipient of contributions by private limited companies, increasing its share of the total from 13.6 to 25.2 per cent in the same years.[1]

Congress's veneer was visibly fading. The results of the 1967 general elections registered an embarrassing defeat for the Congress in eight states. A larger number of candidates in the fray and a greater voter turnout pointed to the intensification of political competition and growing participation in the electoral process. If the limitations of the Congress's social bases of support had begun to pinch, the statistical figures masked the extent of the discomfort. There was a marginal drop in the total vote cast in favour of Congress candidates for the Lok Sabha, from 45 per cent in 1962 to 41 per cent in 1967. In state assembly elections, Congress's proportion of voter support fell to 42 per cent, down more than 3 per cent from 1962.[2]

Yet there were some optimistic signs in this otherwise gloomy scenario. The voting patterns were far too varied to suggest a fundamental rejection of Congress ideology, whether the commitment to centralized authority, secularism or even socialism. In states like Madhya Pradesh, Bihar, Rajasthan and Gujarat the voters had opted for scions of princely families. Communists had been the choice in West Bengal and Kerala while Hindu communalists found favour in the towns and cities of the north Indian heartland. Parties promising populist reforms and contesting the centre's Hindi-only policy came out on top in the south. None of the opposition groupings, including the communists, had scored their successes through a new style of politics. They had at best modified Congress's well-tried method of vertical patterns of mobilization with rural bigwigs who commanded the allegiance of castes and powerful local factions.

These were all indicators of the potential for a Congress revival at the next hustings. Though cut down to size, the Congress was still the only party with a national following. The sheer variety of regional political patterns combined with a general heightening of social conflict along class and caste lines had serious ramifications for political stability at the state level. Violations of parliamentary norms and constitutional powers in many states took on alarming proportions almost as soon as the election results were announced. This guaranteed a continued role for central authority in the person of the state governor, the non-elected kingmaker in the politics of fluidity that marked the terrain in many non-Congress dominated states. So

[1] Bhambhri, *Bureaucracy and Politics in India*, p.29.
[2] Francine Frankel, *India's Political Economy, 1947–1977: the Gradual Revolution*, Princeton, 1978, p. 353.

despite the visible lunge towards regionalism recorded in the 1967 electoral results, the implications for state politics gave Congress at the centre plenty of opportunities to try and best its rivals.

For Indira Gandhi there were other silver linings to the clouds. The failure of the party bosses to deliver the vote banks released her from the awkward position of being a pliant instrument of powerful regional patrons. It was convenient that some of her more redoubtable rivals like K. Kamaraj Nadar, S. K. Patil and Atulya Ghosh had gone down in defeat. With her eventual triumph over the old syndicate bosses now imminent, Mrs Gandhi began considering ways of turning Congress's present weaknesses into future strengths. The results of the 1967 elections had made it plain to those occupying positions at the political centre that the challenge of regionalism was now being posed by political forces outside the pale of the Congress. A simple partnership with the civil bureaucracy was no longer sufficient to maintain Congress hegemony or central authority. Assisted by an inner cabinet consisting of experienced and trusted bureaucrats, Indira Gandhi set about the task of restoring the sagging political fortunes of the Congress with alacrity. Noting the distinct radicalization of the social base along class, caste, tribal and linguistic lines, she opted for an explicitly populist socio-economic programme. In June 1969 Mrs Gandhi deftly outmanoeuvred the party bosses by supporting an independent, V. V. Giri, for party president against the official Congress candidate, Sanjiva Reddy. By November 1969 Mrs Gandhi was endorsing leftist political positions within the party articulated by the Congress Forum for Socialist Action. Mohan Kumaramangalam, a former communist, became her key political and economic strategist.

The tactical shift in the Congress's electoral strategy followed naturally. Since intermediate castes and classes, notably the big farmers and the middle to richer peasants, formed the principal power base of the opposition to the Congress at the state level, the aim was to link the top and bottom layers of agrarian society by buttressing the waning political clout of high caste, old landed elites and by professing to champion the common interests of subordinate castes and classes which transcended local and regional arenas. This was done by ridding the Congress of the oligarchical deadwood in 1969 without damaging the old connections forged by the political centre with the civil bureaucracy, the police, the military and sizeable fractions of the industrial capitalist class.

After the Congress split in 1969 Mrs Gandhi formed a minority government with the support of the Communist Party of India and the Dravida Munnetra Kazhagam. She also sought alliances with populist leaders in the states. In Karnataka she cast aside Nijalangappa, an old Congress hand who had the support of the higher castes, in favour of Devaraj Urs who had the backing of the Harijans or the scheduled castes. In Gujarat, which had been the stronghold of her most rebarbative rival among the syndicate bosses, Morarji Desai, Mrs Gandhi began mobilizing support among the lower castes – Khastriyas, Harijans, Adivasis and the Muslims – a policy that came to be known in the later 1970s as the KHAM strategy. The critical electoral state of Uttar Pradesh provides the best illustration of her strategy of linking the top and the bottom layers. Here she depended on H. N. Bahuguna who had a following among Harijans and Muslims and higher castes like the Rajput Thakurs and the Brahmins to do down the erstwhile Congress boss Charan Singh, who had the backing of middle castes such as the Kurmis and Ahirs in eastern UP and Jat farmers in western UP. A similar strategy was adopted in other states, for instance Andhra Pradesh in the south.

Efforts to deepen the Congress's social bases of support were matched by a series of left-leaning policy measures. These included the nationalization of banks in 1969, steps to check the further concentration of wealth in the hands of the larger industrial houses through a more restricted licensing policy and the abolition of privy purses to princely families. In January 1970 Jagjivan Ram, a Harijan, was slotted in as Congress president and the working committee reiterated the goal of turning the party into an effective instrument of social transformation. Special advisory committees and cells were created within the Congress to monitor the problems facing minorities, scheduled castes, backward classes and industrial labour. But these plans, noble in prospectus, were in sharp contrast to the actual disarray of state and district units following the Congress split. To obviate the problem the working committee extended the office terms of all Congress committees and officers for a year and authorized the state Congress committees to fill the vacancies. In what was an indication of things to come Mrs Gandhi began appointing favoured men as chief ministers, a departure from the established norm of selecting those who had the support of state assembly parties. After 1971, elections to state Congress committees and their offices, especially the post of president, were superseded by direct appointments by the All-India Congress president. Weaknesses of Congress party organization and the ensuing loss of legitimacy at the local levels were matched by an onslaught against the Congress's new populist directions led by the Indian judiciary. Claiming the inviolability of fundamental rights, the supreme court issued a series of judgements which slammed the brakes on Mrs Gandhi's policy of bank nationalization and abolition of privy purses. These judicial checks on executive directed legislative action, even if cast in a conservative mould, underline a feature of the institutional balance within the Indian state that was conspicuous by its absence in neighbouring Pakistan.

It was against this background that Indira Gandhi decided to put her populist alliance building to the electoral test. In 1971 she called a snap election and for the first time instituted the policy of delinking elections to the central and state assemblies. The bifurcation of national and state political arenas was intended to release the Congress's national fortunes from state issues and regional bosses which had worked to its disadvantage in the 1967 elections. By holding elections to the Lok Sabha before the state elections Mrs Gandhi was trying to push the pendulum in favour of the centre where her personal stature and the populist slogan of *garibi hatao* would ensure Congress's success. A strong majority at the centre would better place the Congress to influence the course of state elections. But while giving the Congress at the all-India level more room to manoeuvre, the long-term effects of this structural change in the Indian political system was to make local politics more autonomous from national politics.

For now Mrs Gandhi's socio-economic programme and alliance with populist leaders in the states produced handsome dividends in the 1971 parliamentary and 1972 state elections. The simple but loaded slogan *garibi hatao* appeared to do the conjurer's trick. The Congress won a two-thirds majority in the Lok Sabha and polled 43 per cent of the popular vote. The state assembly elections, hot on the heels of India's successful military intervention in East Pakistan, also registered a resounding success for the Congress (Ruling) led by Indira Gandhi. But it was easier to win the elections than to translate the Congress's populist programme into practice. The implications of Congress's new populist directions, especially at the level of regional political economies, threatened to leave Mrs Gandhi high and dry at the centre. In choosing to ally with populist regional leaders to do down the syndicate, Mrs Gandhi had underestimated the resilience of old rural power structures. Still ensconced in regional political economies, the erstwhile Congress bosses were ready and able to mobilize their middle to richer peasant supporters – many of whom had penetrated the state police and civil service – to blunt the edge of a centrally backed populist challenge. The inability of Congress state ministries to push through their populist programmes or govern effectively in Bihar and Gujarat is a comment on the strength of dominant castes and classes in withstanding attacks mounted by the leaders of emergent and newly empowered subordinate castes and classes. Above all, it underlines the continuing autonomy of regional political economies in the face of a seemingly omnipotent and centralized Indian state structure.

Mrs Gandhi's failure to cash in on the Congress's electoral gains had much to do with her anxieties about the potentially constraining effects of autonomous regional political economies on the centralized structures of decision-making in India. Rebuilding the Congress organization on the basis of her new and broader-based electoral alliances promised to considerably enhance, not diminish, the power of popular regional leaders in extracting concessions from the centre. So even where the new populism was relatively successful, as in the key state of Uttar Pradesh between 1972 and 1975, the central executive began to eye state level populist leaders and organizations with suspicion. Men like Bahuguna and Chandra Shekhar in UP and Devaraj Urs in Karnataka were seen as potential claimants to power at the centre on the basis of their populist mobilization in the states. The response, short-sighted though it may have been, was to completely abandon any semblance of inner-party democracy within the Congress and to hoist state and local leaders from the top.

Yet events which have been explained mainly in terms of Indira Gandhi's flawed leadership qualities, and more specifically her personal paranoia, are more meaningfully analysed in the context of the structural contradictions within the Indian state structure and economy. The dramatic hike in international oil prices in 1973 was a particularly bad piece of timing for incipient populist experiments in all three countries of the South Asian subcontinent. It worsened India's already precarious balance of payments position and sent shock waves throughout the economy. Rising prices, food shortages, industrial stagnation and massive unemployment, especially among college graduates, led to street protests and outbreaks of violence in many parts of the country. International economic pressures compounded Congress's difficulties in delivering on its electoral promises and widened the organizational cracks in district and state level units. With the notion of a strong centre as the concomitant of Indian unity and national weal ingrained in her political philosophy, Mrs Gandhi responded by further concentrating powers in her own hands. While the attractions of ruling by diktat hastened the institutional atrophy of the Congress party underway since the Nehru era, the process should be attributed less to quirks in her personality than to the imperatives of sustaining the centralized character of the Indian state structure.

What is clear is that the continued exercise of executive power from the centre was directly at odds with the demonstrated resilience of dominant castes and the potential problems which populist power could pose at the level of regional political economies. The age-old dialectic between centralism and regionalism in Indian history had come to assume new dimensions with the deepening and widening of the political process. Mobilizing ever larger segments of the unprivileged strata without the will or the ability to actuate qualitative changes in their socio-economic predicament was redefining politics in ways which severely tested the institutional capacities of a centralized state structure. It was the disjunction between state posturing from above and multiple social changes below that created the conditions for personalized rule and the politics of deinstitutionalization. Mrs Gandhi's efforts to counter regional challenges bore a striking similarity to the policies of the colonial and the military dominated Pakistani states, albeit with rather different consequences in a society accustomed by now to using its democratic right to turn out unpopular parties and leaders from electoral office.

Amidst growing popular disenchantment and an intensification of the opposition's efforts to dislodge her government, Mrs Gandhi raised the spectre of internal and external conspiracies against the state. The equation of national integrity and unity with Congress rule at the centre was a well-rehearsed line to legitimize coercive state action. In March 1974 Jayaprakash Narayan, a highly venerated Gandhian socialist popularly known as JP, had stepped in to give a fillip to the opposition's movement in Bihar and soon became the acknowledged leader of a nation-wide Indira *hatao* campaign. In a volley of singeing attacks, JP held Mrs Gandhi directly responsible for the rampant corruption in the country and dubbed her rule authoritarian. Mrs Gandhi for her part accused JP of conniving with the Hindu Jan Sangh and the American CIA. At a time when she was finding it difficult to retain the upper hand in an acrimonious political debate with a strong opposition, the Allahabad high court's ruling invalidating her election from Rai Bareilly in 1971 on account of the misuse of government machinery came as a bolt from the dark.

By resorting to the emergency on 26 June 1975 the besieged prime minister hoped to clip the opposition's wings by deflecting both sorts of regional challenges and projecting the centre as the only source of supra-local and supra-state populist programmes. This mode of bolstering central authority through an overt authoritarianism based on pressing the civil, police and military institutions of the state in the service of the ruling party more blatantly than ever appeared to work reasonably well only in the short term. Called upon to implement unpopular policies, non-elected officials resented being tarred by the brush of popular antipathy towards Mrs Gandhi's government. The worst excesses of the emergency, and certainly the best remembered, were associated with her son Sanjay Gandhi's thoughtless and highhanded activities in the name of population control and urban beautification. Sanjay's programme of forced vasectomies and clearing the capital of its slums targeted the poor and lowly, leading the wits to comment that having failed to get rid of poverty the Congress had taken to getting rid of the poor.

With the growing alienation of the non-elected institutions of the state – especially members of the civil bureaucracy, the police and the judiciary – as well as the subordinate groups in northern India which had rallied to the populist programmes of the Congress since 1969, the option of overt authoritarianism was swept aside in the 1977 elections. The formally demo-cratic nature of the Indian state had reasserted itself against Mrs Gandhi's new, if ultimately misguided, populist directions and, more emphatically, her brief flirtation with overt authoritarianism.

Bhuttoism or populism? The case of Pakistan

There are many fascinating parallels between Indira Gandhi's and Zulfikar Ali Bhutto's populist experiments. Both have been accused of personalizing power, mauling the institutions of the state and subverting the populist dream. Yet these charges reveal less and obscure more. Even the most imaginative exercise in counterfactual history would be hard pressed to prove the success of populism in India and Pakistan in the absence of an Indira Gandhi or a Zulfikar Ali Bhutto. To lose sight of the context in which the two played their respective populist cards is to mistake jokers for the missing aces. Both rose to the commanding heights despite being closely associated with the discredited dispensations populism was seeking to displace. Both drew their main political appeal from links with the structures of the old world rather than any demonstrated personal qualities or ideological commitment that might have helped usher in a new world of populism. A comparison of Mrs Gandhi and Bhutto underlines the ways in which the existing structures of the Indian and Pakistani states and political economies not only ensured their emergence to power but continued to delimit their manoeuverability and, by extension, the parameters of their populist policies.

Contrary to the prevalent view, the post-1971 Pakistani state structure was only marginally different from the one preceding it. The institutional imbalance within the state remained substantially unchanged despite the assumption of presidential office by an elected leader backed by a party with bases of support in two of the four remaining provinces. On the face of it, rampant anti-bureaucratic sentiment coupled with the humiliation of the army provided a perfect opening to tilt the institutional balance against the non-elected institutions of the state. But the legacies of military rule had greatly reduced such prospects as existed for genuine grassroots political party organizations. In contrast to India where populism has been presented both as the cause and effect of political deinstitutionalization, in Pakistan the scope for party building suffered from prolonged bouts of direct state intervention in the political process. As the 1970 electoral results had shown, political horizons in Pakistan had become even more regionally fragmented than before. Worse still, the personal influence of candidates at the level of the constituency mattered more than their adherence to specific socio-economic policies at the national level.

Yet Ayub's so-called decade of development had released a plethora of energies frustrated by a consistent trend towards the political and economic denial of those with limited or no access to state patronage. The primacy of the state together with policies aimed at taking the country down the capitalist road to development had appreciably heightened class tensions in rural and urban areas alike. And while these enlivened the political debate on provincial autonomy among the relatively privileged, the underlying class basis of social grievances augured well for a politics of a left-leaning variety. Correctly gauging the trends, Zulfikar Ali Bhutto had pieced together an alliance with members of the political left despite his close association with a regime that had been expressedly capitalist in orientation. Born into one of the largest landowning families in Sind, Bhutto may have been an unlikely leader of a party committed to reversing the capitalist bias of the state and enforcing a socialist transformation of the Pakistani economy. Yet his emergence as the leading populist figure of the times flowed directly from a military and bureaucratic dominated state system geared to thwarting the development of party organizations and, by implication, the political ambitions of educated urban middle classes. Needing someone with national stature around whom to rally, a small group of mainly urban educated professionals committed to socialism and populist reforms turned to Bhutto. An intelligent and charismatic politician, Bhutto had served in Ayub's cabinet since 1958 in various capacities. He had been an early advocate of a pro-China slant in Pakistan's foreign policy and well known for his anti-imperialist views and hardline position vis-à-vis India. Bhutto had fallen out with Ayub over the Tashkent accord with India, accusing his old patron of bartering away Pakistan's chance to wrench Kashmir out of New Delhi's control. It was an immensely popular stance and one that added to Bhutto's fame and notoriety in ways which his less privileged associates could only imagine emulating.

The Pakistan People's Party was a product of this marriage of convenience between two sides of unequal political stature. So there was plenty of space for tension and conflict between the PPP's left-leaning ideologues – for instance the venerable ex-bureaucrat J. A. Rahim and the public accountant turned popular representative, Mubashir Hasan – and the man of landed origins who had been selected to lead it. Simply put, if recourse to populism was the most effective strategy to leaven the ill effects of Pakistan's widening economic and social disparities, the politician chosen to direct it was one of the main beneficiaries of the very military–bureaucratic state structure that posed the biggest obstacle to its implementation.

This line of argument is intended to stretch the scope of the lenses through which politicians and their performances tend to be analysed in India and Pakistan. It is common to cheerfully greet an ascendant politician with a barrage of expectations whose chances of realization are only remotely related to the reality. And it is all too common to berate the same individual when on the downward incline for personally failing to deliver the goods. What is missing in both points of views is any allowance for the context informing the individual's options and choice of actions. The tendency to exaggerate the capacities of individual human agency are remarkably comparable in Indian and Pakistani societies and need correctives in the form of a keener sense of the historical contexts which not only generate illusions but also the corresponding disillusionments.

However opportunistic, Bhutto and Mrs Gandhi's populist rhetoric was an appropriate and timely response to the socio-economic grievances that were seething below. Both created the illusion of impending changes that for the most part were improbable given the hard structural realities which continued to underpin relations between state and society in the two countries. In the case of India, the Congress split of 1969 had weakened the very vehicle which might conceivably have lent substance to centrally directed populist policies at the level of regional political economies. And while Mrs Gandhi deliberately avoided organizing Congress's new social bases of support because of her fear of a populist regional challenge against the centre, this had as much to do with the centralizing imperatives of the existing Indian state structure as with her own personal paranoia. Short of retailoring relations between centre and state from scratch, the success of populism in the absence of a coherent party organization at the district and local levels of society seemed to demand greater centralization of powers in prime ministerial hands. To castigate Mrs Gandhi for personalizing powers without noting the centralizing tendencies that populism was helping accentuate due to the weaknesses of the Congress party's local units is to take an unacceptably partial view of historical processes.

Similarly, the existing state structure in Pakistan was predisposed towards a concentration of powers in Bhutto's hands, the more so since the PPP despite its electoral successes was hardly a disciplined political party organization with established internal rules and procedures. It is true that like his Indian counterpart Bhutto also neglected to place the PPP's electoral support at the district and local levels on a more permanent organizational footing. Apart from threatening to give impetus to centrifugal forces that were directly contrary to the centralized basis of the Pakistani state, the PPP could be used to challenge Bhutto's own control over the party. As for his personal insecurities bordering on paranoia, given the long-drawn history of military and bureaucratic dominance of the Pakistani state it cannot be denied that these had a much stronger empirical basis than Mrs Gandhi's across the border. Indeed the main contrast between Bhutto's and Mrs Gandhi's location to power stemmed from the very different institutional balance within the Pakistani and the Indian state structures. While Bhutto needed to build up the PPP as an institutional counterweight to the non-elected arms of the state rather more urgently than Mrs Gandhi, both overstepped the bounds of safety in relying upon them to parry threats to their continuation in office at the centre.

The reliance of both leaders to a greater or lesser extent on the non-elected institutions of the state, especially the bureaucracy, conceals some of the more striking contrasts in their respective attempts to gild the populist lily. Yet differences rooted in the pre-existing institutional balance within the state structures had an important bearing on the political space available to them to initiate their populist programmes. The symbiosis between the Congress party and the non-elected institutions, though showing some signs of wear and tear, gave Mrs Gandhi relatively greater leverage. Bhutto on the other hand had to reckon with the well-established supremacy of non-elected institutions whose upper echelons took exception to the ascendancy of politicians they generally held in contempt. This explains why Bhutto directed his institutional reforms at the civil bureaucracy and the military, while Mrs Gandhi restricted her meddling to the officious demand that state officials, the IAS in particular, demonstrate 'commitment' and loyalty to the ruling party's agenda.

Taking his cues from a people stunned by military defeat and resentful of the high profile of the civil bureaucracy during the Ayub era, Bhutto instituted reforms aimed at curbing the autonomy of the two main non-elected institutions of the Pakistani state. Yet Bhutto stopped short of creating a system of checks and balances whereby members of the non-elected institutions would not only be accountable to parliament but directly answerable to the people in courts of law. A measure of the man's personal limitations, it is also an indication of the sweeping nature of the institutional reforms Pakistan needed after 1971 if it was to make a clean break with the past.

The political implications of the PPP's restricted social bases of support deepened Bhutto's nervousness about the intentions of the army high command which had pushed him into office to regroup and reconsider its strategy in the aftermath of a shattering military defeat. More than any other politician, Bhutto had first-hand knowledge of the conniving and colluding ways of the military and the bureaucracy. And he was uncertain of his ability to call the shots in a parliament which in spite of the PPP majority was a close reflection of a largely fragmented and volatile electorate. So Bhutto opted for reforms that would strengthen his own position rather than that of parliament or the judiciary vis-à-vis the military and the civil bureaucracy.

Steps were taken to neutralize the military's role in Pakistani politics. Debates criticizing the military's involvement in politics were encouraged through a continuation of Ayub's system of press advice. Officials in an overworked ministry of information wryly told startled and enervated journalists that venality still paid better dividends than truth in a formally democratic Pakistan that was to be governed by an elected civilian leader under martial law until the promulgation of a new constitution. Expectations of a more open society were belied by the close monitoring of the press. The heavily guarded metal doors at army headquarters in Rawalpindi were symbolic of the persisting distance between Pakistan's premier institution and civil society. In an atmosphere conducive to reporting, not debating, it was not possible to avoid giving uninformed opinion the impression that the reforms were switching the balance between the military and the civilian leadership. On the face of it, Bhutto was hitting hard at a military institution he repeatedly accused of 'Bonapartist' tendencies. Several senior officers were removed from office; the military high command was restructured; the post of commander-in-chief was abolished; the tenure of the seniormost member of the army, the chief of staff, was reduced and a firm decision taken not to grant extensions to any of the service chiefs. A special clause in the 1973 constitution made it illegal for the military to abrogate the constitution.

Yet none of these measures gave elected institutions the power to whittle down the military's large claims on the state exchequer, a critical factor in the continued infirmity of both economic development and political processes in the country. The loss of the eastern wing was a reasonable enough pretext to prune the state's debilitating external security requirements. Instead military expenditure continued to absorb well over 40 per cent of the centre's annual budget. Given the political will Bhutto might have used his Simla agreement of July 1972 with Indira Gandhi to begin recasting the state's regional defence imperatives, a prerequisite to constraining the influence of army headquarters in domestic politics. But a politician whose domestic fortunes soared in proportion to his anti-Indian rhetoric, Bhutto never intended the Simla accord to become a prelude to a fresh chapter in Pakistan's relations with its regional rival. Interested only in negotiating the return of the 93,000 Pakistani prisoners of war taken by the Indian army in Bangladesh, he showed no signs of softening his government's stance towards New Delhi in the aftermath of Simla. This was proof of his unwillingness to incur the wrath of a military institution which past experience had taught him to regard as the final arbiter of Pakistan's destiny. And indeed, the cost of maintaining the coercive arms of the state rose appreciably under the Bhutto regime. In 1974, India's successful detonation of a nuclear device saw Bhutto championing the cause of Pakistan's nuclear programme more energetically than before. This posture brought him into open diplomatic confrontation with the Pakistan army's already distanced patrons in Washington and won him few new friends among military officers leery of his blowing hot and cold at their expense. Many of them had been infuriated with his early decision to set up a para-military force – the federal security force – with the explicit intention of minimizing the regime's dependence on the military during times of civil unrest. The adverse reaction of army headquarters to the FSF saw Bhutto sanctioning successive increases in salaries, allowances and other benefits for senior and junior members of all three services.

His efforts to revamp the administrative services proved to be equally contradictory. In 1973 Bhutto abolished the CSP cadre and merged it into a linear all-Pakistan unified grade structure. Castigating the old structure for nesting corruption and inefficiency by keeping out talent and technical expertise, Bhutto introduced the lateral entry system to draw fresh blood into the civil service and the police. The egalitarianism of the reforms was abreast with the PPP's socialism and initially at least earned Bhutto fewer enemies than it did friends. Non-CSP members of the civil service delighted in the deflation of their overmighty CSP colleagues who like the IAS enjoyed a privileged status on account of having passed a special qualifying exam held under the purview of the public services commission. Yet most CSP officers continued to wield wide-ranging powers in sensitive spots across the length and breadth of the state administration. So although the CSP were forced to shed some of their former airs, there was nothing in the reform package that effectively curtailed the powers of the administrative services. On the contrary, there is every reason to believe that the powers of most civil bureaucrats grew during the populist era. The nationalization of thirty-one private sector industries that had followed on the heels of the PPP's advent to power had seen a rapid expansion of the public sector and considerably extended the regime's scope for the distribution of political patronage. Indeed virtually all of Bhutto's popular policies – whether land reform, new legislation safeguarding the interests of labour, the nationalization of key industries and the extension of state control over the banking and insurance sector – provided immeasurable opportunities for graft and corruption. Notwithstanding the lateral entry system, the main beneficiaries of public sector expansion were for the most part the very civil bureaucrats whom the regime was supposed to be giving a much needed dressing down.

The essentially cosmetic nature of Bhutto's institutional reforms, and the absence of any significant ones under Indira Gandhi, hints at the delicate tight-rope walk required of a 'populist' politician in power. Schooled in the art of governance under a military–bureaucratic regime, Bhutto recognized the obstacles to implementing even the most nominal reforms without the compliance of the administrative machinery and, in the final analysis, the military. This foreclosed the possibility of a genuine shake up of the two institutions which had the greatest stake in the old world. Together with his reasons for not building up the PPP's organization, Bhutto's need to secure the tacit support of the civil bureaucracy and the military, and increasingly from the police, the FSF and also the judiciary, meant a dependence on state authority which contravened the very populist image he was so eager to project.

Caught in the web of new and emerging discrepancies between the structural context and his populist initiatives, Bhutto leaned more and more on the coercive instruments of state authority. So long as he managed to remain at the helm of state power he could offset the PPP's organizational weaknesses by extending patronage to privileged social groups and, failing that, by impelling them to cross over to his side. So the harbinger of a new social order based on redistributive justice swiftly turned to cultivating the one which had originally fanned his political ambitions. Shortly after assuming office Bhutto began weeding out most of the PPP's radical members and mending fences with bigger landlords whom he effusively denounced in his public rallies. This numbed loyal party workers into inaction at a time when the PPP's land and labour reforms as well as promises of allotments of state land to slum dwellers was rousing the rural and the urban downtrodden. The urban intelligentsia was as divided as ever about the merits of the regime but united in opposing Bhutto's recourse to authoritarian powers. With the judiciary as ineffectual as ever and the press meekly chanting government directives, civil liberties remained suppressed while the FSF was given a free rein to quash all opposition to the regime.

In 1973 in a move which was to give a strong provincial dimension to the widening opposition to the regime, Bhutto rid himself of the non-PPP governments in Baluchistan and the NWFP. Charging them with anti-state activities in collusion with Kabul and New Delhi, he began showing utter disregard for the much celebrated provincial autonomy provisions in the 1973 constitution. Indeed the constitution was constantly chopped and changed by a pliant parliament to give Bhutto, now the prime minister, extraordinary powers. This provided legal cover for a variety of political misadventures. The decision to try Wali Khan, the leader of the National Awami Party which had been one of the two coalition partners in Baluchistan and the NWFP, for conspiring against the state was an uncanny replay of the Ayub regime's Agartala case against Sheikh Mujibur Rahman and the Awami League. Later in the year Bhutto took the ominous step of calling in the army to crush a tribal uprising in Baluchistan. As the situation in the province took on civil war proportions, Bhutto began clawing dangerously close to the men in khaki. The undoing of the Bhutto regime by the army high command and the political opposition, whether jointly or severally, was now a matter of time.

A rapidly changing domestic and international environment emboldened social groups like big business, who had been directly affected by the PPP's nationalization policies, into filling the opposition's coffers. The American CIA's covert action against Salvador Allende's government in Chile was widely interpreted as the beginning of the end of the socialist wave that seemed to have gripped the international system since the late 1960s. And indeed after 1973 international pressures on the economy and also on domestic politics left Bhutto with an unacceptably poor hand of cards. Dramatically inflated oil revenues encouraged many Arab states, notably Saudi Arabia, to extend their external profiles by lending monetary support to religious parties committed to raising the ideological banner of Islam in the Muslim world. Attracted by the money but privately repelled by the ideology, the PPP government maintained an equivocal stance towards religious groups such as the fundamentalist Jamat-i-Islami as they augmented their bank balances and, by extension, their political clout. This brought in some Arab aid to the state exchequer, but not nearly enough to lighten the unbearable burden of a devastating oil import bill. Monetary and political intervention in Pakistan's affairs by oil-rich Arab states was paralleled by Washington's froth and fury at Bhutto's dismissive attitude towards its demand that he refrain from proceeding with the nuclear programme. So his many domestic enemies had quite a selection from which to choose their international allies in attempting to eject the PPP out of office.

Nonplussed by these developments Bhutto continued to repose faith in his personal support among the poor and lowly, especially in the Punjab and Sind. In an extraordinary lapse of judgement, he mistook the push of populism with the pull of Bhuttoism, just what his detractors accused him of. A crafty strategist of the Pakistani political scene with an ability to prod and capture the popular imagination, Bhutto may have won the war of populism if he had not lost his horses before the final battle. In his later years in office he further diluted the PPP's populist platform, stifled all remaining avenues for the freedom of expression and, most disingenuously, played to the whims of a petty and scornful religious gallery.

Having carelessly squandered the PPP's remarkable success in strengthening its appeal among the underprivileged strata in Pakistani society, Bhutto expected to use the combined attractions of state power and Bhuttoism to trump his rivals at the hustings he scheduled for early 1977. Bhutto won, but that was easy. It was the post-electoral scene that defeated him. Populist sentiments unmatched by an effective party organization proved to be fatal for a regime facing a determined effort by nine disparate political groupings – the Pakistan National Alliance – to seal Bhutto's fate once and for all. Charging the regime with massive electoral rigging, the PNA took to the streets in a display of strength which could only have been countered by a committed party organization. Sadly for Bhutto, neither his personal appeal nor the coercive instruments of the state could save the situation. Generous financial support from disaffected industrial and commercial groups allowed the opposition to bring business to a standstill for prolonged periods in key cities and towns across the country. The rural areas of Punjab and Sind remained quiescent, while labour in the main stayed away from the PNA-led demonstrations. This was evidence of the PPP's continuing support among lower income groups. But none of this mattered very much against political rivals who apart from being more determined and better organized seemed to occupy the moral high ground. Bhutto turned in vain to a restive army high command confident of its ability to carry out a successful coup. Bhutto's five years in office stand out in Pakistan's history as a folktale of a lost era in which the central actor fell well below expectations but the mere mention of whose name could resurrect memories of hoping for a better future.

The populist interlude in Bangladesh

The populist phase was even more short-lived and tragic in Bangladesh than in Pakistan. As with Mrs Gandhi in India and Bhutto in Pakistan, populism in Bangladesh immediately invokes the personality of Sheikh Mujibur Rahman. Analysts of Bangladesh nevertheless have shown greater sensitivity to the extenuating circumstances facing the newly created state in evaluating Mujib's populist policies. And indeed it is impossible to ignore the awesome constraints which a war-ravaged economy and a political scene riddled with diverse and conflicting social groups imposed on Mujib and the Awami League government. What makes the Bangladeshi experiment with populism particularly intriguing is that unlike his counterparts in India and Pakistan, Mujib relied far more on the Awami League's political networks than on the non-elected institutions of the state. Effective steps were taken to build the ruling party's organizational machinery down to the district level and elective control over the administrative arms of the state was sought to be established. Yet Mujib failed since the Awami League reflected the broader ideological divisions in Bangladeshi society which more than outweighed the merits of its organization. This raises a set of inter-related questions: (i) is a coherent party organization committed to populist reforms a contradiction in terms and (ii) if so can populism ever really succeed in the economic backwaters of the international capitalist system? Post-independence Bangladesh offers the glimpses of a plausible answer.

In January 1972 Mujib had returned from a prison in Pakistan to lead an Awami League government in the newly independent state of Bangladesh. The first flush of independence propelled Mujib to the commanding heights of popularity. As the fount of authority he used his personal stature to strike a fragile working balance between the conflicting social groups constituting the Bangladeshi political spectrum. Mujib initially moved towards a system of parliamentary democracy and announced a package of populist economic measures, including land reforms and the nationalization of the few industries the country possessed. A section of militant youth organized in student fronts, however, fiercely opposed parliamentary democracy and wanted to establish a revolutionary government to reverse the Awami League's dependence on the old power base among the intermediate social strata – surplus farmers, small and middling businessmen as well as urban professionals. Radical students lit the initial fires of opposition to the regime. Under the cumulative weight of economic stagnation and political tensions within both the elected and non-elected institutions of the state these came to engulf wider segments of society, forcing the regime into a repressive gear and pushing open the door for the first military intervention.

Once state power had been won the loosely sewn patchwork quilt of Bengali resistance to West Pakistani dominance began falling to pieces. The six-point programme had in the main represented the interests of the Bengali middle classes. In the context of a united Pakistan it provided the symbol of Bengali nationalism around which the Awami League successfully rallied the lower ranks of the social order in rural and urban areas alike. But in the changed circumstances of a sovereign Bangladesh, the Awami League's six points had little emotive appeal. The bitterly fought civil war had expanded the sphere of political participation to include the smaller peasantry and labour. This was grist to the mill of militant students who subscribed to an eleven-point programme for the socialist transformation of the economy. From their point of view none of Mujib's reforms went far enough in undermining the old structures of power and privilege which had collaborated with the Pakistani regime.

Conflicts over the ideological orientation of the state infected the Awami League, splitting it neatly down the middle. One segment led by the finance minister, Tajuddin Ahmed, wanted to move in the socialist direction with help from New Delhi and Moscow while another, spearheaded by the minister of trade and commerce, Khondkar Mushtaq Ahmed, was emphatically pro-American and preferred a mixed economy based on Western aid. For now the pro-socialist group appeared to have the upper hand. Together with nationalism, secularism and democracy, socialism was one of the four principles of 'Mujibism' incorporated in the constitution, which came into effect exactly one year after Bangladesh's liberation on 16 December 1971. Yet the commitment to a socialist economy was marred by disagreements within the ruling party and the hard realities of a desperately poor country. The result was the absence of clear policy directives and utter chaos in economic management.

Adding to the problems of Mujib's government were the very different experiences of those who had participated in the liberation struggle. While most of the Awami League leadership had either gone into exile in India or to gaol in Pakistan it was the Mukti Bahini, literally the liberation army, which had fought against the Pakistani military. A small section wanted to see the Mukti Bahini transformed into a 'productive' army which would contribute to, not drain, the country's strained financial resources. Yet the dominant elements in concurrence with Mujib favoured the establishment of a military institution styled on the colonial model. In what was an unhappy portent for the future of democracy in the new state, Mujib and the Awami League proved singularly incapable of squaring the interests of the military, some of whom had fought in the liberation war while others had been repatriated from Pakistan. Uncertain of the army's support, Mujib followed Bhutto's example by setting up his own para-military force, the Rakkhi Bahini. Membership of this new security force was based entirely on demonstrated loyalty to Mujib and the Awami League. The creation of the Rakkhi Bahini was a precursor to the regime's growing resort to authoritarian powers after the autumn of 1973 as its reforms failed to meet popular expectations and the national economy fell into complete disarray.

Mujib's regime was better placed to check the powers of the civil bureaucracy. Once again the legacy of the liberation struggle had created serious rifts within the state bureaucracy between those who had fled to Calcutta and others who, because they stayed, had no choice but to 'collaborate' with the Pakistani military command. The repatriation of civil servants from Pakistan, quislings in the popular mind, lowered the prestige of the administrative bureaucracy further still. Dazed and demoralized, civil bureaucrats proved amenable to the dictates of elective representatives. Yet the implications of bureaucratic subservience to the political arms of the state were not altogether salutary. Heightening social conflict coupled with rivalries within the Awami League set the bureaucracy at sixes and sevens along political lines. This made it even more difficult for the regime to carry out its post-war reconstruction polices. In March 1972, the government's nationalization policies led to a dramatic expansion of the public sector which now accounted for an estimated 86 per cent of the total industrial assets. Instead of selecting from the available pool of skilled bureaucrats, the regime opted to appoint political favourites to top jobs in the newly nationalized industries. This was consistent with the imperative of disbursing state patronage – plum jobs, permits and licences – through the political networks of the Awami League. Good for the consolidation of the regime's support base, this was a bad recipe for public sector efficiency.

With more than enough trouble sizzling on its plate, the regime in March 1973 sought to renew its popular mandate. The elections registered a sweeping victory for the Awami League which won 291 seats in a house of 300 and polled 73 per cent of the total votes cast. Yet this apparently thumping democratic endorsement of Mujibism barely disguised the regime's drift towards authoritarianism. To garner an absolute majority, the Awami League resorted to strong-armed tactics, primarily through the trusted agency of the Rakkhi Bahini, to intimidate opposition candidates and voters. The confidence which the election result engendered in the Awami League camp was more than countered by the sullen reception in sizeable quarters to its terrific victory. And in any case, the single-mindedness of the voting public did not reflect the deepening divisions that were cutting into the social fabric.

The regime's faltering democratic resolve coincided with the abandonment of socialist pretences. This left nationalism and secularism as the two remaining pillars of the state's official ideology. Neither could whip up the sort of support Mujib and the Awami League needed to weather the economic storm unleashed by the sudden increase in international oil prices. By 1974 Bangladesh was in the grip of a full-scale famine. During 1974 and 1975 the gross domestic product increased by 2 per cent while population grew by 3 per cent. The national economy suffered from low productivity, an excessive money supply, deficit financing and galloping inflation. There was a three-fold increase in prices with the result that real wages plummeted. The bottom 30 to 40 per cent of the population were the worst sufferers. These economic woes were magnified as the state looked to international donor agencies for a way out of an escalating financial crisis. The loosening of the reins on domestic and foreign private investment followed naturally and brought with it the hated hand of American involvement in both the economic and the political spheres. Here was the basis for an alliance between a disaffected army, put off by the Rakkhi Bahini's growing share of the annual budget, and ascendant capitalist classes, eager to use state power to enhance the processes of private capital accumulation.

Against a backdrop of economic disaffections Mujib made a last-ditch attempt to keep the ship from sinking. In early 1975 he attempted to install a one-party socialist state and began moving in a distinctly authoritarian direction. Mujib dissolved all political parties and formed a new national party, BAKSAL or the Bangladesh Peasants and Workers Awami League. It did not require cunning to realize that this was simply the old Awami League parading in a new populist garb. If the former Awami League had been an unsteady bastion built on the rivalries and shifting allegiances of the intermediate social strata, Mujib's BAKSAL in making a play for the support of the smaller peasantry and labour was more akin to a crumbling house of cards than an organization capable of implementing populist reforms. Yet the biggest irony of all was Mujib's pathetic reiteration of his government's commitment to socialism at a time when Bangladesh was becoming an international icon for the state with the fastest moving begging bowl.

So far from being reassuring, the fusion of populism and authoritarianism generated an even greater crisis of confidence in the regime's capacity to drive the economy out of the hole. Many of the Awami League's former supporters among the affluent middle classes – surplus farmers and business groups especially – and also members of the intelligentsia were sceptical and uneasy about Mujib's ultimate intentions. The decision to establish multipurpose cooperatives in the rural areas where the produce would be equally divided between the tillers, the owners and the government worried surplus farmers who read it as a conceivable step towards the eventual confiscation of private property by the state. Business groups for their part were tired and wary of the flustered regime's blueprints for economic revival. Sensing their moment, a small group of former and serving junior army officers took matters in hand and fired the fatal shots. In August 1975 Mujib and his family were brutally assassinated in a military coup widely believed to be backed by the American CIA. The elevation of Khondkar Mushtaq Ahmed to presidential office by the army seemed to confirm these suspicions. It is unlikely that the historical evidence will ever fully corroborate this conspiratorial view of the tragedy.

Populism reconsidered

The abortive populist initiatives in India, Pakistan and Bangladesh underline the importance of the overall balance of forces within state and civil society in determining the success or failure of party agendas. In each of the three cases the adoption of the populist creed was in response to particular historical conjunctures where the uneven spread of capitalist orientated economic development during the previous decade had led to a precarious balance not only between different social classes and regions but also between them and a centralized post-colonial state. The need for a new social covenant to maintain the legitimacy of the state called for a spate of redistributive reforms without actually disturbing the old alliances with dominant social groups. It is this contradictory requirement of change yet continuity, of evolution in the name of revolution, of running furiously in the same spot, which gives the populist era in the South Asian subcontinent and indeed in most parts of the world its duplicitous character. It also tells why the opportunities afforded by populism turned out to be mirages in the sand and why the passions that discovery elicited were smothered in an overt display of authoritarianism in all three states.

If the early 1970s demanded a show of greater governmental responsiveness to political and economic discontentments, there was much of the established order that was firmly intact to resist a fundamental restructuring of relations between state and society. The splintering of the political arenas along lines of class, caste, language and region militated against party programmes that were either too ideologically precise or addressed to specific social groups at the exclusion of others. Without a significantly changed basis for centre–state relations, the road to power in centralized post-colonial state systems depended upon political parties stretching their networks of social support as diffusely as possible, couching their appeals in generalities which because they had to appear to offer something to all and sundry carried the very real possibility of delivering nothing substantial to anyone.

The emergence of parties with populist manifestos was the product of a context in which the fluidity of social dynamics had yet to be mirrored by changes within existing state structures. In India and Pakistan the parties were headed by leaders with strong roots in the old structures of power and privilege. In the absence of any major organizational restructuring of the state, Mrs Gandhi's and Bhutto's essentially tactical rather than deeply-held ideological commitment to populist policies fostered a reliance on the non-elected institutions of the state, albeit more so in Pakistan than in India. Instead of building up the Congress and PPP organizations by incorporating their newly expanded social bases of support, Mrs Gandhi and Bhutto felt threatened by regional and populist challenges from within their parties that in turn could dislodge the centralized structures of decision making. The centralizing logic of the existing state structure, nominal reforms of the non-elected institutions in post-1971 Pakistan notwithstanding, predisposed Mrs Gandhi and Bhutto towards concentrating power in their own hands. In Bangladesh, Mujib enjoyed similar powers but for different reasons. Unlike India and Pakistan where the institutional balance within the state had largely endured the economic transformation of existing social structures, Bangladesh had emerged from a bloody and hard fought war of liberation with a popular political party with nation-wide bases of support, a weakened civil bureaucracy and a considerably strengthened but highly politicized army. On the face of it, Mujib worked through the Awami League's party organization to establish state control over society. But the radicalization of the Awami League's social bases during the liberation struggle forced Mujib into contradictory postures which alienated his allies from the intermediate strata without consolidating support among the lower classes.

Without the systemic contexts in India, Pakistan and Bangladesh being biased in favour of centralized executive authority it is doubtful whether authoritarian strains in their personalities alone would have allowed Indira,

Bhutto or Mujib to assume complete control over their party's populist initiatives. Needing the support of subordinate social groups to stay in power, none of them was minded to go against the grain of state imperatives and opt for a package of redistributive reforms which might conceivably have built them spontaneous but solid bases of support that even in the absence of a coherent political party organization might have kept the dominant social classes and their allies within the non-elected institutions at bay. The contradictions of populism combined with the structural constraints, domestic and international, were clearly beyond the control of the illustrious trio. Yet it may not have been altogether impossible to concentrate energies on widening the scope of redistributive reforms. Here Mrs Gandhi and Bhutto proved more unwilling than Mujib to break with the dominant alliances within state and society and fashion a new style of politics. But then Mujib was presiding over a state where the non-elected institutions were relatively less cohesive than in either India or Pakistan. Moreover, the dominant social groups in the latter two countries were far better entrenched at the level of regional political economies to pose threats to central state authority than was the case with Bangladesh's culturally more homogeneous yet politically more divided ruling middle classes. Unfortunately, the few political advantages Mujib possessed over his opposite numbers in India and Pakistan were more than cancelled by the perilous constraints, both domestic and international, on Bangladesh's economy.

Clearly then, the collapse of populism, though not the rush into the authoritarian embrace, owed more to the structural constraints than the culpability of the individual leaders. But the imperfections of populism cannot be confused with the impossibility of redistributive reforms even in the constrained and constraining circumstances in which states in the subcontinent negotiate terms with domestic society, regional neighbours and the larger international system.

Reclaiming democratic ground in India, 1977–1993

In the sixth general elections India's voters had vented their anger at the suspension of democratic processes with a pounding rejection of overt authoritarianism. The 1977 elections seemed to mark the end of Congress domination in Indian politics. Indira Gandhi, the populist turned autocrat, was given an electoral snub in her own constituency of Rai Bareilly in Uttar Pradesh. But with the benefit of hindsight 1977 appears to have ushered in a new era where Congress's continued claims to the central authority of the Indian state were under more effective challenge from a variety of regionally based political forces, whether of the conservative or the populist ilk. The expanding arena of democratic politics and the accompanying erosion of the

Congress's organizational and electoral bases of support had worked to the advantage of regional political parties and compounded the problem of concentrating political and economic power in the hands of the central state.

Yet the later years of the populist era had given ample warning of how India's centralized state structure was likely to treat the growing assertiveness of regional political forces. Although Mrs Gandhi's invocation of the draconian powers in the Indian constitution failed to strike a sympathetic chord in a political culture in which Nandy has discerned strains of amoral authoritarianism, reclaiming the democratic ground through the ritual of elections was no barrier to the assertion of authoritarianism, more covert than overt, through the non-elected institutions of the state. During the Nehruvian period the Congress's nation-wide organizational machinery was a mitigating influence on the political centre's inclination to resort to overt authoritarianism at the state level. In the aftermath of populism the Congress party and its national alternative, the loosely put together Janata coalition, were effectively reduced to representing specific regions. The result was an increasing tendency for overt authoritarianism projected by the centre at the regional level to co-exist with formal democracy at the all-India level. The more so since the fit between populism and regionalism tended to be tighter and more readily translatable into practice than the inevitable generalities and platitudinous rhetoric of a centrally orchestrated populism. A continued exploration of the unfolding dialectic between the state structure and political processes after 1977 helps in highlighting the dynamics of these developments.

The Janata party was formed in 1977 following the merger of the Congress (Organization) led by Morarji Desai, the Bharatiya Lok Dal led by Charan Singh, the Jan Sangh led by Atal Behari Vajpayee, the Congress for Democracy led by Jagjivan Ram and H. N. Bahuguna and the Socialists. The formation of a single party out of so many disparate groups was facilitated by the moral authority wielded by the aging J. P. Narayan who followed Gandhi's footsteps by refusing to hold any party or government position. The Janata won impressively in Congress's traditional strongholds in northern and central India, including Uttar Pradesh, Bihar, Punjab, Haryana, Madhya Pradesh, Rajasthan, Orissa and Assam. The Congress emerged from the 1977 elections with a distinctively regional face, winning in the four southern states of Tamil Nadu, Karnataka, Kerala and Andhra Pradesh.

A multi-party coalition committed to restoring democracy and decentralizing power, the Janata party better reflected the conflicting interests within and between India's regional political economies. But its main asset was also its biggest liability. Resting on the support of oligarchs as well as the disaffected populist leaders whose support Mrs Gandhi had wilfully forfeited, Janata could neither pull nor push in the same direction. This, rather than the contending interests of its component parties, was the more important reason why Janata disintegrated with such sweet rapidity. In mid-1979, the octogenarian prime minister Morarji Desai lost his majority in parliament and his place at the helm of the government was taken by Charan Singh, a Jat leader hailing from western UP who had the support of rich farmers and backward castes in northern India. Although Charan Singh never faced the Lok Sabha, he managed during the brief tenure of the Janata party in office to engineer a significant shift in the state's economic policies in favour of the agrarian sector. Charan Singh, however, did not have the necessary parliamentary support to win a vote of confidence as prime minister. He remained merely as caretaker until new general elections in January 1980.

Under the Janata party it was primarily those who dominated the regional political economies of northern India rather than disaffected states outside the Hindi belt which had temporarily occupied a niche in New Delhi. Indira Gandhi made her comeback initially with the support of Devraj Urs, the most successful state level populist of the south. Urs ensured Mrs Gandhi's by-election victory from Chikmagalur in Karnataka in 1978. Earlier in the year the Congress had split for the third time when a segment tried to remove Indira Gandhi from the leadership of the party, holding her responsible for the electoral defeat of 1977. Anti-Indira moves from within the Congress were matched by the Janata's efforts to ensure that popular disaffection with her authoritarian persona was not a fleeting phenomenon but the end of Mrs Gandhi's claims to national power. In what widely came to be perceived a persecution campaign against the former prime minister the Janata government established a judicial commission headed by Justice Shah to investigate the excesses of the emergency. A parliamentary privilege committee went to the extent of unseating her after she had won from Chikmagalur. But state-level elections in Karnataka and Andhra Pradesh established Mrs Gandhi's faction now known as the Congress (I) for Indira as the more powerful or real Congress.

With the political tide turning against the Janata, Mrs Gandhi began plotting her return to the national stage. Urs, who had masterminded the Karnataka victory for the Congress (I), was deemed to be expendable once the subordinate castes, classes and religious minorities in the north began showing clear signs of disillusionment with the agrarianism of Janata's predominantly middle to richer caste and class conglomeration, and the urban communalism of its commercial supporters. On the eve of the 1980 elections Indira Gandhi struck a deal with Bahuguna and named him the general secretary of her party. This was designed to win back the support of Harijans and Muslims in the UP. The KHAM strategy was also revitalized in Gujarat and successfully neutralized Morarji Desai. The Congress won a decisive victory in the 1980 parliamentary elections, successfully overturning the electoral verdict of 1977 in the northern and central states while at the same time holding on to the advantage in the south. Since the Janata party had dismissed the Congress-led state governments in nine northern and central states in the aftermath of their victory in parliamentary elections in 1977, the Congress returned the compliment in 1980 and managed to slot in Congress-led state governments in most of these states. In a slight variation of Mrs Gandhi's tactic in 1971–2 to delink parliamentary and state elections, an attempt was made in 1977 and in 1980 to bring the momentum of a parliamentary victory to bear on the outcome of state-level elections.

The strategy had borne fruit in the short term. But in the long term, far from guaranteeing the alignment of state politics with configurations of power at the centre, it provided the structural basis for a growing divergence between regional and central political imperatives. Electoral success at the regional level called for populist programmes fashioned by the specific concerns at the state and local levels of society. Yet these frequently clashed with the more broadly construed imperatives of the political centre, creating greater dissonance between the forces of regionalism and centralism at a time when nation-wide party organizations seemed to have become relics of the past. To keep the social dynamics underlying political processes at the regional level within the parameters of India's essentially unitary state structure, those occupying the political centre had to lean heavily on the non-elected institutions, the civil bureaucracy, the police and, ultimately, the military. So the delinking of state and parliamentary elections furnished the political system with scenarios where the quantum of democracy at the regional level, even if rendered imperfect by the cupidity of public representatives and institutions, was in inverse proportion to the manifestations of autocracy by the presiding centre.

This is one of the reasons why the restoration of Mrs Gandhi's Congress (I) at the centre could not resurrect the old era of Congress domination. Although memories of populism paved the way for the Congress's return to power, Mrs Gandhi diluted her populist programme on the economic front after 1982 and made tentative moves in the direction of market orientated liberalization. This period was also marked by the central leadership's highhanded interference in the affairs of the states. New Delhi's brazen manipulation of party factions in the different regions was paralleled by a greater confidence in centrally appointed state governors and, of course, members of the IAS and the IPS. Congress chief ministers were changed at the whim of Mrs Gandhi who was both prime minister and president of the party. With the Congress high command abjuring internal party elections, political disaffections at the state, district and local levels could only be voiced through exit from the party. Unable to square the needs of their constituencies with pressures from above, influential state-level leaders and social groups began veering towards specifically regional parties. The myopia of the central Congress leadership's stratagem was dramatically revealed in the astonishing victory of a newly formed regional party, the Telugu Desam led by N. T. Rama Rao, in the 1983 state elections in Andhra Pradesh. In 1984 in what was an overtly authoritarian measure carried out under constitutional cover the centre toppled elected state governments in Andhra Pradesh and Kashmir, which only served to fan the fires of a deepening populist regionalism in both these states.

Yet the most disastrous handling of regional politics by the centre took place in the strategically vital state of the Punjab. While out of power the Congress (I) had encouraged a Sikh faction led by Jarnail Singh Bhindranwale to challenge the mainstream Sikh party, the Akali Dal, which had two ministers in the central cabinet and was the senior partner in a coalition government in the Punjab. In the early 1980s the Akali Dal launched an agitation for more state autonomy on the basis of the Anandpur Sahib resolution first passed in 1973 and amended in 1978. Bhindranwale's more extremist faction turned to violent methods and gained the upper hand as negotiations between the Akali leadership and the central government failed to make any headway. In the face of new and more determined regional challenges to central authority, especially from the Punjab, New Delhi finessed the art of authoritarian governance wearing the velvet glove of democratic constitutionalism. Since the blows administered could not delude an ever-vigilant Indian press corps, the political centre sought legitimacy for its actions by subtly but surely substituting populism and secularism with an implicit ideology of communalism. In June 1984 Indira Gandhi took the fateful decision to deploy the Indian army against Sikh militants occupying the Golden Temple in Amritsar. The military action led to a deep psychological alienation of the Sikh community. On 31 October 1984 Mrs Gandhi was assassinated by two of her Sikh bodyguards.

Using communalism as a counterweight to regionalism was hardly a novelty in Indian politics. Deployed by the colonial state against both Indian nationalist and separatist Muslim politics, it had provided the Congress high command in 1947 with the means to cut Jinnah's and the Muslim League's demands down to size. Yet there was an important new dimension in the centre's evocation of communalism in the 1980s. Encountering implacable opposition from an array of regional forces, the political centre gave Hindu majoritarian communalism its head. Sheer desperation perhaps, but it did seem to do the trick. The 1984 electoral experience persuaded the Congress under Rajiv Gandhi of the efficacy of the explicitly anti-Sikh and implicity Hindu communal card in maintaining parliamentary majorities as well as central authority. The main refrain of Rajiv Gandhi's speeches during the election campaign was that the country must be united to defeat the Anandpur Sahib resolution which in his view embodied a clear secessionist demand. Riding the sympathy wave following his mother's assassination, the Congress bagged a record 79 per cent of the Lok Sabha seats and 49 per cent of the popular vote in December 1984. But in the context of the delinking of national and state politics the Congress did not perform as well in state elections held in March 1985. In fact, the Congress managed to lose control of the state assemblies in Karnataka and Sikkim and was also defeated in Andhra Pradesh.

Projected as a Mr Clean unspoiled by the corrupt and corrupting influences of power politics, Rajiv was seen as the torch bearer of a new generation poised to take India into the twenty-first century. Unable to shed his Doon schoolboy syndrome, Rajiv's approach to politics and economics was unabashedly elitist. The 1985 budget was a rich man's fantasy and a symptom just how out of touch the prime minister and his inner coterie were with the popular pulse. Liberalization of imports and state controls of the domestic economy offended the bureaucracy without bringing any tangible benefits to significant sections of the Indian populace, particularly in the field of employment. Basking in the glow of his newly won victory Rajiv Gandhi signed accords with the Akali Dal in Punjab and the Asom Gana Parishad in Assam which brought these parties to power in state-level elections. Yet substantive elements of the accords that might have defused the regional time bombs were simply not implemented. The Congress lost to leftist political formations in Kerala and West Bengal in 1987, but it was Congress's defeat at the hands of the Lok Dal led by the irrepressible Jat leader Devi Lal in Haryana which provided the first sign of Rajiv Gandhi's vulnerability in the Hindi-speaking heartland. Corruption scandals surrounding the Bofors arms deal and mismanagement of relations with neighbours, particularly Sri Lanka, eroded the credibility of Rajiv's government. The resignation of his former finance and defence minister, V. P. Singh, provided the political opposition with a focal point in the campaign to pull Rajiv Gandhi down.

While Rajiv shared his mother's knack for making enemies out of allies, he lacked her agility in keeping one step ahead of political rivals. The Rajiv Gandhi regime had presided over a clear sliding back from both populism and secularism as the main props of central authority in India. As the 1989 elections made clear, Congress's would-be poker player had, unbeknown to himself, allowed those more ideologically committed to a Hindu Rashtra to turn the tables on him. The Bharatiya Janata Party, the old Jan Sangh in a more populist guise, scored the most points on the communal card while the Congress's hesitance to play the populist card provided rich electoral dividends to the Janata Dal. The Dal in any case had a heavy stack of agrarian cards, including the King of Manda, and managed to form a minority government with support from both communalists and communists. V. P. Singh's much publicized centralist credentials, established during his tenure as finance and defence minister and then as Rajiv's most high-profiled political opponent, made him an acceptable national alternative. The 1989 electoral verdict should be considered as a watershed in India's political development not only because of its implications for the Nehru–Gandhi dynasty and the Congress but, more precisely, because it registered the most decisive success of regional political forces in exercising state power directly from the centre.

As in 1977 this was a victory for the dominant among north India's regional political formations, though a better coordinated and more broadly based one. But here was the rub. Regional parties outside the Hindi belt whose electoral gains and agitations appeared to have laid siege to the centre during the eighties paid heavily for their local sins; they were routed by the Congress in the southern states. The uneven successes of regionalism left central political authority with the irresistible temptation of relying more and more on the ideological starch provided by the BJP's brand of communalism.

On the face of it, the new configuration of political forces at the centre might have had a better chance of reordering the priorities, if not the direction, of India's political economy of development. But any economic reorientation privileging the agrarian sector and the big farmers and the middle to richer peasants within it had to contend with the non-elective institutions of the Indian state, the bureaucracy in particular, and the counterweight of powerful industrial capitalist interests. The difficulties in squaring an agrarian regional economic orientation with the centre's broader based sectoral imperatives brought the contradictions between formal democracy and covert authoritarianism within the Indian state to the surface in a subtle but sure manner. Even the kingmaker Devi Lal could not steal a leaf out of Charan Singh's book in trying to deliver on the Dal's electoral promises. Indeed the Janata Dal had little option but to abandon the fire and fury of its agrarianism and settle down to working within the established parameters of the compromise between formal democracy and covert authoritarianism. The growing importance of money in the acquisition of political power in any case made it impossible for the Janata Dal to ride roughshod over the interests of the stalwarts of Indian industrial and finance capitalism. The most that the Dal's supporters could expect was to keep agrarian subsidies on an even sharper upward incline and to use political power at the central and regional levels to stake a claim for an ever larger share of an already sprawling network of state patronage

– concessional financing, plum jobs, lucrative government contracts and the like.

A Janata Dal minority government relying on the support of the BJP on the right and communists on the left was an inherently unstable arrangement. Seeking to carve out a vote bank for himself, V. P. Singh announced in August 1990 that his government would implement the long-standing recommendations of the Mandal commission to reserve jobs in government and places in educational institutions for the backward castes. This led to a string of street protests by upper-caste youths and, more ominously, to the intensification of the BJP's campaign to build a temple to Rama – the Hindu mythical god – on the very site of a historic mosque – the Babri masjid in Ayodhya. After some hesitation the V. P. Singh government supported the Bihar state government's decision to arrest Lal Krishna Advani, the leader of the BJP, and the UP state government's measures to stop Hindu militants from desecrating the mosque. The withdrawal of BJP support ensured the defeat of the V. P. Singh government in a parliamentary vote of confidence in November 1990.

In one of the more curious twists in India's democratic politics a small gang of barely sixty parliamentarians led by the erstwhile Young Turk of Mrs Gandhi's populist days, Chandra Shekhar, formed the government with Congress support. Chandra Shekhar's group had split away from the Janata Dal to form the Janata Dal (S) for socialists. Once the Janata Dal (S) and the Congress fell out, another reference to India's vast electorate became inevitable. In the violent elections of May and June 1991, punctuated by the tragic assassination of Rajiv Gandhi, the Congress managed to emerge as the largest single party in parliament. It did so by barely staving off the challenge of a loose alliance of the National Front led by the Janata Dal and the Left Front led by the CPI-M as well as the BJP. Particularly striking was the precipitous decline in the Congress vote in north Indian states. The BJP not only won a majority of parliamentary seats from UP, but also formed the state government. It was also triumphant in Madhya Pradesh, Rajasthan and Himachal Pradesh while the Janata Dal emerged victorious in Bihar. For the first time in India's political history a party decimated in the Hindi-speaking heartland nevertheless managed to put together a government at the centre.

The Congress minority government of P.V. Narasimha Rao unfurled an elaborate economic reform programme with a clear accent on privatization and liberalization. Intended to dig the national economy out of the quagmire of deficits and debts since the early 1980s, the new policy marked a break with the statist socialist principles of the past. Yet the change of direction stemmed less from an ideological conviction than pragmatic considerations of how best to deal with the immediate problem of a growing fiscal and financial crisis. The seismic shock administered by the Indian state's abject failure to prevent the destruction of the Babri mosque in December 1992 put a weighty question mark on the course of the economic reform. Allegations of close links between corruption scandals in the Bombay stock market and the prime minister's office deflated the enthusiasm with which the programme of liberalization had been received in business circles.

In the 1990s a deeply discredited Congress regime came to preside over a new and dangerous conjuncture in the overlapping dialectics of nationalism and communalism as well as centralism and regionalism. The pariah-like status of the BJP in the eyes of other political parties after the demolition of the mosque gave only a temporary reprieve to the enfeebled Congress government at the centre. Its decision to dismiss the BJP state governments in Madhya Pradesh, Rajasthan and Himachal Pradesh along with the UP government for its conniving role in the events at Ayodhya was almost calculated to backfire. By the summer of 1993 the BJP was prepared to vote with the Left and National fronts which brought a no-confidence motion in the Lok Sabha chastising the Rao government for its corruption, economic mismanagement and failure to slow the pace of deteriorating communal relations in many parts of the country. The survival of the government in July 1993 by the narrowest parliamentary vote in history signposted a new phase in India's lengthening political paralysis.

With widespread social disorder and the political party system in a state of atrophy, the continuities of government were provided by the tarnished but as yet unbroken non-elected institutions of the state, particularly the civil bureaucracy and the police. The salience of the non-elected institutions in India's state structure was not lost on the BJP and its even more extremist allies such as the Bombay-based Shiv Sena whose sympathizers have been systematically infiltrating not only the civil bureaucracy and the police but also the judiciary and the army. It is this communalization of state institutions that has transformed what used to be periodic outbreaks of communal riots into vicious and organized pogroms against members of India's religious minorities, Muslims in particular. The nexus between the forces of Hindutva and segments of India's non-elected institutions represents on the one hand a conservative reaction along religious, caste and class lines in northern and parts of western India. On the other the discourse of national unity articulated by these regionally grounded forces of communalism claims that they would be more effective and ruthless defenders of the Indian centre against recalcitrant peripheries and suspect religious minorities than the politically bankrupt Congress. In any case, the writ of the centre in such troubled peripheries as Kashmir, Punjab and Assam has for some time been maintained by the coercive arms of the state, including the 'apolitical' Indian military.

The combination of formal democracy and covert authoritarianism had, of course, always characterized the post-colonial Indian state. Keen observers of Indian politics were becoming accustomed to the spectacle of a formally democratic centre masking its application of increasing doses of overt authoritarianism in many regions. What has been unique about India in the 1990s is that attempts are being made to enact the charade in troubled regions with a firmer determination not to undertake any fundamental structural reforms at the centre. Justified on the grounds of preserving national unity, this unbending posture of the Indian centre is likely to stoke the embers of regionalism in even the more cataleptic parts of the country. The alternative proposed by the BJP and its associates aims at buttressing nationalism and centralism through a bid for state power resting on a potent and pernicious combination of their regional power bases and an all-India Hindu communal ideology. An implicit inversion of the old equation between centralism and secularism, the BJP's gamble, if it pays off, might harden the centre in the short term but hasten the longer-term process of India's regional fragmentation. Regardless of the eventual outcome of the battles being fought in the political arenas, the authoritarian features of the Indian state structure are likely to be accentuated in this period of uncertainty. Having lost much of its democratic gloss ever since the waning of Mrs Gandhi's populist politics, the Indian state in the 1990s has become even more tractable to comparison with the overt authoritarianism of military dominated Pakistan and Bangladesh.

Resurgent authoritarianism and the democratic compulsion in Pakistan and Bangladesh

With the dismantling of Bhutto's and Mujib's populist regimes, Pakistan and Bangladesh slipped into a long and trying night of military rule. Gone were the populist pretences which the socio-economic and political disaffections of the late 1960s and early 1970s had thrust upon the ruling configurations. This was to be a phase aimed at fortifying the old world of privilege against the minor infractions made by an enthused but unempowered world of underprivilege. The brutal treatment meted out to the two leaders who had dared engendering illusions of hope among the lower social strata signalled the resolve to brook no nonsense from any quarter opposed to the authoritarian option. Deprived ever so often of civil liberties, the people of both countries could not quite envisage what the pertinacious military jackboot was about to perpetrate in the name of political stability, economic efficiency and social morality.

The similarities between the Pakistani and Bangladeshi experience under post-populist authoritarianism are not confined to the coincidence of two military rulers bearing the same name. Although General Zia-ur-Rahman of

Bangladesh beat General Zia-ul-Haq to state power by two years, their agendas for depoliticization and strategies to build up a support base to assert legitimacy shared much in common. Once General Hussain Muhammad Ershad assumed state power in 1981 the convergences between Bangladesh and Pakistan became even more perceptible. Since outright authoritarianism retreated in the face of democratic compulsions somewhat earlier in Pakistan, an analysis of the theme with reference to that country would appear to take historical precedence.

Upon seizing power General Zia-ul-Haq tried picking up the loose threads his military predecessors had failed to work into the unfolding weave of the state-society dialectic in Pakistan. But while matching earlier attempts at reinforcing central authority, the altered scenario of post-populist Pakistan called for some innovative measures. For one thing, Zia had to break the back of the PPP's populist challenge before he could begin consolidating his own regime. For another, his moment in history owed much to the PNA's successful mobilization of support among industrial and commercial groups who were the main constituents of religious parties averring Islam as their creed. Unable to eradicate the aura of Bhuttoism, Zia raised the banner of Islam to give moral cover to the more unpardonable sins his regime had to commit in veering Pakistani society away from the haunting precipice of populism.

Militarism and Islam were to be the twin pillars of the Zia regime, a formidable blend in a politically polarized and increasingly pulverized society. This allowed for an unashamed display of the state's coercive will in squelching all murmurs of dissent from the PPP's demoralized ranks. Bludgeoning the opposition into submission was easier than evoking enthusiasm for the regime's anti-populist and conservative policies. It was only by issuing a barrage of martial law regulations and getting a select group of civil bureaucrats to mastermind a propaganda campaign equating all politics with venality that the regime staked its initial claim to state power. Following Ayub's example, Zia enlisted the help of the most seasoned bureaucrat available, Ghulam Ishaq Khan, who because he had served in various capacities under every government since the creation of Pakistan had an awe-inspiring knowledge of the mechanics of administrative governance. If Zia was the pious and humble soldier Allah had chosen to pull Pakistani society out of the depths of moral turpitude, then Ishaq was responsible for charting the wilier aspects of the ennobling turnaround.

As Zia's chief economic adviser, Ishaq revoked many of the PPP's economic policies, some of which he had helped shape, with a view to establishing the regime's credentials among dominant social classes in both rural and urban areas. The spectre of fresh land reforms was banished from the political discourse. Reassurances against further nationalization and the shackling of labour were meant to attract private sector investment. Bhutto's ill-advised nationalization of small agro-based industries like rice husking and flour milling was promptly reversed – a reward for the role commercial groups had played in the PNA movement. Yet Ishaq, who knew something about the rapacity and inefficiency of Pakistani entrepreneurs from his days in the Ayub regime, advised against the denationalization of industries. A large public sector held obvious attractions for a regime needing to distribute patronage to its main constituents in the military and, to a lesser extent, the civil services. The regime's industrial policy occasioned a dip in public sector investment without a corresponding increase in private sector contributions. Established industrial houses preferred the relatively safer investment climate offered by trading and the service sector as a whole. The inevitable drag on the economy's employment generation capacities was sought to be countered by encouraging the export of Pakistani manpower to the oil-rich countries of the Middle East. This brought in much needed foreign exchange remittances and created a convenient time lag before the employment requirements of Pakistan's rapidly expanding labour market could force changes in a politically expedient but economically ambivalent industrial policy.

And indeed it was in the political sphere that the regime remained most vulnerable. With the 1973 constitution's clause against military intervention threatening the legitimacy of his regime, Zia began by promising elections within ninety days of assuming power. The offer was recanted as soon as it emerged that Bhutto out of power was stronger than he had been in office. Zia had taken the precaution of suspending specific clauses of the constitution rather than abrogating it altogether. With the PPP challenging the legality of the coup, Zia reiterated his intention of holding elections. So long as the legal niceties were kept in place, the supreme court could give the regime a favourable hearing in the *Begum Nusrat Bhutto vs. chief of army staff et al.* case. True to its past, the supreme court legalized the military intervention, invoking the time-honoured 'doctrine of necessity' but conditioned it with the holding of 'free and fair' elections under the 1973 constitution at an unspecified date.

This was the respite Zia needed as he awaited the supreme court's judgement on the Punjab high court's conviction of Bhutto in a murder case. Though a seven-bench supreme court upheld the high court ruling, it split along provincial lines with all three non-Punjabi judges finding the evidence too circumstantial to charge Bhutto with murder. A concerted international effort to avert Bhutto's impending judicial execution failed to sway a military ruler who could feel the hangman's noose tightening around his own neck each time he considered sparing the life of his principal opponent. On 4 April 1979 Bhutto was physically eliminated from the

Pakistani political scene. Seeing Bhutto's ghost lurking with renewed vigour in his daughter Benazir, Zia cancelled elections and banned all political parties.

After April 1979, aided and abetted by a select group of army and civil officials, Zia initiated a systematic campaign to extend the military's dominance beyond the state structure to all aspects of civil society. Where Ayub had been content to rely on the bureaucratic instruments of state control, Zia intended his regime to be not only overtly authoritarian but plainly military in character. Discouraging signs on the domestic political horizon merely served to fire Zia's ire. The Muslim League and the Jamat-i-Islami who had earlier supported the regime openly distanced themselves once he made the politically unpalatable announcement cancelling elections indefinitely. Upon consulting the dusty notebooks on colonial political control and the elisions introduced during the Ayub era, Zia was persuaded that localizing political horizons was the best assurance for the stability of his regime. The holding of non-party elections to local bodies in September 1979 aimed at driving a wedge between the different levels of the political system, making the twin tasks of militarization and Islamization of society that much easier to accomplish. To Zia's dismay the local election results registered an unexpected victory for candidates with known allegiances to the PPP. The synchronization of domestic repulsion and international condemnation at Bhutto's execution had left Zia isolated beyond measure. The regime was visibly teetering at a time when relations with the United States had gone from bad to worse on account of Pakistan's nuclear programme. With American military supplies in abeyance and the aid-to-Pakistan consortium refusing to reschedule debt repayments, Zia wanted something to turn up from somewhere.

In December 1979 the Soviet invasion of Afghanistan gave him just what was needed to establish his regime's non-existent international stock without which the domestic agenda of repression seemed destined to end in tears. That the push of Soviet imperialism may have received impetus from the pull of Pakistani involvement in destablizing the pro-Communist government in Kabul is not beyond historical supposition. Throughout the fifties senior military and civil officials had used the prospect of Soviet communism spilling into the subcontinent to impress Pakistan's strategic vulnerability upon the erstwhile colonial masters and Washington. By the beginning of the 1980s that potential had been realized, dramatically altering Pakistan's geo-strategic position and qualifying the regime for massive transfusions of Western military and economic aid. Able to invoke the external threat to Pakistan's security more convincingly, the Zia regime could fight its domestic political battles with elan.

Among the fragile yet strategically vital targets was a malleable judiciary and an even more compromised national press. In the most infamous attack on Pakistan's already denigrated judiciary, the provisional constitutional order of March 1981 for the first time scrapped the right of habeas corpus, prohibited the courts from reviewing any of the executive's political actions, including that of martial law itself and, worse still, gave the military regime powers to arbitrarily replace judges. These strikes at the democratic jugular were faithfully reported by a press enchained by stringent pre-censorship of newspapers and journals, forced closures and the cryptic but loaded message of 'self-censorship'. A press which had never known autonomy in the history of Pakistan was enlisted into the service of building Zia's artifact of an Islamic social order. Any journalist imprudent enough to test the regime's low threshold of patience could expect to receive a flogging sentence for preaching sedition and, failing that, for breaching the frontiers of the state's Islamic ideology.

That the regime was so little loved comes as no surprise. But it would be overly simplistic to attribute its ability to outlast all other Pakistani military regimes to the reign of terror that was unleashed in every sphere and at all levels of civil society. Without support from significant elements in society, some of whom were bitterly opposed to Bhutto and his populist rhetoric while others had spotted opportunities in allying with the regime, the military institution even with the help of the civil bureaucracy and the religious lobby could not have underwritten Zia's eleven-year survival in office. Neither the military, nor the civil bureaucracy or for that matter the religiously minded social groups constituted monolithic constituencies who could give undiluted backing to the regime.

Only a section of the military, primarily drawn from the army, was directly engaged in martial law activity. The air force and navy as ever had no say in the army high command's decision to assume state power and so were restricted to watching the spectacle from the sidelines. Within the army itself support for Zia's shock therapy of Pakistani society was by no means absolute. It was restricted in the main to those directly engaged in the martial law administration and others who had contacts or were enterprising enough to partake of the regime's magnanimous cultivation of its military constituency through the usual nostrums – top jobs in government and public enterprises, permits, licences and defence contracts – sure steps to rapid upward mobility. Many senior and junior officers nursing ideas of professionalism were appalled by Zia's extension of military intervention into the virtual colonization of Pakistani society.

Much the same sentiment pervaded segments of the civil services, including elements of the federal bureaucracy. The latter in particular resented being reduced to a wholly subordinate role by the regime's policy of grafting military officers to key jobs in the central and provincial administrations, public sector industries as well as other semi-government and autonomous organizations. The implicit, if not always explicit, rivalry between the two main non-elected institutions of the Pakistani state distinguished Zia's regime from those of Ayub and Yahya.

As for those who had lauded the takeover on account of Zia's religious leanings, specifically the Jamat-i-Islami and its supporters among commercial and trading groups, the regime's Islamization policies were too cosmetic to warm their hearts. The decision to postpone elections indefinitely made it more untenable for the Jamat, which prided itself as one of the vanguards of democracy, to continue to give unqualified support to Zia. In the ensuing ideological and political confusions the more religiously inclined strata opted for the politic posture of pressing Zia in the Islamic direction but reserving the right of dissent whenever the regime undermined basic democratic principles.

This makes it all the more important to consider how Zia managed to stretch the regime's networks of political collaboration outside the military, the civil bureaucracy and the trading and commercial groups whom he had tried luring with his Islamic appeal. In a country where parties had never managed to strike roots, the Zia regime's systematic campaign to discredit politicians and politics gave renewed significance to the old personalized networks of *biraderi* or clan-based ties. *Biraderi* and tribal considerations had always played a part in electoral calculations, much in the same way as caste had in Indian politics. While Pakistan's limited electoral experience is a warning against making a hard and fast proposition, the 1970 election results did appear to suggest that in the relatively more urbanized and commercialized areas political affiliations had begun cutting across the exclusively personalized ties of family and the larger kinship group. In India's party based formal democracy, horizontal associations along caste lines at least came under the broad organizational umbrella of political groupings at the state, if not the central level. But under the rules of Zia's non-party political system individual candidates had no reason to forge any kind of vertical ties. The focus of electoral energies was squarely on the locality or at best the district. In this virtual denationalization and de-provincialization of political issues, the local repute of the candidate together with monetary infusions was the best insurance of success. Keeping political horizons close to the base of society was not a step towards building democracy at the grassroots. Divorced from the larger issues at the central and provincial levels, the narrowly defined concerns of politicians tended to foster a much greater reliance on the local arms of the state. The marriage of personalized politics and the ostensibly rule-bound local layers of the centralized state was a haven for corruption and electoral malpractices.

This was a perfect context in which a military regime needing a measure of legitimacy could try and secure an adequate base of support among fractions of the dominant social classes. In 1981 the regime set up an advisory body – the Majlis-i-Shoora – consisting of individuals selected from all walks of society. But this symbol of Zia's 'Islamic democracy' elicited more contempt than it did respect, leaving the general pondering the safest route to extending his version of local elections to the provincial and national levels. It took a few more years before Zia felt confident about getting the 'positive' results he wanted from the general elections. By the time the elections were held the regime had warded off a determined opposition effort to force Zia's hand. Known as the movement for the restoration of democracy, or the MRD, it was an alliance of all important political parties including the PPP led jointly by Nusrat and Benazir Bhutto. The MRD evoked a strong response in the Bhuttos' home province of Sind but, in what was a sign of the regime's success in exercising control over local politics, failed to ignite the majority province of the Punjab. The regime's policies of differential patronage and selective mobilization had won over substantial segments of Punjab's dominant socio-economic strata, landlords and industrialists and, most promisingly, emergent commercial groups.

The non-party elections of March 1985 to the local bodies as well as the provincial and central assemblies advertised the regime's success in conveying a simple truth: the rewards for collaboration with the state outweighed those of petulant dissent from the political wilderness. As Benazir who had ordered the PPP to boycott the elections discovered to her cost, the attractions of gaining access to state power and patronage were far more tempting than the magnetism of individuals and parties. The Zia regime's masterly social engineering had altered the face of the Pakistani political spectrum, irreversibly it seems with the benefit of hindsight. Not only had the PPP's populism been appropriated by candidates preferring to feather their nests by supporting the military regime but many of its members had participated in the elections in violation of party discipline. That the balance between state and society had tipped in favour of the regime and against the political opposition was patent. Instead of the low turnout predicted due to the MRD's boycott, the regime's careful and extensive political spadework in the localities brought more than 50 per cent of the voters to the polling booths. Least surprising was the socio-economic complexion of the new assemblies. Despite a large number of political greenhorns who may have been more appropriate as municipal councillors than members of the national and provincial assemblies, the vast majority represented the propertied classes the regime had wooed hard and now won over.

Yet it was one thing to achieve 'positive' electoral results and quite another to strike a workable balance between a military regime and its civilian extension. Having established some sort of a claim to legitimacy, Zia was in no mood to weaken his position by abandoning the office of chief of army staff. This most skilful of all Pakistani political strategists knew better than anyone else that power in the existing state structure was nothing without control over the men in military uniform. But tying the knots of dependence between a quasi-military regime and a subservient political system was not without its costs. Zia's handpicked Sindhi prime minister, Mohammad Khan Junejo, soon discovered that the advantages of non-party elections translated into serious disadvantages once autonomous MNAs congregated in the assembly chambers. By now a speed reader of the colonial notebooks on political control, Zia instructed Junejo to establish a party from within the assembly. With Zia playing midwife, Junejo fathered a new party which was promptly named the Pakistan Muslim League to hush speculations about the strange circumstances of its birth.

Enlisting members for the Pakistan Muslim League meant paying the asking price of individual MNAs, most of whom were understandably anxious to recover campaign costs and fatten their bank balances for the next time around in the exorbitantly expensive political system Zia had built. With the monetization of local politics spreading to the provincial and national levels, the effects of insouciant loans given to the regime's business and commercial supporters began to bear down more heavily on the state's dwindling financial reserves. Before Zia seized power the centre's debt reservicing charges had managed to keep up with its revenue receipts. By 1985 interest payments were outstripping receipts and were poised to surpass the military budget. The state's financial travails assumed startling proportions once the logic of a controlled political system began multiplying the avenues of corruption and fraud.

Until his death in a mysterious air crash in August 1988 Zia remained as ringmaster of a subservient, fragmented, highly monetized, corrupt and violent political system. The bankruptcy of the central exchequer and the astounding affluence of privileged segments of society, civil and military, presented real obstacles to a reordering of the state's economic priorities. Together with the prolonged suspension of representative government, growing provincial and intra-provincial disparities heightened tensions between the Punjab and the non-Punjabi provinces as well as significant linguistic minorities within them. This made it more arduous for the political opposition to mount a united challenge to the regime. The more so since the regime wilfully cultivated a style of politics based on encouraging the ventilation of grievances in localized and, failing that, linguistically specific moulds. The sudden rise of the Muhajir Qaumi Movement in the city of Karachi and also Hyderabad, claiming recognition as the fifth nationality of Pakistan for those who had migrated from India at the time of partition, bore testimony to the detrimental legacies of Zia's attempts to militarize and Islamize society by slapping the lid shut on any semblance of a national politics.

Zia's support for the Afghan resistance movement brought in much needed foreign aid, but failed to steer the economy out of its many bottlenecks. The presence of over three million Afghan refugees on Pakistani soil sharpened the lines of social conflict by creating a parallel arms and drugs economy widely believed to be linked with the army's notorious interservices intelligence wing. As arms and drugs money filtered into the social mainstream, unemployed youths brandishing weapons of death began reenacting their own local versions of state militarization. In Sind, armed cadres of the MQM fought skirmishes against Pathans and Punjabis and then declared total war on indigenous Sindhi speakers. Society armed to the teeth in a security obsessed state that had exerted so much of its efforts in confirming its monopoly over the instruments of coercion is a supreme paradox of Zia's eleven-year rule.

Islamization was the other side of the coin Zia had tossed into the ring upon assuming power. The results were quite as paradoxical as those of militarization. For a man who vowed to return Pakistan to the pristine purity of early Islamic society, Zia could do no more than target his social reform programmes to the most vulnerable and inarticulate segments of society, specifically women and religious minorities. The consequences of his politically stabilizing, economically revitalizing and morally regenerating regime are there for all to see – seething hatred among linguistic communities despite the common bond of religion, economic chaos, the practical collapse of the civil, police and judicial services and widespread corruption at every level of society. This great soldier of Allah quite as much as the Satanic populist he had self-righteously replaced ended up becoming thoroughly entangled in the stirring language of his own political rhetoric.

To take on from where Zia left required an effort beyond the capacity of ordinary mortals, not least because his departure had appeared to remove the last citadel in the way of a long repressed democratic compulsion. For a people denied the fruits of democracy for the better part of their history the November 1988 party based general election was something to be relished. The victory of Benazir Bhutto's Pakistan People's Party in the national elections was very restricted. Not only did the PPP fall short of a clear majority in the national assembly but its actual percentage of the popular vote was a mere 2 per cent more than its nearest rival the Islamic Democratic Alliance – a coalition of the warring factions of the Pakistan Muslim League, the Jamat-i-Islami and smaller parties mediated by the army's inter-services intelligence. Yet for many who were marginalized or had suffered directly under the general's iron rule, notably in Sind, the prospect of the PPP forming the national government symbolized a victory far greater than was reflected in the election results.

That the elections did not produce stable governments at either the centre or the provinces had much to do with the depoliticization sought by the Zia regime and the access to state power and patronage enjoyed by the Islamic Democratic Alliance during the election campaign. To offset the worst effects of the IDA's control over the institutionalized channels of patronage, Benazir pragmatically – perhaps too pragmatically – resorted to an untidy mixture of populism and accommodations with landed notables. These electoral compromises disappointed committed party workers but, in a tribute to her father's memory, did not deter significant sections of the subordinate strata in the Punjab and Sind from voting for the PPP. With the advent of a genuinely representative government these underprivileged groups felt they could begin to hope once again. Even for the relatively better off, especially members of the intelligentsia, Benazir' s advent held out the promise of an open government, a decline in the influence of religious obscurantists and a redressal of policies that had led to the fragmentation of Pakistani society into minuscule and alarmingly well-armed factions.

The women of Pakistan for their part celebrated Benazir's assumption of office in quiet expectation. A decade of military rule punctuated by state-sponsored Islamization had led to a qualitative deterioration in their already low status in Pakistani society. A series of crassly sexist laws had been passed by Zia to put some stuffing into the hollow carcass of his Islamization programme. Though dismayed by Benazir's attempts to present herself as a national leader rather than the advocate of their rights, the vast majority of women rallied to her support once the PPP committed itself to repeal all discriminatory laws against women. However, with an extremely tenuous majority in parliament and a consistent volley of low-lying attacks from the religious opposition, Benazir avoided stirring up the Islamic hornet's nest. The offensive laws remained on the statute books even as the fact of a woman prime minister gained Pakistan international acclaim for Islamic moderation.

The symbolic connotations of Benazir's advent were clearly widely at odds with the structural constraints which she inherited. By far the most important of these was the long-standing imbalance between elected and non-elected institutions in the Pakistani state. Registered within years of independence the supremacy of the non-elected institutions had been fully confirmed during the Zia era. The entrenched institutional dominance of a mainly Punjabi army and federal bureaucracy cast the democratically elected government of Benazir Bhutto, whose principal power base was in

Sind, in the role of loyal opposition to the pre-existing state structure. A state structure accustomed to high defence expenditure and dominated by the non-elected institutions – namely the military and the civil bureaucracy – is not easily amenable to a transformation that readily acknowledges the ascendancy of the elected institutions – parliament in particular. The army high command's decision to rest content with dominance rather than direct intervention has been based on a careful calculation of the advantages and disadvantages of playing umpire in a highly polarized and increasingly violent political arena.

Facing a resource crunch and a crippling defence budget, the PPP government was unable to initiate new development projects which might have strengthened its social bases of support. In a context where politics had become hopelessly monetized and politicians locked in a venal dependence on the administrative apparatus to carry out development tasks in their constituencies, a state exchequer in arrears was a serious handicap for any government. And indeed, Benazir's government was acutely vulnerable to the blackmailing tactics of its own supporters in parliament. With the sphere of state patronage divided between Benazir's government at the federal level and Mian Nawaz Sharif's IDA government in the Punjab, ideologically uncommitted supporters of her Pakistan People's Party, including cabinet ministers, sought to extort government monies on threat of defection. This is what contributed to the deluge of criticism against Benazir's government which was blamed for breaking all previous records of jobbery and corruption. The opposition's willingness to pay handsome sums of money to buy up opportunists in the PPP's ranks left Benazir with an unacceptably wobbly majority in parliament. She was soon presented with the unenviable choice of going down gracefully by resigning or trying to beat the system at its own game.

On 6 August 1990 Benazir was dismissed unceremoniously after being completely outmanoeuvred by the keepers of the system who had laid down the rules of the game she was just beginning to learn. In addition to the fiscal crisis and structural imbalances within the state, Zia's 1985 constitution which aimed at perpetuating a quasi-military rule had invested the president with vast discretionary powers to override as well as dismiss an elected prime minister. The president, Ghulam Ishaq Khan, who together with the chief of army staff formed the linchpin of Pakistan's military–bureaucratic state structure, had no hesitation in using his powers to sack the prime minister with the backing of the military high command. It was history repeating itself with some added twists. Although Ishaq dissolved all the assemblies and took the constitutionally correct course by calling fresh elections within the prescribed period, the partisan nature of the gameplan was patently evident. The Islamic Democratic Alliance's governments in the Punjab and, during the October 1990 elections, also at the centre and the provinces were able to use their privileged access to the institutionalized channels of state patronage and manipulation to assemble the votes needed to defeat Benazir Bhutto's People's Democratic Alliance. The electoral stakes were particularly high given the interplay of domestic, regional and international factors. Unused as well as newly discovered 'development funds' were distributed to IDA candidates, especially in the electorally vital province of the Punjab. The administrative machinery was galvanized to undertake the most rapid road-building, sanitation and electrification exercises ever witnessed in the rural localities, and select voters treated with jobs and notes to pull the tricks out of the ballot box.

This is not to exculpate Benazir for her government's abysmal tenure in office or the poor electoral showing of her party. During the twenty-odd months that she hung on to power, not a single piece of legislation was placed before parliament by the treasury benches – a record that is unlikely to be surpassed easily. Exerting her energies in such demeaning tasks as horse-trading – a much used word in subcontinental political discourse to describe the buying and selling of elected members' votes – she had even less time than her father to attend to the PPP's ramshackle party machinery. The PPP's organizational disarray and loss of credibility in the key electoral province of the Punjab contributed to something of an electoral swing in certain constituencies. Yet ultimately it was access to state power and patronage, and firm support from the presidency, the civil bureaucracy and the intelligence networks of the army high command, which helped the IDA to make a royal showing at the hustings.

The formation of Mian Nawaz Sharif's IDA government at the centre as well as in all of the four provinces signalled important changes on the Pakistani political landscape. By far the most striking was the fact of a Punjabi prime minister with an urban industrial rather than a rural landed background. A first in Pakistan's history, it would not have been possible without the concerted support of key elements in the military–bureaucratic axis which during the Zia era had selected and then groomed Mian Nawaz Sharif for the job. The pro-industrial bias of Nawaz Sharif's programme for the liberalization and privatization of the economy appealed to business groups eager to escape the maze of bureaucratic red tape. Many of the prime minister's landed and commercial political associates also assented to his leadership. In the Punjab particularly hopes were aroused of the province's industrial takeoff, some of the boons of which would inevitably fall in the laps of those with agrarian and commercial capital to invest.

With the political dice loaded in his favour and support from the presidency and the military high command, Mian Nawaz Sharif's government was able to score a useful point in the troubled domain of Pakistan's Islamic ideology. Having worsted the PPP on the Islamic issue, the IDA government had to make some gesture to pacify its restless religious constituency. Yet the demand for the implementation of the Shariat bill passed by the senate just prior to Benazir's ouster did not have the approval of the military high command and a majority of the IDA's own members in the assembly. This was the green signal the government needed to seek smooth passage in parliament for a much watered down version of the original Shariat bill. An enabling rather than a binding piece of legislation, the Shariat bill was a propaganda device in the good tradition of the departed general. Though it met with truculent criticism from the religious parties, including the Jamat-i-Islami, the adoption of the Shariat for the time being put a damper on the ideological debate. So, for the first time in Pakistan's history, the military–bureaucratic state's democratic as well as ideological credentials appeared to be in fine fettle.

The 1990 election results marked the successful completion of a long process during which a military–bureaucratic dominated state had tried broadening its social bases of support and impressing control over the political process. Zia's social engineering and the attractions of an expanding network of official patronage had given rise to a political system where futures seemed better assured in collaboration with rather than in resistance to the state structure. While improving the prospects of working arrangements between the elected and non-elected institutions, the high-handed manipulations that led to an artificial harmonization of the political process and the state structure had extracted a hefty price in terms of social conflict along regional, class and linguistic lines. The discrepancy between a state-sponsored political system and a rapidly splintering social base did not auger well for Pakistan's incipient experiment with formal democracy and covert authoritarianism.

Despite an absolute majority in parliament and a relatively firm handle on the provinces, Mian Nawaz Sharif found himself confronting many of the same perils which led to the early demise of Benazir Bhutto's government. With the president and the army chief calling the shots from the control rooms, Nawaz Sharif concentrated on pushing through his economic programme and consolidating his political support. Yet tasks which befitted his brief and prime ministerial position soon proved to be difficult in a power-sharing arrangement with an interventionary presidency and a formidable army high command. Since the mid-1980s Pakistani politics had become so highly monetized that the success and survival of an elected prime minister depended on the ability to stretch control over the spheres of official patronage. As Nawaz Sharif sought to enlarge his share of state patronage and control of the political economy, he found himself trampling on territory the president and the army chief strictly regarded as their own.

Considering that the Pakistani state and political edifice rest on a structural fault – defence projections outweigh resource availability – it is easy to understand why the restoration of some semblance of democratic processes led to a distinct stiffening of competition between elected and non-elected institutions. Forced to do without American military aid since the autumn of 1990 – due to the nuclear programme and the changed strategic perspectives of the post-cold war international system – and unwilling to accept any alteration in its regional security imperative, the Pakistani army high command had wagered on a massive domestic resource generation effort. Here the legacies of military authoritarianism, the role of illicit money and weapons in politics and class-based social conflict manifested along regional, linguistic and sectarian lines, proved to be daunting. Some distorted successes in private capital accumulation did not amount to a strengthening of the resource base of the state. The much celebrated democratization of Pakistan had simply established a highly monetized electoral system in which a ruling party led by a businessman was not above resorting to questionable financial manoeuvres.

Apparently reaching the limits of the sphere of state patronage assigned to him as the elected prime minister, Nawaz Sharif allegedly toyed with the idea of laying claim to major defence contracts falling under the purview of the military high command. Whether prompted by greed or the desire to curb the military institution's powers of patronage, the two are admittedly not mutually exclusive, the prime minister's tinkering with the established basis of apportioning financial rewards in Pakistan's political economy of defence was a serious infringement. The prime minister came into collision course with the president when as part of his larger agenda he demanded a say in the appointment of the new chief of army staff following the sudden death of General Asif Nawaz Janjua.

So if there is logic in the madness of Pakistan's palace intrigues it lies in the battle over the controlling levers of the political economy. Many federal bureaucrats and senior army officers came to resent Nawaz Sharif's deployment of his massive financial portfolio in politics, as much as they had feared Zulfikar Ali Bhutto's populist mobilization. In the formally democratic politics of post-authoritarian Pakistan, power flowed from the hand operating the till as never before. The manipulations of the political process by state institutions in 1990 had not effaced the incongruence between an elected government and a political economy of defence. When push came to shove, it was not the democrat but capitalist political operator in Nawaz Sharif which led him to consider trimming the president's overbearing constitutional powers under Zia's eighth amendment of 1985. Threatened by his growing economic muscle and potential capacity to wield decisive control of the political process, the prime minister's old and new opponents rushed to embrace the bastions of the establishment in the name of saving the country from extensive corruption and financial mismanagement.

On 18 April 1993, an angry but supremely confident president, Ghulam Ishaq Khan, ousted the prime minister and the cabinet and dissolved the national assembly for the second time in three years. Her powers of empathy failing, Benazir Bhutto welcomed the move as poetic justice. On 25 May in an unprecedented ruling the supreme court, which had in the past invariably endorsed constitutionally questionable manoeuvres of the military and the bureaucracy, declared the presidential order illegal and reinstated Nawaz Sharif's government and the national assembly. Clashes between the non-elected institutions and the political process had, however, proceeded too far to permit the easy implementation of the judicial decision. In the past, contests of this sort had always been won by the non-elected institutions of the state. But Nawaz Sharif's success in carving up a support base in the Punjab, including the provincial bureaucracy, made the outcome of this particular wrangle more uncertain. A dramatically changed post-cold war international context coupled with a significantly altered domestic political scenario placed a different accent on the calculations of the military high command. Yet the final arbiter of Pakistan's destiny did not fail to make its presence known. As the presidential and the prime ministerial factions bickered and disgraced themselves in the struggle for the political control of the Punjab, the new army chief of staff, General Abdul Waheed Kakar, moved in to broker a settlement. On 18 July both the prime minister and the president resigned after calling for the dissolution of the national assembly and a fresh round of general elections. Interim governments at the centre and the provinces, consisting of non-political elements, retired bureaucrats and military officials in the main, were formed to create the conditions for free and fair elections. Although the people had precious little to do with the intrigues at the top, yet another reference to them had become inescapable. If periodic elections could only wash away the cesspool of its politics, Pakistan in 1993 seemed better poised than ever to refurbish its façade of formal democracy.

In the general elections of October 1993 a mere 40 per cent of a visibly lethargic and apathetic electorate turned out to exercise their right to vote. The Pakistan People's Party led by Benazir Bhutto emerged a nose ahead of the faction of the Pakistan Muslim League headed by Mian Nawaz Sharif. With the assistance of smaller parties and the blessings of the non-elected institutions of the state, the PPP was able to form a government at the centre. Yet a hung parliament at the centre and a drawn and quartered provincial field can hardly be seen as a healthy political development in a country where the civil bureaucracy and the army have for the most part remained dominant within the state structure. Insofar as the new electoral arithmetic is a fair reflection of a fragmented polity – itself a product of prolonged bouts of military and quasi-military rule – Pakistan in the 1990s has a democratic dispensation both at the national and provincial levels, albeit one with a greatly strained capacity to curb the authoritarian features of the state. So while the tussle between democratic politics and an authoritarian state has entered a fresh phase, the prospects of the former triumphing over the latter are uncertain at best. Democracy and authoritarianism in the Pakistani context are so thoroughly imbricated as to foreclose the possibility of any straightforward resolution following even a reasonably free and fair electoral exercise.

The elementary lessons of Pakistan's tentative steps beyond the well demarcated field of overt military authoritarianism towards an uncharted democratic future make for a sobering comparison with its sibling state in the far north-eastern corner of the subcontinent. Bangladesh, which began its transition to democracy two years after Pakistan, had come under military rule in August 1975. Before the similarities of the experience under resurgent military authoritarianism in the two countries can be uncovered, it is worth noting the main difference at the very outset. Unlike the Pakistani army which has preserved the hierarchical and rigid discipline of its colonial counterpart, the Bangladesh army's involvement in a war of liberation had weakened the structural grip of the high command over the middling and lower ranks. To date all military takeovers in Pakistan have been led by the top-ranking general, whether the commander-in-chief in the case of Ayub and Yahya or the chief of army staff in Zia's instance. At no time has the decision to intervene been challenged from either within the army or the two other services. The institutional coherence of the Pakistan army together with the overall organizational structure of the defence establishment has safeguarded against breaches in the ranks. By contrast, the Bangladesh army has been rent with divisions and, consequently, shown itself to be more prone to bloody coups led by men other than the commanding officer. The legacies of the liberation struggle – a structurally unstable army, an infirm and divided bureaucracy and a generally more politicized society – has tended to give more scope to opposition parties than in Pakistan. One of the primary goals of its two military rulers, Zia-ur-Rahman and Ershad, was to replace the more immediate legacies for the old and, wittingly or unwittingly, force Bangladesh into greater conformity with the dominant trends in the erstwhile metropolis.

After Mujib's assassination in a military coup the pro-American politician, Khondkar Mushtaq Ahmed, had briefly served as president and the country placed under martial law. A pro-Awami League counter-coup in November 1975 led by Brigadier Khaled Musharraf, the chief of general staff, was squashed. At this time the entire Awami League political leadership, including the left-leaning ex-prime minister Tajuddin Ahmed, were ruthlessly murdered inside a Dacca prison. The new regime also faced early challenges from the Biplobi Gana Bahani – Revolutionary Peoples Army – led by a Colonel Taher within the armed forces, which had close links with a left-wing political party called the Jatiya Samajtantrik Dal (Nationalist Socialist Party). During 1976 the regime spent the better part of its energies parrying assaults from within as well as outside the military. A coup led by a faction loyal to Khaled Musharraf and another by the air force chief was thwarted. Threatened by all sides, the regime perked up the expenditure on defence and internal security and doubled the size of the police force. This helped strengthen the position of Zia-ur-Rahman who had become the chief of army staff in 1975, but did not formally take over as president until April 1977. In steps which invoked the memory of Ayub Khan and presaged the measures of his namesake in Pakistan, Zia-ur-Rahman opted to consolidate his hold on state power by restoring the positions of civilian bureaucrats and military officers who had been denied the fruits of state patronage during the Mujib period.

In 1975–6 defence accounted for only 7 per cent of the national budget, but this was revised upwards so that it was 20 per cent of the entire budget. The size of the army grew from 60,000 in 1974–5 to 90,000 in 1976–7. Mujib's creation, the Rakkhi Bahini, which like Bhutto's FSF had been an irritant for the military top brass, was disbanded and select elements merged into the regular army. Many of the special privileges enjoyed by army personnel during the Pakistan period were reinstated. Expenditure on civil administration was also increased and bureaucrats given more clout in Zia's cabinet and the central secretariat as well as the divisional and district levels of the administration. Former members of the CSP were put in charge of twelve out of the nineteen districts. Bureaucrats also controlled the national economic council, the planning commission and thirty-eight major public corporations.

Much in the manner of Pakistan's military, the Zia regime in Bangladesh initially relied on the support of Saudi funded Islamic political groups. While nationalism had been one of the four principles of Mujibism, Zia-ur-Rahman made it the centrepiece of his regime's political ideology with added emphasis on unity, sovereignty and independence. But as in Zia's Pakistan, neither Islamic nor nationalist rhetoric could provide Zia-ur-Rahman's regime with an adequate social base of support or a modicum of legitimacy. So Zia moved towards the formation of gram parishads, village councils, in 1976 which were renamed swanirvar gram sarkars – self-sufficient village governments – in 1980. Like Ayub's basic democracies system these local governments were controlled by the bureaucracy, the only difference being that these were village governments rather than union-level governments. The same logic as later guided Zia-ul-Haq into dividing and insulating political horizons in Pakistan informed Zia-ur-Rahman's efforts to muster support in the localities. Winning over the leaders of local society through the extension of state patronage and development funds was a safe way of establishing control over the political system. This is why in both cases local body elections preceded those to the higher levels – giving the regimes plenty of opportunity to gauge political trends before taking the big step of holding elections to the national parliament.

In May 1977 Zia held a referendum on the basis of a nineteen-point policy programme promising to succour the private sector and achieving self-sufficiency in food production by instituting measures of population control and promoting agricultural development. Claiming 99.5 per cent support and an 85 per cent voter turnout Zia felt confident enough to try and assert complete control over the state apparatus. In June 1978 in a presidential election closely monitored by the civil bureaucracy Zia declared himself the victor. He then followed Ayub's and after 1985 also Zia-ul-Haq's pattern in Pakistan by creating a political party called the Bangladesh Nationalist Party which was designed to hold a majority in a parliament to be set up in 1979. Parented by military–bureaucratic state structures, the BNP and the Pakistan Muslim League, the main component of the IDA, share some common birth marks. Apart from being congenitally anti-Indian, both claim to be firmly set against secularism and socialism. If not for the differences between the Bangladeshi and Pakistani social structures, the BNP and the IDA might pass for fraternal twins. Despite an industrialist as prime minister, the IDA in Pakistan has been predominantly agricultural in composition. When it was formed one-third of the central executive committee of the BNP was composed of businessmen and less than 12 per cent were agriculturists. In parliamentary elections held in February 1979 the BNP won 41 per cent of the votes and two-thirds of the seats. Outside parliament the Awami League and the Jatiya Samajtantrik Dal remained the most trenchant political opponents of the regime.

In contrast to the situation that confronted Zia-ul-Haq in Pakistan, it proved relatively easier for Zia-ur-Rahman to manipulate the political process than confirm his authority over the Bangladesh army. And indeed it was instability within the army which led to Zia's downfall. Although Zia himself had been a freedom fighter, by 1981 only two of fifty major generals and brigadiers were men who had fought with the Mukti Bahini in 1971. The rest were all repatriates from West Pakistan. Only 15 per cent of the soldiers consisted of freedom fighters, 25 per cent were repatriated and 60 per cent were new recruits. Zia had faced as many as nineteen abortive coups between 1977 and 1981. On 30 May 1981 Zia was killed in Chittagong, allegedly by a faction of freedom fighters. Zia's death and the almost instantaneous killing of his alleged assassin removed the only two remaining veterans of the liberation army.

The main benefactor of these developments was General Ershad, chief of staff of the Bangladeshi army, who had been repatriated from Pakistan in 1973. In what was symptomatic of the precarious nature of the military institution, Ershad like his predecessor managed only gradually to consolidate his power and deferred the assumption of presidential office until 1984. Taking his cues from the military rulers in the subcontinent, Ershad too began building his base of support by strengthening his hold over the lower levels of the administration. The time-honoured second tier – the thana – was raised to the status of upazila or subdistrict and given enhanced administrative functions. Ershad went even further than Zia-ur-Rahman in establishing rapport with the business community by handing over thirty-three jute mills, twenty-five textile mills and thirty-one other industrial units to the private sector in 1984. He formed his own party, the Janadal (the People's Party) in December 1983. Elections were promised according to the established military tradition, first at the union and the subdistrict level, to be followed by parliamentary and presidential elections.

The Awami League led by Mujib's daughter, Hasina Wajid, and the Bangladesh Nationalist Party led by Zia-ur-Rahman's widow, Khaleda Zia, provided an intense challenge to Ershad's political engineering. Together with the lesser political parties they protested against the regime's intention to hold elections under martial law, demanded the restoration of fundamental rights and the holding of parliamentary elections before the local. Ershad refused to budge and echoed Zia-ul-Haq in Pakistan by accusing politicians of creating conditions which had necessitated martial law. Local elections were deemed to be the first step to the genuine empowerment of the ordinary citizen, not fundamental rights of citizenship which no one really understood.

Amid a rising crescendo of protests and general strikes spearheaded by two women opposition leaders – yet another interesting parallel with Pakistan under Zia – Ershad managed to get his way. By holding local body elections first in 1984 Ershad was able to use the newly elected councillors to secure the government's victory for the parliamentary elections. In such a tightly controlled setting the Janadal, now the Jatiya Party, naturally won a majority. Hasina Wajid's Awami League bagged more than a third of the seats but refused to enter parliament, charging the regime with widespread rigging. Ershad's Jatiya Party had now replaced the BNP as the main political vehicle for the distribution of state patronage. A second round of upazila elections held in 1989 further consolidated Ershad's support in the rural constituencies. One of the main grievances of the political opposition was Ershad's attempt to include military and bureaucratic officials as members of the local councils. This amounted to giving the military–bureaucratic state a suffocating hold over the lowest levels of the political system, something even Zia-ul-Haq had not directly attempted.

There were other significant variations between Ershad's Bangladesh and Zia's Pakistan. The most important of these flowed from the very different strategic positioning of the two states. A front line state in Western security calculations following the Soviet invasion, Pakistan enhanced its international and regional profile considerably on account of the support it lent to the Afghan resistance movement. This brought generous flows of foreign aid but also turned the country into a conduit for arms and drugs trafficking. Combined with Zia's manipulation of Islam these contributed to intense and unprecedented social conflict. Bangladesh under Ershad shared some of Pakistan's antipathy towards India and also supported the cause of the Afghan Mujahideen. But its relative lack of importance in geo-strategic terms spared it many of the devastations which military rule combined with regional and international pressures wreaked on the intricate weave of Pakistani society. Economically, however, Bangladesh under military rule remained far worse off than the strategically more exposed Pakistan. Unable to make ends meet without substantial international handouts, Bangladesh's mainly stagnant and aid driven economy was vulnerable to foreign intervention which inevitably extended to the political domain.

By the late 1980s the interplay of domestic, regional and international factors were only faintly pointing to the end of the post-1977 military regime in Pakistan. Despite undeniable successes in moulding the political process, Ershad in many ways was left facing a far more concerted opposition than Zia in Pakistan, who had largely managed to win over substantial segments of the dominant social strata to his side. While he could not prevent his military and bureaucratic associates reading the writing on the wall, Ershad had come to fancy himself as a good enough democrat now that the Jatiya Party had done well in successive local body elections. And so he had to be prised out of office. With the changed calculations of the military–bureaucratic state, the movement for democracy in Bangladesh reached an altogether new pitch during 1990. While the demonstration effect of other democratic movements may have been a factor, it was the excessive corruption of the Ershad regime which contributed to its isolation. The All-Party Students Union, especially the student activists in the universities of Dhaka and Chittagong, played a key role in forcing the Awami League and the BNP-led coalitions of parties to take a united stand against a hated military regime. Gigantic popular demonstrations further convinced many top-ranking military and civil officials that Ershad was a losing bet. He was pressured into stepping down and has since been pegged down with an array of criminal charges.

However, Ershad and the Jatiya Party were not debarred from participating in the general elections held in February 1991. Contrary to most expectations and at least a passing hint of the continuing influence of the military–bureaucratic state over the electoral process, the Awami League trailed behind the BNP at the hustings rather than the other way round. The BNP polled 31 per cent of the popular vote and won 140 seats against the 28 per cent cast in favour of the Awami League which gave it 85 seats in a full house of 300. Proof, if proof is needed, that the effects of political engineering under military rule linger on long after the formal collapse of the regime, was the thirty-five seats secured by Ershad's Jatiya Party and the not at all bad statistical showing of 12 per cent as its share of the popular vote. It was certainly better than the Jamat-i-Islami's eighteen seats and 6 per cent of the popular vote which enabled it to hold the balance in the assembly by supporting the BNP government from the outside.

The reasons for the BNP's success are variously ascribed to its command over the majority of organized student groups in the country, promises of stability and economic development, its anti-Indian stance, support of the private sector and commitment to Islam. This attracted votes from the rural and the urban middle classes, the business community as well as the rural and the urban poor. The Awami League doused its appeals by reviving the memory of Mujib while the BNP appears to have stuck closer to issues of more immediate relevance to the electorate.

At the helm of a conservative political grouping like the IDA in Pakistan, Khaleda Zia was undoubtedly more acceptable to the Bangladeshi military–bureaucratic establishment than Hasina Wajid. The new prime minister showed circumspection towards the embedded complexities of governing Bangladesh by selecting a relatively experienced team consisting of former ministers and retired military and civil officials. Whether the inclusion of military officers and civil bureaucrats will facilitate the transition to democracy or merely confirm the old patterns of governance remains an open question.

Conclusion

The recent history of Pakistan and Bangladesh demonstrates just how difficult it is to reverse the phenomenon of military authoritarianism. The interplay of domestic, regional and international factors during the cold war which established the fact of military dominance in Pakistan cast the state structure into an enduring mould. These factors combined again in the late 1970s to reaffirm institutional imbalances in Pakistan and to create similar ones in Bangladesh. The military–bureaucratic state in both cases utilized their powers of patronage to coopt significant segments of dominant socio-economic elites and to localize political horizons in a manner reminiscent of the colonial state. Elections have been held in both countries of late, but the ritual of voting cannot be confused with the achievement of substantive democracy resting on the social and economic rights of citizenship. Political processes in Pakistan and Bangladesh remain hostage to highly inequitable state structures. Continuing imbalances within the state structures and also between them and civil society foreclose the possibility of a significant reapportioning of political power and economic resources in the very near future.

Yet most perturbing for the subcontinent, even relatively autonomous political processes in India have not generated the kind of pressures needed to force the state structure into undertaking major redistributive measures. Alliances between dominant castes and classes both within the ruling parties and the non-elected institutions of the state have used the democratic rubric to perpetuate economic inequalities and social injustices. Populism in India quite as much as in Pakistan and Bangladesh proved to be a mirage and merely provided grounds for a greater reassertion of authoritarian tendencies rooted in the state structure and the political economy. That after years of diverging political developments, these tendencies are co-existing with formal democracy in all three countries in the 1990s is a matter less of relief than of consternation. What is evident is that without some sort of restructuring of the present equations of dominance and privilege, the subcontinent as a whole, discrepancies encrusted in social structures and political systems notwithstanding, seems inexorably poised for greater conflict along the myriad lines afforded by its class, caste, communal, regional and linguistic divisions. Whether the longer surviving formally democratic state structure in India stands a better chance of forestalling the prospect of spiralling violent conflict than military dominated Pakistan and Bangladesh is a question whose answer is better postponed until after a closer assessment of the contradictions in their respective political economies as well as the proliferating tensions between the centralized states and the component units.

4 The state and political economy, 1947 to c.1993

The study so far has alluded to the ways in which the state and economy influence social dynamics underlying political processes in India, Pakistan and Bangladesh. Exploring this relationship further and making the implicit more explicit is the task to which this chapter now turns. Instead of looking at economic factors to the exclusion of the political, the analysis merges the two in a broad approximation of the approach adopted by the practitioners of political economy. The concept of political economy, located as it is at the interstices of state and economy, assists analyses of social structures and political processes on economic policy choices which for their part seek to mould the patterns of social change. A focus on the political economies in each of the three countries lends an added dimension to the comparative assessments based on an examination of the unfolding dialectic between state structures and political processes.

Since the end of the second world war, most states in the post-colonial world have laid emphasis on planning for development. The experience of the great depression and the war had underscored the merits of state interventions in the economy. With the onset of decolonization the state's role in development processes came to pervade the theory and practice of development economics. Development was to be overseen by the centralizing state which was considered to be the ultimate leveller of inequities and injustices and, by extension, the myriad diversities rooted in developing societies. By planning for development and monitoring the production and distribution of economic resources in society, the centralized state was expected to also expedite processes of national integration. Singular or unitarian concepts of sovereignty were obvious corollaries of the pious hopes the modernization paradigm raised among economists and state managers alike. The accent on the centralization of state structures and the ensuing dysfunctional effects on political processes in much of sub-continental South Asia owed not a little to these grandiose notions of planned economic development leading to national integration. Before considering the implications of centralized states pursuing specific development strategies on the integration of heterogeneous societies, the link between politics and economics needs to be drawn more closely.

As elsewhere, states in the subcontinent engage in economic development processes with a twin-fold purpose: to hasten the pace of capital accumulation and to implement redistributive reforms. Yet the demand for rapid capital accumulation entails that the state win the support of at least a fraction of the dominant social classes, a requirement which not infrequently constrains its ability to bring about redistributive reforms for the subordinate classes. The contradiction is never easy to overcome, much less resolve, whatever the balance between state and society or the particular type of regime in power. One way to establish how the contradiction plays itself out in different contexts and with what effect on decision-making priorities is to consider the extent to which the state is dependent on or, to use a familiar concept in political theory, relatively autonomous from dominant social classes. Far from being a hollow concept induced by abstract theoretical imaginings, the relative autonomy of the state from social classes is a useful way of historically contextualizing the political economies of development in any country. The ideological leanings of those occupying strategic positions within the state apparatus bear upon development policies adopted by ruling configurations. But while ideology certainly merits attention, it is no substitute for real intention and the actual impact. Distinguishing the rhetoric from the substance of state policies aimed at economic transformation is indispensable to a meaningful historical interpretation of development strategies. It is equally necessary to have a sense of the state's organizational capacities – its cohesiveness or fragmentation, and the balance between elected and non-elected institutions.

An investigation of the state–class relationship in the different phases of the post-independence history of India, Pakistan and Bangladesh abets comparisons of their relative capacities in addressing and redressing the gnawing problems of economic inequalities and social injustices. The absence of any significant restructuring of existing associations of dominance and privilege in civil society have since the late 1960s served to magnify competition and conflict in ever-expanding political arenas and sharply increased the transactional costs of governance, forcing greater reliance on the state's coercive apparatus, irrespective of its formally democratic or authoritarian façade.

India's political economy of development

The case of India raises the intriguing question whether state power can be used in an essentially capitalist society, recourse to socialistic rhetoric notwithstanding, to bring about redistributive justice without abandoning the path of democracy. Centralized state power in India has always had to contend with the varied and conflicting interests of its regional political economies. The high degree of political infractions along lines of class, caste, community and the rural–urban divide in the different regions has tempered challenges to the centralized state. Combined with its own broader imperatives, these have prevented the state exclusively reflecting the interests of any specific regional political economy. Both the Janata party's and the Janata Dal's mainly north Indian-based agrarian economic orientation had to be reconciled with the state's broader sectoral imperatives – the need to promote the interests of the industrial and financial magnates as well as those of the non-elected institutions. So the relative autonomy of the Indian state from dominant social classes, its own administrative requirements and the ideological protestations of the national leadership have all contributed to the shaping of its political economy of development.

Among the particularly notable features of India's political economy of development is that in spite of its enormous diversities, which of late have erupted in a veritable epidemic of social conflicts along class, caste, linguistic, regional and religious lines, the central state has until recently remained firmly wedded to the ideals of democracy and planned economic development. Over the years the strains on its social fabric have been reflected increasingly in the workings of civil and police services and placed untold burdens on the state's overall administrative capacities. Without internal administrative coherence many of the basic goals of economic development have badly miscarried. The domestic obstacles to development have been exacerbated by tensions with neighbours, especially Pakistan, which have steeled India's determination to project itself as a major regional military power. Despite a decidedly non-aligned posture, the imperatives of the international capitalist system have not failed to impose their constraining influence on the Indian economy. The history of India's political economy of development is, therefore, best analysed in the context of the interplay of domestic, regional and international factors.

During the 1950s India was held up as a model for Asian economic development. The Indian development effort based on Nehru's vision of a mixed economy was seen as the best answer to the challenge posed by Mao-Zedong's communist experiment in China. Post-colonial India possessed an effective administrative structure, a stable government dominated by a relatively well-organized nationally based political party, an educated elite of sizeable dimensions and an ideological commitment to planned development. Yet by the 1960s the optimism had all but evaporated.

Even with scores of disappointments and failures the Indian development experience, nevertheless, is a most instructive one. When independence was won in 1947 the annual growth rate was a mere 1 per cent and an Indian could on average expect to live for no more than 33 years. In 1943 a famine in Bengal had killed over three million people. By the 1980s, life expectancy in India had gone up to 55 years; there have been no major famines since independence and the annual growth rate was about 4.8 per cent while population grew by 2 per cent. So India clearly had some successes to report. Yet in comparison with other low to middle income countries, many of India's most notable achievements pale into insignificance. Malnutrition as distinct from acute starvation stalks the Indian countryside. More than a third of the rural population suffers from nutritional inadequacies although India has attained self-sufficiency in food. The state has been able to turn a blind eye to the fact of 30 to 40 per cent of the rural population going to bed each night hungry and malnourished because, to quote Amartya Sen, 'persistent orderly hunger does not upset the system'.[1] Although ethnic conflict has ripped apart its social and economic texture, Sri Lanka still compares favourably with India on almost all counts. Endemic hunger is rare and life expectancy stands at 68 years for men and 72 years for women. After forty-seven years of independence, a mere 40 per cent of adult Indians are literate and this in a country with a well-advertised nuclear capacity and well-developed scientific know-how. By contrast, the adult literacy rate in Burma and Sri Lanka is 78 per cent and 87 per cent respectively. While some regions within India, notably Kerala, do creditably on these indicators, the aggregate picture has remained quite dismal.

What all this suggests is that while development has undoubtedly taken place in India, it has occurred alongside rather than broken the vicious cycle of poverty perpetuated by an inequitable distribution of power and assets, high population growth rates and mass illiteracy. Although couched in 'socialist' terms, India's macro-economic efforts have by and large followed the liberal model of planning for capitalist development. An historical assessment of the state–property nexus reveals the political as well as the structural constraints that have hampered the Indian state's ability to carry out any significant redistributive reforms. Without these reforms winning the battle against widespread poverty has remained a distant dream, albeit one which the rising political costs of exploitation and discrimination along lines of class, caste and gender have made more and more unconscionable and perilous for Indian state managers to ignore.

Under the influence of men like Jawaharlal Nehru and Subhas Chandra Bose a segment of the nationalist movement had been spurred on by hopes of rapid economic development under the auspices of a sovereign, indepen-

---

[1] Amartya Sen, 'How is India Doing', *The New York Review of Books*, 16 December 1982.

dent and centralized Indian state. This essentially socialist ideal was countered by Gandhian notions of decentralized and self-sufficient village republics, but had gained the upper hand by the late 1930s in the face of growing disaffection with the colonial state's financial manipulations and indifference towards India's basic development needs. It was towards this end that in 1938 the All-India Congress Committee sanctioned the creation of a national planning committee. Chaired by Nehru and consisting of socialists, communists and leading industrialists, the committee's brief was to prepare blueprints for India's post-independence economic recovery. To avoid ideological disagreements by committing independent India to either the socialist or capitalist road to development, Nehru contented himself with securing the committee's endorsement for central economic planning.

So vagueness about ultimate economic objectives did not extend to the Congress's immediate goal of wresting control over the centralized colonial state. And indeed it is the assumption of the centralized power of the British raj by the Congress, professing an ideology of reformist class conciliation but in fact representing the interests of specific though historically shifting dominant classes and regional bases of support, which provides the crucial context in which to assess India's actual development experience. Despite Nehru's vocal effusions about socialism, his years as prime minister, spanning three national development plans, are marked by a commitment to consolidating the state and initiating import-substitution industrialization through not only a large public sector but also support for the private sector. During the fifties agrarian reforms were initiated with a view to eliminating intermediary landlords or *zamindars* who under the colonial system collected rent from the actual cultivators and paid a prescribed amount as revenue to the state. But the disappearance of the top strata in agrarian society, mostly absentee landlords, worked mainly to the advantage of the Congress's middle to rich peasant supporters rather than peasant smallholding families and landless labourers. In 1959 although Nehru resoundingly failed to secure the party's approval for a blueprint to promote cooperative farming on the Chinese model, the mere suggestion provided the grounds for a serious rift in Congress's north Indian agrarian support base.

Congress's overwhelmingly middle to upper class and caste composition meant that in spite of a seemingly cohesive national party organization it could not but promote the interests of the propertied strata at the expense of the subordinate. The decision to pursue development in a particular kind of liberal democratic context merely expedited the trend and further weakened the Congress's ability to deploy the state's capacities in the interests of redistributive justice. According to the Nehruvian development vision, a gradual and non-violent transformation of the existing social order would

not only be the more democratic way to proceed but would at the same time
sow the seeds of the socialist principles he held so dear. In other words, the
autonomy of the state was circumscribed in the interests of establishing the
Congress party as the organization presiding over a 'democratic consensus'
or, more aptly, a majoritarian consensus fashioned around the middling to
upper strata in rural and urban areas alike.

It is hardly surprising that the early fruits of Indian economic development were reaped mainly by the privileged social groups. Committed to
rapid industrialization and only marginally concerned with the agrarian
sector, which in any case was a state subject and so outside the direct
purview of the centre, Nehru compromised his socialism and endowed it
with the logic of the mixed economy. Nehruvian socialism was perfectly
consistent with indirect state support for private enterprise. So state ownership and national economic planning in the name of socialism promoted
private enterprise in the best capitalist tradition. Much the same sort of
policy was adopted towards the agrarian sector. With over two-thirds of the
Indian electorate huddled in the agrarian sector, it was politically in-
expedient and administratively unfeasible to press hard for a socialist
transformation and much simpler to settle down to nurturing existing
alliances with landed groups who dominated the countryside. Nehru envisaged a gradual enhancement of the state's economic power without altering
the basic ownership pattern. The policy emphasis in the industrial and, to a
more limited extent, the agricultural sector was on production and capital
accumulation, here and now, and shelving efforts at redistribution and the
redressal of poverty for the future.

With the 'morality of postponed gratification'[2] as the guiding principle of
the political centre, early Indian planners adopted a supply-side approach to
development. The main concern was to achieve higher rates of saving and,
in this way, to push up the aggregate levels of public investment in three
main areas – infrastructure, industry and agriculture. This primarily long-
term view of development ignored the constraints which domestic demand
could place on the growth process in the short term.

Operating under Nehru's personal direction the planning commission
carried enormous prestige and stature. During Nehru's long tenure in office
less than two dozen men directed the commission's work, evidence not only
of the highly centralized nature of the exercise but also the limited field of
decision-making in a putative effort involving hundreds of millions. In 1952
the national development council was established with a view to giving voice
to the chief ministers of the states in the national planning operation. Yet,

[2] Lloyd and Susanne Hoeber Rudolph, *In Pursuit of Lakshmi: the Political Economy of the
Indian State*, Chicago, 1987, p. 215.

with Nehru in the chair, the NDC was a more effective institutional channel for those setting the scope and targets of the plan than for those entrusted with the implementation. There was much ado about creating a village-level leadership, free of manipulation by political parties and exclusively engaged in extending the development effort through the education and organization of the lower levels of the rural strata. Yet for all practical purposes, the development effort at the local levels was squarely in the hands of block development officers and a team of badly trained and underpaid workers who took their orders from mainly conservative IAS officers and state ministers. The top-heavy character of the national planning organization and the flimsy vehicles of implementation at the local levels of society flew in the face of the inherently disparate and decentralized tendencies informing India's expanding political arenas at the level of the different regional economies.

While obstacles to implementation certainly played a large part in the problems which came to stymie India's development efforts by the early sixties, there is reason to question the very wisdom of centralized planning in a sprawling country dotted by enormous variations. For one thing, it is debatable whether the goals set by the planning commission entirely corresponded to the realities at the base or were based on broad suppositions. For another, it seems far more plausible that the principles guiding the planning exercise owed more to the imperatives of the centralized state than with those of the constituent units. So to the bottlenecks in implementation and the ambiguities of political will must be added a third possibility of the central planning exercise being at odds with the forces propelling social dynamics at the level of the regional economies, a contradiction often sought to be invoked by the India versus Bharat dichotomy. This is not to imply that the Gandhian ideal of self-sufficient village communities was a closer approximation of Indian realities, but to suggest that although the Nehruvian agenda kept abreast with the more focused, if broadly, construed requirements of the centre it was quite as ahistorical as that of the Mahatma's borrowings from Western misperceptions about an unchanging past. Both views failed to take account of the historically shifting, more diffuse, yet narrowly based, needs of post-independence India's diverse regional political economies.

A cursory glance at the three plan documents written and adopted during the Nehru period reveal some of the pitfalls of centralized planning based on a crude intermingling of the socialist and capitalist modernization paradigms. Bracing themselves for the sacrifices required to transform India into an industrialized country and a major military power in the shortest possible time, the planners paid little heed to the hard realities of resource constraints, inequities enmeshed in the social structures of different regional political economies and the bare-bone needs of a swarming population. The first five-year plan, covering the years 1950 to 1955, was less of a plan than a motley bunch of public investment projects, most of which were already underway as part of the colonial post-war reconstruction effort. Its main focus was on developing industrial infrastructure and public irrigation projects in the agrarian sector. Given a very low base to start from, the plan's achievements were impressive. The 12 per cent targeted increase in national income was surpassed largely due to a sharp jump in the production of food grains from about 52 million tons to 66 million tons.

The second five-year plan (1955–60) made a more concerted break with the past. It was heavily influenced by the planning commission's statistical adviser, P. C. Mahalanobis, and bore some resemblance to the first Soviet five-year plan. Indian planners were convinced, wrongly it could be said with hindsight, that Indian export commodities could not penetrate the protected markets of the advanced industrialized countries. So it was thought wise to impose strict restrictions on imports and concentrate on expanding the productive capacity of the capital goods sector. The goal was to raise savings from the initial low level of 5 per cent in 1950 to 20 per cent by 1975. In other words, the capital goods sector – heavy metals and machinery – would have to grow at an accelerated rate in order to convert higher savings into additional public investments. Here it is worth mentioning that the Mahalanobis model deviated from the 'textiles first strategy' of industrial development followed by a number of countries – Japan being a prominent example – who were late comers in the nineteenth-century race towards industrialization. Convinced that India's poor record of industrialization was part of a determined strategy by imperialism and capitalism to keep it dependent on the advanced countries of the West, the planners banked on the abilities of a huge indigenous market to absorb the outputs of a highly protected domestic capital goods sector. With this rationale, efficiency and competitiveness were relegated to the sidelines of India's capital intensive import substitution drive.

Yet in betting on the capital goods sector, the planners inadvertently contributed to a slowing down of the rate of growth of the consumer goods sector. The second five-year plan was unduly optimistic in its approach towards the agricultural sector, hoping to achieve growth targets without corresponding investment outlays. Agriculture's share of the total investment was slashed by nearly half that of the first five-year plan. The result was predictable. Within fifteen months of the plan Indian agriculture was in the throes of a serious crisis with foodgrain production well below expectations. By the summer of 1957 a 50 per cent hike in food prices sent the wholesale price index spiralling, forcing the central government to import huge quantities of wheat. The planning commission ascribed the miserable failure to enforce price controls and initiate state trading in the unorganized agrarian sector of the economy to hoarding and black marketeering by surplus farmers. Both the food ministry and the states in turn faulted the principle of central planning and market forces – stagnant levels of production due to the absence of adequate agricultural inputs and remunerative prices for commodities which could give incentives to private investment, the increase in urban incomes due to imprudent development outlays and high rates of population growth.[3]

Accusing India's surplus farmers, who formed the backbone of the Congress party in key electoral states like UP, of avidity and illegal profiteering was necessary to justify the soundness of the goals of central planning but awkward for the future cohesion of the dominant ruling configuration. The social effects of a deepening financial crisis, worsened by the food imports and the high costs of defence procurement as well as steel and iron all contributed to the escalation of political rancour between the centre and the states. And this at a time when the central government had reluctantly given way to strident demands for the linguistic reorganization of existing state boundaries. Severe shortages of essential consumer items did little to mollify political tempers stirred by appeals to linguistic identities. Mahalanobis's calculation that labour-intensive village and small-scale industrial production would be sufficient to deliver adequate quantities of consumer goods simply failed to materialize. Besides, the emphasis on capital-intensive public investments did not boost the employment generating capacities of India's labour surplus economy. Finally, the continued need to import intermediate raw materials – essential for the production of many agricultural and industrial consumer items – plunged India into an acute balance of payments crisis which lasted well into the 1970s. An import substitution drive without requisite support from the export sector inevitably created a serious shortage of foreign exchange.

Yet during this period India had built a heavy industrial base and made some strides in establishing its own research and development facilities, a useful accompaniment to the defence procurement effort. By the time the next five-year plan was launched the general index of industrial production had risen from 139 in 1955–6 with 1950 as the base line to 194 in 1960–1. The machinery index had leapt from 192 in 1955–6 to 503 in 1960–1. There was a spectacular growth in the production of iron, steel and chemicals. By contrast, cotton textile manufacturing had languished badly, increasing from 128 in 1955–6 to only 133 in 1960–1.

As the results of the 1957 parliamentary and state assembly elections showed, the cosy assumptions of planners sitting in the comfortable con-

[3] Frankel, *India's Political Economy, 1947–1977*, pp. 131–47.

fines of Lutyens' central secretariat buildings in New Delhi had slowly begun backfiring in the rustic expanses. With the political opposition as divided as ever, the Congress improved its tally of the total votes cast in the national as well as the state elections. But quite as much as the statistical manoeuvres of its chief planners, the election figures masked a distinct erosion of the Congress's support base in a number of states. The central planning logic of postponed gratification of needs and sacrifices today for a rosier tomorrow was not one to kindle enthusiasm among parlously poor segments of society. Even the middle strata had reason to be dismayed at the slow to non-existent improvement in the quality of life. The opposition parties in UP, Bihar and Bombay improved their position at Congress's expense, which failed to win a majority and had to form coalitions with independent members of the assembly.

The time lag between economic grievances and electoral realignments appeared superficially to give the central leadership something of a breather. But the economic objectives set by the central planners were coming to clash with the political imperatives of the Congress party. Despite growing pressure from within the party and big business to give even more incentives to the private sector, Nehru argued that greater investment in the heavy industries orientated public sector was necessitated by India's security requirements. So the third five-year plan for the period 1960 to 1965 continued to follow the logic of the Mahalanobis model for a capital-intensive industrialization. But the planners gave more explicit recognition to the needs of the agrarian sector. While emphasizing the urgent need for reorganizing the rural social structure, the plan perked up investment outlays for agriculture. Rural works programmes received special attention, but did little to transform the agrarian structure. Instead of reaching the lowest strata in rural society, the funnelling of greater development resources to the countryside expedited the commercialization of agriculture, a process in which the main beneficiaries were the rural upper-class supporters of the Congress. Another notable feature of the plan was the allocation towards family planning. Yet for all the platitudes about the state's intention to eventually obliterate illiteracy, the planners seemed in no great hurry to make education the primary goal of development. At any rate, many of the plan outlays were based on hypothetical estimates of available resources. Foreign aid had to be included as an essential ingredient in plan projections to cover the huge budgetary deficits. Since self-reliance was the cornerstone of India's development planning ideology the planners claimed that the aid would be used to expand production in import-substituting industries and promote exports.

Stagnant resources chasing dreams of grandeur are wont to exacerbate problems in any society. The illusion of political stability, administrative cohesion and controlled corruption which Nehru's presence in high office served to keep alive are wholly belied by the facts on the ground. Growing state interventions in the economy created fantastic opportunities for non-elected officials in the civil, police, judicial, revenue and development services to extort favours in cash or in kind in exchange for granting access to public assets and services. The age-old contradiction between rule-bound institutions and a highly personalized social order took on new proportions under the rubric of state-induced economic development processes. Needing access to the state for most things, big and small, businessmen, small contractors, men of trade and commerce, landed groups and politicians all relied on the personal discretion of government officials only too willing to skirt around the rules in order to combat inflationary pressures on their modest monthly salaries. The institutionalization of corruption was one of the more intractable legacies of the centralized planning efforts during the Nehruvian era, compounding the political difficulties flowing from unrealized economic objectives and growing regional disparities.

Although Congress survived at the hustings in 1962, its share of the total vote in parliamentary and state elections was appreciably less than in 1957. Regional, communal, right and left leaning parties all gained at the Congress's expense, especially among the economically least privileged strata – those denied education, unemployed youth and lower income groups. Had Nehru taken concerted steps towards arresting the Congress's decline at this stage and carried out the necessary organizational reforms in the party, the worst effects of the 1967 electoral débâcle might conceivably have been averted. But the stubborn reluctance to reorient planning objectives or countenance a break with the old rural party bosses, whose control over the vote banks had been substantially compromised by unmet economic expectations, is a telling comment on a basic inability to keep in step with his ideals.

In the event, exogenous factors rescued Nehru from taking full responsibility for the inappropriateness of the goals chalked out in the third five-year plan. Its faltering beginning, notwithstanding, the plan went off the rails largely on account of the Indo-China war of 1962 and the Indo-Pakistan war of 1965 which saw a sharp increase in defence spending. Nehru's death in 1964 removed the great steadying hand which had inspired so much confidence in India's development potential. Economists painted a gloomy scenario of the crisis in India's development planning. Some held urban bias to be responsible for this sorry state of affairs, others pointed to the total disregard of foreign trade and the neglect of human resource development. There were elements of truth in all of this. Yet in the final analysis India's development effort was foiled by managers of a centralized state who in reaching for national glory through brisk industrialization and projections of military prowess ended up being hoist by their own petard.

That said, the crisis of Indian planning in the late 1960s should not obscure the achievements of the early development planners. The period of the second and third five-year plans witnessed a remarkably high rate of public investment in proportion to total expenditure and rapid growth rates in industrial production. India was able to diversify its industrial structure and build up a heavily industrial base. There was a substantial increase in the skills base of the Indian population even though little was done to alter the elitist nature of the colonial educational system by directly addressing the problem of mass illiteracy. Given the long-standing stagnation of the agrarian sector under colonialism, post-independence India under Nehru could boast a striking turnabout owing mainly to the expansion of both irrigation and land under cultivation. Among the notable failures was the underestimation of the costs of the import substitution process and indifference towards improving the quality of life for substantial segments of society, in particular those occupying the lowest rungs of the economic pyramid.

But the biggest failure by far was the state's inability to bring about effective agrarian reforms in the early 1950s because of the unwillingness of Nehru's government to alienate the rural elites who dominated the party at the provincial and district levels. While the *zamindari* or landlord system of rent and revenue collection was abolished and tenants given greater security of tenure, there were too many loopholes in the land ceilings legislation and its implementation. In anticipation of the reforms, which were carried out piecemeal by the different states, many *zamindars* bribed the *patwari* – or the local revenue official – and the police to take advantage of the legal lacuna allowing them to hold on to land proven to be under their self-cultivation. Timely evictions of tenants saw *zamindars* acquiring ownership rights over land from which they had previously only exacted rent. Since the ceilings in the early decades were on an individual rather than a family basis, huge amounts remained within the ambit of the very *zamindars* the reforms were supposedly targeting. Others were generously compensated for the land resumed, enabling the more enterprising among them to set up highly profitable agro-based industries. So for all practical purposes the abolition of intermediary interests did not alter the basic contours of the agrarian structure.

Indeed, there is reason to believe that some of the legislation passed was singularly inappropriate. The incongruence between legal categories and rural social classes ensured that reformist legislation remained unclear about who it was supposed to empower. Dominant landholding classes could not only use ambiguities in the law but also deploy their control over the product, credit and even the labour markets to shift the burden of acquiring the benefits of the legislation on to the small peasant, share-cropper and landless labourer. Much the same sort of constraints dictated the state's relations with the industrial classes. Despite the expansion of the public sector, the government and the ruling party, supported by civil bureaucrats, were beholden to the industrial capitalist class. Throughout the time that Nehru remained at the helm, India's private entrepreneurs continued to carp and complain about the barriers to their investing in the heavy industrial sector which, because it was linked with the defence procurement effort, held out the promise of handsome profits. Yet the capitalist classes had much to thank the state for building an industrial infrastructure and curbing the bargaining power of the industrial labour force.

So although the Indian National Congress emerged from the colonial era as a legitimate, if heterogeneous political force, the national leadership chose to consolidate its position by forging an alliance with the civil bureaucracy and compromising with dominant social classes. This assured the stability of the Indian state and preserved a liberal democratic tradition, albeit one which co-existed with authoritarian strains in the institutional structures inherited from the colonial period. But in the long run the ruling party's symbiotic relationship with the civil bureaucracy and promotion of private propertied groups seriously undermined the state's capacity to intervene on behalf of the dispossessed with forceful measures of redistributive justice. The Congress leadership avoided conflict with the dominant social groups and made measured uses of state coercion in accordance with their preferred strategy of class accommodation. This tacit agreement between India's leadership in government, state officials and the owners of property led to a state-supported capitalist rather than a state-sponsored socialist pattern of development.

With Nehru's departure from the political scene, Indira Gandhi continued to rely on the administrative arms of the state and the tacit support of the industrial classes. But unlike her ideologically and, to a lesser extent, politically more obstinate father she blended pragmatism with realpolitik while trying to broaden the Congress's social base of support. After the late 1960s Indira made the removal of *garibi* or poverty the central theme of her populist cum socialistic policy. Sadly for the many millions floundering at the brink of poverty, disease or death, it was a makeshift strategy for the continued survival of Congress hegemony at a time when both Indian politics and economy were manifestly in the throes of a crisis. The pessimism surrounding the social costs of centralized planning had deepened with a sharp fall in food production after two consecutively bad monsoon seasons in 1965–6 and 1966–7. The inevitable cut-back in public investment put the brakes on India's industrial engine and led to the emergence of unused capacity in the heavy capital-goods sector. American wheat aid under the PL 480 programme temporarily alleviated the food crisis. Yet it had become patently evident that a chronic imbalance had arisen between the demand and supply of food, the combined result of high rates of population growth and the exhaustion of possibilities of expanding the area under actual cultivation. In a disquieting development for non-aligned and proudly independent India, Mrs Gandhi's government had to agree to an unpopular devaluation of the rupee in 1966 under strong pressure from Washington. The decision to declare a three-year 'plan holiday' pricked the bubble of India's initial leap towards centrally planned development.

The political sea-changes following the emergence of Indira Gandhi as the populist stabilizer were only partly reflected in the objectives of the fourth five-year plan for the period between 1969 and 1973. In a major departure from the Nehruvian years, planners no longer placed much hope in augmenting agricultural production through a fresh round of land reforms. Though land scarcity had no doubt become an important constraint, there was much to be said in favour of reforming the inequities in India's rural product, credit and labour markets. Yet any such suggestion would have placed the planning commission and the political centre at loggerheads with middling to richer farmers, considerable segments of which continued to provide the Congress's main support base while others had parted company and contributed in no uncertain way to the 1967 electoral shock. The discrepancies between political alignments and economic interests had been considerably sharpened by the time the fourth five-year plan was on the anvil. So far from matching Mrs Gandhi's anti-poverty rhetoric and initiating redistributive programmes for the rural and urban downtrodden, the plan plumped for a technological package aimed at inducing the middling to upper landed strata to enhance their production of agricultural commodities. It is widely known that the US president Lyndon B. Johnson pushed Indian planners in this direction by his refusal to deliver shipments of grain to India in 1968 unless the government adopted new policies bolstering the interests of middling to rich farmers. Increased use of fertilizers and high-yielding varieties of seeds were supposed to usher in a 'green revolution'. Handsome benefits accrued to America's agro-based industries upon gaining entry into India's huge market. But since land reforms in the early 1950s had barely grazed the agrarian power structure, the new technological innovations in Indian agriculture at best produced regionally disparate results. Parts of north-western India with better irrigation facilities, Punjab and Haryana in particular, saw a rapid growth in agricultural output but paid the price of increasing political polarization in the countryside and greater rural–urban migration. There were large parts of rural India which were simply not visited by the 'green revolution' of the late 1960s.

Even as the technological innovations accentuated existing inequalities in the distribution of rural power and resources, and created greater disparities in the development of the different regional political economies, India as a whole was able to shore up its food grain production. So regional variations notwithstanding, the 'green revolution' left a decisive imprint on India's economic and political future. Not only was the political centre drawn more closely into monitoring a largely unorganized agrarian sector but had to so without undermining the interests of the middling to upper rural classes. Needing to keep down agricultural prices for political purposes, and pump food through a public distribution system to the rural poor, the Indira Gandhi government initiated the economically costly policy of adopting price-support schemes on a fairly remunerative basis for wheat and later also for other crops. The origins of what Pranab Bardhan has dubbed India's 'subsidy raj' and 'spoils system'[4] can be traced to this period. The growing monetization of Indian agriculture flowing from the use of energy, oil-based fertilizers and pesticides established a two-way linkage between the agrarian and industrial sectors, making them more sensitive to fluctuations in the international economy. Without subsidizing the rising costs of agricultural inputs and providing cheap credit through government lending agencies to the rural elite, no political configuration could expect to govern from New Delhi.

The contradictory pulls underlying the reformulation of Indian development strategies in the early 1970s owed as much to Indira Gandhi's populist strategy for political mobilization as to the changing structures of economy and society. Her policy preferences were reflected in the fifth five-year plan stretching over the years 1974 to 1979, which put the issue of poverty into the foreground of political discussion. Thus began an era of Indian development plans emphasizing redistribution with growth. The bottom 30 per cent of the impoverished population became a special target group. But forced to maintain subsidies to the agrarian middle and upper classes, the state soon ran into severe resource constraints. It was apparent that without steady inflows of aid, India could not attain a growth rate of more than 5 to 6 per cent, which simply did not allow for any significant reduction in the level of poverty. The dilemma was made worse by the oil shock of 1973 and compelled the redrafting of the fifth five-year plan, especially since it came in the wake of a serious harvest failure in 1972–3.The plan had to be constantly readjusted, an indication of the clear divergence of objectives and performance during the period of the plan. At the height of the inflationary

4 Pranab Bardhan, *The Political Economy of Development in India*, Oxford, 1984.

spiral during 1974–5 India's balance of payments was in a shambles. The deficit was up to nearly $1.2 million, nearly one and a half times in a single year, forcing the government to introduce severe restrictions on imports. Setting appropriate investment levels for commodity producing sectors was clearly no answer to India's economic problems and wholly inadequate for the eradication of poverty.

It was against the backdrop of countrywide labour strikes and rural class struggles that Mrs Gandhi temporarily abandoned the Congress's commitment to democracy and declared an emergency in June 1975. The economic 'successes' of the emergency era were, however, too modest to vindicate the recourse to authoritarianism. By the late 1970s, rates of savings and investments were rising even though there was no corresponding increase in the rate of growth of the gross domestic product. Another positive feature of Mrs Gandhi's period of emergency was the creation of a food reserve and a large increase in foreign exchange reserves. The latter rose from Rs.7.5 billion in 1970–1 to Rs.57.5 billion in 1975–6 in nominal terms.

During the brief Janata interregnum between 1977 and 1979 the central government seemed to loosen its grip on macroeconomic management. The government responded in more uncertain fashion to the second oil shock of 1979 than in 1973. Part of the reason for this lack of resolve and direction was the contradiction between the bureaucratic arms of the state and the interests of the regional political economies whose representatives had managed temporarily to wield central power from New Delhi. Charan Singh's budget of 1979 was an unabashed attempt to promote the interests of surplus farmers in northern India. At a time when the international economic environment imposed a serious resource constraint, the political decision to hike up agricultural subsidies was not something the Indian bureaucracy embraced with enthusiasm.

Indira Gandhi changed some of the economic priorities following her return to power. The sixth five-year plan of 1980 to 1985 proposed a range of measures to eradicate poverty. Emphasis was placed on rural employment programmes aimed at eventually increasing the productivity of small and marginal peasants as well as rural artisans. But other than keeping the huge armies of India's underemployed labour alive from one harvest to another, the employment programmes were too haphazard to be able to raise productivity in the long run. The procurement of food grains for public distribution at low prices served to alienate important groups of surplus peasants and rich farmers despite the rising costs of subsidies. Already during the late years of Indira Gandhi's rule the national leadership had come to the conclusion that with a growing population and limited resources, productivity could only be raised through a wide and effective diffusion of technology. This began a period of tentative liberalization of the import regime from 1982–3 onwards.

After 1985 liberalization became one of the more striking features of Rajiv Gandhi's economic policies. Yet there were all manner of structural difficulties to be surmounted in implementing this policy. For one thing, liberalization aimed at introducing new technologies in Indian industry demanded foreign exchange resources. Since the 1950s India had shied away from playing the world market. The limited importance of the export sector helped India withstand fluctuations in the international economy during the 1970s and 1980s better than many developing countries. Having neglected to promote its export potential in the 1950s or the early 1960s, India opted to enter the world market at a time of much greater competition in the international trade regime. To make matters worse, decades of state protection had resulted in a wide range of manufactured products being of much inferior quality than those available in a consumer conscious capitalist world market. Nor could Indian goods compete in costs. In attempting to finance a liberal import policy the Indian state took a plunge into the debt trap. India had a negligible foreign debt until as late as 1982. In less than a decade it had become the largest debtor country in Asia and the second largest debtor country in the developing world. Having already piled up a foreign debt of over $80 billion the government of India in 1991 had to negotiate an IMF loan to help it tide over a severe foreign exchange crunch which had been greatly exacerbated by the Gulf war.

India's belated liberalization was intended to overcome the problems posed by sliding rates of industrial growth, sluggishness in private investment and the demonstrated limitations of domestic demand. It had to be accompanied by massive subsidies for export industries and efforts to expand the home market through more public expenditure. At the same time agricultural subsidies continued to claim a substantial chunk of the state's strained financial resources. According to one estimate, the subsidy bill rose steeply from Rs.1 billion in 1960–1 to Rs.40 billion in 1983–4 to include massive losses in public sector industries.[5] Together with escalating costs of defence and other kinds of non-development expenditure, for administration and policing purposes in particular,[6] the Indian state has had to disavow most of the guiding principles of the early planners. A more dramatic volte face would be difficult to envisage.

---

[5] Bardhan, 'Dominant Proprietary Classes and India's Democracy' in Atul Kohli (ed.), *India's Democracy: an Analysis of Changing State–Society Relations*, Princeton, 1988, p. 218.

[6] Defence, subsidies and interest payments constitute over 80 per cent of the Indian central government's non-development expenditure and between 50–60 per cent of total current expenditure. Defence expenditure alone increased to nearly 15.8 per cent annually during the period of the sixth five-year plan, compared to a yearly increase of 8 per cent under the fifth five-year plan. Interest payments went up from 1 per cent in the period of the fifth plan to 21.6 per cent during the sixth five-year plan. (S. P. Gupta, *Planning and Development in India: a Critique*, New Delhi, 1988, p. 93.)

Under the Congress government of prime minister Narasimha Rao, India has gone even further in the direction of liberalization and deregulation. By 1992, many of the more stringent bureaucratic barriers to the entry, expansion and diversification of firms were dismantled. Restraining the hand of a venal, lethargic and extraordinarily interventionary administrative bureaucracy was a step in the right direction, but one that is more than likely to cut into the state's already puny social welfare capacities. Many of the old controls on private and foreign investment have been removed. Even the once scorned multinationals are now permitted to own 51 per cent equity. Anti-monopoly measures have been relaxed and programmes for income redistribution put into cold storage. Under IMF directives to reduce the budgetary deficit the Indian central government has cut fertilizer subsidies. The package of reforms has been intended to reenergize industrial growth rates through the introduction of imported technologies which could eventually allow for a more realistic export promotion effort. Yet this kind of economic recovery leaves the state little room to be sensitive to the fragile livelihoods of ordinary low-income people. Without hounding industrial labour into submission and turning the full face of the state's coercive apparatus against instances of popular unrest, India's search for undiluted capitalist dynamism may not succeed in putting the economy on the chosen track. The social and political costs of the new policies may well take an even heavier toll on national unity than the goal of socialist orientated centralized economic planning for capitalist development.

Yet it is one thing to bemoan the inability of India's democratic system to bring about redistributive reforms and quite another to associate them with authoritarian regimes. The issue of redistribution has less to do with the democratic or authoritarian character of regimes than with the state–society dialectic in general and the state–private property nexus in particular. Simply put, India's choice is not one between democracy and authoritarianism so much as one involving structural changes in the relationship between a centralized state and increasingly restive political configurations at the level of the regional economies. Uneven patterns of regional economic development combined with an unwieldy concentration of power at the political centre have thwarted many of the substantive goals of democracy and, in the process, heightened the sense of alienation on the part of ever larger segments of India's diverse peoples. There would appear to be little room for further paradox in post-independence India's highly paradoxical development experience. Yet one that deserves a mention is the spectacle of a centralized state which in the wake of independence extracted sacrifices from the populace to piece together an infrastructure for an integrated economy but omitted to administer the requisite balm to heal old and emerging fractures in the national polity.

The political economy of defence in Pakistan and Bangladesh

Extended periods of military rule in Pakistan and Bangladesh have left an indelible mark on their respective political economies. In the sixties military regimes were acclaimed by many as agents of modernization in the developing world. Democracy resting on a mass mobilization of the social base was believed to be detrimental to both political stability and economic growth. The military institution with its hierarchical structure, established chains of command and rigid discipline seemed well equipped to ensure efficiency in economic management – the much lamented missing ingredient of planned development in so many parts of the world. Unfortunately, few military regimes have lived up to these expectations. Moreover, the salient issue is not whether they are better suited to promote development but rather the kind of development in which they tend to engage.

The Pakistani and Bangladeshi development experiences are an interesting test of the proposition that relatively more efficient economic management is assured under authoritarian military rule. With the history of India's development planning in a liberal democratic framework providing the broad lines of contrast, assessing and comparing the nexus between state and political economy in the two military dominated countries of subcontinental South Asia affords some interesting insights. Three themes warrant special attention. Given the frequency and longevity of military rule in both instances, is it more appropriate to label the political economies of Pakistan and Bangladesh as political economies of defence and how does a political economy of defence compare with India's political economy of development? Secondly, have the political economies of the two countries undergone shifts with changes in regimes and, if so, are these more significant than the ones noted in the case of India? And finally, to what extent, if at all, are the states in Pakistan and Bangladesh relatively more autonomous from the dominant classes than their counterpart in India?

An outstanding difference between India and Pakistan in the initial two decades of independence was the relative cost of defence to the central exchequer. Prior to the war with China in 1962 defence never constituted more than 12 to 14 per cent of the central government expenditure in India. After 1962 there was a steady increase in India's defence expenditure, one that unexpectedly gathered momentum under the Janata government of 1977–8 and maintained its steep upward incline following Indira Gandhi's return to power in 1980–1. Between 1962–3 and 1984–5 there was a fourteen-fold increase in defence expenditure at current prices while GNP grew by less than twelve times.[7] By contrast, the share of defence as a

[7] Y. Lakshmi, *Trends in India's Defence Expenditure*, New Delhi, 1988, pp. 23–4 and 37.

proportion of total government expenditure has been extraordinarily high ever since Pakistan's inception. In the vital first decade after independence, defence along with the cost of civil administration swallowed more than three-quarters of the central government's revenue budget. With the onset of military rule in Pakistan, defence and civil administration continued to claim the lion's share of the central government's resources, leaving little for development purposes. India, on the other hand, continued to spend relatively more on social services even after the border skirmishes with China and the inconclusive war with Pakistan in 1965 gave impetus to defence expansion.

Injections of foreign aid helped keep up the semblance of a centrally planned effort to provide basic social services to a rapidly growing population. Yet the central state's lack of commitment to the social sectors has been conspicuous. A paltry 2.6 per cent of the Pakistani central government's expenditure in 1988 was targeted to education and less than 1 per cent to health. India fared only marginally better in the same year with 2.9 per cent on education and 1.8 per cent on health. Despite its meagre resources the Bangladeshi central government in 1972 was spending 14.8 per cent on education and 5 per cent on health. It is true that education and health in Pakistan and India are provincial and state subjects respectively and so the overall expenditure in these two sectors is higher. Yet Pakistan's social indicators speak for themselves. A mere 30 per cent of Pakistan's total adult population in 1985 was literate while women's literacy stood at a shocking 19 per cent. In the same year, India's literacy rate was 43 per cent and 29 per cent of women qualified as literates. Bangladesh, on the other hand, had an overall literacy rate of 33 per cent with women's literacy at 22 per cent. Although the difference appears marginal, the comparative rates of population growth indicate the importance of higher rates of literacy among Indian and Bangladeshi women. During the eighties, Pakistan's rate of population growth was 3.2 per cent compared to India's and Bangladesh's 2.1 and 2.6 per cent respectively.[8] This more than cancelled out the advantages of Pakistan's higher per capita income and relatively better performance in attaining growth rates in GDP than either India or Bangladesh.

These statistics in themselves would appear to discount a contrast between the political economies of India, Pakistan and Bangladesh. After all, in recent years the state structures in all three countries have been geared to sustaining extremely high rates of non-development expenditure. Yet in relation to India, which spent less on defence in the first decade or so after independence, Pakistan (including present-day Bangladesh) has been

[8] The figures have been culled from the World Bank's publications, *World Development Report 1990* and *World Development Report 1991*.

devoting a disproportionate amount of its resources to security since its creation. The defence budget coupled with the costs of administration, expenditure on para-military forces as well as interest payments on military debt accumulated over the years has greatly limited Pakistan's policy options with disastrous effects on its development trajectory. Given the centralized nature of the state structure it seems reasonable to portray Pakistan's political economy as more defence than development orientated. India of course also possesses a centralized state and defence accounts for about 3.5 per cent of the GDP compared to Pakistan's 6.3 per cent. Yet India's diversified industrial structure, remarkably high rates of saving and, above all, its formally democratic polity, have militated against the pursuit of security requirements at the expense of the development imperative. Pakistan, on the other hand, has always suffered on account of an extremely limited industrial base with the emphasis on the consumer rather than capital goods sector. The relative size of India and undivided Pakistan undoubtedly played a part in the choice of development strategies. But it would be facile to argue that differences between the political economies of the two countries stem from their vastly uneven geographical size. Certainly, Pakistan's appallingly low rates of saving and abject dependence on foreign aid cannot be blamed on its natural attributes alone. These two factors in conjunction with a technically weak industrial structure have necessitated far greater dependence on military imports and, consequently, been much more of a drag on development processes. By the time India began escalating its defence expenditure after the mid-seventies it had already established a fairly diversified industrial structure. In Pakistan the rate of growth of non-productive expenditure on the military and the civil administration has been consistently out of all proportion with productive expenditure. According to one estimate, the increase in value-added per capita of agriculture and industry since 1972 at 1959–60 prices was a mere 1.2 per cent per annum compared with the per capita annual growth of 5.4 per cent for defence and civil administration.

Yet statistical comparisons alone cannot convey the qualitative differences in the political economies of India, Pakistan and Bangladesh. What the figures do not divulge is the extent to which the Pakistani military has been able to translate its dominance over the state structure to become deeply entrenched in the political economy. Military regimes in Pakistan have rewarded senior officers in the defence establishment with top positions in the state structure as well as in semi-government and autonomous organizations. In addition, Pakistan's military dominated state has at each step awarded its principal constituents with land grants, defence contracts, permits, licences and ambassadorial appointments. This has allowed for much greater upward mobility for military officials than in India. There can be no doubt that some civil and military officials in India were duly rewarded for their role in helping preserve the symbiosis with ruling parties, for instance by securing jobs in public sector enterprises or key diplomatic appointments. Yet they have been far less successful than their Pakistani and Bangladeshi counterparts in using government jobs as ladders to private fortune. In a polity that is at least formally democratic, even the most favoured state officials have had to compete with disparate and squabbling regional political elites clamouring to secure privileged access to state patronage.

Apart from the monetary perks and comforts that come from being the trustees of a security conscious state, military personnel and their families have enjoyed access to the best health and educational facilities Pakistan has to offer. Service hospitals and garrison schools dignify the landscape of a country, especially in the province of the Punjab, with a dismal record on providing basic educational and health facilities to the bulk of its population. Military personnel, generally speaking, are better educated than most other segments of civil society. Sharply deteriorating educational standards, suffocating curbs on the press and the deliberate neglect of the arts, have done much to reduce the knowledge differentials between military personnel and the small pockets of a civil intelligentsia Pakistan possesses.

Yet the most impressive result of more than forty years of dominance over the state apparatus has been the military establishment's extensive tentacles throughout the economy. Each of the three defence services in Pakistan have trusts and foundations with large investments in the national economy. The Fauji Foundation run by the army has eight manufacturing units, including sugar, fertilizer, cereals, liquid gas, metals and a gas field, as well as transportation companies, schools, hospitals and investments in defence production industries. The largest private sector group in industry has assets worth 50 per cent of just four units of the Fauji Foundation. The incomes of these units are exempt from taxation and legislation regarding the manufacturing sector. They do not, for instance, have to disclose their assets or make their shares available for public subscription.[9]

Although comparable information on Bangladesh is not available, the shift towards a military–bureaucratic state under General Zia-ur-Rahman and the policies pursued by General Ershad suggest that its external aid dependent political economy has done more to promote the interests of senior defence and civil officials than the development requirements of its teeming millions. This is borne out by the fact that already in 1975 most of

[9] 'Shahid Kardar, 'The Political Economy of Contemporary Pakistan', in Sugata Bose and Ayesha Jalal (eds.), *Nationalism, Democracy and Development: Reappraising South Asian States and Politics* (forthcoming).

the key public corporations were being run by members of the non-elected institutions of the state, the civil bureaucracy, the police and the military. The trend gathered further momentum once Generals Zia and Ershad actively began currying favour with the private sector. Much in the same vein as Pakistan, enterprising military and civil officials could use their privileged positions within the state structure to acquire permits, licences and aid-related government contracts, thus expediting their entry into the upper echelons of the economy.

So it is the entrenched interests of the non-elected institutions, the military in particular, within the state structure and the opportunities this affords for legal and extra-legal privileges which justifies labelling Pakistan and Bangladesh as the political economies of defence. A political economy of defence by its very nature encumbers the state's development activities, especially when economic resources are scarce and the appetites of the non-elected institutions insatiable. But to understand why the political economies of both Pakistan and Bangladesh became defence rather than development orientated requires an investigation of the relationship between political and economic power in the two countries. The very dominance of the non-elected institutions in Pakistan and Bangladesh points to a disjunction between state power and class power. So it is important to consider the nature of the links between the non-elected institutions and the dominant social classes. Is it a case of 'organic' collaboration, as some theorists have tried to assert, or simply a matter of expediency in response to effective social and political engineering by the military–bureaucratic state structures?

Political power in Pakistan came to be concentrated in the hands of the civil bureaucracy and the military very early on in the day. But while their dominance within the state structure has been undeniable, they would not have succeeded in their project of exercising control over the economy and society without the tacit support of at least some of the dominant social classes. These have been identified as the big landowning families of West Pakistan and the nascent industrial bourgeoisie. Although both have remained junior partners in the firm that has managed Pakistan's affairs since the early fifties, they have not failed to extract economic compensation for their subordinate role in the power structure. Despite an inability to turn economic power into direct political control, the dominant social classes in Pakistan have done quite as well as their Indian counterparts in negotiating terms with the state in support of their material and other interests.

Tentative attempts by the Pakistani state to bring about land reforms in the pre-1971 period were successfully circumvented by West Pakistan's big landowners. As in India the reforms were intended to strengthen the position of the intermediate strata in relation to the very large landowners. Yet this is where the similarity ends. In India the super-large and mainly absentee landlords for the most part were politically weakened by their past collaboration with the colonial state. By contrast, the bigger landlords of West Pakistan remained indomitable in the post-independence period by virtue of their control over the Muslim League. In India it was the middling to richer farmers and peasants who dominated the Congress party and so were able to turn the land reforms of the early 1950s to their advantage. Land reforms in Pakistan, on the other hand, have met with stiff resistance from the bigger landlords irrespective of the democratic or authoritarian nature of the regime. The fact that neither the Indian nor, until very recently, the Pakistani state has found it easy to impose an agricultural income tax is an indication of the limitations on their relative autonomy of action from the dominant agrarian social classes. Yet in India the intermediate strata in agrarian society have been the main constraining influence on state efforts to initiate redistributive reforms. In Pakistan the issue has been significantly knottier on account of the continued importance of the bigger landlords and the willingness of the middling strata to ally with them against state encroachments on agricultural interests. That in August 1993 an interim caretaker government, consisting mainly of technocrats from international organizations as well as retired civil bureaucrats and military personnel, felt compelled to impose an agricultural income tax was more a comment on Pakistan's dire fiscal straits than a true measure of the state's new found autonomy from the landed classes.

As early as 1952–3 Punjab's bigger landlords subverted an attempt by the more progressive wing of the Muslim League to initiate redistributive reforms by refusing to bring their produce to the market and precipitating a man-made 'famine' in that province. This pattern continued during the late fifties and sixties when Ayub's military regime attempted to bring about a land reform favouring the middling landlords. Special care, however, was taken not to unduly ruffle the bigger landlords. Consequently, the land reforms orchestrated by a military regime made even less of an impact on the agrarian structure than the preceding intermediary tenurial reforms in India. Ayub's land reforms announced in 1959 fixed the ceiling on land ownership at 500 acres of irrigated and 1,000 acres of unirrigated land. But as in the case of the Indian land reforms of the early fifties, the ceilings were on individual rather than family holdings. This allowed most of the larger landlords, bunched in the Punjab and Sind where the agrarian structure is far more skewed than in Pakistan's other provinces, to retain land well in excess of the ceilings. Special loopholes rewarding the more productive landlords and excluding orchards from the prescribed ceilings further diluted the efficacy of the reform legislation. For instance, an individual landlord could retain land above the ceiling as long as this was equal to 36,000 produce index units, defined as the total value of output per acre. The productivity index was based on pre-independence revenue settlements. Since the value of output depended on quality of land and prevailing prices, the PIU's fixed before 1947 underestimated the actual productivity of the land in 1959.

These lacunae effectively derailed the land reform, proving yet again that legislation itself can be the root of the problem rather than the process of implementation. Just how badly Pakistan needed a land reform can be gleaned from the fact that the average holdings of each declarant in the country was 7,028 acres while it was an astonishing 11,810 acres in the Punjab. After the resumptions had been made, the average per declarant in Pakistan was still as high as 4,033 acres and 7,489 acres in the Punjab. Much of the estimated 1.9 million resumed by the state was of the poorest quality. Indeed, as much as 57 per cent was uncultivated while the landlords were handsomely compensated to the tune of Rs.89.2 million.[10] This sham of a redistributive land reform was consistent in one respect. Ayub made no pretence of trying to improve the livelihoods of the lowest strata in rural society. The better part of the resumed land was sold at nominal prices to army and civil officials, thus creating a loyal constituency for the military regime among middling level landlords.

The reluctance of Pakistan's mainly Punjabi-dominated military and bureaucratic state to implement effective land reforms or impose an agricultural income tax, strongly demanded by the nascent industrial groups and also by Bengali middle-class professionals, has been presented as evidence of its 'organic alliance' with the landed elite of West Pakistan. Such an argument lays emphasis on the lack of any real class-based conflict between state managers and landed groups. Yet in looking solely at the economic motivation of the alliance it loses sight of the political differences between non-elected state officials and landlord politicians. So what has been the politics of compromise should not be confused with the politics of 'organic' collaboration. Non-elected officials are often prepared to forgo purely economic interests for the sake of the politically advantageous arrangement of perpetuating and enhancing state authority under their institutional dominance. Indeed even after the break up of Pakistan and the emergence of a leader and a ruling party ostensibly committed to a socialist

---

[10] Much has been written on the failure of the land reforms in Pakistan. The basic data are to be found in *Land Reform in West Pakistan*, especially vol. 3, Government of Pakistan, Lahore, 1967. Additional information used here has been referred to by various authors, including M. H. Khan, *Underdevelopment and Agrarian Structure in Pakistan*, Lahore, 1981 and Akmal Hussain, 'Land Reforms in Pakistan: a Reconsideration', in Iqbal Khan (ed.), *Fresh Perspectives on India and Pakistan*, Oxford, 1985, pp. 206–17.

transformation, the bigger landlords were able to take advantage of loopholes in state legislation to retain the better part of their most productive land.

Much radical rhetoric adorned Zulfikar Ali Bhutto's land reforms of 1972. Yet as in 1959, the drafters of the legislation were more concerned about winning popular legitimacy than delivering substantial benefits to the poor.[11] As in 1959 the ceilings were on individual rather than on family ownership. An individual landowner could hold up to 150 acres of irrigated and 300 acres of unirrigated land. Once again productivity was sought to be rewarded. The equivalent of 12,000 PIUs with a gratuity of an extra 2,000 PIUs for owners of tubewells and tractors could be held in excess of the ceiling. As a result the actual ceiling in the Punjab and Sind was well above the prescribed limit.[12] Land resumed by the state was much less than in 1959 of which a substantial amount was uncultivated. The 1972 reforms made no real impact on the power of the larger landlords and were more in the way of a window dressing than a genuine attempt at redistribution. But, unlike the Ayub regime, some of the vested land acquired was parcelled out to the poorest strata in agrarian society. Although a mere 1 per cent of the landless tenants and small peasant holders directly benefited from the reforms, the social and political effect was out of all proportion to the economic.

The PPP regime was seen to have diminished the social status of the bigger landlords even as it had failed to deliver on the electoral promises of giving land to the tiller. So although the redistributional effects of the reforms were practically non-existent in the Punjab and Sind, the treatment meted out to the landlords shored up hopes among the lowest strata. And in the NWFP where the power of the bigger landlords had been negligible in comparison with Punjab and Sind, the reforms actually worked to the advantage of the landless tenants, 33 per cent of whom became owner cultivators. Continued pockets of support for the PPP in the NWFP and the deeply ingrained psychology of populism in parts of the Punjab and Sind is testimony to the political success of a land reform whose economic consequences were marginal.

The political significance of the 1972 land reforms becomes clearer when set against the backdrop of the socio-economic changes wrought by the 'green revolution'. With the introduction of new technologies in the late

[11] That this has been one of the primary motivations behind most of the land reform legislations in South Asia is skilfully and convincingly demonstrated in Ronald Herring, Land to the Tiller, New Haven, 1983.

[12] According to one estimate, landowners in the Punjab could legally hold as many as 932 acres while those in Sind did even better with 1,120 acres. (Khan, Underdevelopment and Agrarian Structure in Pakistan, chapter 5; also cited in Akmal Hussain, 'Land Reforms in Pakistan: a Reconsideration', Khan (ed.), Fresh Perspectives on India and Pakistan, p. 209.)

sixties middling and very large landlords augmented their economic clout at the expense of the small peasants and landless labourers. The size of operational holdings in Pakistan is considerably larger than in India and Bangladesh. In 1972 less than a third of the holdings in Pakistan were smaller than 5 acres and accounted for a mere 5 per cent of the total area under cultivation. Medium-size farms of between 12.5 and 50 acres were 7.6 per cent of the total rural households and cultivated 18.8 per cent of the total farm area. Farms larger than 50 acres accounted for just over 3 per cent of the rural households but cultivated as much as 24 per cent of the total area. By comparison, marginal and small farmers in India constitute as many as 80 per cent of the rural households and cultivate a third of the total farm area. With an already more skewed ownership pattern Pakistan's experience under the green revolution served to sharpen differentials not only between the middle and lower strata as in parts of India, but also strengthened the economic and extra-economic powers of coercion available to the super-large landlords over small peasant holders and landless labourers. Middle to larger landholders were able to use their privileged access to the local arms of the state to secure cheap loans as well as inputs and so manipulate the inter-related land, product, credit and labour markets even more effectively than before. Unable to finance the rising costs of cultivation many small to marginal owners in the Punjab leased out land to middling and larger landlords, anxious to enlarge their holdings in order to take full advantage of the Pakistani state's policy of subsidizing farm mechanization. The intro-duction of tractors and other farm machinery had a deleterious effect on rural employment.

It was the growing polarization in the countryside, particularly in the Punjab, which gave Bhutto and the PPP an opportunity to confound the 1970 electoral calculations of the military–bureaucratic state. At a time when the rural poor were undergoing a qualitative deterioration in their ability to negotiate terms with the rich, the PPP's populism created an illusion of empowerment whose psychological appeal outweighed and, ulti-mately, outlived its substantive effects. Even after Bhutto began actively wooing the larger landlords, the rural poor of the Punjab and Sind con-tinued to see him and the PPP as the harbingers of a new social order, the mere evocation of which was seen to have tempered the traditional arro-gance of 'feudal' exploiters. This is why the assumption of state power by General Zia-ul-Haq was not a reversal in agrarian relations as such, but a shift in the psychology of the political idiom in the countryside. Once the flicker of democracy had gone out, it was back to the well-tried methods of collaboration with the military–bureaucratic state. The Zia era further underlines the success of the landed elite in cutting their losses by substitut-ing the direct exercise of political power at the level of the state with economic power and control over their local bailiwicks.

In Bangladesh, both before and after independence, the scale of inequalities in the agrarian sector were nowhere near as marked as in Pakistan. Yet at the same time the levels of poverty are undoubtedly greater than in Pakistan and many parts of India. Already in 1951 the zamindari abolition act had eliminated the landlord element from the East Bengal rural scene. The richer peasants of East Pakistan were the poorer cousins of the landlords and rich farmers of the western wing. During the early sixties, for instance, holdings over 12.5 acres accounted for 3.5 per cent of the rural households and cultivated just under 19 per cent of the total farm area. By 1967–8, the number of holdings above 12.5 acres had declined by 21 per cent and the area under their cultivation by 23 per cent. During the same period the number of rural households with holdings below 2.5 acres went up from 51 to 57 per cent while those with less than one acre rose slightly from 24 to 25 per cent. In both instances there was an expansion of the area under cultivation, from about 16 to 21 per cent in the case of farms under 2.5 acres and from 3.2 to 4.3 per cent for farms below one acre.[13] The tendency towards smaller and smaller farm holdings was matched by the growing numbers of unemployed which jumped from 18 per cent of total rural households in 1961 to 38 per cent in 1973–4.[14] Clearly, then, the picture of the Bangladeshi countryside is one of unmitigated impoverishment.

After it emerged as a sovereign country in 1971 Sheikh Mujibur Rahman imposed land ceilings of about 33 acres and abolished land revenue on holdings below 8 acres through a series of presidential ordinances. The reforms typically skirted around the problem of growing landlessness. Although Bangladesh did not experience a 'green revolution' of the sort that occurred in Pakistan and India, certain pockets saw technological innovations in the form of new fertilizers and high-yielding seeds whose supply to the peasants has been controlled since 1975 by a military–bureaucratic state. Richer peasants consolidated their slight edge in landholding by their ability to have better access to state patronage and, by implication, to capital-intensive agricultural technology. By 1977 there was a discernible trend towards medium to larger sized farmers, reversing the pattern of the 1960s and hinting at the growing incidence of distress sales and renting out by smaller peasants due to unaffordable costs of cultivation. As elsewhere in the subcontinent, the surplus peasants in Bangladesh have been able to syphon off new capital-intensive inputs, institutional credits and foreign aid at a time when the predicament of the land poor and the landless labourers

[13] I. J. Singh, *The Great Ascent: the Rural Poor in South Asia*, Baltimore, 1990, p. 89.
[14] Cited in Kirsten Westergaard, *State and Rural Society in Bangladesh*, London, 1985, p. 105. On the process of pauperization in rural Bangladesh see also Willem Van Schendel, *Peasant Nobility: the Odds of Life in Rural Bangladesh*, Assen, 1982; Shapan Adnan and H. Zillur Rahman, 'Peasant Classes and Land Mobility: Structural Reproduction and Change in Bangladesh', in *Bangladesh Historical Studies*, 3 (1978), pp. 161–215; Willem Van Schendel and Aminul Haque Faraizi, *Rural Labourers in Bengal*, Rotterdam, 1984.

has been worsening. Some tentative attempts were made in 1984 by the Ershad regime to strengthen land reform measures, but these remained weak on prospectus as well as implementation.

In a country where agriculture still constitutes the highest percentage of the gross domestic product and provides over 90 per cent of the export earnings, it is remarkable that the agrarian sector's share of the state's total development resources in 1978–9 was less than 25 per cent. While this can be attributed to the urban bias found in other developing countries, there can be no question that the trend was greatly facilitated by Bangladesh's transformation into a military–bureaucratic state under the regimes of Generals Zia-ur-Rahman and Ershad. The erstwhile backwater of West Bengal's industrial hinterlands and then the proverbial milch cow of West Pakistani colonialism, post-independence Bangladesh naturally aspired for rapid economic development through an expansion of its manufacturing capacities. Yet, paradoxically, the neglect of the agrarian sector is more an echo of the historical injustices suffered under successive colonial overlords than the voice of a self-confident, independent and rapidly industrializing country.

At the time of the British withdrawal in 1947 the industrial classes of Pakistan were much weaker than in India. Given the narrow resource base the Pakistani state's first priority was to encourage capital accumulation in the industrial sector. But unlike India which focused on the capital goods sector, Pakistan took the more conventional path to import substitution by investing in consumer goods industries – textile and jute manufactures in particular. Pakistan's first five-year plan (1955–60) was an elaborate document authored by members of the planning commission in close consort with the Harvard advisory group. Apart from setting the tone of Pakistan's aid dependent industrial strategy – 35 per cent of the development expenditure was to be financed by the USA – its only notable achievement lay in the fact of being completed and published before the end of the plan period. So Pakistan's critical first decade was a planless one, even as the planning bug began pervading the minds of state managers given to extreme ad hocism in economic policy making.

The only constant was the recognition of a serious resource constraint and the need to industrialize, here and now, in order to meet the rising costs of defence. Keeping the terms of trade tilted against the agriculture sector held out the promise of short-term benefits, especially during the Korean war boom. By refusing to follow Britain's and India's example and devalue the rupee, Pakistan was able to peg its exchange rate artificially high and, in this way, acquire capital on the cheap for the import and import substituting sector. The price of wage goods was also held down; infant industries were protected and the industrial sector given access to foreign exchange earned by the agricultural sector at less than the actual cost to the economy. This meant that the agricultural sector was selling its output to the industrial sector at low prices and purchasing manufactured commodities at prices higher than in the world market. The initial beneficiaries of the Pakistani state's pro-industrial bias were Muslim trading castes who migrated from the Indian state of Gujarat to settle in Karachi – Memons, Bohras and Khojas – and some Punjabi families like the Sheikhs and Chinotis.

Primarily a land of small peasant holders and a large professional middle class, East Pakistan had no significant Muslim business class. Although the eastern wing during the fifties contributed between one-half and nearly three-quarters of the foreign exchange earnings, it was the hardest hit by the state's policy of squeezing the small peasantry by maintaining a high exchange rate. With less than one-third of the total domestic investment and less than one-third of the commodity imports, East Pakistan was a victim of a concerted policy to base industries in the western wing. The Pakistan industrial development corporation was created with the explicit purpose of assisting select private capitalists to set up industrial enterprises. Yet in 1959 only 11 per cent of the industrial assets were controlled by Bengalis; of these less than one-third were in the hands of Muslims with Hindu entrepreneurs accounting for the rest.

The difference in the social structure of the two wings worked to the advantage of civil bureaucrats and the military. It was the fear of the Bengali majority exercising its democratic right to dominate the state apparatus and reapportioning the distribution of financial resources between West and East Pakistan which provided the basis for a tacit alliance between state officials and the West Pakistani landed elite and business classes. With the onset of military rule, the pro-industrial development strategies of the Pakistani state were loaded even more heavily against the eastern wing. State-supported industrialization took on a wholly different meaning in Pakistan than in India where the private sector benefited indirectly from investments in infrastructure. Close monitoring of financial and fiscal policy by the state and the channeling of funds to chosen members of the private sector through its appendages – the Pakistan industrial credit and investment corporation (PICIC) and the industrial development bank of Pakistan (IDBP) in particular – set the stage for a highly concentrated structure of industrial ownership.

The Ayub regime's industrial strategy went into full swing during the second five-year plan (1960–5). As much as 50 per cent of the planned expenditure was to be met by external resources, consisting of aid as well as loans. Direct controls on private enterprise were relaxed and investments encouraged in practically any sphere of the industrial sector in which it wished to operate. Government institutions like the PICIC and IDBP served as conduits disbursing foreign resources to buffet private industrial investment. According to one estimate, 40 per cent of total private investment in industry and as much as 70 per cent of its foreign component was financed by loans through these state agencies.[15] The domestic resource component of industrial investment was negligible, underscoring a vital difference between the Pakistani and Indian industrial development strategies. In addition a variety of fiscal, monetary and commercial policies aimed at stimulating private investment and profitability in favoured industries. Apart from tax holidays and generous depreciation allowances, the government introduced an ingenious mechanism known as the bonus voucher scheme which allowed exporters to inflate their earnings overnight and turn the accumulated capital into additional investments. Exporters were given vouchers equivalent to 10–40 per cent of the value of the exported goods which they could sell on the open market to importers at a fantastic premium.

Yet for all its cultivation of the private sector, the Ayub regime's industrial development strategy would have been doomed without the abundance of external resources made available by its international patrons. Despite the range of incentives on offer, Pakistan failed to attract direct foreign investment which remained wholly insignificant throughout the period of the second (1960–5) and third five-year plan (1965–70).[16] The high profitability of private investments and an impressive growth rate of 20 per cent in the industrial sector attained under the second five-year plan was a result of aid dependent development. Industrial investments and profits began to sag after the suspension of American aid following the Indo-Pakistan war in 1965. The period of the third five-year plan (1965–70) consequently was one of greater controls on the private sector, a stiffer import regime and the derailment of the planned strategy to turn from consumer to capital goods industrialization. Among the many adverse implications of this sort of dependent development was a growing debt burden and an aid-addicted national economy.

But by far the most important consequence on the Pakistani political economy of the industrialization strategy pursued during the Ayub era was the staggering concentration of wealth in the hands of a few business houses. State-aided capitalist development fostered strong linkages between industrial and finance capital. Between 21 and 44 business houses controlled the entire gamut of industrial, banking and insurance services and also occupied positions in PICIC, the premier investment agency. Almost 65 per cent of

[15] Rashid Amjad, *Private Industrial Investment in Pakistan 1960–1970*, Cambridge, 1982, pp. 56 and 173.
[16] Ibid., p. 23; also Lawrence J. White, *Industrial Concentration and Economic Power in Pakistan*, Princeton, 1974.

the total loans extended by PICIC were bagged by 37 industrial houses with the largest 13 appropriating 70 per cent.[17] While many of the top business houses had operations in both wings of the country, the vast majority were based in West Pakistan which was the main recipient of externally boosted private industrial investments. To the list of mainly Karachi-based industrialists were added the names of well-connected entrepreneurs from other parts of the country, including big landowners mainly from Punjab and a smattering from Sind and the NWFP. During the period of the third five-year plan the regime tried broadening its social bases of support by stretching the network of industrial ownership to those not belonging to monopoly houses. Efforts were made to rope East Pakistani trading and commercial groups into the Ayub regime's military–bureaucratic cum industrial corral through grants of permits, licences and government contracts. But the emergence of a small nascent Bengali industrial class proved inconsequential by comparison with the regional disparity which the policy of functional inequality produced.

During the much vaunted decade of development the per capita gross domestic product of East Pakistan grew by only 17 per cent at 1959–60 constant prices compared to 42 per cent in West Pakistan.[18] Inter-regional resource transfers imperilled the already fragile living standards in the predominantly agrarian eastern wing. The Stolypinian philosophy of betting on the strong translated in Ayubian parlance as ignoring the weak. When Ayub seized state power the East Pakistan's per capita income was 30 per cent less than that of West Pakistan. By the time he was thrown out of office in 1969 the differential was as much as 61 per cent.[19] Seen in the context of declining real wages for the industrial and the rural labour force, the gap in the per capita income between the two wings becomes even more politically fraught. It was the deepening of regional and class inequalities during the Ayub era which provided the East Pakistani political opposition with the impetus to extricate themselves from the clutches of the West Pakistani military–bureaucratic–industrial establishment.

In the immediate aftermath of independence attempts were made to nationalize Bangladesh's small industrial base. Under Mujib's leadership the state gained control over 86 per cent of the country's industrial assets compared to only 35 per cent before 1971. But uncertainties induced by fierce debates over the shortest road to industrialization and the country's insatiable need for external resources saw the Awami League government winking at socialism while moving in the capitalist direction. The coming of

---

[17] Amjad, *Private Industrial Investment in Pakistan*, pp. 49–50.
[18] Cited in Khalid Bin Sayeed, *Politics in Pakistan: the Nature and Direction of Change*, New York, 1980, p. 57.
[19] Omar Noman, *The Political Economy of Pakistan, 1947–1985*, p. 41.

military rule in 1975 signalled a process of denationalization of industries. If the early 1970s show a broad analogy in the relationship between the state and industry in Pakistan and Bangladesh, the late 1970s and 1980s in Bangladesh accord more with the early Pakistan experience of the 1950s when the state had attempted to succour a nascent industrial capitalist class. The military regime of General Ershad extended the denationalization process to the banking sector and made an even more concerted effort than its predecessor to bolster private enterprise. It is not surprising, therefore, that industrialists provide a disproportionate share of the leadership of military sponsored political parties such as the Bangladesh National Party and the Jatiya Party.

As in Pakistan, Bangladesh's military–bureaucratic state structure has remained heavily dependent on external aid and advice. Since gaining its independence roughly 80 per cent of Bangladesh's plan expenditure has been financed by foreign sources, the United States in particular. Aid-related corruption has been the bane of Bangladesh. State support for the private sector coupled with massive external aid flows has allowed a small segment of Bangladeshi entrepreneurs and civil and military officials to line their pockets and pursue life styles of conspicuous consumption that are obscene considering the woeful fate of millions below the poverty line. New islands of private affluence in a stagnant ocean of public squalor has given the post-independence Bangladeshi political, economic and social scene a menacing new dimension.

While Bangladesh's economy continues to be overwhelmingly aid dependent, the situation in Pakistan altered radically after the late 1970s. Despite large infusions of foreign loans during the Zia regime, Pakistan's main source of external resources in the 1980s came in the form of remittances from the Middle East. The delinking of the rupee from the dollar helped bolster the value of the remittances so that they provided as much as 40 per cent of total foreign exchange earnings and accounted for nearly 8 per cent of the GNP.[20] Together with a lucrative narcotics trade running into billions of dollars, the remittances disguised the full extent of the resource constraints on the Pakistan economy. Efforts at domestic resource mobilization have borne pitiful results in spite of the government's efforts to cash in on a rapidly growing black economy. Hopelessly low savings rates and the petering out of remittances after the peak year of 1984 forced dramatic readjustments in development outlays initially projected in the sixth five-year plan for the period 1984 to 1989. Since the mid-1980s Pakistan has faced considerable obstacles in qualifying for loans from international agencies with serious consequences for flagging growth rates, once the best

[20] Noman, *The Political Economy of Pakistan*, p. 157.

defence of its development policies. Loans extracted after hard bargaining from the IMF and the World Bank as well as the aid-to-Pakistan consortium have been accompanied by strict conditionalities.

Pakistan is desperately trying to kick old habits to prevent the economy slipping more deeply into the mire of its myriad structural constraints. The need for new sources of energy has become a major obstacle in the next stage of Pakistan's industrialization strategy. But with defence and debt reservicing constituting more than 50 per cent of the central government's expenditure, investments in infrastructural development fall well short of industrial targets. Inevitable cut-backs in the already meagre resources available for health, education and housing have assumed nightmarish proportions. Pakistan is currently scouring the globe for assistance simply to maintain its inordinately low allocations to social sector development.

Having failed to make even the most nominal investment in human capital, Pakistan's development prospects look somewhat bleak at a time when the international economic environment has limited the prospects of fresh infusions of external assistance. Yet without some sort of resource miracle Pakistan's economic development prospects are no better than those of an estimated million heroin addicts it came to harbour in its midst during eleven years of Zia's military rule. In recent years, the problem of external dependence in Pakistan has been essentially one of trade and budgetary deficits and a large foreign debt. The external debt in mid-1990 amounted to $18.1 billion, a staggering 44 per cent of the GNP. This compares with India's much higher absolute figure of nearly $84 billion of foreign debt but lower percentage, roughly 30 per cent of GNP. Debt reservicing costs in Pakistan have increased from 22 per cent of export earnings in 1975–6 to 30.5 per cent in 1988–9. And the share of external resources in the financing of development expenditure has increased from 42 per cent in 1980–1 to 74 per cent in 1989–90. The suspension of all American aid, economic and military, since the autumn of 1990 has forced Pakistan to borrow from commercial banks at exorbitantly high interest rates. Debt reservicing has overtaken defence expenditure as the largest item in Pakistan's annual budget, giving an added twist to the political economy of defence.

During the 1990s moves towards liberalization, privatization and deregulation were symptomatic of the state's dire financial straits. But the combined burden of Pakistan's political history and development experience weighs heavily on the effort. All the more so since influential segments of the bureaucracy are in no mood to undergo a diminution of powers which their institutional ethic and instincts of self-preservation teaches them to guard jealously. State-sponsored liberalization unmatched by prudent economic decentralization and a measure of equality of economic opportunity to those outside the bounds of the privileged minority is no answer to the problems of a country whose political economy has been more a shambles of privatized greed than a vehicle of collective self-reliance. It is as yet too early to give a verdict on Pakistan's attempts to break out of its hidebound statist economy. But one thing is clear. Given the history of a highly concentrated industrial ownership structure, the emergence of small and medium-sized businesses in the Punjab during the Zia era notwithstanding, the liberalization of the Pakistani economy is more likely to enhance the financial portfolios of the few against the many and heighten conflict between and within the different regions. By contrast, India's liberalization regime, if it is not nipped in the bud by the bureaucratic arms of the state, seems better poised to deliver benefits to a regionally more diverse collection of small and medium entrepreneurs.

Conclusion

Unlike India's political economy of development in a formally liberal democratic mould, the political economy of defence in Pakistan and Bangladesh has rested on a particular kind of relative autonomy of the state from the dominant social classes. It is imperative to draw an analytic distinction between institutional dominance and class dominance. While these two aspects may coincide or overlap to a certain degree, there can be little question about the salience of the power of non-elective institutions rather than class power. The state's powers of patronage has made it a principal agent of class formation in all three countries. But the fact of military rule and the prolonged suspension of political processes has enabled the Pakistani and Bangladeshi states to refine the art of social engineering to a much larger extent than the Indian state. So while the relatively autonomous logic of politics in India has thrown up different and changing regional social configurations, all demanding a share of state patronage, the military-bureaucratic states of Pakistan and Bangladesh have been able to determine whom to include and exclude from the development process. The boons of development in India may not have been spectacular, certainly in the realm of redistribution, but are more widely shared than in the two military dominated states. Since the late seventies there are signs in both Pakistan and Bangladesh of a growing congruence of interest between the dominant social classes, swelled by members of the non-elective institutions who have used their positions within the state apparatus to acquire substantial property. Yet these trends do not augur well for a shift in the foreseeable future away from a political economy of defence to a political economy of development.

5   Central power and regional dissidence

For all their historical specificities subcontinental South Asian states and societies have kept a march ahead of the rest of the world in at least one important respect. The recent surge in assertions on 'ethnic' identity and demands for national sovereignty in the erstwhile Soviet Union, Eastern Europe, the Middle East, the United Kingdom, Canada and elsewhere is an old and familiar occurrence in the subcontinent. Indeed, the dialectic between centralism and regionalism has played a pivotal part in the more dramatic developments in subcontinental history. Frequently overlaid by communal, sub-regional, caste and class factors, the fluctuating balance between centre and region nevertheless has been something of a constant. Unflinching faith in the virtues of a strong central state authority proceeds from a clear recognition of the subcontinent's perplexing diversities, most with recorded histories of periodic defiance of attempts to bring the far-flung frontiers of geographical India under a single political banner.

As if the weight of pre-colonial history was not burden enough, the partition of India in 1947 followed by the disintegration of Pakistan in 1971 have served as sharp reminders of the potency of centrifugal tendencies in the subcontinent. Far from encouraging greater flexibility towards the fact of diversity, both developments have turned the hearts and minds of influential segments in political society, to say nothing about the guardians of the state, against loosening the screws of centralized structures. Yet stolid defence of centralized authority in South Asia has tended to be in inverse proportion to the real strength of the political centres, both colonial and post-colonial. Masking weakness with coercive power is not the same as making effective use of the centralized state. And it is the growing in-effectiveness of centralized authority that signifies the extent to which federalism in this over-populated, socially disparate, economically deprived and politically divisive corner of the globe has frayed at the edges.

During the closing decades of the twentieth century centralized state authority in South Asia has been wrestling uncertainly with an array of challenges from movements of social dissidence. The Indian union is plagued by several regional campaigns – especially the Sikh agitation in

Punjab for autonomy, if not secession, and the increasingly strident movement for separation orchestrated by the United Liberation Front of Assam.
In neighbouring Pakistan, which in 1971 witnessed the only successful
secessionist movement in a newly independent state and where there have
been long-standing tensions between the Punjab and the non-Punjabi
provinces, the southern province of Sind since the 1980s has become a
battlefield for alarmingly well-armed rival social and linguistic groups. In
Sri Lanka, the Liberation Tigers of Tamil Eelam are waging a guerilla war
for the recognition of the Tamils as a sovereign nation and the establishment
of a separate state in the northern regions of the island. Even Bangladesh has
faced an armed separatist campaign by Chakma Buddhists in the hill tracts
of Chittagong district. The major states of South Asia, irrespective of
variations in size, are beset with broadly similar challenges to central state
authority. Each of these is not merely confined to particular regions or even
the boundaries of existing states, but has far-reaching implications for
inter-state relations in South Asia. By far the most serious problem in the
region is the popularly backed armed uprising in Kashmir which raises the
spectre of nuclear war between India and Pakistan. An acute manifestation
of India's federal dilemma, Kashmir also exemplifies the inter-connectedness of domestic, regional and international problems. It is a supreme irony
of the times that a region with a long history of working out creative political
arrangements based on layers of sovereignty appears today to have declared
sovereignty a non-negotiable issue.

While regional dissidence against central authority has been a recurring
theme in modern South Asia, threats to existing federal equations have
recently acquired a new intensity. A bewildering number of social groups
are asserting the ideology of difference with a vengeance, making nonsense
of the modernization paradigm's confident assumptions of national integration through centrally planned economic development. It is worth considering why elaborate efforts at coordinated planning under central auspices so
adversely affected the quest for national unity in South Asia. Is it simply
because centralized states were unable to deliver the fruits of economic
development widely and equitably that social groups have taken to forging
new identities out of old in order to give expression to their resentments and
aspirations? Those who subscribe to political cultural interpretations would
fault this line of enquiry for being economically deterministic. Yet what
then are the dynamics informing the politics of difference in South Asia?

The expression of difference, whether in the form of regionalism, sub-
regionalism or communitarianism, is channelled only in part into the formal
electoral or institutional arenas of politics. Most of these erupt in streets and
neighbourhoods of rural and urban areas in the form of what is commonly
termed 'ethnic' conflict or even an epidemic of the disease of ethnicity.

Some theorists of political culture have tried attributing the assertion of distinctive identities by social groups to a resurgent 'primordialism'. Refined variants of this thesis include proponents of the modernity of tradition argument who spot much that is old in what appears to be new. Yet neither are able to explain why 'ethnic' differences degenerate into violent clashes in certain societies and not in others or, for that matter, why rival 'ethnic' groups with a relatively harmonious history of co-existence erupt in open conflict at any given moment in time. Instead of being historical givens identities are constantly forged and reforged at local and supra-local levels in response and reaction to complex social, economic and political processes whose origins can be traced to wider national and international dynamics. These complexities cannot be understood or interpreted adequately by invoking the catch-all notion of 'ethnicity' given currency by analysts of political culture.

The dominant discourse on ethnicity is loaded, even if unconsciously, in favour of those who propagate the monotheistic creed of a single unified nation. Difference or diversity within this discourse is defined as the polar opposite of a unifying tendency invested with a rational and higher moral virtue. Even more sophisticated variants of work on the formation of cultural communities, however defined, have not always elucidated the links between socio-economic and political processes in particular and state and civil society in general. Rediscovering culture to correct an earlier over-emphasis on politics and economics could be made more meaningful if in deciphering the shifting patterns viewers did not lose sight of the larger historical kaleidoscope. As it stands, cultural interpretations of communitarian identities convey quite the wrong message to those still clinging to the worn out dictums learnt during the heyday of the modernization paradigm. Asserting the autonomy of culture is almost tantamount to denying the role of existing structures of states and political economies in provoking communitarian sentiments. By imputing a measure of cultural insularity to specific social groups, such arguments seem to reinforce the old proposition that the answer to resurgent communitarianism in South Asia lies in more effective policies of national integration.

It is difficult to see how the inclusionary idiom of integration, which inspired policies of centralization and homogenization and in conjunction with the uneven distribution of economic and political rewards led social groups to stress a particular identity out of many, can help break the grip of 'ethnicity'. Developed as a negative counterpoise to the positive goal of national integration, the discourse on 'ethnicity' has thrived on category crunching. This has involved compressing the historically more pervasive phenomena of multiple and shifting social identities into easily distinguish-able characteristics which can then be aggregated to define a particular community. The parallel with the methods of census enumeration adopted by the colonial masters from the late nineteenth century to make sense of South Asian societies is undeniable. It might be better, certainly more refreshing, to slip out of the methodological straitjacket of 'ethnicity' and abandon the shallow rhetoric of national integration. That the compartmentalization of society into neat 'ethnic' categories on the one hand, and the imposition of a monolithic national ideology by centralized states on the other has not furthered the goal of national unity in any South Asian country is hardly surprising. Diversity in a negotiated unity, not an imposed unity on an all-pervasive diversity, would appear to be the better course for South Asian futures. This is why the following historical analysis of the problems between the centre and regions in the subcontinent rejects explanations of social conflict in terms of 'ethnic' attributes. There is no inevitability or immutability about social and cultural differences resulting in political clashes. Quite the contrary. Social identities in South Asia, as indeed anywhere in the world, are constantly in the historical process of formation as they react against and co-exist with structures of states and political economies.

Tensions between centre and region in South Asia have had less to do with its inherent cultural diversities than with the historical circumstances of the immediate post-colonial period. The main priority of those presiding over the transition from colonialism was to assert central authority over territories that were so culturally distinct and economically disparate as to defy being welded into a single unified nation state. Yet in the aftermath of independence from colonial rule the ideology of inclusionary nationalisms in conjunction with state power sought to bundle the rich mosaic of sensibilities and aspirations among South Asia's peoples into unified wholes. Instead of freely negotiated political and economic unions from below, such concessions as were made to the principle of federalism, whether real or on paper, were handed down from above. The result, notwithstanding differences in types of regimes, was state structures that were unitary in substance and only nominally federal in form. Clashes between state authority and regional sentiments were, therefore, an implicit part of the pact of dominance established in post-colonial South Asia. The price which regional elites extracted for their tacit acceptance of federal arrangements assuring central supremacy has been a major hurdle in translating the normative ideals of democracy into practice. Concerned only with winning the support of dominant regional political configurations rather than instituting the rights of citizenship, especially social and economic, centralized states in South Asia have upheld their structural imperatives by negating the very principles which make for substantive democracy. The validity of these observations can be gleaned from an investigation of the problems of regionalism and state authority in the formally democratic polity of India and a brief comparison with similarly placed Sri Lanka followed by an analysis of centre–province tensions in military dominated Pakistan and Bangladesh.

India's democratic federalism?

One of the reasons Congress single-mindedly coveted the strong central authority of the colonial state was to quickly snuff out any reassertion of the centrifugal tendencies which had played such a decisive part in the transition to British rule. Yet it was easier to adopt unitarianism as the dominant creed of post-independence India than to ensure centralized control over regions which even under colonialism had enjoyed some measure of autonomy. Here the anguish of partition and the salve of centrally directed planned economic development provided the managers of post-independence India with powerful legitimation to curb autonomists in the Hindu-majority provinces and rope in the 500-odd quasi-sovereign princely states into the Indian union. By upholding its pre-independence commitment to the idea of federalism, the Congress fashioned the semblance of an accord between the centre and the constituent units even as its symbiosis with the non-elected institutions enabled the functioning of India as an essentially unitary state.

With a multitude of languages and dialects, not to mention a wide range of religious and cultural diversities, India's need for a federal system was more an imperative than a matter of political choice. Yet instead of creating a genuinely federal system, India's early state managers were more concerned about making central powers commensurate with the goal of an integrated and united India. Defenders of states' rights were cajoled or coaxed into silence. This was not too difficult once the drafting committee of the constituent assembly declared that the Indian federation was not the result of negotiated agreements with the constituent units. The component parts of the federation, so the argument went, were not independent, autonomous or indestructible states. So the issue of states voluntarily entering the union did not arise. By extension, there could be no question of allowing states to secede from what was envisaged as an indivisible sovereign union of India.[1] But until 1963 when a constitutional amendment specifically invested the union government with powers to preserve and maintain the unity of India there was some ambiguity surrounding the issue of secession. Under the original fundamental rights provision of the constitution it had been legal to advocate secession from the union.

[1] See M. C. Setalvad, *Union and State Relations Under the Indian Constitution*, Calcutta, 1974, pp. 28–31.

Yet this barely compensated for the dimunition of states' rights. Taking an imported construct of indivisible sovereignty, which even under the British had proven only partially implementable, the drafters of the Indian constitution imbued it with a tendentious reading of history to craft a truly unique concept of federalism. Pragmatism triumphed over principle. The notion of a federalism based on divided sovereignty was rejected out of hand. And while the distribution of sovereign powers in a federal system was acknowledged in principle by the provision of three lists of subjects, the constituent units in India were made subject to a single unitary constitution based on the government of India act of 1935. Not only were state legislatures, the Vidhan Sabhas, assigned relatively less important subjects, but elected representation at the centre based on population proportions alone discriminated against the smaller states. Although the constitution provided for a bicameral parliament, India's representative democracy had no elected chamber comparable, for example, to the American senate with equal or even weighted voice for all the constituent units. Representation to the Lok Sabha was understandably based on population. Yet the indirectly elected Rajya Sabha, which was supposed to be a council of states, did little more than replicate the system of representation in the lower house. So even in the legislative arena little heed was paid to any sort of principle of federalism.

By far the most contentious point between the proponents of central vs. states' rights was the allocation of financial powers. Consonant with the objective of planned economic development, the Indian states control only minor items of revenue income – land revenue for instance which is highly inelastic – while the bulk goes to the centre. The states are consequently dependent on the centre for grants-in-aid, loans, development outlays as well as their shares of the consolidated revenues of the union. Demands for a larger proportion of the proceeds from income tax, union excise duties as well as a portion of corporate tax has been a standard refrain even as the states concede that the centre is the appropriate authority to levy, collect and distribute them. In 1952 the first finance commission, set up at five-yearly intervals to determine the share out of union revenues, reported that the states fell short of their annual administrative expenses by at least 15 per cent. It recommended that the states' share of income tax be increased from 50 to 55 per cent; of this 80 per cent was to be allocated on the basis of population and 20 per cent on the basis of collection.[2] Under the sixth finance commission in 1972, 80 per cent of the income tax revenue was earmarked for the states while their share of union excise duty remained at 20 per cent.[3]

[2] S. N. Jain, Subhash C. Kashyap and N. Srinivasan (eds.), *The Union and the States*, New Delhi, 1972, p. 61.

[3] B. S. Grewal, *Centre–State Financial Relations in India*, Patiala, 1975, p. 205.

The period between the first and the fourth five-year plan evidenced the states' growing dependence on central disbursements. These include grants-in-aid, development outlays and loans. In 1972 more than 40 per cent of the total expenditure of the states was being met by financial transfers from the centre. After 1979 with the exception of the more backward ones the majority of the states were relying less on direct central transfers and meeting a larger percentage of their revenue expenditure. But even if the states are no more dependent on the centre than they were in the 1950s,[4] it is difficult to make light of the inverted pride which the habit of indebtedness tends to breed. With resource constraints dictating against a sustained central effort to bail out states in financial trouble, the fissures in Indian federalism have grown wider. That the centrally biased federal financial structure itself has become a key source of friction between New Delhi and the states is indisputable. Under the second five-year plan there was a rise from Rs.194 crores to Rs.900 crores in tied union loans to the states. By the time of the third finance commission in 1961, the indebtedness of the states to the centre had assumed alarming proportions.[5] Unable until after the late 1970s – and then too only nominally due to diminishing public investments in infrastructural development – to effectively tap their own resources the states have been forced to borrow from the centre to reservice the debt. The proportion of such repayments to total state borrowings rose from 9 per cent in the first plan period to 33 per cent in the third plan and was in the vicinity of 40 per cent during the fourth plan.[6]

Keeping the constituent units tied to the tangled apron strings of a centre facing a regionally based political backlash from the late sixties and a financial crunch since the early eighties has had an adverse impact on the federal balance. The states have exploited the lack of coordination between the planning commission and the various finance commissions to secure larger development outlays from the one and non-plan monies from the other. Despite the centralized nature of India's federal finances, the in-built inefficiencies of the structure have provided opportunities for a downward seepage of initiative. The growing crevices in the political arenas, deepened by the erosion of the Congress's organizational structure and the delinking of national and state level elections after the early seventies, proved detrimental for centre–state relations. These have had to be countered by reliance on the authoritarian aspects of Indian federalism, namely its inherently unitary administrative structure.

On the face of it, a centrally appointed governor and a cabinet headed by

[4] Paul R. Brass, 'Pluralism, Regionalism and Decentralizing Tendencies in Contemporary Indian Politics', in A. Jeyaratnam Wilson and Denis Dalton (eds.), *The States of South Asia: Problems of National Integration*, London, 1982, pp. 231–2.
[5] Jain et al. (eds.), *The Union and the States*, p. 62. [6] Ibid., p. 12.

the chief minister replicates the presidential and prime ministerial equation at the centre. Appearances apart, the state governor, like the members of all-India administrative and police services, is for all practical purposes an active agent of the centre at the state level. Unlike the president whose powers are carefully spelled out in the constitution, a governor has certain discretionary functions which do not require the prior advice of the state's elected council of ministers. The only sanction against the governor's powers of discretion is that they require presidential approval and have to be in accordance with his oath to preserve, protect and defend the constitution. This effectively translates into carrying out the will of the president who is constitutionally bound to act on the advice of the central cabinet. So while the Indian president is little more than a ceremonial figurehead, the governor has considerable scope to influence the course of state politics. For instance, a gubernatorial appointee has virtually unrestricted powers to dissolve the state legislature if satisfied that it is no longer representative of the electorate. Given that floor crossing has been the bane of South Asian politics, the governor can use legislative defections as a pretext to call for fresh elections. In addition, the governor has to approve bills passed by state assemblies – a provision which effectively ensures central control over the legislative domains in the constituent units.

Even without governors' powers, the Indian centre has a range of constitutional provisions to check political developments at the state level. If the centre feels that a state is not being administered according to the constitution, the elected government headed by the chief minister can be dismissed and the state brought under what is euphemistically known as president's rule. So long as the same party held power at the centre and the states, the resort to president's rule was an exception rather than the norm. The first controversial instance of president's rule was in 1959 when the Congress government at the centre deployed its constitutional powers to oust the communist government of Kerala. After the 1967 elections, and increasingly since 1977, governor's powers and president's rule have been used in tandem to dismiss state governments ruled by parties other than the one in office at the centre. The central government in New Delhi has constitutional sanction to poach on both the legislative and executive domains of the states and can concede or refuse their regular budgetary needs as well as capital expenditure.

Considering the unitary character of the administrative arrangements, centre–state relations in India infract most accepted definitions of federalism. For instance, under the constitution the states are responsible for law and order. But New Delhi is constitutionally empowered to put the central reserve police into action in a state without the prior approval of its elected government. States seeking to contest the centre's actions in courts of law have to reckon with a highly streamlined and integrated system of administrative justice. The Indian supreme court is at the apex of a judicial hierarchy, consisting of civil, criminal and revenue courts, with each state possessing its own high court. Rulings by high courts can be overturned by the supreme court; there is no distinction between federal and state issues as is the case in the United States of America. In unexceptional times, a rarity in recent decades, the members of the IAS and the IPS can by and large be relied upon to underwrite the centre's powers at the state level in matters pertaining to developmental as well as day to day administration.

Borrowing freely from the colonial masters in the initial stages, the Indian state structure moved towards greater centralization even as the dynamics of expanding political arenas have pointed more and more in the direction of regionalism and decentralization. The predictable clashes between the centre and the states voiced most stridently in the political arenas have been echoed within the formal structures preserving federal relations – especially financial and administrative – making for a highly tenuous display of the unity, integrity and indestructibility of the Indian state. Recourse to overt authoritarianism in various regions seized by the impulse to assert distinctive cultural identities has now become an imperative for a formally democratic centre still committed to the inclusionary ideology of national unity. A closer scrutiny of the interplay between the structural rigidities and political fluidities of its federalism reveals why electoral democracy has proven to be a rudderless ship in the hard rocked sea of India's cultural diversities.

As early as the 1920s, the Congress had promised a culturally sensitive democratic federalism based on the linguistic reorganization of existing provincial boundaries. These were correctly seen to be arbitrary creations for the convenience of colonial administrators. Yet no sooner had independence been won that the Congress under Nehru tried blocking vociferous demands for a reorganization of state boundaries along linguistic lines. During the early 1950s Nehru's speeches were peppered with attacks on linguistic federalists whom he accused of stirring fissiparous tendencies and frequently equated with terrorists, communists and religious communalists. In Nehru's opinion the demand for linguistic provinces would push India into 'a boiling cauldron of redistribution' at a time when the consolidation of central authority had to be the first priority.

The voice of sweet reasonableness had missed the popular pulse. On 20 October 1952, Potti Sriramalu – a Gandhian – began a fast unto death unless the centre conceded the principle of a separate state of Andhra based on the eleven Telugu-speaking districts of Madras. Nehru was unmoved. On 15 December 1952 Sriramalu died of starvation. This was ironically enough the same day that Nehru presented the preamble of his first five-year plan for India's development to the Lok Sabha, describing it as the 'first attempt to create national awareness of the unity of the country'. News of the Telugu leader's death incited riots in all eleven Telugu districts of Madras. On 18 December 1952, a frazzled central cabinet announced that the state of Andhra would be created.

In 1953, the states' reorganization commission was set up and in 1956 the implementation of its report began in earnest. In all the report provided for fourteen states and six union territories. The rules of thumb guiding the commission's recommendations encapsulate the Indian centre's attitude towards regional demands.[7] First, the commission refused to have any truck with political groupings calling for outright secession from the union. Aimed at dissuading secessionists in north-eastern India – the Nagas, Mizos as well as other tribal groups – and also among the Tamils in the south, the principle has determined the centre's response to regionalists ever since. Second, there was no question of taking on board regional demands based on religious affinities – an obvious throwback to the partition experience. Third, there was to be no quixotic application of the language principle in demarcating state boundaries. Without demonstrated popular support linguistic states would not be created simply because of a dominant language being spoken in a particular region. And finally, demands for linguistic states were given no quarter if they were opposed by one or more of the language groups. This was the rationale for rejecting demands for the reorganization of Bombay and Punjab along linguistic lines. The commission's refusal to consider dividing Bombay province into Marathi and Gujarati states was due to the fact that Congress's Gujarati supporters dominated Bombay business while Marathi speakers were in a majority. The problem snowballed in the late fifties. In 1960 there were violent language riots in Bombay. The Marathi speakers eventually succeeded in forcing the centre's hand and Gujarat was separated from Maharashtra which included the city of Bombay.

In the Punjab there was a long-standing demand for a Punjabi-speaking subah. Since the Indian constitution prohibited political groupings from couching their demands in the religious idiom the dominant faction of the premier Sikh party, the Akali Dal, led by Sant Fateh Singh made its claims on linguistic rather than communal grounds. Master Tara Singh, the other prominent Sikh leader at the time, made no bones about wanting a Sikh-majority province. He was ingloriously edged out of the Akali Dal with the help of a Congress leadership averse to dealing with anyone toeing a communal line. Confusions in Akali ranks ensured that the Punjab problem

[7] Based on Paul R. Brass's analysis of the Indian centre's attitudes towards regional demands. See his *Language, Religion and Politics in North India*, Cambridge, 1974, pp. 17–19.

was less of a thorn in the centre's side than Bombay. A segment of the Sikhs supported Pratap Singh Kairon, the leader of the state Congress party, who promoted the concept of a greater Punjab in order to qualify for a larger share of the central kitty. Moreover, the demand for a Punjabi-speaking subah was opposed by Hindi speakers and Hindu speakers of Punjabi who saw it as a veiled attempt to establish Sikh supremacy over the state. It was not until 1966 that the demand for a Punjabi subah was conceded by the government of Indira Gandhi. The state was reorganized into three units, the Punjab, Himachal Pradesh and Haryana. Continuing opposition from Hindi speakers and Hindus with Punjabi as their mother tongue has prevented the completion of the reorganization process, one of the reasons why India's Punjab problem has proven to be a particularly sticky one.

Yet in the early decades the most serious secessionist challenge came from the southern state of Tamil Nadu. C. N. Annadurai, founder of the Dravida Munnetra Kazhagam, sought to counterbalance the dominance of the Hindi-speaking north by first promoting a Dravidian nationality and culture and then espousing a strident Tamil nationalism. At its height, Tamil nationalism found symbolic expression in the burning of the Indian flag and constitution. The linguistic reorganization of Madras province and the creation of Tamil Nadu dampened the secessionist fervour. During the Sino-Indian war Annadurai, in a prison cell at the time, dropped the DMK's demand for secession. This gave the Congress at the centre an opportunity to amend the Indian constitution and formalize what until then had been in practice informally in the north-eastern parts of the country, namely the use of brute force to squelch all secessionist tendencies. The DMK's electoral triumph over the Congress in 1967 created the conditions for a more palatable accommodation of Tamil nationalism within the parameters of the Indian union. Tamil Nadu along with the north-eastern states of Nagaland and Mizoram represent the Indian centre's most notable successes in turning the tides of secession, the first by mainly democratic means and the other two through outright coercion followed by political concessions. In its handling of regional demands, whether secessionist or not, the Indian centre has sought to draw upon these earlier experiences. But in the very different context of the eighties, complete success has so far eluded the centre in many regions and left it tugging ever more desperately at the lengthening sleeves of the state's coercive arms.

If language was the key issue in the fifties and sixties, regional autonomy from New Delhi in financial, administrative and political matters has dominated relations between centre and state since the eighties. This was not because the question of India's national language had been resolved but that flexibility was shown towards the multifarious linguistic groups constituting the different regions. Since flexibility has been conspicuously absent in other spheres it is important to consider how India, that veritable babel of tongues, managed to contain an issue which at one point seemed to threaten the unity, integrity and indestructibility of the union. After independence, proponents of Hindi demanded its recognition as the national language of India and, by implication, as the sole official language of intra-government communication. This was fervently contested by spokesmen of vernacular languages in the non-Hindi regions. Enforcing Hindi as the national language insulted their cultural sensibilities and would impair non-Hindi speakers seeking jobs in public services. It was in response to the challenge from the non-Hindi-speaking regions, spearheaded by the southern states, that Nehru proposed his three language formula. According to this formula, Hindi would be the official language of India, English the link language and regional languages of each state would be compulsory in the school curricula. The constitution provided for a fifteen-year interim period to complete the transition to Hindi. In 1965 when parliament was scheduled to reconsider the issue little progress had been made. Instead regional languages had become more firmly entrenched, making their displacement well-nigh impossible. So despite sporadic efforts by the Hindi lobby to revive the issue, India has settled for a multilingual pluralism with English serving as the most important language of communication.

India's prudent handling of the language question has been in stark contrast with the refusal to entertain demands for substantially renegotiated centre–state relations. Measured doses of cultural autonomy unmatched by a formal relaxation of financial and administrative controls has accentuated regional sentiments in varying measure, especially among the educated middling strata who benefited most from the creation of linguistic states. Diehard supporters of state centralization interpret this as proof of the poor judgement which informed the linguistic reorganization of state boundaries. Dissenters from this point of view have demonstrated that the implications of incorporating regional movements into the national mainstream have been more constructive for India's political and economic development than was predicted by the prophets of doom.[8] The debate continues unabated. Yet it is clear that the completion of the linguistic reorganization of state boundaries in the fifties and sixties in itself was insufficient in alleviating centre–state tensions which resurfaced during the past decade with not only unprecedented intensity but also simultaneity. By the 1980s the mushrooming of regional political parties and the shrinking bases of support of national political parties amplified the problems arising from a concentration of political and economic power in the hands of the centralized state.

[8] See Jyotirindra Das Gupta, 'Ethnicity, Democracy and Development in India: Assam in a General Perspective', in Kohli (ed.), *India's Democracy*, pp. 144–68. The best known dooms-

In the initial decades of independence the centralized state structure of India partly tempered by a nationally organized political party, the Indian National Congress, was able to counter the centrifugal pulls of a predominantly linguistic regionalism. But the expanding sphere of democratic politics and the withering away of the Congress's organizational and electoral bases of support has seen state authority in India resting more and more on the non-elected institutions of the state, the civil bureaucracy, the police and the military. Increasing recourse to covert authoritarianism coupled with the failure of the centralized national state to act as the great leveller of economic inequities and social injustices has led to deepening tensions between the centre and the different regional political economies of India. And this in spite of the clear emphasis in all the plan documents since the mid-fifties on removing inter-regional disparities through appropriately weighted allocations of public sector investments per capita. Donning the cap of a redistributive centre, New Delhi has an impressive track record of making larger per capita plan outlays to the less developed states. But statistics beguile. The value of total plan outlays in removing regional disparities has to be captured in quality, not quantity. Even if there is no real evidence of political parties at the centre punishing states who have rejected them at the polls, there is every reason to believe that inter-regional income disparities have increased significantly with the rich states growing richer and the poor looking poorer.[9] The introduction of technology and rapid urbanization in turn have served to aggravate intra-regional disparities, leading some analysts to call for a spatial rather than a state by state approach to development. On this view the district rather than the state should be the basic unit in the planning exercise.[10] Intended to obviate intra-regional inequalities in the ultimate hope of easing inter-regional disparities the proposed method of determining planning targets is not likely to kindle much enthusiasm in state capitals.

Critical changes in the centre–state dialectic from the late 1960s had been forcing a major review of the planning process. The sixth five-year plan made decentralization of the planning process an explicit part of India's development strategy. Significantly enough, the emphasis was on functional, financial and administrative decentralization to the district level rather than from the centre to the states. Given the great variation in the

day view is to be found in Selig Harrison, *India: the Most Dangerous Decades*, Princeton, 1960.

[9] For a detailed examination of regional disparities see Gupta, *Planning and Development in India*, section IV, pp. 243–69 and K. R. G. Nair (ed.), *Regional Disparities in India: Papers presented at the All-India Conference on Regional Disparities in India at New Delhi, April 1979*, New Delhi, 1981.

[10] L. S. Bhat, 'The Cases for Spatial Planning and Decentralisation of the Planning Process', in Nair (ed.), *Regional Disparities in India*.

quality of different state administrations this declared goal of central planning has at best remained a pious paper principle. Regional autonomists are wont to see it as an attempt to build artificial bridges between the political centre and the districts in order to bypass the state governments. The colonial experience of localization as well as the Pakistani and Bangladeshi examples of linking the centre with local government bodies at the district and village levels would appear to lend some credence to these apprehensions.

The more so since the ostensible revision of the objectives of centrally planned economic development have been at odds with a marked trend towards the concentration of political power at the centre. Here it is worth reiterating that the centralization which India witnessed after the fourth general election flowed more from the weaknesses than the strengths of ruling parties in office at New Delhi. In this sense centralization of powers in executive hands, simplistically attributed to the cult of personality in Indian political culture, is compensating for the loss of effective central control over electoral politics at the level of the different regional economies. During the 1980s a reaction to these over centralizing tendencies was evident in the election of various regional parties to power at the state level. The most spectacular example of the phenomenon was the 1983 victory of the newly formed Telugu Desam party in the Andhra state elections. More dangerous for the centre were powerful agitational and, in some instances, armed movements of regional and sub-regional dissidence. The three most serious challenges in the past decade have been posed by the Punjab, Assam and Kashmir. In each of the three cases regional dissidence was more in the way of an anti-systemic reaction to a constitutional framework patterned on the patron–client model than on an equitable partnership between the centre and the states. Repeated raps on the knuckles by the political centre have inflamed regional sentiments. Regional movements are for the most part led by elites frustrated at being treated as misguided wards in need of New Delhi's correctional therapy. The assertion of distinctive cultural identities in such a context simply appears to be the most effective means of mobilizing support among newly inducted social groups more familiar with local idioms and closer to the grassroots than the earlier assortment which gave the Congress party its regional bases.

In Punjab the Akali Dal, which until 1966 had been in the vanguard of an agitation for a Punjabi-speaking linguistic state, claimed in the 1970s and the 1980s sovereign national status, though not necessarily a separate state, for the Sikh religious community. The reasons for the Akali Dal's turnabout reveal how culture can be refashioned into a forceful vehicle of political and economic protest. Encouraged in no small measure by the policies of the British colonial state, the Sikhs had over the years constructed a distinctive identity which blended the myth of martial races with the hard-headed realities of a predominantly agrarian society.[11] Yet a common cultural identity did not assure the Akali Dal the support of all Sikhs. As mentioned earlier some Sikhs were supporters of the Congress party led by Pratap Singh Kairon, who became chief minister of the Punjab in 1957, and believed that the Sikhs would do better in a bigger province and more power at the centre. It was only after Kairon's death in 1964 and the emergence of Sant Fateh Singh as the predominant leader of the Akali Dal that the political centre felt comfortable about conceding the demand for a Punjabi subah. After 1966, the Sikhs had a 56 per cent majority in the Punjab. But the Akalis, with their main support base restricted to Jat farmers, discovered that they still had to ally with other parties to form a stable government at the state level. This gave the centre greater opportunities to manipulate the various political factions in the state.

The coming of the 'green revolution' provided an economic dimension to Sikh disaffections. Although the Punjab did remarkably well, Jat farmers resented the centre's procurement of their wheat crop at below market prices. One calculation gives Punjab the top position among Indian states in terms of per capita agricultural production.[12] So the centre's redistributional role, according to which wheat from surplus states is distributed at subsidized prices to deficit areas, is seen to have had an adverse effect on the state economy. Since the late 1960s Punjab has had one of the highest per capita incomes in India. By the time of the fifth five-year plan the Punjab was meeting over 90 per cent of its total expenditure. Between the first and sixth five-year plans the share of central assistance in the Punjab's total outlays dropped from 86.5 to 15.3 per cent.[13] Declining dependence on central resource transfers and relatively high rates of growth in state domestic product excited hopes of extending Punjab's prosperity into the industrial sphere. Those with investible capital were put out by the constraints which an unwieldy federal bureaucracy placed on their efforts to set up industries. Small-scale agro-based industries seemed a poor reward for the Punjab's contribution towards feeding the rest of India.

The status of Chandigarh, the state capital of the Punjab prior to the reorganization, was left pending in 1966. Haryana demanded compensation for the loss of its main urban centre to the Punjab. In 1970 Mrs Gandhi announced that Punjab could have Chandigarh in return for Rs.10 crores and the districts of Fazilka and Abohar to the state of Haryana. This was interpreted by the Akali Dal as a purely political manoeuvre; the proposal

[11] For an excellent analysis of Sikh identity formation see Richard G. Fox, *Lions of the Punjab: Culture in the Making*, Berkeley, 1985.
[12] See K. R. G. Nair, *Regional Experience in a Developing Economy*, New York, 1983, appendix.
[13] Gupta, *Planning and Development in India*, pp. 260–1.

was rejected out of hand. Even more acrimonious has been the dispute over Punjab's share of river waters which the Akalis view as a deliberate attempt by the centre to sabotage the state's agrarian economy. To this long and weighty list of complaints the Sikhs have appended the issue of discrimination in recruitment to the army, one of their traditional bastions within the state structure since the colonial period. Under the new recruitment policy announced in 1974 the Punjab's share was pushed down from a high of 20 to 2.5 per cent. Though a mere 2 per cent of the total population of India, many Sikhs were not above construing this as discriminating against their entry into the one institution of the state where they have consistently excelled.

Against this backdrop the defeat of the Akali Dal in the 1971–2 elections by the Congress led to demands for a Sikh homeland. In October 1973, the Akalis adopted the Anandpur Sahib resolution for Sikh autonomy. The resolution was later amended in 1978. Its main feature was the insistence that the centre's interference be restricted to defence, foreign affairs, currency and general communications. All other departments, including railways after 1978, should be handed over to the states who would make contributions to the centre in proportion to their representation in parliament. The basis chosen to determine state contributions to central revenues is significant considering that the Punjab, when conditions permit elections, sends only thirteen members to the Indian Lok Sabha. Although the resolution claimed that the Sikhs were a *qaom*, which could mean a people or a nation, it did not unequivocally demand a separate sovereign Sikh state. What the Akalis seemed to be angling for was a substantially renegotiated centre–state relationship, one which would not penalize states with higher rates of productivity to maintain the façade of a redistributive centre.

As in the case of the Muslim League's Lahore resolution of 1940 there was plenty of room here for bargaining. Yet instead of negotiating with the Akalis, Mrs Gandhi and her associates chose to view the Anandpur Sahib resolution as a subterfuge for eventual secession from the union. This gave the central leadership a handle to exploit divisions among various Sikh factions and sects. Together with her Punjabi lieutenant, Giani Zail Singh, Mrs Gandhi started wooing one of the more militant and communally inclined Sikh leaders, Jarnail Singh Bhindranwale. In 1979 and 1980 Bhindranwale campaigned for Congress candidates against the Akalis. The Akalis did badly in the 1980 elections and began making increasing use of religious symbolism to revive their sagging political fortunes. Meanwhile, Bhindranwale and his men resorted to more and more extreme measures, targeting the Hindu population of the Punjab with a spate of murders. The Congress dominated centre not only chose to ignore the threat Bhindranwale was coming to pose but refused to negotiate with the more moderate

Akalis. The failure of the Akalis to wrest concessions from the centre added to Bhindranwale's stature and, in the process, shattered any hope of peace in the Punjab. Bhindranwale's followers acquired sophisticated weapons and launched a violent campaign for the attainment of a separate Sikh homeland – Khalistan.

Negotiations between the Indian state and Sikh representatives were fitful; agreements remained unimplemented as the Punjab was convulsed in waves of terror and counter-terror.The deep psychological alienation caused by the Indian army's assault on the Golden Temple in June 1984 – aimed at removing Bhindranwale and his men from the premises – the assassination of Indira Gandhi in October 1984, and the anti-Sikh riots in New Delhi of November 1984, have not been healed. Both Rajiv Gandhi and V. P. Singh during early months of their prime ministership lost opportunities for achieving a political settlement in the Punjab. The government of Narasimha Rao has been no more imaginative. In February 1992 a farcical election boycotted by all but one of the Akali Dal factions was held under the supervision of the security forces. Populist terrorism countered by state terrorism can only furnish short-term results. The agony of the Punjab is far from over. Daily exchanges between Sikh militants and security forces that had taken on tragic proportions in what was once a microcosm of India's developmental successes had become less common by 1993. But presiding over the relative calm of a graveyard could turn out to be a dubious advantage for the new chief minister Beant Singh. The restoration of some semblance of law and order is necessary but not a sufficient remedy for a political resolution of the Punjab imbroglio. Punjab's strategic location and the disproportionate number of Sikhs in the army continue to present dilemmas for the Indian state. New Delhi's claims of Pakistani intervention in arming and training Sikh militants gives the Punjab problem a troubling international dimension.

While this strategically important north-western state remains a festering sore, India's north-east has once again erupted in militant campaigns of regional dissidence. The epicentre since the 1980s has been Assam, linguistically the most diverse of the states in India. It also has had one of the highest rates of population growth and the lowest per capita incomes in the country. Although it boasts high rates of agricultural productivity per capita, Assam straggles behind Punjab on almost every development indicator. It is also hopelessly dependent on central transfers, managing to raise about 46 per cent of total expenditure from state resources under the fifth five-year plan. At an average nearly three-quarters of the plan outlays have been funded by the centre.[14] While these figures point to the difficulties of a

[14] Ibid., pp. 260–1.

sustained campaign against its key economic benefactor, they delineate the flagging economic development of a state whose cultural heterogeneities have taken on violent manifestations in an expanding political arena.

Feelings of neglect, injustice and exclusion from the national development effort motivated Assamese nationalism. Like the Sikhs in the Punjab the Assamese want control and management of their own resources and prefer to be partners than hapless clients of an indomitable and distant political centre. The present boundaries of the states are as recent as 1972 and have been particularly prone to trespassing by Muslim migrants from Bangladesh. Fearful of being reduced to a minority in their own province, the Assamese have been demanding a 'sons of the soil' policy to counter the influence of Bengali Hindus who have historically dominated the government and the professional services as well as Bengali Muslim cultivators. The growing wedge between Assamese and Bengalis has taken place within a context of the increasing deprivation of the state in the allocation of financial resources. Until the discovery and production of oil in Bombay during the late 1970s, Assam was the main reservoir of domestic oil in India. Although it still supplies 60 per cent of India's crude oil production, it receives less than 3 per cent of the value of the oil as royalties from the centre. Assam is a resource rich state but is debarred by India's federal framework from enjoying the boons of its natural wealth. Over 50 per cent of the tea production in India takes places in Assam which also is the largest supplier of plywood and has considerable reserves of coal.[15]

Spokesmen of the Assamese national movement, students and urban professionals in the main, have consistently pointed to the artificial dependence on the centre which the existing federal arrangements force upon the state. Stringent measures against migrants and control over natural resources would enable the state to pursue development policies aimed at improving economic productivity, not the consolidated revenues of the union. The fact that Assam has a baker's dozen in the Lok Sabha and even fewer in the Rajya Sabha is a source of bitter resentment. Drawing support from educated middle-class Assamese, the regional autonomy movement initially thrived on strident anti-Bengali Hindu and anti-New Delhi rhetoric. As the movement fanned into the rural areas, Bengali Muslims became the primary targets, giving the situation an explosive communal dimension. Thwarted political and economic aspirations have bred a virulent kind of cultural chauvinism.

Years of violent agitation in Assam eventually persuaded the newly elected government of Rajiv Gandhi to pursue the path of conciliation. In

---

[15] Jyotirindra Das Gupta, 'Ethnicity, Democracy and Development in India: Assam in a General Perspective', in Kohli (ed.), *India's Democracy*, pp. 157–8.

August 1985 the centre signed an accord with Assamese militants which made certain concessions to protecting the 'sons of the soil' against intrusive 'foreigners'. More symbolic than substantive, the accord was a calculated step towards the holding of state elections. These were won by the pre-eminent regional party, the Asom Gana Parishad or the Assamese People's Council led by the 32-year-old Prafulla Mahanta, who became the youngest ever chief minister in India's history. But in the absence of any recasting of centre–state relations, Mahanta and his party failed to satisfy the aspirations of dissatisfied Assamese youth by following the constitutional path. Coopted into the national mainstream the Asom Gana Parishad was reduced to playing the centre's game on the regional stage. In the past few years a more radical organization, the United Liberation Front of Assam (ULFA), has launched an armed struggle against the Indian union in alliance with like-minded groups in the neighbouring tribal states. Having artfully split the Assamese regional movement the centre is in no mood to accommodate ULFA extremists who are currently on the most wanted list of the state's security apparatus in north-eastern India.

Overstretched and demoralized by its recent experiences as the centre's domestic rod of order, the Indian military has been engaged in the demeaning exercise of reconquering a people it had helped extricate from the jaws of the country's premier enemy. The problem of Kashmir, or more accurately that of Jammu and Kashmir, has many unique features which cannot be analysed within the boundaries of the presently constituted nation-states in the region. On the one hand, Kashmir poses an acute dilemma for India's federal equation and on the other has regional and international dimensions which sets it apart from other dissident states in the union. Kashmir is the only state in India on which Pakistan has territorial claims. During the late forties and fifties the United Nations security council endorsed the principle of self-determination for Kashmiris, albeit one limited to joining India or Pakistan. An artificial status quo, based on military and political manoeuvres by the two countries and the denial of the right of self-determination by Kashmiris, has been a principal source of instability in the region. It has already sparked off two of three Indo-Pakistan wars and in the 1990s threatened once again to engulf the two subcontinental rivals in a contest neither one can afford. With India controlling 63 per cent of the state and Pakistan the rest, the pacification of this predominantly Muslim state is one of the biggest challenges to have landed at New Delhi's doorstep. A detailed analysis of the dispute between the two countries warrants a separate study. Without losing sight of the dispute, here it will suffice to consider why the people of a state impelled by their foremost leader, Sheikh Abdullah, to opt for a secular and democratic future over an ostensibly Islamic one, and granted special status under article 370 of the Indian constitution, came to be seized by the virus of secession. Unlike the Tamils who first preached secession and later became defenders of the Indian union, most Kashmiris initially chose to hitch their wagons to India only to abruptly unfasten the bolts and bring the relationship to a grinding halt.

Since late 1989 the Kashmir valley has been astir with a popularly backed armed insurgency aimed at severing all links with the Indian union. New Delhi has predictably charged Islamabad with complicity. Pakistan's neutrality towards an uprising it has for years tried in vain to engineer is difficult to envisage. Yet it would be an exercise in historical fatuity to maintain that New Delhi's recent nightmare in Kashmir is entirely a Pakistani concoction. Seeing India's troubles as gifts from abroad is a standard line of defence. But in the past Kashmir has led to military confrontations between India and Pakistan without a widespread popular revolt against the union. So Pakistan's new found prowess in masterminding the recent Kashmiri revolt, even if conceivable, cannot be an adequate explanation for the unprecedented developments that have activated a people, long the butt of criticism for expecting others to fight their battles.

More than thirty political groupings in Indian Kashmir, and also in Pakistani-held Kashmir, are currently demanding the exercise of their right to self-determination. This had been promised to them by Nehru in November 1947 after New Delhi accepted the Hindu Maharaja's decision to accede to the Indian union. The implicit conditionality of the accession was later denied by India. Efforts by the United Nations to resolve the dispute and hold a plebiscite faltered on Indian and Pakistani intransigence. For many Kashmiris wedded to the idea of autonomy New Delhi's resistance to a plebiscite under UN auspices has come to symbolize their captive status within the union. According to the official Indian view Jammu and Kashmir became an integral part of the union through a slow and voluntary process set in motion as early as 1954 when the state's constituent assembly voted for accession to the union. The only caveat to this has been article 370 of the constitution which prohibits non-Kashmiris from buying land in the state. A putative symbol of the state's special status in the union, the article has come under attack by Hindu parties who accuse the centre of pampering Kashmiri Muslims and, in this way, keeping them outside the national mainstream. In point of fact, the article is an extension of a law passed in 1920 by the Maharaja to prevent the alienation of Hindu landed property to prospective Muslim buyers from the Punjab. Nothing in the article guarantees the people of the state basic democratic rights, much less autonomy. Wholly irrelevant to the demands for self-determination reverberating in the Kashmir valley, it has become a convenient distraction for New Delhi as proponents and opponents of the article nervously debate the future of Jammu and Kashmir in the Indian union.

Why the Indian union has felt obliged to perpetuate the myth of Jammu and Kashmir's special constitutional status merits consideration. No such reserve had guided its attitude towards the other princely states. But then Jammu and Kashmir always has been something of a red herring in New Delhi's path. At the time of partition this north Indian princely state had an area of about 86,000 square miles, consisting of half a dozen religiously and culturally heterogeneous regions. Muslims predominated in the Vale of Kashmir, the most populous and relatively more prosperous part of the state, as well as in Poonch district, Baltistan and the Gilgit region. Muslims formed 61 per cent of the total population of Jammu but Hindus had a majority in the eastern districts of the province and Buddhists in Ladakh. The population of the whole state, including the frontier districts of Gilgit and Ladakh, was about four million, of which 80 per cent were Muslim.

The fact of a Muslim majority, though concentrated in the valley, took on added significance once the British decided to partition India along supposedly religious lines. Jinnah and the Muslim League naturally staked a claim on the state. The Congress refused to concede the claim, arguing that its pragmatic acceptance of partition was not extendable to the League's two nation theory. Professing a secular democratic disposition the Congress dominated centre justified its claims on Kashmir on strategic and economic grounds. Despite Jinnah's earlier demand that the state be given the right to opt out of both unions the matter settled as one between accession to India or Pakistan. Once Maharaja Hari Singh had signed the instruments of accession to the Indian union, Nehru quickly offered the premiership of the state to Sheikh Abdullah. By far the most influential of Kashmiri leaders since pre-independence days until his death in 1982, Abdullah's political career wavered between seeking accommodation with New Delhi and asserting unqualified autonomy from the union. He had risen to prominence in the 1930s as the leader of a popular movement against the Maharaja's autocracy orchestrated by a political organization called the All-Jammu and Kashmir Muslim Conference set up in 1932. In 1938 the Muslim Conference converted itself into a secular organization called the National Conference under Sheikh Abdullah. A breakaway faction led by Abdullah's close associate, Ghulam Abbas, and Sardar Ibrahim went under the name of the Muslim Conference and later allied itself with the Muslim League. The National Conference, considered to be in the vanguard of a people's movement against the pro-British Maharaja, received encouragement and moral support from the Indian National Congress.

Indebted to the Congress and put off by the tactics of the Muslim League, Abdullah strongly favoured the independence of Kashmir and, failing that, accession to India with adequate safeguards for its autonomy. Nehru's offer of a plebiscite was interpreted by Abdullah as evidence that the Maharaja's accession was conditional and would be fully confirmed only after securing necessary guarantees for state autonomy. By 1953 these expectations had been dashed by New Delhi's furtive attempts to brace factions within the National Conference more amenable to granting the union greater sway over the affairs of the state. In that year Abdullah was thrown into gaol and his lieutenant, Bakshi Ghulam Mohammad, slotted into place to do the centre's bidding. The results were impressive. In 1951 an electoral sham had produced a forty-five member constituent assembly. All were members of the National Conference who had been elected unopposed after the opposition candidates were browbeaten into withdrawing their nomination papers. With Abdullah safely out of the way the constituent assembly's unrepresentative character became even more pronounced. On 14 May 1954 this hand-picked constituent assembly voted to extend the centre's jurisdiction beyond defence, foreign affairs and communications to cover all subjects on the union list. Another bill passed at the same time divested the council of ministers of powers to be the final interpreters of the state constitution. These put paid to Kashmiri dreams of autonomy. A chronology of the historical landmarks in the state's relations with the centre makes for telling reading. In 1958 an amendment to article 312 of the Indian constitution saw Jammu and Kashmir coming under the purview of the all-India services from which it had been specifically excluded as a gesture to its special status in the union. The state's financial autonomy was extinguished in the same year. One year later the state high court was stripped of its role as the highest court of appeal and placed under the gaze of the Indian supreme court. By 1961 the national election commission had been empowered to organize elections in the state. With its non-elected arms in place, it was easier for New Delhi to dominate the political chess game in the state. In 1963 Bakshi Ghulam Mohammad was checkmated under the defence of India rules. A succession of Kashmiri leaders received the same summary treatment. In March 1965, the special designations of sadar-i-riyasat and wazir-i-azam for the Jammu and Kashmir governor and chief minister respectively were scrapped. By 1971 the all-India central services were playing knights to the state politicians' pawns in a manner reminiscent of neighbouring Pakistan. Jammu and Kashmir has paid dearly for a special status which with the passage of time was special only in eliciting a sterner kind of structural authoritarianism from the Indian state.

By the mid-seventies New Delhi decided to cast all caution to the winds. On 24 February 1975, a suitably chastened Abdullah signed an accord with Indira Gandhi making Jammu and Kashmir 'a constituent unit' of the Indian union, thus bringing the centrally scripted drama to an appropriate climax. Henceforth, the Indian parliament could override the state legislature on any matter affecting the territorial integrity of the union. Self-determination for the Kashmiris was now history. In a reenactment of the dynastic succession at the centre, Abdullah's son Farooq assumed his father's mantle in 1982 and proceeded to fall flatly into the Congress's lap. But Farooq liked globetrotting better than administering a state, which despite central outlays for development, remains one of the poorest and least industrialized in India. He soon managed to discredit himself with the centre's gubernatorial appointee, Jagmohan, and was sent packing. His successor fared no better and was removed with equal impudence by the governor. Back in office, but not a wit wiser, Farooq forged an alliance with the Congress which destroyed the little credibility he possessed with the people of the state. A royally rigged election in 1987 parried a serious threat to the National Conference and the Congress from a coalition of parties calling themselves the Muslim United Front. This set the valley alight, resentments rained bullets and mortar as a once peaceful people embraced blood and death to be released of the ignominy of colonized subjecthood.

The centre's throttling of democratic aspirations in the valley had kept abreast of an invidious policy of turning a blind eye to, if not actually provoking, efforts by Hindu right-wing parties from Jammu and northern India to give a saffron colouring to the politics of the state. This spurred the communal elements among Kashmiri Muslims to unfurl the green banner in defence of their Islamic identity. Conducted under the rubric of a formally secular Indian state the communalization of Jammu and Kashmir's political arenas, especially during the eighties, further weakened the centre's hold over a people who had long tired of walking the thorny garden path to democratic secularism. As mosque and temple faced off in symbolic counterpoint, demands for Kashmiri self-determination were overborne by the delicate communal balance in the state. Intended as the democratic right of all inhabitants of the state, it has become the battle cry of Kashmiri Muslims and an anathema to Hindus in the valley and Jammu as well as for Buddhists in Ladakh.

Non-Muslim opposition to the principle of self-determination forecloses the possibility of the Indian centre conceding the demand in any shape or form. Majoritarian communalism, after all, has been since the early 1980s New Delhi's favourite ideological weapon against movements of regional dissidence. The dramatic demographic changes that have occurred in the state since partition are a source of added comfort. By the time of the 1981 Indian census the proportion of Muslims to the total population had fallen to 64.19 per cent and Hindus had attained a comfortable majority in Jammu. The loss of Azad Kashmir to Pakistan has something to do with the overall decline in the percentage of Muslims in the state. Kashmiri nationalists, however, see it as a deliberate policy by secular India to encourage the settlement of non-Muslims in the only Muslim-majority state in the union. Dismissing these charges out of hand, New Delhi has since the late 1980s made a big play of Hindu families fleeing the valley to escape the terror unleashed by the Kashmiri militants.

While the communal situation in the state has decidedly worsened, it is important not to lose sight of the underlying causes. Economic deprivations have given a cutting edge to charges of central duplicity towards democratic and secular dynamics in the state. The advocates of Kashmiri autonomy point to the state's relative lack of development, the disproportionate share of non-Muslims in government employment and the niggardly central investments in public sector development. Central resource transfers, subsidies and supplies of basic necessities such as food are seen as part of a concerted policy to keep the state at the perpetual beck and call of the union. For once the statistics can be marshalled in support of this conspiratorial view of New Delhi's policy to push up the economic costs of the state's secession from the union. Although Jammu and Kashmir has the lowest gross per capita investment in centrally financed public enterprises, it was able to meet 32 per cent and 42 per cent of its expenditure from internal resources under the fourth and the fifth five-year plan respectively. This compares poorly to the majority of the Indian states during the same period.[16] The lavish life styles and well-advertised corruption of successive National Conference governments, specifically in disbursing patronage to the chosen few, has embittered educated Kashmiris and frustrated the ambitions of a small but enthusiastic group of entrepreneurs.

The gradual etiolation of the state's autonomy, repeatedly rigged elections, blatant central interference in its internal politics, the activities of Hindu communal groups and, last but not least, efforts to Sanskritize the Kashmiri language and weed out the few remaining symbols of traditional Muslim education have all led to a severe disillusionment with India's secular democracy and development prospectus. Anger with India does not translate into a desire for union with Pakistan. The politically subservient and economically underdeveloped status of Azad Kashmir in military dominated Islamic Pakistan is not lost on Muslims in the valley. Pro-Pakistan sentiments among certain Kashmiri militant groups are based on the pragmatic calculations of a struggle with an overmighty foe. For the vast majority of Kashmiris, it is the repeated denial of the political as well as the economic and social rights of citizenship combined with the inversion of secularism to promote a crude form of Hindu communalism that has led them to agitate for complete independence from India.

[16] Gupta, *Planning and Development in India*, pp. 260–1.

During the last few years Kashmiris have weathered one of the largest ever deployment of Indian security forces to sustain an emotionally charged campaign against New Delhi. While a large number of Kashmiris seem prepared for a long drawn out fight for freedom from India, it is by no means clear that they want incorporation in Pakistan. The Jammu and Kashmir Liberation Front, which is deemed to be the largest and best organized of the groups, has been calling for a secular and sovereign state with equal citizenship rights for all Kashmiris, irrespective of religion. More numerous, but not necessarily more powerful, fundamentalist groups have been appealing to the religious sentiments of the Muslim majority in Kashmir in order to establish an Islamic state in close alliance or a confederal arrangement with Pakistan. In the absence of any reference to the people, the strength of popular opinion must remain a matter of conjecture. But there is no question that deep disappointment with their status in the Indian union and doubts about a future in military dominated Pakistan has made the option of independence more attractive to Kashmiris. India and Pakistan have always argued that there has never been any question of a sovereign and independent Kashmir. Deliberations on Kashmir at the United Nations as well as the various security council resolutions passed between 1948 and 1957 were based on the same principle. Long the main point of contention between India and Pakistan, the people of Kashmir have served notice on both to change their attitude and come to terms with the new realities at the social base. Kashmir may well prove to be the decisive factor in the reordering of the federal equation not only in India but also in Pakistan.

Barely capable of dealing with its multifarious domestic discontents, India has tried performing the improbable role of a regional fire brigade in two major instances. The most dramatic of these was the Indian military intervention in East Pakistan in 1971. The 1980s saw another, though far less successful, instance of Indian intervention in a neighbouring country's federal dilemma at a time that New Delhi itself had been placed under virtual siege by an array of regional forces. The opportunity for India's regional projection of its redoubtable military machine came as the clamour for sovereign nationhood gathered momentum among the Tamil minority of Sri Lanka. Although most Sinhala speakers, who form the majority of Sri Lanka's population, are Buddhists and a majority of the Tamils are Hindus, the linguistic divide has been rather more important than the religious one. Sri Lanka's post-colonial state structure was heavily centralized and the centre came to be dominated by the Sinhalese majority. A blatantly chauvinistic policy by the Sinhala majority against the Tamils in the initial years of independence sowed the seeds for bitter conflict in the late 1970s. As in the case of Indian Punjab, Assam and Kashmir, the political fratricide in Sri

Lanka has a strong economic dimension. During the 1950s and the 1960s Sri Lanka was a veritable model of successful planned development in South Asia. A state-supported rice subsidy programme and food stamps ensured against endemic hunger. Yet as in many other Third World countries the fruits of economic development in Sri Lanka were extremely uneven. By the late 1970s the agrarian sector was practically stagnant. Sri Lanka's remarkable achievements in the sphere of education – some 87 per cent are literate – were not paralleled by job opportunities. Between 1971 and 1976 the labour force grew at the rate of 125,000 per annum while employment rose at the rate of just 85,000 a year. By 1977 20 per cent of the labour force was unemployed.[17] The assumption of office in 1977 by the United National Party led by Junius Jayawardene and the adoption of a liberalization policy aimed at greater incorporation in the capitalist world system led to a serious deterioration of the economic situation. Growing economic distress contributed to the political explosions which have become the norm rather than the exception in Sri Lanka in recent decades. The problem became particularly acute when Tamils were targeted during riots in the capital city of Colombo in 1983. The Tamils who form a majority in the northern province of Jaffna took up arms under the leadership of the Liberation Tigers of Tamil Eelam (LTTE), who have been demanding a sovereign Tamil state in the northern and the eastern parts of the island. The Indian government initially supported the Tamil rebels. But the military contingent it sent, ostensibly to enforce an agreement between the Sri Lankan government and the rebels to keep the peace, promptly got embroiled in a war with Tamil guerillas who refused to be pliable clients. The appearance of the Indian troops as the common enemy opened the way for talks between the Sri Lankan government and the LTTE and the withdrawal of Indian troops in early 1990. The talks soon collapsed leaving the two warring parties arrayed against each other in a dangerous military stalemate interrupted all too frequently by political assassinations and insouciant violence.

This survey of the dynamics impelling movements of regional and linguistic dissidence in formally democratic India and Sri Lanka spells out their inter-connections with the overall nature of the state. Popularly elected regimes aided by the non-elected institutions of the state have had no qualms about discarding democratic practices whilst tackling the problem of regional dissidence. Even if statistics are allowed to lie, there can be no doubt that centrally planned development has offered no satisfactory answer to inequities between and within the different regional political economies. So one of the main justifications for sustaining federal structures with a unitary bias appears to have been negated. Without a better balance

---

[17] Stanley J. Tambiah, *Sri Lanka: Ethnic Fratricide and the Dismantling of Democracy*, London, 1986, pp. 56–7.

of political and economic power between the centre and the states, movements of regional autonomy, if not outright secession, are likely to grow in frequency as well as intensity. Votaries of the centralized state can no longer expect the familiar cry of balkanization to rescue them from the deepening quagmire of regional dissidence.

The history of the subcontinent is ample testimony against seeing cultural difference as an overwhelming compulsion leading to secessionist demands. It is time culture was relieved of its unchanging and insular moorings and viewed as a constant process of redefinition in response or reaction to larger economic and political structures. Having chosen language out of all the other attributes in social grouping, the Indian state gave legality to the articulation of political demands in the very compartmentalized and exclusionary categories its ideology of inclusionary nationalism was intended to contest. Recent efforts to manipulate communal divisions among linguistic communities and turning the full face of state authoritarianism on certain regions is more a recipe for madness than central efficacy. Treating culture as a patchwork quilt, not a seamless garment of exclusion, might at least hold out the prospect of co-existence in difference. By implicitly denying the much more pervasive historical phenomena of multiple social identities, concessions to certain strands in culture without corresponding changes in the political and economic structures underpinning centre–state relations has perpetuated and created fresh tensions in India's federal equation. The multiple social identities of the disparate peoples constituting India, and indeed South Asia as a whole, demand more than piecemeal appeasement of specific cultural values. They need political and economic structures capable of accommodating them.

Dissidence and rebellion under military authoritarianism

If India's formal democracy has had such a chequered record handling regional dissidence, military authoritarianism could not be expected to do much better. Despite the bond of Islam, Pakistan retains the unenviable distinction of being the only country in the post-colonial world to have experienced a successful secessionist movement. It also provides the most vivid illustration of the proposition that centre–province conflicts have less to do with the inherent volatility of cultural or 'ethnic' divisions in heterogeneous societies than with the complex and shifting ways in which social identities are forged and refashioned in response or resistance to structures of states and political economies. State-directed processes of political as well as economic inclusion and exclusion rather than the fact of cultural diversity per se have been at the nub of Pakistan's problems in piecing together some semblance of a nested federalism.

Rehearsing the fault lines of the Pakistani state structure might help clarify the point. The limitations of the economic resource base and the disproportionate requirements of the military establishment saw a newly constructed centre blunting the autonomy of political processes in order to better dictate the terms of accommodation with the provinces. If some elements of consensus dignified relations between the centre and states in Nehruvian India, coercion was the most daunting legacy of state formation on Pakistan's emerging federalism. So although Pakistan followed the Indian pattern of borrowing heavily from the 1935 act, including the distribution of powers between the centre and the provinces, the unitary aspects in its federal configuration were much starker in practice. With the exception of the 1973 constitution which made some tentative attempts to reflect the aspirations of the provinces, neither the 1956 nor the 1962 documents showed much appetite for federal principles. And this despite the Lahore resolution of 1940 – the presumed magna carta of the proposed association of Muslim-majority provinces in India – offering 'sovereign' and 'autonomous' status to constituent units within independent Muslim states in the north-west and the north-east of the subcontinent. The not so implicit concession to confederalism was swept under the carpet soon after independence. Countering the Bengali majority was the foremost concern of the harried architects of Pakistan's constitutional future. To complicate matters all four of Pakistan's provinces in the west have been home to a culturally and linguistically hybrid population, including the Punjab where Seraiki speakers dominate the southern parts. More than India, the Pakistani centre has manipulated intra-regional cultural diversities to deprive entire provinces of their political and economic rights.

While some Indian states might fret over their inadequate representation in the non-elected institutions, no single region exercises complete dominance over them. By contrast, the institutional dominance of a predominantly Punjabi military and federal bureaucracy has at each step heightened the sense of alienation on the part of the non-Punjabi provinces and significant linguistic minorities within them. Prolonged suspension of representative government, the absence of well-organized national parties coupled with the politics of differential patronage have led to recurrent clashes between a centralized administrative structure and a regionally disparate society. Efforts to invoke a monolithic Islamic national identity to deny the populace the comfort of multiple affiliations has confounded Pakistan's task of weaning a highly differentiated amalgam of provincial sentiments away from the temptations of outright secession. The breakaway of Bangladesh in 1971 was simply the most dramatic manifestation of this problem. Winds of dissent, directed more at the centre than towards secession, have continued to blow in Pakistan's culturally diverse and economically highly differentiated western provinces.

An artifact of decolonization, Pakistan has laboured hard to justify its creation to the outside world. Unable to meet the objectives of its own ideational justification as the homeland for India's Muslim minority, the managers of Pakistan compensated by creating a state structure which is ideologically averse to the bare manifestation of difference. Instead of treading delicately to win the allegiance of linguistically and culturally diverse constituent units, the state structure has been geared to promoting a costly process of militarization tempered by a thin and rather crude veneer of Islamic legitimacy. The failure of the state's ideological protestations in giving any sense of common purpose to a heterogeneous society has been more pronounced due to Pakistan's singular inability to allocate its scarce resources equitably between the different provinces. As in India, provincial disaffections in Pakistan are cast in cultural moulds to express feelings of political inefficacy flowing from unmet expectations of job opportunities, better social services and an adequate share of the state's financial resources. Yet compared to India, Pakistan's aid inebriated political economy of defence has been relatively less successful in coughing up resources to keep the provinces pulling in the same direction. While matching India's emphasis on the centralization of authority in the pursuit of development policies aimed at maximizing revenue and postponing social welfare measures, Pakistan has been able to sustain the strategy only by conferring direct control over the state to non-elected institutions carrying a legacy of uneven recruitment patterns from the colonial era.

Punjabis from the middle and upper economic strata were the main recruits to the civil bureaucracy and, especially, the military – thus exacerbating the problem of constructing a state structure capable of accommodating diverse linguistic and socio-economic groups. Like its subcontinental neighbour, Pakistan's federal problem has stemmed from its highly centralized state system. The military–bureaucratic dominance of the central state apparatus has been a prohibitive factor in the accommodation of non-Punjabi regional interests. Unable to assert themselves in democratic arenas or seek advance through representation in the non-elected institutions, Bengalis, Pathans, Baluchis and Sindhis have at different moments considered the merits of formally exiting from the national mainstream.

Soon after its establishment Pakistan was forced to take stock of the poor representation of non-Punjabis in the non-elected institutions. A quota system of recruitment to the services based on regional affiliations was devised but failed to give adequate or equitable representation to the different provinces or the linguistic minorities within them. In the early years of independence, Bengalis in the eastern wing accounted for just over half of the country's total population but were woefully underrepresented in the civil bureaucracy and the military. Since these institutions rose to a position of dominance within the state structure and democratic political processes were aborted in the late 1950s it is possible to see why regional dissidence in Pakistan cannot be understood without reference to the nature of the state. During the Ayub era Bengalis still constituted only 5 per cent of the officer corps of the army, 15 per cent in the air force and 20 per cent in the navy. Bengalis continued to be underrepresented in the CSP at a time of growing pressure for entry due to a 162 per cent increase in college enrolment in the eastern wing.[18]

There was of course a strong cultural dimension to Bengali alienation. They deeply resented the early attempt to impose Urdu as the sole national language. Even Jinnah, the much venerated champion of minority rights, showed little appreciation for the cultural sensitivities of a people who had come through at a crucial moment in the late thirties to save him and the Muslim League from political extinction. The paradox is all the greater given that Jinnah with his Anglicized sartorial persona was hardly the most convincing proponent of the Urdu language. As early as February 1952 state repression of a student-led language movement in East Bengal gave post-partition Bengali nationalism its first martyrs. Yet it would be unacceptably telelogical to sketch a linear progression between this initial expression of defensive linguistic regionalism and Bengali nationalism's coming of age in the late 1960s.

More than elsewhere East Bengal presents the most vivid example of how culture as process interacts with political and economic structures to give rise to alternate strains within it at different moments. Just prior to 1947 religion had appeared to subsume predominantly Muslim East Bengal's linguistic and cultural ties with the economically more powerful but Hindu-dominated West Bengal. By the sixties East Pakistan's religious affinities with West Pakistan had been eroded by an overwhelming sense of political denial and economic exploitation. But while the Islamic ideology of the West Pakistani-dominated military–bureaucratic state was countered by linguistic regionalism, there was no attempt to seek reunification with West Bengal. In more recent years Bangladesh, now a sovereign and independent state, has taken to reemphasizing its Islamic credentials, not so much in opposition to but in accordance with its rich cultural and linguistic heritage. Clearly then, the process by which social groups select one cultural identity out of the many they possess needs to be identified and placed in the broader political and economic context.

Consistently denied an equitable share of state resources, the eastern wing's predicament substantially worsened with the suspension of democratic processes in Pakistan. And this despite the fact that the infusion of external aid in the early sixties increased the total amount of direct central

18 Rounaq Jahan, *Pakistan: Failure in National Integration*, Dacca (second edition), 1977, pp. 62 and 106.

grants-in-aid to the province. Yet it was the centrally directed nature of public sector investments, not aggregate figures of development outlays, which explain why the provincial economy lagged behind the western wing on almost all fronts. The growth orientated strategies of economic development pursued by the military regime of Ayub Khan during the sixties widened regional disparities. East Pakistan with its lower per capita income became a handy dumping ground for over-priced and generally poor-quality West Pakistani manufactures. Even the West Pakistani-dominated planning commission was hard put to deny the accelerating pace of income disparities between the two provincial economies. The slower growth rates of the East Pakistani economy despite larger central outlays were attributed to the introduction of new agricultural technologies in West Pakistan. Efforts to explain away the causes of regional disparity to forces beyond the control of the central government met with contemptuous retorts from emotionally charged political circles in East Pakistan.

With the politics of exclusion and the economics of inequality giving impetus to the Awami League's campaign for provincial autonomy, the situation in East Pakistan did eventually slip out of the centre's control. The clash between the imperatives of the military–bureaucratic state and Bengali politics ultimately proved irreconcilable. Given the history, this was hardly an astonishing conclusion to an unhappy union. It is the scale of the atrocities which the Pakistani military high command thought fit to perpetrate in the name of preserving national integrity which will continue to astound the voices of sanity in South Asia for many generations to come.

If the creation of a Muslim homeland with no say in the future of co-religionists in India was not a political abortion of the two nation theory then the secession of Bangladesh had surely exposed the inadequacies of the Islamic adhesive in holding together Pakistan's linguistically and culturally diverse social groups. But accustomed to rewriting history, not learning its lessons, the ideological cheerleaders of the Pakistani state turned to reemphasizing the Islamic bond with renewed vigour. If it was not the fact of creeping Hinduism which had made the Bengalis indurate in the face of the Islamic appeal then the fault lay with the Pakistani state for failing to enforce religion in all walks of life. The uses made of Islam in post-1971 Pakistan have been brazen, bizarre and brutish, though not always in that order. There has been a distinct sharpening of tensions in Pakistan's remaining provinces where linguistic and cultural identities are fusing with political and economic grievances to short circuit the melting mechanisms of state-sponsored programmes of Islamization in effect since the late 1970s.

In structural terms the breakaway of the eastern wing removed the only existing obstacle to unfettered Punjabi dominance within the state structure, albeit one exercised by certain social classes hailing from the relatively better off districts in the province. Between 1955 and 1971 the western wing had been brought under one unit to obscure the distinctive identities of the less numerous linguistic groups in Sind, the NWFP and Baluchistan. Until its dismantling by the military regime of General Yahya Khan the one-unit system remained the main target of attack by all parties in West Pakistan except those directly dependent on state patronage for their political survival. In an apparent inversion of the Indian example where concessions to language were countered by continued central controls on the constituent units, the Pakistani state opted to stump linguistic regionalism by creating a single administrative system over the western wing. That the recognition by one and denial by the other produced similar results – linguistic identity has been a key issue in both countries – further underscores the importance of assessing culture with reference to the broader political and economic context.

After the loss of the Bengali majority in 1971 Punjabis constituted nearly 60 per cent of the population of Pakistan and supplied 70 per cent of the personnel of the military. Punjabis dominate the federal bureaucracy and form a large percentage of the provincial civil services and police forces in Sind and Baluchistan. Most disquietingly for the proponents of a democratic federalism, no system of weighted representation has been devised to ensure that the combined strength of the smaller provinces in the national assembly is equal to, if not greater than, that of the Punjab. For a country which made its place on the map of the world through conscientious objection to majoritarian rule and whose pre-1971 political development was based on rejecting the fact of a Bengali majority in the eastern wing, the notion of weighted representation is not nearly as far-fetched as might seem at first sight. Zulfikar Ali Bhutto might have learnt something about the plight of minorities as one of the few Sindhis with privileged access to central state authority during Ayub's regime. But then being a central politician from a non-Punjabi background has tended to be more of a handicap than an advantage in addressing tricky issues like Pakistan's federal dilemma. Superficially at least the new constitution of 1973 promulgated by Bhutto's government appeared to be responsive to the smaller provinces. It gave them equal representation with the Punjab in the senate, the upper house of a two-chamber legislature. But under the 1973 constitution the senate had no financial powers, a serious defect from the point of view of the non-Punjabi provinces marvelling at the Punjab's centrally assisted growth trajectory from the confines of Pakistan's political basement.

The 1973 constitution, nevertheless, was a potential prelude to a significant recasting of Pakistan's federal configuration. At the helm of a political party, Bhutto understandably was interested in spreading the

PPP's net of support as widely as possible. Towards that end steps were taken to increase central resource transfers to each of the four provinces. But politically inspired central handouts were no substitute for the financial autonomy demanded by the provinces. As in India, Pakistan's fiscal structure has been tipped in the centre's favour with the provinces controlling only the most inelastic sources of revenue. Recently there have been some tentative steps towards enlarging the provincial share of the centre's consolidated revenues. Yet historically, provincial dependence on the centre in Pakistan has been much greater than in India. According to one calculation, Pakistani provinces in general manage to finance under 20 per cent of their development and non-development expenditure.[19] They consequently have had to rely on various federal subsidies and financial allocations recommended by the national finance commission, the planning commission and the ministry of finance.

Pakistani provinces have sought to exploit the loopholes in the federal financial structure to their advantage. Before the changes instituted by Mian Nawaz Sharif's IDA government in 1991, one way of qualifying for greater amounts of federal revenues had been to declare deficit budgets, leaving the centre to make up the difference. During the initial years of the PPP regime this appears to have been the decided policy of the non-Punjabi provinces. By 1973–4 the Punjab too had caught on and gone into the business of declaring deficit budgets year in and year out. Fairly sophisticated doctoring of figures in the provincial secretariats of Sind, NWFP and Baluchistan by financial experts, not infrequently Punjabis, has been more detrimental for the centre than the Punjab. During the 1970s a higher percentage of the provincial revenue expenditure was being met by central resource transfers. But most of the federal revenues continued to be raised and spent in the Punjab and the industrial belt in and around the city of Karachi. Punjab is also the main beneficiary of central subsidies, concessional credit and direct public sector investments. The sectoral rather than provincial basis of the centre's development outlays disguises the full extent of the disparity in financial allocations to the provinces. Per capita income by province forms no part of the statistical juggling carried out by the planning commission. The authors of the sixth five-year plan (1983–8) went so far as to assert that 'per capita income is not a meaningful concept for areas within a country [sic]'.[20] With the Punjab leading the other provinces by a wide margin on all development indices, there can be no question that central allocations have consistently deepened inter-regional inequalities irrespective of the formal character of the regime in Islamabad.

[19] Shahid Kardar, *The Political Economy of Pakistan*, Lahore, 1987, p. 14.
[20] *The Sixth Five Year Plan: 1983–1988*, Planning Commission, Government of Pakistan, May 1983, p. 185.

Needing the support of the Punjab to remain in power, Bhutto was not prepared to push new fangled ideas of a cooperative federalism in Pakistan to his political detriment. Without the political will no constitutional document could correct the course of centre–province relations in Pakistan. But then Bhutto, while occasionally claiming to be a social democrat, never thought much of being a federalist. The provincial autonomy provisions of the 1973 constitution, like the rest of the much lauded document, were honoured more in the breach than in its observance. Once subtler political manipulations failed to consolidate the PPP's support in the two provinces where it suffered an electoral rebuff in 1970, Bhutto came out into the open against the 'anti-state' elements the military–bureaucratic state was most accustomed to dealing with. The non-PPP government in Baluchistan was unceremoniously dismissed and the one in the NWFP resigned in protest. When a full-scale tribal insurrection broke out in Baluchistan in 1973–4 Bhutto's government called in the military to put it down by force. The opportunity for a political resolution to the centre–province problem in Pakistan had been squandered in a manner that must have won Bhutto a round of applause from his strongest detractors in the highest echelons of the non-elected institutions of the state.

The federal dilemma became more acute, especially in Sind, during the eleven long years of military and quasi-military rule under General Zia-ul-Haq. In 1985 when Zia gave a civilian face to his military regime as many as 56 per cent of the posts in the federal government secretariat and related departments were held by the Punjab. Rural Sind had a mere 3 per cent, the NWFP 11 per cent, and Baluchistan about 2.5 per cent. Urban Sind, Karachi and Hyderabad in particular, consisting of Urdu-speaking Muhajirs and Punjabis, held 25 per cent of these posts. In public sector corporations Punjab had an estimated 41 per cent of the middle and senior posts, urban Sind 47 per cent, rural Sind 3.5 per cent, NWFP 6 per cent and Baluchistan a paltry 1 per cent.[21]

Since the fiscal powers of the constituent units have been extremely limited, the institutionalization of regional imbalances within the state structure gave added intensity to centre–province as well as inter-provincial tensions. These are mistakenly ascribed to cultural differences and their proneness to periodic 'ethnic' outbreaks. A closer look at each of the three non-Punjabi provinces, and the reaction to their grievances in the Punjab, suggests why 'ethnicity' as the key analytical variable distorts more than it explains the socio-economic and political discontentments which are the springboards of centre–province struggles in Pakistan.

Take the case of Baluchistan, the largest, least populated and most

---

[21] Kardar, *The Political Economy of Pakistan*, p. 11.

impoverished of the four provinces of Pakistan. It covers as much as 40 per cent of the total land mass of the country but has just over 5 per cent of the total population. Baluchistan's literacy rate is appalling even by Pakistani standards. A mere 8.5 per cent of the people are literate compared to a national average of about 30 per cent. Until its formal abolition by the PPP government in 1976, the sardari or tribal system in Baluchistan militated against the infusion of central resources for the development of the province. During the first three five-year plans total development outlays to the province were a mere Rs.25 million.[22] Per capita incomes in Baluchistan are appreciably lower than elsewhere in the country which together with the poorly developed nature of the social and physical infrastructure has forced the majority of the Baluchis to try and eke out a living in Sind and parts of the Punjab. Baluchi speakers have been reduced to a minority of about 36 per cent in a province which is also home to Pathans (25 per cent), Brahuis (21 per cent), Makranis and Lassis.

Like the Assamese the Baluch have turned their wrath against both migrants from other provinces and the central government. Despite a history of sustained opposition to central authority, British and Pakistani, Baluch nationalism has floundered on account of its tribal social structure. The bewildering multiplicity of tribal and linguistic affiliations matched by serious intra-regional economic inequities have precluded the possibility of a Baluchi directed provincial nationalism. Even if the Baluchis could forge a common front with Brahuis, Makranis and Lassis, a difficult proposition given a history of uneasy tribal co-existence, the local Pathans have had their own agendas to impress upon the Pakistani central government. Pathans dominate the civil services, trade and commerce in the province. Historically Pathan, Sindhi and Punjabi merchants have maintained a stranglehold over the commercial life of Quetta, the only really urbanized part of the province. The Ayub regime parcelled out land in the fertile agricultural tracts of the Pat Feeder area to Punjabi military and civil bureaucrats. Non-Baluchis dominate the few industries the province possesses. All eighty-five established industrial units in Baluchistan are owned by non-Baluchis. Fifty of these are located in Quetta, which has a 60 per cent Pathan population. The rest are in the Hub, a primarily non-Baluch area.

In the 1970–1 elections eight out of the twenty provincial assembly seats were bagged by Baluchi and Brahui tribal leaders belonging to the National Awami Party. It was forced to form a coalition with the Jamiat-ul-Ulema-i-Islam, whose main bases of support are in the Pathan areas. As the dominant partner in the coalition the NAP tried to push for a socio-economic pro-

[22] *The Sixth Five Year Plan, 1983–88*, p. 187.

gramme akin to the 'sons of the soil' policy in many parts of India. The NAP's plan to remove Punjabi, Sindhi and Pathan bureaucrats in Baluchistan was strongly contested by the central government. Violent opposition to the NAP's policies from within the province provided the Bhutto regime with a pretext to deploy the Pakistan military against Baluchi tribesmen – Mengals, Marris and Bugtis in particular. Fearful of the implications for Iranian Baluchistan, the Shah provided generous monetary and moral support to Islamabad. During 1973–4, army operations against the rebellious tribesmen assisted by aerial bombing delivered a crushing blow to Baluchi nationalism whose firepower proved wholly inadequate in the face of the combined might of the Pakistani and Iranian states.

With most of the Baluch nationalist leadership dead, gaoled or exiled, the centre swiftly put the finishing touches to the humbling of the province. Under Zia's military regime the centre tried coopting segments of the existing provincial elite, both Baluch and Pathan, by dangling bags of development monies. Between 1970–1 and 1982–3 there was a five-fold increase in Baluchistan's annual development plan. The sixth five-year plan for the period 1983–8 made a big play of developing the social and physical infrastructure of the province. But the gap between intention and implementation proved impossible to bridge. The plan went off the rails on account of the centre's financial troubles. Detractors of the Zia regime were unimpressed by its sudden compassion for Baluchistan. Like his predecessor and one-time patron, Zia's interest in Baluchistan flowed directly from strategic considerations. The much publicized increases in federally supported provincial development outlays were mostly aimed at defence related public sector projects. Transportation and communications were given priority in the annual development plans, especially once the Soviet invasion of Afghanistan had further heightened the strategic importance of the province.

Baluch nationalists have scoffed at the emphasis on building roads and communications facilities, which are correctly seen to be part of the centre's gameplan to extend its control over Baluchistan's inhospitable terrain. What the province needs more than anything else is the capacity to mobilize its own resources for development. Most of these end up in the hands of the federal government or are funneled out as profits by non-Baluchis engaged in commercial, agricultural and industrial activities in the province. For instance, Baluchistan produces 80 per cent of Pakistan's natural gas requirements which saves nearly Rs.8 billion annually in foreign exchange to the central exchequer. But during the 1980s Baluchistan received under Rs.0.6 billion as royalties.[23] In 1991 an award by a resurrected national finance

---

[23] Kardar, *The Political Economy of Pakistan*, pp. 9–10.

commission left the province only marginally better off in its overall share of the centre's consolidated revenues. Efforts to tap the province's rich mineral resources could do more in putting Baluchistan on the road to self-sustaining development. These characteristically have been long on rhetoric and short on implementation.

The continued retardation of Baluchistan's development potential and the creation of new pockets of wealth based on a burgeoning drug trade has contributed to a considerable polarization of the political base. Employment opportunities have been few and far between and the provincial labour force failed to partake of the Gulf bonanza in anything but the most nominal fashion. Educated Baluchi youth have been particularly trenchant in their criticisms of the Pakistani centre. Though many are sceptical of their future in a Punjabi-dominated military–bureaucratic state structure and political economy of defence, the chilling experience of the 1973–4 insurgency appears to have put the damper on Baluchi militancy for the time being. The close link between drug barons and politicians has given a new face to the politics of the province. Since the autumn of 1988 combinations of Baluch, Brahui, Pathan and other tribal sardars have sought to govern the province by offering direct or tacit support to the ruling configurations at the centre. A younger generation of tribal sardars is playing a leading role in the coalitions that have come to prominence at the provincial level. But the temporary and superficial alignment of parties at the provincial and central levels has done little to deflect attention from the growing incidence of conflict within the province. Clashes of an inter-tribal, sectarian and linguistic kind are now common occurrences. Recently a party claiming support among the Pathans and Afghan refugees in Baluchistan and the NWFP has taken to demanding the reorganization of provinces along linguistic lines with a view to achieving a Greater Pukthunkhawa or Pathan province. While the centre can take considerable comfort in the spectacle of Pathans being pitted against Baluchis, the demand has dangerous implications for the other Pakistani provinces, all of which are administrative rather than linguistically coherent units. With the continuing civil war in Afghanistan threatening Pakistan's internal stability, a linguistic reorganization of the provinces would be akin to removing the roof in the middle of a hurricane.

The idea of a greater Pathan province is unlikely to electrify the NWFP in the foreseeable future. Of the three smaller provinces, the NWFP has become better incorporated into the Pakistani state structure and political economy than the rest during the past few decades. The early threat posed by a movement for a Pakthunistan has lost potency. Despite common linguistic ties, indigenous Pathans came to resent the demands placed on the provincial economy by a sprawling population of Afghan refugees. More importantly, Pathans are represented in substantial numbers in the civil service and the army, and also in business circles, the labour force in Karachi and important service sectors like transportation and construction. About 13.5 per cent of the Pakistani population, Pathans have provided 15–20 per cent of the military personnel. A number of army and air force institutions are located in the NWFP. Unlike the Baluchis and the Sindhis, the Pathans are masters of their own fate at the provincial level with a predominant share of the civil and police services. After Generals Ayub and Yahya, president Ghulam Ishaq Khan was the most high profiled Pathan in Pakistan's history. Many key civil servants in and around the presidency were also Pathans. Some Pathans like the Hotis, the Khanzadas, General Habibullah, Gohar Ayub and the Saifullahs rank among the biggest Pakistani industrial capitalists. Substantial segments among the Pathans therefore have developed a stake in the existing status quo.

Economic benefits from participation in the national life of Pakistan have not been entirely restricted to the provincial elite alone. After the Punjab the province benefited the most from the large-scale migration of Pakistani labour to the Gulf states. Well over 0.3 million Pathans went to the Middle East and were sending back more than half a billion dollars annually to their places of origin. During the Afghan war the more enterprising and unscrupulous prospered by engaging in smuggling of foreign goods, guns and drugs. Although the NWFP lags behind Punjab and urban Sind on most indices of development, its foothold in the power structure has given the Pathans a much greater degree of self-confidence about their future in Pakistan than can be said for either the Baluchis or the indigenous inhabitants of Sind.

During the military rule of Zia-ul-Haq it was Bhutto's home province of Sind which became the main venue of provincial dissidence. There was of course a prior history of Sindhi discontents but a close examination of Sind undermines any notion that Pakistan has been in the grips of an 'ethnic' conflict. Muhajirs or Urdu-speaking refugees poured into Sind at the time of partition. Throughout the fifties, sixties and seventies, there was a constant influx of Pathans and Punjabis into Sind. Consequently, less than half of the population consists of Sindhi speakers while 22 per cent are Muhajirs who account for well over 50 per cent of the urban population. Non-Sindhis form an overwhelming majority in the main industrial concentrations. The membership of Pakistan's big business groups had initially been drawn heavily from the Memon, Bohra and Khoja trading castes from Gujarat. Of the teeming 8 million plus population of Karachi, 54.3 per cent are Muhajirs, the Sindhis are a mere 6.3 per cent and the rest are Pathans and Punjabis. Some 40 per cent of the city's population lives in urban slums, the gift of Ayub's decade of development. Large tracts of valuable Sindhi agricultural land have been granted to Punjabi military and civilian officials. As much as 60 per cent of Sind's population, mostly rural *haris* or tenants, are thought to languish quietly below the poverty line. The Sindhis did not benefit from the Middle East bonanza of the late 1970s and 1980s. The civil bureaucracy in the province is largely non-Sindhi as is the police. And of course the judicial murder of Bhutto in 1979 provided Sindhis with a martyr.

While in office Bhutto had channelled more development resources into Sind – excluding Karachi – than any previous regime in Pakistan's history. Even Sindhi middle-class opponents of the PPP conceded that Bhutto's policies had generated employment in the province. They were particularly delighted with the 1972 decision to make Sindhi the sole official language of the province. The policy was in counterdistinction to that in other provinces where Urdu was the official language of governmental communication. Violent language riots between Sindhi and Urdu speakers in key urban areas were an early sign of the seething hatred which was to grip the two linguistic groups in the eighties. Sensing the volatility of the situation Bhutto intervened by issuing an ordinance superseding the Sindhi language act. For the next twelve years no one eligible for employment in the provincial civil service was to be discriminated against simply on account of an inability to communicate in either Sindhi or Urdu. Despite the dilution of a policy which symbolized their deep-seated resentments against refugee settlers, Sindhi speakers had reason to be grateful to Bhutto. During the PPP era many Sindhis secured employment in the provincial civil service to the dismay of the Muhajirs who ever since the Ayub era had been in tough competition with Punjabis and Pathans for jobs in the public and the private sectors.

After Zia's coup Sindhi recruits to the provincial civil service were dismissed on the grounds that they were political appointees. By February 1978 some 1,746 Sindhis had been thrown out of the provincial service. Indigenous Sindhis who constitute no more than 2 per cent of the armed forces and a mere 5 per cent of the federal service control 500 out of some 2,000 industrial units in the province. Punjabi and Urdu-speaking Muhajirs not only dominate the wholesale and retail trade but also transportation, credit and construction services in the province. Punjabi civil and military officials were also the main beneficiaries of government largesse in the distribution of agricultural and urban land. So it is easy to traverse the depths of Sindhi antipathy towards the Zia regime which frankly projected the interests of a non-Sindhi military–bureaucratic–industrial alliance.

Rural Sind was transformed during the 1980s into a cauldron of discontent. In 1983 a Sindhi uprising was put down by the armed might of the state. In urban Sind where Sindhi speakers are heavily outnumbered by

Urdu-speaking Muhajirs and other linguistic groups, the Muhajir Qaumi Movement made a meteoric entry into Pakistan's political landscape. The MQM was formed in March 1984. Beginning its career as the All-Pakistan Muhajir Students Organization, it demanded recognition for the Muhajirs as a fifth nationality in Pakistan at a time when the political process was held in abeyance by a military regime which deemed the articulation of sectional interests to be less dangerous than the growth of a nationally based political party. With a highly disciplined semi-fascistic organization, the MQM eclipsed the religious parties like the Jamat-i-Islami on the Karachi political horizon. During the latter half of the 1980s the urban centres of Sind, particularly Karachi and Hyderabad, became battle zones for ferocious conflicts between well armed rival linguistic communities. Drug mafias operating under the umbrella of the national logistical cell of the army and its intelligence wing, the ISI, are believed to have extended monetary support to the competing groups. During the eighties riots erupted between Muhajirs and Pathans, Muhajirs and Punjabis and Muhajirs and Sindhis. Although the Sindhi–Muhajir dimension has received more attention of late, the struggle between Punjabis and Muhajirs over the spoils of the political economy and the state may well be the structurally more significant conflict.[24]

Rural Sind's disenchantment with the military–bureaucratic state of Pakistan was reflected in the sweeping victory of Benazir Bhutto's PPP in the elections of 1988. The MQM captured most of the seats in urban Sind and extended support to the PPP government at the centre. IDA-ruled Punjab was cast into the unprecedented role of opposing the federal government. The PPP and the MQM failed to work out a modus vivendi in Sind, and a reign of anarchy descended on the rural and the urban areas of the province. Dacoities, kidnappings, murders and armed encounters with the security forces became the order of the day. The situation in the rural areas remained substantially unchanged following Benazir's dismissal in August 1990 and the installation after the October elections of an MQM–IDA coalition government in the province. Until the death of Sind's chief minister, Jam Sadiq Ali, a systematic campaign was carried out against the PPP supporters in the province. Jam simultaneously used the attractions of state patronage to win over many of the PPP's more influential supporters among Sindhi landlords and religious leaders. But with many of these elements protecting the dacoits, Jam's political coup against Benazir did not restore the sanctity of life and property in the province. The provincial police force itself appeared as a den of dacoits. If not directly involved with

---

[24] For different perspectives on the current problems in Sindh see A. Akbar Zaidi (ed.), *Regional Imbalances and the National Question in Pakistan*, Lahore, 1992.

the dacoits, the Sind police eagerly took to extorting monies from both criminals and victims.

Jam's failure to rectify a deteriorating law and order situation was a serious source of worry to a federal government desperately seeking foreign investments to revive the national economy. In June 1992 following Jam's death and a series of murders and kidnappings of businessmen as well as foreign nationals, the army high command took matters in hand. The decision of the chief of army staff General Asif Nawaz Janjua to target the MQM strongholds in Karachi gave the operation a semblance of non-partisanship which was imperative in the highly polarized and volatile situation pertaining in Sind. Although the new chief of army staff, General Abdul Waheed Kakar, vowed to continue with the policy of neutrality, the problems of Sind still await a political resolution.

Only an erroneous reading of the macabre developments in Sind can lead to the conclusion that the problem is the result of 'ethnic' conflict with secession as the obvious goal. While prolonged political denial matched by unmitigated economic deprivation stung the Sindhis into challenging the military–bureaucratic state structure's exclusionary policies, many voted for inclusion through the ballot box in the 1988 and the 1990 elections. Secession has been the goal of a marginal fringe in Sind politics led by the veteran politician G. M. Syed, who having spent the better part of his life under house arrest understandably sees no future in Pakistan. But in an ironic twist to the politics of the province, many of Syed's diehard supporters joined forces with the IDA's hatchet man, Jam Sadiq Ali, and the MQM to try and obliterate the PPP in the rural areas of the province. Realpolitik, not ethnic discord, has been the propelling factor in the alignment of political forces in Sind. Eleven years of military rule left an indelible mark on the province, sharpening the problems of both urbanization and rural deprivation. The menace of a parallel arms and drugs economy has been the cause, not the product, of conflict among the various linguistic groups in the province. Monetary rewards on offer from drug barons and the merchants of death have put a premium on perpetuating civil uncertainty in Sind. The administrative and police services are in a state of disgrace, made the worse by the high-handed interference of politicians many of whom are in open complicity with criminal elements on both sides of the linguistic divide. And while the underlying causes of Sind's slow death are undeniably political and economic in nature, traceable to a most inequitable state structure, it would be a travesty of history to view its would-be rebels come lately as the harbingers of a more equitable and just social order.

This is not to suggest that military bayonets will be sufficient to root out the ills that have come to beset Sind and, consequently, Pakistan as a whole. The death and displacement of Punjabi settlers in Sind is portentous for

Pakistan's future federal balance. Many Punjabis have reacted angrily to Sindhis and Muhajirs couching their disillusionments in more and more improbable idioms of difference. Attempts to stir up a Punjabi backlash by the more chauvinistic elements in that province have so far failed to materialize. Punjabi supremacy is as yet an alien concept for those denied direct access to the state. The main beneficiary of a military–bureaucratic dominated state structure and political economy of defence, the Punjab has large pockets of underprivilege which have suffered quite as much as their opposite numbers in the smaller provinces from political denial and economic deprivation under extended periods of overt authoritarianism. But Punjabi bashing, be it by Sindhis or Muhajirs, is unlikely to pass without a response. The ultimate tragedy of Pakistan's political development will be enacted when the underprivileged in the majority province become the cannon fodder at the command of the institutionalized structures of political and economic privilege to blast unempowered non-Punjabis into submission.

Whether Pakistan can avoid such a fate is as yet unclear. In the formal political arenas of Pakistan the Punjabi-dominated IDA had succeeded in 1990 in forming governments not only at the federal level but also in all of the provinces. Much publicity attended the IDA government's success in getting all the provinces to agree to the national finance commission's allocation of federal revenues to provinces according to population. But the award skirted around the uneven needs and capacities of the provinces and came under bitter attack by non-IDA parties in all the provinces. Most significant was the virtual revolt by the IDA government in the NWFP which accused the central government of reducing the province's share of federal finances by scrapping the practice of special subventions to backward areas. In another attempt to redress long-standing tensions in interprovincial relations, the IDA government at the centre signed an accord with all the provinces for the distribution of the Indus river's water resources. This too failed to meet the criteria of each province's individual needs and capacities. It is consequently insensitive to the inequality of results which has been at the heart of inter-regional and intra-regional disparities in Pakistan.

Conscious of the disruptive power of linguistic regionalism, the centre has yet to devise a sound formula for redressing the manifold structural problems within the Pakistani state and the political economy. Neither of the agreements claimed as the crowning achievement of the IDA government in the sphere of federal relations comes close to addressing the causes of disaffections and discontentments in Sind and also Baluchistan to the satisfaction of the various linguistic groups constituting them. The military–bureaucratic–industrial axis at the federal centre and a concordat of industrial and landed magnates at the provincial level might provide the gloss of stability. Yet so long as regional inequities persist within the state structure and vast sections of the poor in provinces like Sind and Baluchistan remain unempowered, Pakistan's federal dilemma will continue to bedevil the future of the country.

Conclusion

What this enquiry into the federal equations in India and Pakistan has revealed is just how inappropriate the existing state structures have proven to be in accommodating multiple social identities in a context shaped by regional diversities and inequities. The interplay of culture as process with structures of states and political economy in both countries has accentuated the lines of difference as disenchanted social groups have met with little success in redressing their grievances in the formal arenas of politics. Despite the formally democratic and military authoritarian character of the Indian and the Pakistani states respectively, processes of inclusion and exclusion have been the more important factor in determining the frequency and intensity of regional and sub-regional dissidence. Indian political democracy tainted by authoritarian strains within the state structure has alternated between inclusionary and exclusionary policies to contain fissiparous tendencies. Military authoritarianism in Pakistan for its part has sought to coopt provinces by extending differential state patronage to fractions of regional and sub-regional elites. Turning on the coercive powers of centralized states has always been an option of ultimate resort in particularly intractable cases in both India and Pakistan. The results have not been dramatically different.

Until the 1980s the holding of elections at regular intervals together with the right of free speech and an autonomous press and judiciary distinguished Indian federalism from its Pakistani counterpart. The Indian centre occasionally earned a reprieve from insistent centrifugal pressures as regional parties moderated their stance in power or so discredited themselves as to be voted out by the electorate. But more recently elections when held have either been rigged or boycotted in states witnessing the more extreme forms of regional dissidence. The consequent loss of credibility suffered by Indian democracy has tarnished its image of superiority to state controlled electoral exercises performed in Pakistan. In the 1990s 'democratic' India has unleashed military and para-military repression on recalcitrant regions on an even bigger scale than 'authoritarian' Pakistan.

So in the state's attitude towards regional aspirations there has been little qualitative difference between formally democratic India and military dominated Pakistan. Both are characterized by the lack of equitable or effective representation of constituent units at the centre as well as the absence of a judicious measure of financial and administrative decentralization. The longer history of India's formal democracy has enabled its regional political economies and electoral processes to maintain greater resilience against central interference. Pakistan's regional social and economic formations by contrast have been more amenable to political manipulation by a military–bureaucratic dominated centre. This leaves more space at the margins in India for centre–region tensions to be tackled through a dynamic process of bargaining and negotiation. In Pakistan there appears to be less room for manoeuvre between the hard choices of cooptation on the centre's terms or costly anti-state defiance.

That the combination of structural constraints is less formidable in India offers no guarantee that its state managers will demonstrate more political will and imagination than their counterparts in Pakistan in accommodating multiple identities and regionally articulated aspirations. So long as the ruling configurations in both countries are more concerned with retaining the features of centralized authority than strengthening the rights of citizenship at the social base, the imperative of alliance building with dominant regional forces will continue to result in a notional federalism devoid of the substance of democracy. The spectre of violent conflict looms equally large in both countries. After all an easing, if not long-term resolution, of South Asia's centre–region contradictions can only take place in the context of a fundamental renegotiation of state–civil society relations. With states increasingly inclined to enhance and deploy coercive power to fend off threats from turbulent regions, federalism in South Asia has turned out to be little more than a façade despite the recurrent resort and recent return to formal democratic processes in India and Pakistan respectively.

6 Societies, cultures and ideologies: hybrids in contrived monoliths

Threading the intricacies of multiple social, cultural and ideological meanings informing subcontinental South Asian states and politics is a task befitting a team of artful tapestry makers. Subcontinental societies in their varied regional and sub-regional cultural and ideological hues defy unidimensional patterning onto neat seamless folds. At each step in their historical evolution they have devised their own modes of resistance, both passive and active, to the dominant frames within which centralized states have sought to embroider a coherent national identity. Partly expressed in the dialectic of state and political processes, social dynamics at the regional and local levels also need to be decoded in terms of their own relatively autonomous, if never wholly insular, cultural and ideological idioms. Neither static nor unchanging, these represent the hybrid and improvised responses of different social formations to the centralized state's efforts at constructing and imposing monolithic cultural and ideological meanings.

The dialogue between state and societal cultural and ideological semantics waxes and wanes according to the level of political and economic incorporation of specific regions. But at no stage does it fade away to establish the omnipotence of state-sponsored symbols and meanings. Resistance to the dominant discourse promoted by the state has been an immutable feature of South Asian societies and psyches. Shaped in overlapping realms of the public and the private, these contestations have given cultural processes a certain measure of autonomy from the state, even as they are influenced by the larger political and economic context. True of the colonial era, it has been equally so in the post-colonial period where inclusionary ideologies, whether secular or religious, articulated by nationalist leaders have in conjunction with state power attempted to use culture as a means of establishing legitimacy as well as social control. The choice of which cultural strands to project as authentically national has depended on the ideological agendas of the leadership. Insofar as these agendas have been set by the extent of their following and stature, societal diversities have played a role in the construction of national monoliths. But monoliths once in place seek to contain, if not obscure, the fact of diversities. The uneasy co-existence of inherently hybrid cultural and ideological meanings with monolithic idioms has given a unique accent to the evolving dialectic between subcontinental states and societies.

It is one which can best be deciphered by looking at some of the key organizational principles of subcontinental societies, the cultural and ideological variations they display, and the ways in which they have fashioned and in turn been refashioned by structures of states and political economies. Despite their multiple diversities, societies in the subcontinent historically have shared certain broad features to make comparison permissible without losing sight of the specificities which distinguish region from region and one form of social grouping from the other. Inevitably selective in scope the analysis of social formations will then consider the role of locally and regionally defined cultures and ideologies in the plural before turning to uncover the interplay between them and state orchestrated national culture and ideology in the singular.

Interpreting subcontinental social mosaics

Spatial location and the affinities of language have been the most important defining features in subcontinental diversities. But within each space and linguistic grouping a complex set of social relations provides the individual with additional sources of identification. Three stand out in particular: those of caste, class and community. Caste and class might form the social bases of linguistic community in a generic sense. But in the subcontinental context community has come to acquire a rather special connotation. It refers primarily, if not exclusively, to the religious bond. Caste is on the one hand a unique feature of the Hindu social order but on the other has significant undertones in Muslim, Sikh and even Christian social hierarchies. In parts of north-western India and Pakistan, clan or *biraderi* patrilineal kinship ties rather than caste form an important strand in social networks. Caste and class are in one sense diametrically opposed social categories and in another they overlap to a considerable degree. The community of religion binds the followers in an overarching solidarity, both ritual and doctrinal, but is frequently undercut by identities along caste, class, clan and linguistic lines. To select one of several as the main organizational principle of subcontinental societies is to obfuscate the manifold ways in which all interact and balance one another. Castes, clans, classes and communities in their various permutations and combinations together constitute the subcontinental social mosaics that it is the purpose here to define and interpret.

A comparative exercise in analysing the cultural idioms and social ideologies of domination and resistance can best be launched by placing the spotlight on the caste–class and clan–class dialectics within linguistically defined spaces or regions in India and Pakistan. The state in both countries has had to take normative ideological stands vis-à-vis structures and ideologies of hierarchy at the societal level. No social institution or ideology of hierarchy has mesmerized anthropologists and sociologists more than the Indian caste system. Recent historical scholarship has clarified, however, that the Indian caste system in the singular was largely a late nineteenth-century colonial reinvention of tradition.

This is not to suggest that caste was an artifact of colonial imaginings. The caste system in its pristine form was elaborated in the Vedic age, roughly lasting from 1500 to 800 B.C. The *Rig Veda* delineates four major castes by *varna* which literally means colour. At the top of the hierarchy are the Brahmins – the priestly or sacerdotal elite – followed by the Kshatriyas – the warrior castes. The third caste, the Vaishyas, are often misinterpreted in recent times to be confined to trading groups when in fact they were meant to include a wide range of people, including agriculturists, traders and cattle raisers. At the bottom of the hierarchical system are the Shudras or the menial labourers. The Shudras themselves became differentiated between superior and inferior. Discrimination against the Shudras by the other castes was in turn practised by the superior Shudras against those who were considered to be impure by virtue of their social occupations. The latter were ostracized from the *varna* system altogether and constitute the bulk of the scheduled castes of today.

While deriving religious sanction from Hindu scriptures, caste by *varna* has hardly ever provided an accurate representation of sociological facts. The four major castes serve primarily as points of reference to define the status of numerous social groupings by *jati* which locks people into occupational categories defined by birth. Contrary to common perceptions, levels of mobility for *jatis* have never been static or unchanging. Castes by *jati* are usually bounded by localities and have different nomenclatures in different parts of India. The enormous variety and highly localized character of *jati* affiliations makes generalizations about a caste grouping in a regional or even a sub-regional setting a hazardous enterprise.

This is one reason why caste by *varna* has become a convenient shorthand for a social system which fascinates even as it befuddles the uninitiated. While caste has been an important indigenous classificatory scheme, Indians have never defined nor divided up their social universe exclusively in terms of caste. There are innumerable local terms in usage of a class character. For instance, in every regional Indian language there are terms for sharecropper, labourer, small peasant, rich peasant, landlord, money-lender and so forth. Like the colonial rulers, investigators of Indian society have been so enamoured by caste that they have paid insufficient attention to the classification of Indian society on schemes other than caste. It is possible, however, in interpreting Indian society in the contemporary period to find a caste and class nexus. The two categories do not overlap completely but in many areas they exhibit a broad congruence of structures. Social discrimination by caste and economic oppression by class in many instances go hand in hand even if there is no neat fit between these two distinct structures. Put somewhat differently, there are important class oppositions and inequalities in Indian regional and sub-regional formations which tend to get articulated along caste lines. It is not caste of age-old tradition but caste as linked to historically changing class-based social relations of production and exploitation which gives it the centrality it appears to enjoy in India's regionally defined cultural and political formations.

Historically, caste boundaries approximating the four-tiered *varna* system have been rather more marked in the northern than in the southern parts of India. For instance, in rural northern India there are Brahmins and Rajput Thakurs – the latter are clan as much as caste-based – who are mostly drawn from the upper landed strata. Kurmis, Ahirs and Yadavs are the middling castes, or the so-called 'clean' agricultural castes, and are more often than not middling farmers and peasants. Chamars and Pasis are the lowest castes and swell the ranks of landless labourers. These were the sorts of downtrodden castes that were referred to by Gandhi as Harijans, or children of God, and have come to be known as scheduled castes in the terminology of the Indian constitution. In southern India, however, there are only three distinguishable castes – the Brahmins, the non-Brahmins and the scheduled castes and tribes. Previously Brahmins, a mere 3 per cent of the population, dominated the government services and cultural life of the south. Since the 1920s non-Brahmin movements have contributed to the steady etiolation of Brahmin dominance, thus narrowing over time the arena of conflict between the upper castes in the south. Except in matters concerning marriage and commensality, caste has a relatively weaker hold in West Bengal and the north-eastern states where class, linguistic and regional loyalties are much stronger. Despite immense regional variations in the caste system it is commonplace to view India as the bastion of Brahmins, Thakurs and a handful of others known as the forward castes. Although about 17.6 per cent of the total population, the forward castes exercise a disproportionate measure of political and economic power. Brahmins constitute a mere 5.5 per cent of the total population of India but with 37.6 per cent as their share form the largest single caste grouping in the prestigious IAS. During the eighties upper castes, including those castes by *jati* claiming Kshatriya and Vaishya *varna* rank, accounted for 68 per cent of the IAS posts and also cornered most of the top jobs in the public and private sectors. Scheduled castes and tribes are about 28 per cent of the population but are hopelessly underrepresented in government service. And this despite the policy of protective discrimination which allocates 15 and 7.5 per cent respectively of the openings in the IAS to scheduled castes and tribes. In between these two layers are an estimated 3,000 to 4,000 intermediate castes by *jati*, known as the other backward castes or OBCs, which comprise nearly 43.7 per cent of the Indian population.

All three caste layers are divided into different linguistic and cultural groups, further distinguished by economic standing. Not all members of the forward castes are rich just as there are speckles of wealth among the scheduled castes even as they may continue to suffer the common stigma of social inferiority with their less well off caste fellows. The so-called other backward castes are in many regions the better off farmers and peasant proprietors who benefited from *zamindari* abolition in the fifties. While economic prosperity and improved social standing has led to the political mobilization and ensuing empowerment of the OBCs in certain states, they are like the top and the bottom levels of the caste pile far too numerous and diffuse to permit any valid generalization about their preferred cultural or ideological idioms.

But if regional, linguistic, economic and cultural variations discount the possibility of treating caste equations on an all-India scale, why does caste play such a major role in Indian political discourse? Here the role of the colonial and the post-colonial state is of great relevance. It was the state that invested caste, which possessed varying degrees of social importance in different regions, with a measure of all-India political significance. British census enumeration in the nineteenth century led to a rank ordering of regional and sub-regional caste affiliations by *jati*. The chosen categorization of Indian society provoked a rash of caste movements claiming higher status in a manner not wholly dissimilar to the politics of Muslims following the granting of separate electorates in the early twentieth century. By the same token, the colonial policy of establishing special quotas for the 'backward' or 'depressed' castes, as the untouchables were referred to by British officialdom, created a certain vested interest in backwardness. As in the case of the Muslims, the compartmentalization of social groupings according to specific criteria contributed to a welter of contradictions. Claims of economic backwardness tended to be matched by assertions of higher caste status. So many lowly castes foreswore 'unclean' practices and by claiming to have become Sanskritized demanded higher caste status. Many claimed Brahmin or Kshatriya status; others simply switched to more high sounding names. Declaring themselves to be Kshatriyas was both a cultural and ideological act of protest against a hierarchical Brahminical system as well as a way of asserting a higher status within it – a tactic which served to legitimize an inherently unjust but at the same time relatively accommodative social order. There are innumerable examples where upwardly mobile as well as economically underprivileged castes rewrote their caste histories to qualify for higher ritual status. In the absence of an institutionalized priesthood, much less doctrinal uniformity, Hinduism as a historical phenomenon was able to accommodate movements of social protest at the regional and sub-regional levels. These more often than not sought to challenge the structures of hierarchy by appropriating and, subsequently, recasting some of its main idioms. Only in very rare instances did acts of protest and resistance result in the construction of cultural and ideological idioms that fell outside the pale of Hinduism altogether.

The British policy of distributing differential patronage to certain castes and communities gave impetus to the supra-local organization of these groups. By far the most far-reaching change in this direction came in the conglomeration of a large number of local untouchable castes into the category of depressed classes. One of the ablest and most influential leaders of the untouchables in the late colonial period was B. R. Ambedkar who belonged to the Mahar caste of Maharashtra. He mobilized his caste brethren to take advantage of the educational opportunities and political reservations offered by the colonial state. Ambedkar made searing attacks against the Brahminical social order in his political and philosophical writings. Gandhi countered Ambedkar's appeal by condemning the practice of untouchability but upholding the *varna*-based caste hierarchy as an organic part of Hindu society. In the Mahatma's view the untouchables performed functions intrinsic for the self-perpetuation of the Hindu social order which only needed to alter its views of their ritual impurity. This ideological justification of *varna* hierarchy was later accompanied by Gandhi's refusal to countenance separate electorates for the depressed classes, the latter-day scheduled castes, during the constitutional negotiations leading to the government of India act of 1935. By threatening to fast unto death Gandhi succeeded in bringing Ambedkar around to the idea of dropping separate electorates and instead accepting adequate reservations in elective bodies for the scheduled castes. Ambedkar's cooptation within the nationalist mainstream, however, remained more symbolic than actual. Although he played a major part in the drafting of the constitution, Ambedkar persisted with his tirades against the caste system which he declared had to be abolished if India was to make a genuine advance towards political democracy. In the 1950s Ambedkar, put off by the Congress leadership's lack of commitment to social reform, called upon the Mahars to convert to Buddhism.

Fears of untouchables converting to other religions was deeply ingrained in Hindu upper-caste psyches. This was why Gandhi had fought tooth and nail against the British attempt to grant separate electorates to the scheduled castes. The strategy was consistent with the emerging nationalist paradigm of a single nation, cutting across differences along caste, class, religious, linguistic and regional lines. Two main strands informed this construction aimed at presenting a joint front against colonialism. One based itself on reinterpretations of the Hindu cultural tradition whose assumed historic universality allowed for the blending of differences into overarching unities. It mattered little whether the ideologues could substantiate their claims of Hinduism's universality in history. Reference to scriptural and mythological texts as well as theoretical political tracts strove to give credence to the idea of an Indian nation resting on shared cultural symbols. An integral part of the ideological repertoire of late nineteenth-century nationalists, this strand was given a much longer lease of life and connected to popular Hindu religious symbols by Gandhi's invocation of the post-independence utopia, *Ram Rajya*. While the meanings and interpretations of this utopian vision varied greatly across regions, castes and classes, it provided a useful umbrella for shielding differences, spurring mass mobilization and projecting a semblance of cultural unity against an alien power.

The second strand derived from the secular ideas and ideals of European nationalism and while minimizing evocations of a universal Hindu cultural unity also denied the fact of cultural difference and distinctiveness, especially along religious lines. Even those who acknowledged the reality of social identities at least partly fashioned along lines of religious affiliation advocated cross-communal political alliances for the present in the expectation that other common social and economic interests would erase communally based contradictions in the long run. A secular nationalist like Jawaharlal Nehru was ideologically disinclined to concede the existence of a distinct Muslim cultural identity. He had looked through the telescope, he once declared, to spot Hindu–Muslim differences but had been unable to see any. Yet ironically, once he rose to the pinnacle of political power, the Pandit's telescopic view assumed a convenient myopia towards an ostensibly religiously determined division of the subcontinent. As prime minister after 1947 he presided over a state spouting a rigidly secular ideology co-existing with crucial regional and sub-regional political arenas in which an implicit, if not explicit, Hindu communalism remained a potent force. So political ideology in post-independence India was articulated at multiple levels. The secular garb worn by the centre did not extend over the various layers of Indian polities where Hindu communalism continued to be an important strategy in the attempt to blunt the edge of caste and class conflicts.

The post-independence Indian state declared itself to be committed to the principle of equality and firmly set against discrimination on grounds of religious or caste affiliation. Yet given the contradictory nature of the nationalist legacy, clarity of intent was matched by ambiguity of policy. Separate electorates for Muslims were scrapped, drawing only muffled murmurs of protest from the few remaining stalwarts of a greatly weakened and discredited All-India Muslim League. The dismantling of institutionalized sanctions against Muslim participation in mainstream electoral politics was consistent with a brand of secularism which considered dilution, if not the actual disavowal, of religious identity to be a logical extension of allegiance to the 'nation'. By equating secular and nationalist credentials, the post-colonial Indian state in effect delegitimized the expression of minority fears and aspirations in an idiom other than that dictating its version of secular-nationalism. While guaranteeing the constitutional freedom to practice one's faith, Indian secular-nationalism made it easy to misconstrue concern for one's religious community as disloyalty to the nation. So a policy, manifestly designed to bring India's religious minorities into the nationalist mainstream, barred them from nurturing their multiple identities in a unitary, secular nation-state.

When it came to taking a stand on the disabilities of caste, the Indian state equivocated between outlawing untouchability and providing the framework for its perpetuation. Part of the problem, of course, lies in the very concept of equality, a complex jumble of meanings with contrary implications. At its simplest, equality rejects all distinctions irrespective of differences in capability. But given the existence of uneven capabilities among individuals and social groups a simple application of the principle of equality can only lead to inequality of result. Sensitivity towards unequal capabilities, however, demands an inequality of approach which undermines the notion of equality of opportunity without distinction.

The clash between these two quite different conceptions of equality is writ large in the Indian state's policies of affirmative action or, more accurately, protective discrimination. Undertaking to protect those who in its view had been discriminated against in the past was not a matter of moral judgement alone. It entailed striking a delicate balance between two conflicting interests – those whose relatively privileged position predisposed them to demanding equality of opportunity and those like the untouchables who needed compensation for their unequal capabilities derived from longstanding social and economic deprivations. With as many as 78 per cent of the members of the constituent assembly drawn from the upper castes, the Indian state opted for the path of least resistance. The constitutional document incorporated the notion of equal opportunity in the fundamental rights section and compensatory or protective discrimination in the directive principles of state policy which are not justiciable in any court of law. Article 16 of the constitution qualifies the equal opportunity provision in the fundamental rights by including special provisions for the scheduled castes and tribes, Harijans and Adivasis in popular parlance. The adoption of protective discrimination as state policy has entailed the reservation of jobs in government, seats in legislatures and places in universities for members of the scheduled castes and tribes, that is the historically disadvantaged castes and tribes listed in the relevant sections of the Indian constitution. A constituent assembly that had firmly rejected the principle of separate electorates and reservations for religious minorities on grounds of the state's secular ideology had no hesitation extending safeguards to those whose caste status placed them at the bottom of the Hindu social pyramid.

The contradiction between the state's secular ideology and a definition of disadvantage based on location within the Brahminical social order was only one among many. Assurances of equal opportunity in the fundamental rights provisions have remained at odds with the protective discrimination provided by the directive principles of state policy. The fundamental rights are guarantees to individual citizens while the directive principles offer special consideration to groups or certain classes of citizens. By treating inequality in aggregate terms the policy of protective discrimination makes no allowance for the relative inequality and poverty of individuals, women, children and the elderly for instance, within disadvantaged social groups. With the spread of capitalist relations of production more and more women, especially from the scheduled castes and tribes, have been seeking employment outside the home. Often engaged in strenuous and laborious tasks these women at the bottom of the economic pile are usually paid lower wages than men and denied basic employment benefits. The redressal of disadvantage based on caste and community affiliations prevents the rectification of inequalities along lines of gender and generation, particularly at the lower rungs of the social order. The more so since the policy encourages the construction and articulation of caste identities, giving a nebulous secular ideological cover to a social system which despite its relevance in regional and sub-regional contexts is rooted in Brahminical conceptions of the Hindu religion. By strengthening the solidarities of caste, the constitutional provisions unwittingly reproduce rather than eliminate the structural conditions of social and economic marginality in India.

Moreover, legal provisions in themselves do not actuate processes of effective implementation. While compensatory discrimination has allowed for a limited measure of redistribution through greater representation of the better placed members of the scheduled castes and tribes in legislatures, both at the centre and the states, governmental employment and educational institutions, it has been more than offset by the lingering stigma of untouchability at the social level. Access to education, government employment and state patronage based on reservations may in fact have hampered rather than strengthened the autonomy of the more privileged and talented members of the scheduled castes and tribes. Reservations of seats in legislatures, both at the centre and in the states, for the scheduled castes and tribes are based on population proportions but have to be filled by votes cast by general electorates. The scheduled tribes are relatively more concentrated in constituencies specifically reserved for them. But the scheduled castes are far more dispersed geographically with the result that in 1962 they did not constitute a majority in any of the reserved constituencies and formed 30 per cent of the population in only thirteen. What this means is that candidates from the scheduled castes and tribes have to seek the support of political parties, often with platforms appealing to caste interests that are diametrically opposed to their own. So despite the reservation of seats in the Lok Sabha and the state assemblies it is arguable whether elected representatives of the scheduled caste and tribes are free agents capable of advancing the interests of their main constituents. Similarly, the advantages of job reservations in government service so far have been limited in their impact. The beneficiaries of reservations have had to reckon with the resentment of not only fellow employees but also overseers on whose good will their placement and promotion prospects squarely rest. In any case, quotas apply to current appointments rather than available posts and, consequently, the representation of the scheduled castes and tribes has been well below the prescribed level of reservations. The prospect of reserved jobs has no doubt encouraged more members of the scheduled castes and tribes to secure an education. But arguably, many have responded to the challenge with less rigour than might be expected of those anticipating stiff competition at the tail end of a school, college or university education. And predictably women, while savouring the advancement of some of their caste fellows, have seen no improvement and even a deterioration in employment prospects and working conditions.

If the impact of compensatory discrimination at the very best has been uncertain, it continues to elicit implacable opposition from those excluded from the scheme of reservations. This has been most pronounced in the case of the so-called backward castes or classes who have been clamouring for special treatment ever since the promulgation of the Indian constitution. Apart from the scheduled castes and tribes, articles 15 and 16 of the constitution mention other backward classes as the third category deserving special consideration by the state. The problem of formulating an objective method to gauge backwardness, which unlike 'untouchability' was open to varied interpretations, delayed the granting of reservations at an all-India level. It was as early as 1953 that the central government set up a backward classes commission. Though expressing misgivings about using caste as the basis of identifying backwardness the commission in its report of 1955 listed well over two thousand castes as socially and economically disadvantaged. The report was rejected by the Nehru government on the grounds that its measure of backwardness was neither objective nor convincing.

Letting the matter rest suited the upper caste, and particularly Brahmin, dominated elected and non-elected institutions at the central level. But the Indian state's ambivalent attitude towards historically disadvantaged social groups defined in terms of caste had served to create arenas of virulent social conflict at all levels of the different regional political economies. While successive Congress central governments sat on the fence, many states on their own initiative adopted reservations in response to organized demands by economically and politically powerful backward castes and classes for protection against social discrimination. This process was more marked in the southern states where non-Brahmin or anti-Brahmin social movements were particularly strong. In many northern states, by contrast, society at the local and regional levels was permeated by caste-based ideologies of domination and control. An air of arrogant superiority was not just the monopoly of castes such as the Bhumihar Brahmins and the Rajput Thakurs of the Gangetic plain but also of agricultural castes such as the Patidar rich peasants of Gujarat that had been enjoying a measure of upward mobility since the days of the nationalist movement in the 1920s and 1930s. Throughout India's post-independence history the central state's equivocal normative position on equality had to contend with caste-based ideologies of hierarchy deeply embedded in local and regional cultures. Ill-defined policies of protective discrimination stood little chance on their own of achieving the kind of compensatory equality that was loudly avouched as a crucial component of state ideology. It was only in regions where some impetus came from below in the form of anti-upper caste social reform movements that the hiatus between the Indian state's normative position and regional social reality narrowed in any significant measure. The denting of Brahminical dominance by intermediate social groups did not denote the victory of the downtrodden castes and classes. It merely enhanced the power of those claiming to be the other backward castes and classes. The Indian state's ideological promise to redress historical disadvantage along caste lines was turned to good advantage by groups who were well placed and skilful enough to borrow that idiom at the level of regional social formations.

By the seventies most of the southern states had adopted policies of reservations for backward castes in government and educational institutions. This was a symptom of the growing electoral and political importance of backward castes, organized into associations seeking to deploy the fact of social disadvantage within the Brahminical system into an ideological rallying cry for the mobilization of their caste fellows cutting across class differences. The ability of state governments in the south to introduce reservations had much to do with the politics of accommodation worked out between the forward and the backward classes. In other words, reservations in the south did not aim to displace the forward castes, many of whom had emerged from the landowning Shudra peasantry, so much as to secure the political cooptation of the backward castes. By contrast, the sharper lines of division between upper and intermediate castes in the north led to violent agitations and clashes against all attempts to implement reservation policies for the backward castes. This was especially true for Bihar and UP where the Congress relied on the support of the upper and the lower castes to parry the rising challenge of the backward castes. Playing the two ends of the social spectrum against the middle had worked reasonably well for the Congress until 1977 when the Janata party, drawing support from agriculturally dominant backward castes in northern India, trumped the premier national party at the hustings.

The formation of a new backward caste commission in 1978 headed by B. P. Mandal indicated the growing ability of the middling agricultural castes in north India's regional political economy to directly influence the centre stage of politics. Caste was made an explicit criterion of the commission's recommendations for reservations. As many as 3,248 castes or communities constituting 52.4 per cent of the total population were identified as backward. But by the time the commission's report was presented to parliament, the Congress under Indira Gandhi had regained the saddle to make sure that the document gathered more dust than mileage. In 1989 the victory of the Janata Dal under V. P. Singh provided an opening for the advocates of reservations for other backward castes. Needing to strengthen his political constituency in the face of mounting pressures from Hindu right-wing forces led by the Bharatiya Janata Party and also his own lieutenant Devi Lal, the leader of the Jat farmers of Haryana, V. P. Singh declared his intention to implement the Mandal commission's report. To the 22.5 per cent reservation for scheduled castes and tribes was now added another slab of 27 per cent reservations for other backward castes in certain central government posts. The announcement fomented violent protests by upper-caste youth in key urban centres of northern India. Singh's gamble had badly misfired and contributed to the fall of his government in November 1990. The less than subtle attempt to play caste divisions against the politics of an emerging Hindu communalism induced the defection of upper-caste Hindu professional and service groups to the BJP. One result of this was a further erosion of the India's state's secular façade. The corroded façade was administered a fresh coat of paint by the supreme court's decision in November 1992 to uphold the legality of reservations for the backward castes in addition to a directive to the BJP state government in UP not to demolish the Babri mosque. But on 6 December the pick-axes of Hindu chauvinism made certain that India's secular façade, the authority of the state's highest judicial institution included, crumbled amid the ruins of Ayodhya.

If caste has proven an uncertain bet in piecing together a broad-based network for all-India political mobilization, the policies of class conciliation articulated from the centre have been no more successful in breaking down the hierarchies of caste dominance at the level of regional social formations. Of course there was a certain parallel between the ambiguities of the Indian state's normative position on caste and its ambivalence in pursuing policies aimed at redressing the grosser inequities of class. For a brief moment in the era of Indira Gandhi's populism there was a hint of a deliberate attempt by the political centre to mobilize support along lines of class. Yet the overall thrust of *garibi hatao* designed to galvanize the subordinate classes in all regions when translated into electoral practice soon disaggregated into diverse patterns formed by locally bounded caste, tribal and communal affiliations. So in Gujarat Mrs Gandhi's centrally orchestrated class-based populism took the form of what came to be known as the KHAM strategy – an acronym for an electoral coalition based on the Kshatriyas, Harijans, Adivasis and Muslims. In UP Mrs Gandhi's populism involved forging an alliance between the upper castes, including the Brahmins and the Rajput Thakurs, and lower castes as well as minorities such as the Harijans and Muslims against middling agricultural castes and clans. Later in the 1980s in a variation of Indira Gandhi's strategy, the Janata Dal sought to wean away the Muslims from the Congress by propounding the so-called MAJGAR platform – constituting Muslims, Ahirs, Jats, Gujars, Rajputs and other backward castes. This caste and community based alliance at the regional level was given the all-India ideological gloss of social justice, though not quite the socialism of the Indira Gandhi variety.

Explicitly class-based resistance has not been entirely absent in India's contemporary history. In fact two important states, Kerala and West Bengal, have had communist governments. In the late 1960s West Bengal witnessed a class-based agrarian uprising which captured the imagination of radicals far beyond the locale within which it took place. The revolt whose epicentre was the village of Naxalbari in the northern part of West Bengal lasted from March to June 1967 and involved around 15,000 to 20,000 poor peasants. It was led by the extreme left wing of the Communist Party of India–Marxist, a party whose mainstream was the main constituent of a United Front government which had just dislodged the Congress in state elections. The peasants of Naxalbari had been supported by radical students in the urban centres. Once the widespread agrarian revolution failed to materialize as the countryside refused to adopt the declared policy of annihilating individual class enemies, the Naxalite movement degenerated into an erratic campaign of urban terrorism. The Naxalites were imitated in some other parts of India, notably in Srikakulam district in Andhra Pradesh. More importantly, the Naxalbari uprising, confined though it was to a small part of northern Bengal, had a disproportionate impact on political psyches in India. Yet the shadow of caste has lingered even in regions which have witnessed communist-led class-based politics. The radical politics of Kerala for instance have often been expressed in progressive caste movements. In sections of Bihar and Andhra the social imprint of caste and tribe intermeshes with an undeclared class war that has been raging in the countryside. The Naxalites who were crushed in the early 1970s by the coercive arms of the state have been undergoing something of a revival in both Bihar and Andhra Pradesh.

West Bengal has been governed since 1977 by a left front government led by the CPI-M. It has followed a cautious but clearly class-based policy of consolidating its electoral power base in the rural areas among middle peasants while delivering some palliative reforms to sharecroppers and labourers. Firmly entrenched in the elected *panchayats* or local governments at the village level, the CPI-M has provided one of the most stable yet moderately progressive state governments in independent India. But working within the confines of India's parliamentary democracy, the CPI-M has been far too constrained to deliver anything of substance to the poorest of the poor.

Neither caste nor class-based organization and articulation of politics in India has adequately addressed discrimination and exploitation along lines of gender and generation. Women, children and the elderly have been the farthest removed from sharing the spoils of the politics of patronage as well as reaping the rewards of moderately progressive caste and class movements. Except in parts of south India where matrilineal systems have invested women with a measure of social status, gender relations have remained wholly skewed within patriarchical structures at various levels of the socio-economic hierarchy. While the women of the poorest labouring strata may be relatively less constrained by the culturally informed restrictions on their mobility than those belonging to upper castes and classes, their status at the lowest rungs of the social ladder leaves them acutely vulnerable to a combination of economic and sexual exploitation. The persistence of gender related discrimination within the context of caste-based politics is hardly remarkable. But it has been the lack of sensitivity towards women displayed by ideologies of class-based resistance which merits underlining. The successful instances of class politics in India have been at best moderately radical rather than revolutionary in their vision. In West Bengal the CPI-M led government has assiduously cultivated the constituency of the middling landholding peasantry and not the large class of landless rural labourers. Consequently, they have buttressed the patriarchal values of the propertied strata. Keeping their own women's front organizations firmly subordinated, the communists have done little to alter the highly exploitative gender division of labour within peasant families. In recent years autonomous movements ideologically committed to promoting specifically women's causes and concerns have begun making something of an impression in certain regions of India by operating outside the framework of mainstream political parties.

The state's normative commitment to equality and social justice has undoubtedly altered attitudes and engendered debates on the need to undermine the legitimacy of caste-based discrimination. Yet shifts in the normative sphere have not yet succeeded in dislodging the multitudinous structures of social, cultural and economic oppression and discrimination to be found at the level of India's different regional political economies and social structures. In choosing to alleviate disadvantage along caste lines while tentatively seeking to conciliate conflicts along those of class, the state has strengthened the very multiple and particularistic affinities which its secular and socialist creed was supposed to have replaced and channelled into the universalistic pool of a singular all-India nationalism. In any event, the central state's secular posture has always shown an extraordinary degree of pragmatic tolerance, not so much to religious and cultural difference but to caste and communally defined ideologies of dominance and even occasionally of resistance. Small wonder that the Indian state's secular, socialistic and democratic self-definitions and self-projections have turned it into an island in a sea astir with the identities of distinction and exclusion.

The social mosaic in predominantly Muslim Pakistan is only marginally less complex than in India. A product of Islam's accommodations with its Indian environment, Pakistan regional formations are for the most part based on a syncretic weave of Muslim and Hindu religious and social practices and beliefs. But while saintly worship and notions of pollution are well in evidence at the level of popular and folk religious and social practices, the doctrinal rigidity emphasized by Muslim theologians has by no means failed to make an impact. As in the case of the historically evolved Brahminical order in India, interactive processes of tension, accommodation and appropriation between popular and doctrinal Islam have over the centuries helped shape regional formations that are more distinctly Muslim than the Buddhist or Hindu social stratums from which they emerged. The specificities of Pakistani Islam are more conducive to being interpreted in a framework which acknowledges the multiple blendings and fusions of folk and elite religion, of saintly and theological commentaries and of local and supra-local systems of power and dominance.

Unlike Hindu India, caste-like social forms of organization in the various regions of Pakistan have very different connotations and implications at the level of everyday culture and political practice. Tribal and *biraderi* or clan-based patrilineal kinship ties play an important part in social and political organization. Insofar as they stress the importance of genealogical descent in their locally bound organization and systems of authority, tribal and *biraderi* solidarities in principle broadly approximate each other at both the ideational and structural levels. But while *biraderis* share the tribal ideology of the extended kinship in marriage patterns and other forms of social interaction, they have under the impact of economic change associated with processes of urbanization become structurally far more diffuse and flexible in their norms of allegiance to a single male head of the local clan. Since the colonial period, however, there has been a tendency to conflate the two structures of social organization. The terms *zat*, literally endogamous marriage group but also referring to occupational status, *qaum*, an umbrella term signifying a community based on local or supra-local descent as well as religion, and *biraderi*, were all treated by British officialdom as the equivalents of tribe. In fact, *biraderi* is more accurately a local sub-clan or a sub-tribe within the broader based kinship grouping of *qaum*.

Although tribes and *biraderis* refer to themselves as belonging to certain *qaums* and *zats*, there are subtle distinctions between these broadly similar social structures owing to demographic peculiarities and the uneven spread of urbanization in Pakistan's different regional formations. For instance, the tribal idiom and form of organization has been more pervasive in the North West Frontier Province, Baluchistan and parts of Sind than in the Punjab, where with the exception of the southern districts settled by migrant Baluch tribes, *biraderi* ties are more common. In the NWFP, which is demographically relatively more homogenous than other parts of Pakistan, the shared language of the Pukhtuns or Pathan tribes, expressed in the common social code of Pukhtunwali, makes for a stronger sense of regional cultural identity despite the internal differentiation along lines of clan. Only in recent times have processes of urbanization in the NWFP acquired momentum and begun fracturing purely clan-based affiliations. In Baluchistan where rates of urbanization have been even slower the regional social formation is differentiated by membership in Baluch, Brahui, Pukhtun and other tribes. The social structure of Sind was shaped in the pre-independence period by a west–east migration of mainly Baluch and Brahui tribes as well as a north–south movement of Punjabi clans. Additional migrations from the Muslim-minority provinces of India at the time of partition and also of Punjabis and Pathans, attracted by the relative economic dynamism of the province in the post-independence period, has lent complexity and disparity to the regional social formation in Sind where the rural–urban divide has become especially marked. The clan-based social structure of the Punjab has been rendered looser and more diffuse principally due to the twin influences of periodic migrations from outside and rapid commercialization and urbanization in the twentieth century.

Demographic specificities and variations in patterns of urbanization have served to qualify the social, cultural and ideological implications of tribal and *biraderi* structures in Pakistan's regional formations. Owing nothing to Islamic religious doctrine, these vertical and horizontal clan-based social bonds operate differently from caste by *jati* which assigns not only occupational but also ritual status rooted in structures of power and dominance. Tribes are rarely linked to specific social occupations and there is a wide measure of economic differentiation within the membership of the clan. While certain locally bound *biraderis* have been historically linked with specific occupations, and even places of origin, they are now mainly symbols of identity rather than an accurate or meaningful description of societal status and differentiation. For instance, the Mughal and Rajput or the warrior *qaums* generally belonged to the wielders of political power in the locality; the Syeds and Quereshis drew their lineage from *pirs* or local religious leaders based around a Sufi shrine; Pathans, Afghans and Kashmiris from their territorially defined basis of descent; Bhattis, Sheikhs and Khojas hailed from the trading groups while Arains, Jats and Gujars were rural artisans, cultivators and menial labourers respectively. But with the expansion of commercialization, urbanization and closer integration into the broader capitalist world economy there has been much intermixing of *qaums* or *biraderis* in terms of social functions. Today members of the Rajput or Jat *biraderi* are just as likely to be engaged in trade as the Sheikhs and Bhattis are in agricultural activities.

The breadth of clan-based solidarities in Pakistan's regional formations makes it even more difficult to generalize with any amount of accuracy about their cultural and political characteristics than is true for occupational castes by *jati* in India. Despite the strong affinities with Islam, especially as manifested in the uniformity of ritual observance, clan-based social structures are defined by regional and local cultures. In spite of the authority exercised by the mullah and *pir* of the local mosque or shrine, customary law and practice has remained a powerful lever in the hands of tribal and *biraderi* elders against processes of homogenization periodically resorted to by the more doctrinally committed guardians of the faith in the urban areas. This is not an invocation of a simple duality between rural and urban religion or between the so-called low and high traditions of Islam. Rather, it is a reiteration of the essentially Muslim yet locally and regionally specific universes which are the culturally constitutive elements of the social collage that is Pakistan. Specificities and syncretic accretions have historically never been a barrier to dynamic interaction with broader Islamic currents, but at the same time have retained the imprint of local and regional social structures with their distinctive and autonomously evolved cultural practices.

Islam clearly plays a part in the articulation and motivation of clan-based politics. But this can be established with any measure of precision only after an empirical verification of the actual strength of tribal and *biraderi* solidarities at the level of specific localities and regions. Despite the staggered pace of economic development and urbanization in the different regions, clan-based kinship ties are no longer necessarily the strongest or only factor in political motivation. In an earlier period, the overarching authority of say a Bugti, Mengal or Marri sardar in Baluchistan, of the Baluch Leghari and Mazaari chiefs in southern Punjab, of the Afridi or Khattak maliks in the NWFP or the heads of the Khuro and Soomro clans in Sind may have been a sufficient indicator of how the predilections of the reigning leader was likely to influence the ideological or political preferences of their respective tribes. Yet with the increasing breakdown in rights of primogeniture, to say nothing of the impact of widening socio-economic and political horizons, none of these tribes has been free of factional rivalries. The loosening of tribal bonds and the emergence of multiple sources of authority linked to structures of economic power and dominance in the locality effectively foreclose the possibility of entire clans strictly following a directive issued from above. The problem is even more pronounced in the case of *biraderis*, especially in the urban areas of the Punjab. With class-based differentiation and occupational interests undercutting, if not quite replacing, the social identities of patrilineal kinship groups in both urban and rural Punjab, analysing the political role of extended clan ties is an extremely knotty exercise.

While there are few parallels between caste associations in India and exclusively *biraderi* or tribal-based political groupings in Pakistan, local clan solidarities have always exercised a decisive influence on electoral processes during the colonial and the post-colonial periods. British perceptions of north-western Indian social formations as primarily tribal and the subsequent ordering of the colonial state's patronage system to fit that definition created a vested interest in 'tribalism' even among clans more akin to the looser *biraderi* structures. This was particularly true of the Punjab where the colonial discourse ferreted out would-be agricultural 'tribes' from supposedly non-agricultural 'tribes' while streamlining the land tenure and revenue collecting system. The Punjab land alienation act of 1901 gave impetus to the construction of a supra-communal agricultural cultural idiom geared to collaboration with the colonial state. Within that idiom not only Hindus and Sikhs but also Muslim landed and popular religious leaders sought refuge from periodic ideological onslaughts launched by more communally minded urban groups, such as the Arya Samaj, the Singh Sabhas and an array of doctrinally committed Islamic ulema. Despite the British decision to create a separate all-India Muslim category in 1909, predominantly Muslim rural Punjab effectively resisted encroachments from urban communal parties like the All-India Muslim League. By the same token, Sind, the NWFP and Baluchistan with their overwhelming Muslim majorities continued to shun the communally determined political agendas of the Muslim League.

In the Muslim-majority eastern districts of Bengal the colonial invention of an all-India Muslim political category had been roughly coterminous with a relatively autonomous process of redefining religious identity. During the late nineteenth and early twentieth century Bengali Muslim society discarded some of its syncreticist cultural practices and self-consciously adopted Arabic names. As in the north-western regions of the subcontinent Bengali Islam was shaped by a dialogue and debate between the doctrinal and mediational varieties of the faith. Despite the adoption of some tenets of cultural exclusivity to bolster their ideological rejection of a Hindu dominated socio-economic order, Bengali Muslims did not permit orthodox reformist religion to swamp the popular syncreticism that had been a key strand in their Islamic identity, especially in the rural areas. Even in the urban centres where reformist orthodoxy was more pervasive mediational *pir*-based forms of worship were widely practised. The 1920s and 1930s witnessed both communitarian and class-based mobilization of a predominantly Muslim smallholding peasantry. Devoid of the *biraderi*-style social networks that characterized the politics of rural elites in the north-west, the non-communal and cross-communal strategies forged by Bengali Muslims in rural areas had something of a populist dimension. The specifically Muslim politics sought to be fostered in response to colonial constitutional manoeuvres was much more of an urban phenomenon in Bengal.

The net result of the contradictory constructions of the colonial state at the local and all-India levels was to infuse clan solidarities, whether tribal or *biraderi*-based, in the north-west or class and communitarian bonds in the north-east, with political meaning within the protected walls of specifically Muslim constituencies. Electoral calculations in these separate constituencies revolved around local issues rather than the agendas of parties at the provincial level, much less the All-India Muslim League, which despite a history of trials and tribulations remained steadfast in its determination to put stuffing into the British classification of Muslims as a distinctive political category. After the 1920s, the Indian National Congress under Gandhi

partly succeeded in skirting around the ambiguities of its ideological posturing and claiming the varied social affiliations at the local and regional
levels as compatible with a singular nationalist impulse. By contrast, the
All-India Muslim League, while making minor inroads in the urban centres
where kinship ties were more fluid, continued to be spurned at the local and
regional levels of rural politics in the Muslim-majority areas in both north-
western and north-eastern India. The intermeshing of clan and class solidarities with special electorates for Muslims at all levels of representation
placed political party organizations linking locality, region and nation at a
serious discount.

This colonial legacy gave a fillip to the inbuilt cultural and ideological
autonomy of the predominantly Muslim regional social formations claimed
by the Muslim League. The more so since Islam in adapting to subcontinental conditions had borne the local and regional imprint quite as
much as it had altered the contours of their syncretic cultural idioms. If the
assumed cultural unities of Islam on a subcontinental level had failed to
translate into a coherent or solid all-India Muslim politics, attempts to
evoke religion as the ideological basis of the new state were shot through
with contradictions and conflict. For one thing, there was no agreement
among the guardians of the faith or the managers of the state as to what
should constitute the ideal of a socially uniform doctrinally based cultural
monolith called Islam. For another, the choice of an Islamic idiom open to
wide and contrary interpretations as the dominant variant in the construction of an inclusionary national ideology for Pakistan was acutely vulnerable
to deflection and appropriation by the different local and regional social
formations. Making a virtue out of vagueness was one way to try and square
the concentric circles of Islam as religion, Islam as culture and Islam as
ideology. Yet this merely served to confound the problem of claiming
Islamic cultural moorings for relations between the state and a regionally
heterogeneous society. Apart from the difficulties in defining an Islamic
identity in a context where it invoked a multiplicity of meanings, Pakistan's
early managers vacillated between asserting an Islamic basis for the state
and finding ways to keep the religious guardians at bay. Lip service to an
Islamic ideology they could barely define was one thing, reordering the
structures of the state and political economy to fit the conflicting views of
the religious groups and the imperatives of governance was quite another.

These confusions in the control rooms at the top impeded the project of
giving substantive content to the Islamic ideology that was being proclaimed as the main self-justification of the Pakistani state. In the meantime
Islam as religion and culture continued to impart relatively autonomous
meanings to the disparate and changing clan and class-based regional and
local social formations. Having invoked Islam as an ideological monolith in

the state-sponsored discourse, however, it was possible to claim the multi-faceted and frequently unorthodox practices of Muslims in the different regions and localities as part and parcel of a single cultural tradition. But this still did not alter the basic fact that the meanings attached to Islam in religious and cultural practices in locality and region differed in essentials from the monolithic ideological protestations of the nation-state that was in the making.

So it is not at all remarkable that specifically religious parties in Pakistan have done poorly on the few occasions that their Islamic platforms were put to the test at the hustings, whether local, provincial or national. Parties mouthing Islamic platitudes at the ideological level but in fact pressing agendas of socio-economic reform and, not infrequently, manipulating the clan-based structures in the localities have generally tended to meet with greater success. Such was the posture of the Muslim League before the military intervention of 1958 and also of the Pakistan People's Party during the first general elections held in December 1970 on the basis of universal adult franchise. But this appropriation of Islam in political discourse cannot detract from the fundamental importance of the relatively autonomous logic of local and regional social formations which are more rooted in changing structures of power and dominance at these levels than in an overarching affinity to religious doctrine or its attendant symbols per se.

The gulf separating an officially fabricated legitimizing Islamic ideology from the changing social and economic dynamics informing politics has had large and paradoxical consequences for relations between state and society. Clan-based social networks in the Pakistani context have weathered lengthy spells of military dictatorship which typically undermined party organizations, such as they existed, and sought to localize the nature of electoral politics. On the face of it, Ayub's basic democracies system aimed at empowering a newly emergent intermediary rural strata. Yet in point of fact the localized character of the basic democracies system ensured the continuing importance of kinship ties, albeit expressed increasingly in economic and class-based dominance, rather than in structures of authority embedded in clan hierarchies. Borrowing from the colonial state's lexicons on political manipulation and control, the Ayub regime tried to drive a wedge between its networks of collaboration in the rural areas and the more articulate pockets of opposition in the urban areas. While not wholly immune from structures of clan and kinship allegiance, urban social groups were more amenable to broad-based political organization along lines of class or, more aptly, sectional and occupational interests.

During the urban protests against Ayub Khan's military rule in 1968–9 organized industrial labour was in the forefront alongside radical students. The anti-Ayub movement was later joined in by white-collar workers like clerical staff, doctors, lawyers, engineers and central government employ-ees. So prolonged periods of depoliticization and the absence of political party organizations could not forestall the emergence of partially organized and spontaneous non-clan-based resistance to a repressive state structure. Zulfikar Ali Bhutto during his brief tenure in power managed to lose the support of the labour unions as well as student and professional groups. When street protests erupted in 1977 against Bhutto's alleged rigging of the elections, labour was conspicuous by its absence. But its place had been more than adequately filled by the urban commercial groups who supported the Pakistan National Alliance – a nine-party coalition ranging from the extreme right to the left of the political spectrum. Some of these commercial groups had been upset by Bhutto's nationalization of agro-processing industries such as rice husking and cotton ginning. Interestingly, the class-based grievances of traders and merchants were articulated in a religious mould. The hard core of the anti-Bhutto movement centred around two re-ligious parties, the Jamat-i-Islami and the Jamiat-i-Ulema-i-Pakistan. The declared aim of the PNA movement was to achieve Nizam-i-Mustapha (the system of the Prophet Mohammad). General Zia-ul-Haq, who utilized the turmoil to his advantage, borrowed the Islamic rhetoric but showed a keen awareness of the limited electoral base of specifically Islamic parties. Con-sequently, he chose to coopt a broader range of socio-economic elites. A state-sponsored programme of Islamization was more than balanced by pragmatic individuals capable of combining their personal stature with the manipulation of clan-based tribal and *biraderi* ties in the local arenas of Pakistani politics. Zia the great soldier of Islam left as his legacy a style of politics associated more with individuals commanding the affiliations of localized clans, than the all-pervasive unities of a religious ideology. This is not to say that a religious issue could not be effectively deployed towards political ends. Benazir Bhutto's opposition to the Shariat bill left her open to the charge of being anti-Islam and was one of the many catalytic factors in the dismissal of her government. Yet when the 1990 elections were held both the pro-establishment Islamic Democratic Alliance and the PPP-led People's Democratic Alliance paid far more attention to individuals with bases of support in the localities on the one hand, and the arithmetic of tribal and *biraderi* equations on the other than to issues of class or even religion.

So although Pakistan describes itself as an Islamic republic, religion rarely has been the primary motivating factor in political calculations. In the localized horizons of the party political system built by Zia, the personal following and financial clout of the candidate along with the demography of clan ties, however loose and ruptured, are the most important factors in clinching electoral victory. As in the colonial period when landed power exercised through clan networks in conjunction with separate electorates for Muslims rendered the role of all-India or even provincially based political or religious ideologies ineffectual at the local levels, the current fragmentation of the Pakistani polity stands in sharp contrast to the monolithic Islamic self-projections of the central state. In selecting Islam as the main ingredient in defining national identity the Pakistani state was attempting to turn the colonial construct of Muslims as a separate political category and the accompanying notion of the 'two nation' theory into a potent legitimizing ideology. Yet the extended suspension of political processes by authoritarian post-colonial institutions has hindered the emergence of organized or semi-organized layers that can mediate the multiple religious, cultural and ideological meanings between the central state and local and regional social formations. The official discourse of inclusionary nationalism far from contributing to the evolution of a collective ethos has been the main obstacle to the accommodation of distinctive but significant strands of local and regionally defined belief systems and practices. The dilemma is a particularly acute one. All levels and segments of Pakistani society draw upon Islam without wholly submerging their linguistic and regionally based cultural beliefs and practices or their economic and political interests within its rituals or doctrine. The relative autonomy of culture at the level of local and regional social formations has not only contested a reductionist state ideology based exclusively on religion but sought to affirm difference and distinctiveness in the politics of linguistic regionalism or sub-regionalism, the highest possible common denominator available in a state that has been federal in form but unitary and undemocratic in spirit.

Linguistic regionalism has not been the worry of a military authoritarian state structure professing an Islamic ideology alone. Formally democratic India with its creed of secularism also has had to vie with regional dissidence based on linguistic affiliations throughout its post-independence history. India's and Pakistan's contrasting official ideologies and the more nuanced differences in state structures makes it especially intriguing to consider why, despite variations in their respective locally and regionally informed social mosaics, linguistic rather than caste or clan-based affinities have proven to be the more powerful mobilizing factor in the enunciation of demands for regional and sub-regional autonomy.

Language as culture and ideology

Even though linguistic affinity more often than not has been the highest common factor in the articulation and organization of regional dissidence and resistance against central power, the role of language as culture and ideology in the politics of South Asia remains curiously understudied. Part of the reason for this may be that the bond of language is accepted as a given and not subjected to in-depth scholarly analysis. But more than that many scholars have tended to follow the trail of central policy makers by focusing on the structural dimensions of language as one of the more important principles in the demarcation of state and provincial boundaries. Consequently, language as culture and ideology has provided no more than a hazy backdrop to the arresting foreground of conflicts between region and centre and also within regions in post-colonial South Asia. Since language has provided the emotive edge to many of these conflicts it merits a sharper focus in historical analysis of subcontinental societies.

Colonial and post-colonial states generally have been averse to or only grudgingly accepted language as the main basis for the territorial organization of administrative boundaries. This was despite the fact that language or more accurately linguistic diversity was acknowledged in colonial discourse, if not translated into policy. Financial, strategic and political imperatives of the colonial state weighed against a systematic or across the board implementation of a linguistic reorganization of provincial boundaries. In 1936 the creation of Orissa was one of the rare instances when the colonial state explicitly conceded the linguistic principle. The pertinence of language as culture in regional social formations and the discrepancy between colonial discourse and colonial policy enabled nationalist opponents of the raj to turn it into an important item on their ideological agenda. Nationalist poetics since the late nineteenth century had been expressed in vernacular languages. Only bold leaps of poetic imagination had been able to transfigure Bengal or Tamil Nad as the motherland into the overarching image of a mother India. The Indian National Congress harnessed this potent anti-colonial force, but was also wary of its divisive potential. In the early twentieth century the Congress not only organized its own provincial units along linguistic lines but promised a linguistic reorganization of provinces once independence had been won. Yet no sooner was central power within sight that the Congress hedged and backtracked on its well advertised commitment to the linguistic affinities of India's peoples. In a mirror image of the colonial bosses, the Congress's central leadership voiced their unease about using language as the sole criterion for the territorial reorganization of India's political landscape. National unity and security were now touted as the most important considerations in administering the newly independent territories. It was a fitting transition from anti-colonial resisters to would-be post-colonial hegemons.

The All-India Muslim League for its part had always played down the linguistic specificities of the Muslim-majority provinces. Having asserted a distinctive Muslim political identity the League sought to strengthen the religious bond through the medium of the Urdu language at the supraregional level. While the use of Urdu evoked a positive response among the upper and middling strata of Muslims in the urban centres of the Punjab, the role of regional vernaculars remained the most important factor in the political mobilization of the Muslim-majority provinces of north-western and north-eastern India. Islamic symbols played a large part in rallying support for the League among diverse Muslim linguistic groups, but perceptions of them in the emerging consciousness was informed by idioms embedded in local and regional cultures. Certainly the link between Islam and Urdu was embraced more enthusiastically in the Muslim-minority provinces, especially the UP, than in the Muslim-majority provinces which formed part of Pakistan. The disjunction between the all-India discourse of the Muslim League and regional cultural idioms of linguistic social groups became more pronounced after independence. Even if Urdu was a civilizational symbol of subcontinental Muslim culture, its association with the north Indian heartlands of Muslim political power lent it the status of a new imperial immigrant in the territories constituting the new state. The long and well documented history of resistance to a north Indian based Mughal central authority in the Muslim-majority provinces was not a healthy portent for the elevation to national status of a language essentially imported from that region. In choosing Urdu as the national language and glorifying the era of Mughal imperial hegemony on the one hand and promoting an inclusionary Islamic ideology on the other, Pakistan's central leaders had expected to hasten processes of assimilation and secure allegiance to a monolithic notion of state sovereignty. Instead they created an arena of fierce contestation where Urdu, Mughal power and an Islam, more doctrinal than syncretic in complexion, gave a powerful stimulus to the articulation of regional dissent in the linguistic idiom.

The attempted imposition of Urdu and Hindi by the Pakistani and Indian states respectively came to be perceived as broadly analogous affronts to language as culture in the subcontinent's regional social formations. So the post-colonial states provided a major impetus to the metamorphosis of language as culture to language as ideology in the politics of the subcontinent. Although in the case of India no explicit equation existed between religion and language, the partition of 1947 gave a communal bias to the linguistic policy adopted by a 'secular' state. At least a section of the nationalist leadership in the pre-independence period, notably Subhas Chandra Bose and Jawaharlal Nehru, had favoured Hindustani, a blend of Hindi and Urdu, written in the Roman script as the lingua franca for an independent India. But the association of Urdu with the Muslim League's ostensibly separatist politics, its perceived role in sundering the unity of India and, finally, its adoption by the Pakistani state as the national language served to strengthen the position of the advocates of Hindi in the

Devanagri script as the only acceptable national language for India. While at best marginalizing Urdu within its own north Indian environment, the Hindi-only posture ignited widespread protest from the non-Hindi-speaking regions, notably the south. In Pakistan where Urdu was adopted as one of the ideological pillars on which to rest central state authority, the reaction was as inflammatory among Bengali speakers in the eastern wing. Regions which were comfortable with language as culture and had even given voice to more broadly based anti-colonial and religious nationalisms now became the scene of powerful language movements directed against the homogenizing tendencies of the central state.

The more so since language was not merely a sentimental attachment to specific cultural beliefs and practices but the basis on which social groups could secure advancement in professions and services and, in this way, assert their dominance at the regional level. Language as culture had always played a critical role in the definition of regional identities, if not 'homelands', as expressed in such vernacular terms as *desh, nadu* or *watan*. But pragmatic material considerations dictated the recourse to language as an ideology of protest and resistance quite as much as its correlation with regional culture. In the local and regional social formations of both India and Pakistan, language presented itself as a useful mobilizing symbol transcending caste, clan and even class-based interests. It enabled social groups with privileged access to literacy and education to represent regionally defined interests. Where the commonalities of language were fractured by communal affiliations, as in the cases of pre-independence UP, Bengal and the Punjab, linguistically defined identities reemerged as major, though not exclusive, organizing principles of politics within the altered configuration of the state–society framework. The recourse to the community of language by social groups possessing multiple identities has to be understood in the context of historically changing relations between state and civil society during the process of decolonization. Language as an ideology distilled out of its undeniably deep cultural moorings afforded both an ideology of dominance at the regional level and one of resistance against central power.

In post-independence India the earliest uses of language to assert regional dominance as well as challenge central authority was in the Telugu-speaking regions of predominantly Tamil-speaking Madras. Although the Congress leadership had conceded the principle of a Telugu-speaking state of Andhra, preoccupations with national security, unity and the integration of the princely states had relegated the linguistic reorganization of Madras province to the margins of the central state's political agenda. The immediacy of a linguistic 'other' in the form of a Tamil-speaking community powered the Telugu movement in no uncertain fashion. It was the death by starvation of Potti Sriramalu and accompanying riots in the Telugu-speaking districts of Madras which forced the Nehru government to alter its priorities of so-called 'nation-building'. The anti-Hindi agitations of the 1950s and early 1960s in the southern states quickly fell back on parallel linguistic nationalisms. These had been masterminded by the Dravida Munnetra Kazhagam in Tamil Nadu, after an initial haphazard attempt to forge a broad Dravidian counterpoise to the attempted hegemony of the Hindi-speaking north. Tamil, Telugu, Kannada and Malayali linguistic identities offered a better interface to aspects of regional dominance and resistance than a more broadly based Dravidian identity.

So linguistic ideologies came to be constructed in congruence with relations of domination within regions, in counterdistinction to other linguistic identities in neighbouring regions as well as in opposition to impositions by an overweening centre. This was exemplified particularly strongly in the case of the Marathi-speaking territories of Bombay which along with Punjab had been denied the linguistic principle by the states reorganization commission of 1955–6. The 1960 language riots that led to the formation of Maharashtra combined protest against Gujarati and central dominance with cultural symbols of Maratha solidarity. In what was a difference of degree in relation to the south, Maratha society historically had been less sharply stratified along caste and class lines. But even here the dimension of dominance of advantaged social groups within the regional social formation was unmistakable. A Marathi linguistic ideology did not, for instance, accommodate the social and economic grievances of the Mahars – the region's most prominent scheduled caste.

Indian Punjab oscillated between emphases on linguistic and religious identities in achieving the goals of regional dominance, distinctiveness in relation to Hindi-speaking and predominantly Hindu regions such as Haryana and assertion of autonomy vis-à-vis central authority. Since the Indian constitution ruled out the possibility of expressing political demands in religious terms, Sikh leaders tended to stress the linguistic variant of their multiple identities until the concession of the Punjabi subah in 1966. The religious aspect which had never been wholly absent came to the fore once it became clear that the mere creation of a Punjabi-speaking state with a slender Sikh majority could not in itself ensure either regional dominance or a real measure of autonomy. A common Punjabi linguistic cultural idiom shared by Hindus, Muslims and Sikhs alike continued to be pervasive at the societal level. But an exclusively Punjabi linguistic ideology became less and less effectual in the political arena as centralized state power forged alliances with Hindi-speaking neighbouring regions and the Hindu minority within the state. The more overt reliance on a Sikh religious ideology since the 1980s was in large part shaped by contradictions inherent in the policies of the central state. These on the one hand created a space for communalism within its ideological discourse and on the other unleashed its coercive arms on the display of cultural–religious symbols of the Sikh minority.

The Janus-faced stance of the Indian political centre – formally secular in orientation while increasingly relying surreptitiously on communal ideologies – in order to claim national legitimacy in the face of narrowing regional bases of support has imparted an important dimension to movements of regional dissidence not only in the Punjab but also in Assam and Kashmir. In an interesting flashback to the situation in the Muslim-majority provinces in pre-independence India, differences in context notwithstanding, linguistic affinities are competing with religious identities in varying measure. Until the 1970s the Assamese had deployed a linguistic ideology to bolster Asom dominance within the region, contest Bengali Hindu preponderance in the professions and services as well as protest against exploitation and neglect by the centre. Early attempts to fashion an alliance with Muslims in Assam gave way to bitter conflicts between the mainly Hindu Asoms and Bengalis, Hindu and Muslim alike. The expulsion of Muslim peasant immigrants from Bangladesh became the main demand of the Asom Gana Parishad in the early 1980s. In order to counter the Asom campaign of regional dissidence the central state, which was increasingly turning to Hindu majoritarian communalism in northern India, did not hesitate to play the Muslim communal card in Assam in an effort to enlist the support of the minority community. The upshot of this Machiavellian policy was to leave the Muslims defenceless against attacks perpetrated by the more communally minded Assamese Hindus while further alienating the educated middle strata in the state.

Nowhere has the dialectic between religious and linguistic identities been played out with more devastating consequences than in the Indian state of Jammu and Kashmir. The ideology of secular democracy, at least in political rhetoric, had seemed to provide adequate space for the accommodation of a Kashmiri linguistic and regional identity in this Muslim-majority state. Yet the undermining of both secularism and democracy in political practice left Kashmiris groping for an ideology to enforce regional dominance and resist central encroachments on their autonomy. The dilemma was compounded by the deployment of a communal ideology in Jammu, historically a distinctive sub-regional political entity, by Hindu organizations as well as by the Indian centre. Although language as culture continues to be an important component of Kashmiri identity, the lack of a political concordat with Jammu on the issue of autonomy from the central state has given a religious accent to the regional aspirations of the Muslim majority. But it is necessary to distinguish between an attachment to Muslim culture along with a Kashmiri regional identity and the articulation of an Islamic ideology. While some political groups have taken to expounding an inchoate

Islamic ideology and inflamed an already uneasy communal situation, it is by no means clear that the vast majority of Kashmiri Muslims subscribe to an identity based on religious exclusivism. It is simply that the Indian state's politically expedient wooing of Hindu communalism in Jammu and Kashmir as well as an implicit reliance on Hindu majoritarianism in the country as a whole has temporarily turned language as culture into an ineffective ideological resource for Kashmiri Muslims. Linguistic states in India continue to be the most organized units of resistance against centralized power. At the same time rivalries between linguistic and communal groups within states have provided the Indian centre with an important lever in trying to counter regionally based challenges. Language as culture may continue to thrive at the level of day to day living in regional social formations, but cannot unproblematically provide the basis for language as ideology. Linguistically defined ideologies of dominance, distinctiveness and resistance have to constantly contend with a shifting emphasis in national discourse aimed at preserving a monolithic ideology of state sovereignty. The dialectic is particularly fraught in regions where the central state can derive political benefits from the existence of rival communal and linguistic ideologies.

Pakistan despite an overwhelmingly religiously homogeneous population reflects many of the features that have characterized language as culture and as ideology in Indian regional social formations. Self-confident, even arrogant, steps by the central state to hoist Urdu as the national language met with early resistance from far-flung eastern Bengal. Mistaking Muslim Bengal's endorsement of the All-India Muslim League's communal demand for a Pakistan as willingness to submerge its distinctive cultural identity within the national discourse that was being constructed, the central leaders overlooked the possibility of a people being equally committed to a regional language and an overarching religious tradition. Rumblings of protest on the language issue which began as early as the late 1940s erupted into a full-scale linguistic movement led by students in 1952. The killing by police of four students in Dacca during street demonstrations on 21 February 1952 turned that into a martyrs day ever since. Within less than five years of partition ostensibly along religious lines urban educated Bengali Muslims chose to place greater emphasis on their linguistic and cultural identity in forging an ideology of resistance against central state power. With their Muslim identity politically neutralized by its appropriation by the West Pakistani-dominated state, educated Bengali Muslims borrowed from the supra-communal literary and cultural traditions of Bengali nationalism in the pre-partition era. A proud attachment to the Bengali language not only laid the basis for a powerful political ideology of resistance against the central state but also confirmed for the urban educated classes leadership of the movement of regional dissidence during the two decades leading up to 1971.

The Bengalis were not alone in harbouring a sense of cultural alienation from a post-colonial discourse that sought to tailor national unity by using Urdu to stitch together an Islamic canopy. Unlike Hindi in India, Urdu was not the language of any region of Pakistan. At the very moment that the Indian state began reluctantly conceding the linguistic principle, the Pakistani state was ardently seeking to establish administrative unity on its linguistically diverse western wing. In the non-Punjabi provinces the one-unit system of 1955 came to be associated with a Punjabi–Muhajir axis looking to exterminate their distinctive cultural identities. Language as ideology, consequently, found fertile ground in the unfolding saga of centre–province tensions in Pakistan. As in India, the shift from language as culture to language as ideology had much to do with the specificities of regional social formations, namely the presence of rival linguistic communities, and the postures of the central state. For instance, while reactions to one unit were widespread in all the non-Punjabi regions, and though more muted not entirely absent in the Punjab, the migration of Urdu speakers from India into the main urban centres of Sind and their subsequent domination of the economy and government services gave it added meaning in the politics of the province.

Pointing to their well-developed literary tradition which had retained its distinctiveness despite the imperially backed influences of Arabic, Persian and English, leaders of Sindhi society passionately resisted the dominant idioms of the new national discourse. If Bengalis resented a cultural imperialism ventilated by a distant centre, the Sindhis found that new colonial masters had come to settle permanently in their homeland. Once Karachi became the first capital of Pakistan, Sindhis were expected to embrace Urdu, but non-Sindhis did not have to learn the language of their adopted environment. For Bengalis Dacca University became a bastion for the defence of their language and culture. In the case of the Sindhis the centre rescinded the decision to set up a Sind University in Karachi, preferring instead to support a Karachi University in the city as the preserve of an Urdu-speaking intelligentsia. The Sindhi language department at Karachi University was axed. While a Sind University was established in Hyderabad, its standards were allowed to drop below the low levels that, sadly enough, have been the hallmark of the higher educational system in post-colonial Pakistan. The inability of the vast majority of Sindhis to compete for jobs in government or communicate with their compatriots adequately in either Urdu or English was in due course to encourage disparaging stereotypes about their general lethargy and soft-headed approach to the hard realities of life.

The onslaught on regional linguistic cultures gathered momentum during the military regime of Ayub Khan. The systematic denial of linguistically defined regional cultures met with a débâcle in the eastern wing in 1971. But despite the reorganization of provincial boundaries along linguistic lines in 1971 this policy of denial was not wholly abandoned at the level of the national discourse which continued to project Urdu as one of its main ideological planks. The populist interlude in Pakistan's politics, however, brought to the surface some of the main proponents of regional cultures who had been pushed underground by military authoritarian rule. Bhutto's efforts to promote the Sindhi language and provide employment opportunities to Sindhi speakers in the provincial civil service caused resentment among the Urdu-speaking Muhajirs.[1] The decision by the military regime of General Zia-ul-Haq to slam shut the half-opened windows of opportunity for Sindhis and lend tacit, if not overt, political support to the Muhajir Qaumi Movement sharpened the lines of conflict between linguistic communities in the 1980s and early 1990s.

While attention has been riveted on the rivalry between linguistic groups in Sind, language as culture and ideology continues to be of relevance in Pakistan's other provinces. In predominantly Pukhtun-speaking NWFP, language as culture remains an important source of regional identity. But the need to cultivate language as ideology against the centre has been rendered less effective as an emotive force in the absence of an immediate threat from a rival linguistic community. To be sure, the NWFP has a significant Hindko-speaking linguistic minority, but it is not one which presents a real or consistent threat to Pukhtun dominance in the professions and the services. In Baluchistan where many linguistic identities contend for dominance at the level of the regional formation, the central state has had ample opportunity to neutralize movements using language as ideology. The presence of large numbers of Afghan refugees during the 1980s and the growing assertiveness of Baluch parties after the restoration of electoral politics in 1988 has led to demands that the Pukhtun-speaking areas of Baluchistan be separated out and linked to the NWFP to form a greater Pukhtun province. Such a demand is unlikely to be conceded since the acceptance of the linguistic principle in one region cannot but force a substantial redrawing of existing provincial boundaries in Pakistan as a whole. With Baluch speakers straddling the boundary between Sind and Baluchistan, Hindko speakers in the NWFP and Seraiki speakers in southern Punjab, to say nothing of the continuing civil war in Afghanistan, the ramifications of a greater Pukhtun province would be far too complex to merit serious consideration by Islamabad.

---

[1] See above, chapter 5.

The situation in the Punjab is unlike any other in the subcontinent. Ostensibly the dominant region in Pakistan with direct access to state power, the Punjab's distinctive linguistic cultural traditions have been even more submerged than those of other regional formations by the expedient alliance of its dominant social classes with the two main non-elected institutions of the state espousing Urdu as the main ingredient of a national ideology. In the Punjab not only has language as culture suffered from the state's advocacy of Urdu, but language as ideology remains ineffectual on account of a gaping divide between a regional elite linked to state power and the vast majority of underprivileged social groups. Attempts by autonomous literary associations to revitalize Punjabi prose and poetry have faced the wrath of the military–bureaucratic state in much the same manner as their counterparts in the non-Punjabi provinces.

So in contrast to India where Hindi symbolizes the political preeminence of the northern states, recourse to language as ideology in Pakistan's provinces cannot be seen as a reaction to the cultural dominance of the Punjab as a region. It is the institutional clout of a mainly Punjabi military–bureaucratic establishment using an essentially extra-territorial set of cultural symbols which has been the principal source of tensions between the centralized state and distinctive regional social formations. The disjunction between the political and cultural dominance of Punjabis has meant that grievances in the linguistic mode are directed squarely against the policies of political denial and economic exclusion pursued by a centralizing and homogenizing state.

Yet even in India the centre's decision to back off from a stridently pro-Hindi policy has given precedence to the structural relationship rather than ideology in centre–state and inter-state disputes. Although language as ideology played a more crucial role in the articulation of regional dissidence in the immediate post-independence decades, it has remained a powerful mobilizing force in recent decades. But the concession of linguistic states after the mid-fifties and the success of regional parties within some of them has partly blunted the ideological edge and brought structural imbalances into the foreground of centre–state relations. An analogous shift of emphasis from ideology to structure is also discernible in post-1971 Pakistan. However, where regional aspirations were not accommodated within the framework of linguistic states as in Indian Punjab and Kashmir the dialectic of linguistic regionalism and religious communalism has been shaping a dramatic confrontation between region and centre. In the Pakistani province of Sind and in Assam the perception of the major linguistic groups, the Sindhis and the Assamese, of being reduced to minority status within their own domains has kept alive the salience of language as ideology. Yet once again the fierce linguistic rivalries in these two regions can be interpreted meaningfully only in the context of their interaction with the structure and ideology of the central state.

The attempt to impose a national language, whether Hindi or Urdu, was merely one feature in the centralizing state's project of constructing a unifying ideology for the nation-state. Having appropriated the concept of monolithic sovereignty from the colonial era, the post-colonial state in both India and Pakistan attempted to give currency to a welter of idioms capable of transcending the bounds of locality and region. Partly tweezed out of the ideational features present in local and regional social formations these were cast in a rigid mould once they were sought to be transformed into ideological pillars of state monoliths. This explains why despite their inclusionary claims state-sponsored national ideologies have tended to be almost exclusionary in social impact.

Monolithic ideologies and societal dissonance

Nation-states quite as much as individuals can be rather vain when it comes to self-perceptions. At the height of the emergency in November 1976 the Indian parliament passed a mammoth amendment to the constitution which among other things altered the nomenclature of the Indian state. Since that date India has been described in grandiose terms as a 'sovereign socialist, secular, democratic republic'. Proclaiming India to be sovereign nearly forty years after independence may have been somewhat redundant, while the appellations socialist, secular, democratic attempted to assert by the stroke of the pen principles which were being vigorously contested in both the formal and informal arenas of local and regional politics. And there were cynics in 1984 who commented tongue in cheek upon Rajiv Gandhi's succession that it was at best unclear whether India was a monarchy or a republic. While India adorned itself with a plethora of adjectives, the debate whether Pakistan should be Islamic or secular persisted in confusing this predominantly Muslim country's efforts to define a national identity. Although successive constitutions since 1956 with the brief solitary exception of Ayub's constitution in 1962 defined Pakistan as an Islamic republic, doubts about the precise implications of the Shariat bill adopted in 1991 suggest that the question of Islamization has not been resolved to anyone's satisfaction. When Bangladesh broke away from Pakistan in 1971 it described itself as a people's republic and professed secularism as its creed. In 1988 the military regime proclaimed Islam to be the state religion of Bangladesh but stopped short of changing the appellation from people's republic to Islamic republic. Secularism and the role of religion in politics together constitute the most important comparative theme in assessing the role of monolithic ideologies fashioned by South Asian states. This entails a critical scrutiny of not only secular and religious claims but also the meaning and substance of democratic, socialist and republican character-istics of the state. Not to subject the self-definitions of states to rigorous questioning would be to mistake the aura for the essence.

Most contemporary debates in subcontinental South Asia impel a return to the deciding moment of 1947. This is especially so when it comes to analysing the role of a secular or religious ideology as bases of South Asian states. Yet religious differences – frequently encapsulated in the catch-all term communalism – were not the main or sufficient cause for the partition of India. Muslim demands for a share of power after the British withdrawal cannot be simplistically interpreted as an invidious policy to subvert the secular ideals of Indian nationalism. The hollowness of such a contention is exposed when when one considers that Gandhi himself associated the goal of Indian nationalism with *Ram Rajya*. Although Gandhi never intended this as a religious ideal, it was for many Indian Muslims a problematic symbol to embrace with equanimity. Mohammad Ali Jinnah on the other hand had long maintained that he was advancing the question of minorities as a political and not a religious issue which needed to be addressed and resolved. Even after he put forward the Muslim claim to nationhood there was no waning of Jinnah's secular beliefs. As he told the first meeting of Pakistan's constituent assembly on 11 August 1947:

You are free to go to your temples, you are free to go to your mosques or to any other place of worship in this state of Pakistan. You can belong to any religion or caste or creed – that has nothing to do with the business of the state . . . we are starting with this fundamental principle that we are all citizens and equal citizens of one state.[2]

A constitutional lawyer by training, Jinnah could see the difficulties of reconciling the conception of a religious state with the need to confer equal citizenship rights in a modern nation-state. The insight of the founding father was lost upon the ideologues of an Islamic Pakistan. Making a virtue of their exclusion from India, they rushed to adopt an idiom of inclusionary nationalism based on Islam to claim the allegiance of territories constituting the newly created nation-state. Tensions between the imperatives of citizenship in a territorial nation-state and the supra-territorial notion of a Muslim *ummah* was to frustrate Pakistan's search for an identity that is both 'national' and 'Islamic'. It could not be 'national' because in the Islamic conception of the state non-Muslims do not have equal rights of citizenship. And it could not be 'Islamic' if the boundaries of the nation-state, as opposed to religious affiliations, were to distinguish citizens from non-citizens. There was yet a starker contradiction attending the construction of

[2] Quaid-i-Azam Mohammad Ali Jinnah, *Speeches as Governor General of Pakistan 1947–1948*, Karachi, no date, p. 8.

the discourse on Pakistani nationhood. This was the willingness to sever all ties with co-religionists in India whose geographical location denied them the rights of citizenship in the Muslim state even while they were theoretically constitutive elements of not only the *ummah* but, more importantly, the pre-1947 'Muslim nation'.

The disjunction between claims of Muslim 'nationhood' and the winning of 'statehood' has been one of the more profound legacies of decolonization. It is one which has continued to shape the destinies of Muslims in the subcontinent, albeit as citizens of three distinct nation-states. Far from Muslim-majority states raising a shield in defence of their interests, the Muslim minority in India has been left peculiarly vulnerable to charges of dubious loyalty to both the Indian nation-state and the community of Islam. The existence of sovereign Muslim-majority states in the north-western and north-eastern corners of the subcontinent has hugely exacerbated the ever present insinuation of the extra-territorial affinities of India's Muslims. Extremist Hindu organizations such as the Jan Sangh and the RSS have long fulminated against Muslims for their 'foreign' and, therefore, anti-national, origins. Even the historically more circumspect versions of the role of Islam in the subcontinent are wont to associate the term 'Muslim' with a long line of Muslim invaders from the north-west. During the freedom struggle the distinction between Muslim 'communalists' and 'nationalist Muslims', or those who supported the Congress, was not just a matter of semantics. It was representative of an attitude which saw fit to exclude from the nationalist mainstream any Muslim contesting the Congress's vision of the future.

The fact of partition and the conflation of secularism and nationalism in the official discourse of the post-colonial Indian state aggravated the dilemma of Muslims who for a variety of reasons, some ideological but mostly pragmatic, opted out of Pakistan. In their efforts to be good citizens of a secular and democratic state, India's Muslims have had to distance themselves from any displays of concern about their predicament by co-religionists across the border. Particularly true of sections of the Muslim elite in India, it has made for a widening gulf between India's secular Muslim spokesmen anxious to assert their nationalist credentials and the broader masses of Muslims for whom religion remains one of the more important sources of identity. The creation of a truncated Muslim state in 1947 has intensified the vertical and horizontal lines of division among the subcontinent's regionally based Muslim majorities and minorities as well as elites and non-elites. Non-Muslim minorities in Pakistan and Bangladesh are in a similar, perhaps deeper, quandary even though their problem is not nearly as vast in scale as that of Muslims in India. Against the common backdrop of partition neither Islam nor secularism as ideologies of state have managed to alleviate the problem of religious minorities in the subcontinent.

While successive regimes in Pakistan have sought to confirm their adherence to the official ideology of Islam as the *raison d'être* of the state, political leaders in India have tried equally hard to assert their secular credentials. Discrepancies arising from Pakistan's Islamic claims and the imperatives of equal citizenship rights in a territorially defined nation-state defy logical solution. In choosing to define itself as secular and democratic, India at least avoided the ponderous illogicalities of Pakistan's official self-projections. Yet the close association of state secularism with Indian nationalism has given rise to its own peculiar set of contradictions. True for the religious minorities, it has also had a bearing on segments of the majority community who cannot envisage the notion of a secular nationalism devoid of a cultural ethos.

Designed as strategies of mobilization in the main, secularism and communalism have never been rigidly compartmentalized ideologies, whatever the claims of the proponents. While they have influenced official constructions of nationalism in both India and Pakistan, the precise role of the two ideologies has had less to do with the absence or existence of religion in politics per se than with the ways in which they have been deployed by the state to gain legitimacy. In other words, secularism and communalism as such convey little of the differences and similarities between the Indian and the Pakistani states and polities. It is only in conjunction with the official discourse of nationalism that the two ideologies assume relevance. Seen in the context of the dialectic between the state structure and political processes, it is possible to detect not only the reasons for the current stresses on secularism in democratic India but also those that have made Islam an uncertain resource at best in military authoritarian Pakistan.

The term 'secularism' in the Indian context has come to assume a number of meanings. First and foremost a secular ideology seeks to assert that India despite the fact that Hindus constitute 85 per cent of the population is not a Hindu state. Second, all citizens of the state have the constitutional right to profess, practise and propagate their religion. And finally, the state is constitutionally bound not to discriminate on the basis of religion or to favour one religion over another. Indeed, the Indian constitution explicitly prohibits the use of the religious idiom in election campaigns for political office. That the need to assert the Indian state's secularism was intended as the antithesis of partition and Pakistan requires no special perspicacity. The secular posture of the Indian state also aimed at reassuring the religious minorities that their citizenship rights would be protected. Yet in the absence of the effective institutionalization of citizenship rights, irrespective of religious affiliation, India's formal democracy has over time clung more to the 'national' than to the 'secular' side of the equation legitimizing relations between state and society. With the steady etiolation of Congress's democratic base of support, there has been a commensurate loss of credibility in its version of a secular India. The battle between secular and communal forces, whether deriving support from or being contested by regionally based political configurations, is about which can lay a better proprietary claim on the nationalist mantle.

In the immediate aftermath of partition, Congress's adoption of a secular ideology symbolized both the negation of Muslim provincialism and communalism and the affirmation of Indian unity. But the reiteration of secularism in the sweeping constitutional amendment of the emergency period was directed against Hindu rather than Muslim communalism. The forty-second amendment was justified by Indira Gandhi as a necessary weapon to ward off what she saw as a Hindu chauvinistic movement against her regime. Although the opposition movement led by Jayaprakash Narayan contained democratic and egalitarian strands it was supported and deeply infiltrated by the Jan Sangh, the Hindu right-wing party. This gave Mrs Gandhi the ammunition she needed to prop up central authority professedly in the cause of secularism as well as socialism. Though the secular façade in India had provided cover to a multitude of sins, it is true that until about 1980 the rights of religious minorities were by and large upheld by the juridical arms of the state. It is only in the past decade or so that observers have grown chary of spotting the blots in the Indian state's commitment to secularism.

The raging furore over the issue of so-called secularism versus Islam in Pakistan would appear odd only to those who take the oft-repeated claim of religion being the sole determinant of nationality at face value. Resting on a pronounced tension between the imperatives of equal citizenship rights in a modern nation-state and the non-territorial conception of the Muslim community, the claim has served more as a rhetorical device than an easily implementable policy. While providing a pretext for meting out differential treatment to Muslim and non-Muslim 'citizens', many of the more stinging contradictions in a nation-state proclaiming a religiously based nationalism have been kept under wraps during extended periods of military authoritarianism. Prior to the breakaway of Bangladesh, non-Muslims constituted 14 per cent of Pakistan's population; after 1971 their percentage plunged to a mere 3 per cent. Under the terms of the objectives resolution of 1949, the Pakistani state is committed to affording protection to the religious minorities. Yet separate electorates for religious minorities have been kept in place despite repeated charges by their spokesmen that this enforced compartmentalization from the rest of society disempowers Pakistan's non-Muslims further still. Quite apart from the denial of basic political rights to all and sundry, the fact that non-Muslims constitute an insignificant proportion of the Pakistani population has prevented any sort of sustained debate on equal citizenship rights. Indeed, the debate on Islam and secularism in Pakistan for the most part has been largely irrelevant to the mundane concerns informing the lives of the vast majority of the citizens.

Devoid of substantive content and littered with platitudes, the historical significance of the debate lies in capturing the desperate postures of Pakistan's leaders in their search for state legitimacy. For all the lip service its early managers paid to the religious credentials of Pakistan, there has never been any consensus on what was to be the relationship between Islam and the state. Here one can sympathize with their plight. Except for a brief period in the seventh century, and perhaps since 1979 in Iran, there has never been an Islamic state in history. Even the long history of Muslim rule in India offers few clues into the mechanics of Islamic statecraft in the subcontinental setting. So for all the talk about an Islamic state there has been no agreement on what should be its basic features and hardly any historical precedent for translating theory into practice. It is worth pointing out that any definition of an Islamic state which would establish the dominance of the religious leaders was quite unacceptable to the Muslim League leaders and, more importantly in the Pakistani context, to the Western educated and secular orientated civil bureaucrats and army officers. This explains why the 1956 constitution while labelling Pakistan an Islamic republic avoided acquiescing to the dictates of the religious leaders.

The 1973 constitution did make some efforts to win the support of the religious lobby in order to create a semblance of consensus after Pakistan's military defeat of 1971. Sensing that there was no mass support for Islamization in the country, Bhutto made a series of cynical concessions to the religious lobby in the hope of stealing their thunder while at the same time ensuring that Pakistan remained as 'secular' as it always had been since 1947. By far the most detrimental for the future of equal citizenship rights was Bhutto's buckling under pressure to concede the long-standing demand of the religious parties to cast the heterodox Ahmediya community beyond the pale of Islam. Since the early fifties the Ahmediyas had been the targets of religious intolerance for violating a basic tenet of Islam by maintaining that their spiritual leader, Mirza Ghulam Ahmed, had qualities akin to that of a prophet. Upholding the religious guardians' right to determine a Muslim from non-Muslim, when they could not agree on a simple definition of the Faithful, was to set a dangerous precedent as the great populist is known to have conceded in the privacy of his office. The sight of Bhutto unlocking the floodgates to the Islamic storm of the 1980s is one the dwindling ranks of his supporters have found most difficult to live down.

In a country which has yet to write a primer on the political rights of citizenship, much less its social and economic dimensions, selecting the rules of inclusion in and exclusion from the community of Islam seemed designed to confuse, not clarify, the issue of the state's ideological basis. Islam as religion has been open to far too many conflicting interpretations to serve as a stable ideological anchor for the state. Pakistan's sectarian diversities – and not just the major Sunni–Shia divide – make any sort of consensus, not to mention uniformity of opinion, on Islam virtually impossible to achieve. Pakistan's regional and linguistic diversities pose major impediments to the imposition of doctrinal Islam as the only authentic basis for cultural unity. Islam exercises an undeniable hold on the people of Pakistan. Yet the underpinnings of Pakistani society are strongly defined by local and regional cultures, all of which have incorporated Islam without losing their distinctive characteristics.

Even Zia-ul-Haq's Islamization programme after 1977 had to contend with these social complexities. The general who blandly claimed to be Allah's viceregent on earth was highly selective in his attempts to Islamize Pakistan's state, economy and society. While the Pakistani economy largely escaped being overhauled along Islamic lines and the military regime gave short shrift to the egalitarian aspects of Islam, it was women who came to symbolize the regime's Islamization policies and Islamic commitment. A series of discriminatory laws were passed against women. These blurred the distinction between adultery and rape and reduced the value of the evidence given by a woman to half that of the man. Urban middle and upper class women's groups, notably the Women's Action Forum (WAF), showed courage in opposing these inequitable laws but failed to deter a military ruler anxious to make women – those symbols of Muslim social consciousness – the focal point of a state-sponsored Islamization programme. The fact that Zia's efforts to win approval for his state-sponsored programme of Islamization and his own continued rule in a referendum which equated the two issues in December 1984 was boycotted by an overwhelming majority of Pakistanis is evidence enough that for Muslims Islam is a religion which promises social justice and not, as the general seemed to believe, one with an inordinate appetite for punishment.

Benazir Bhutto, although careful to avoid presenting herself as a spokesperson of women's rights, vowed to repeal all discriminatory laws against women. But with an uncertain majority in parliament and facing the brunt of an orthodox Islamic onslaught against her assumption of office she did not rescind Zia's Islamic laws. With her unceremonious dismissal and subsequent electoral defeat, the women of Pakistan were left confronting a resurgent misogynist wave implicitly supported by the state that would have liked to deny them any role at all in the public arenas. Yet the fact that even the Islamic Democratic Alliance soft pedalled on its drive towards Islamization by passing a much attenuated version of the Shariat bill hints at the unfathomable problems involved in trying to establish the supremacy of Islamic law through the mechanism of representative political institutions. An IDA-dominated parliament refused to give its legislative stamp of approval to any bill which amounted to accepting the supremacy of the religious guardians. The contradictions between an Islamic ideology and the existing structures of the Pakistani state and political economy are too real to be steamrolled by executive fiat. Yet this did not prevent the Pakistani president, Ghulam Ishaq Khan, from preempting the parliamentarians by issuing the *diyat* or blood-money ordinance. According to its provisions, the state cannot prosecute a murderer if he or she has been forgiven by the victim's family. In a society where the ascendancy of a Kalashnikov culture has become proverbial, scions of wealthy families can now commit murders and escape legal action by bribing the victim's family. The *diyat* ordinance also makes fair game of reckless driving, another manifestation of a society edging close to the precipice of anarchy. Under the terms the family of a victim in a traffic accident was to receive a stipulated amount in compensation from the driver. A spontaneous nationwide strike by lorry drivers forced the government of Mian Nawaz Sharif to amend the ordinance. All drivers were assured insurance coverage. But this has made the problems of traffic hazards even more intractable. With the *diyat* ordinance on the statute books, roadside suicides may well become a lucrative option for unemployed members of poor and destitute families. The gaping cleavages between a monolithic Islamic state ideology and diverse societal realities are tangible enough.

In contrast to Pakistan's ungainly experiments in translating its Islamic ideology into practice, socialism and secularism have been the two sacred cows of the Indian state since independence. Both have been deployed to secure the legitimacy of central state authority. Indian socialism was wanting in any real policy content until the late 1960s and always has been something of a smoke screen. Yet few Indian leaders prior to the early 1980s had the temerity to renounce socialism altogether since it was symbolic of a commitment to a betterment of the conditions of India's poor. Rajiv Gandhi made a clear break from India's socialist tradition in 1984 by abandoning socialist idioms even for rhetorical effect and instead launching a selective mobilization which excluded a significant majority of the population. But the technocratic and elitist orientation of the mid-1980s soon ran into difficulties. By the end of the decade Rajiv Gandhi himself had taken to invoking socialist slogans in his appeals to voters. So socialism in India might well be in retreat at the level of state policy and ideology, but it is still very much in currency at the level of politics of mobilization.

No regime or political party in India has repudiated secularism in an outright manner. Even Lal Krishna Advani – the leader of the Bharatiya Janata Party which has succeeded the Jan Sangh as the premier Hindu party – glibly criticizes what he calls pseudo-secularism rather than the secular faith itself. According to Advani, a crusader of what he calls 'cultural nationalism', politicians in India have used secularism as an 'euphemism to cloak their intense allergy to religion, and more particularly to Hinduism'. Indian nationalism was steeped in a 'Hindu ethos'. To force the 'nation to disown its essential personality' was 'perverse and baneful'.[3] India, on this view, can be secular and Hindu at the same time. Defining India in Hindu terms is to deny the historical processes of syncretic accretion, especially those resulting from the Muslim encounter, which have made for a composite culture. Yet, however spurious, the argument does have the effect of calling into question the Nehruvian conception of state secularism as not only coterminous with the polity but also representative of Indian nationalism. The post-independence history of India is replete with instances of an officially secular state accommodating, and even actively encouraging, strategies of mobilization along lines of caste and communal equations in many regions. By effecting changes in the political configurations at the regional level, these strategies gave credence to a set of idioms diametrically opposed to the secular posture of the central state.

While parties like the BJP have been able to score debating points more effectively since the late 1980s, the deemphasis on the secular foundations of the Indian state in fact began under Congress tutelage in 1982 and became more emphatic from 1984. Although persisting in the old Congress tactic of wooing Muslims, Rajiv Gandhi's regime thrived on Sikh baiting and an implicit, if not an explicit, form of Hindu chauvinism hitherto unknown at the level of state policy and ideology in India. So the dissonance between the Nehruvian brand of socialism and a changing polity was in evidence before the BJP emerged as a significant force on the Indian political scene. As the conflation of secularism and nationalism at the level of the central state has come under growing pressure from the overlapping spheres of secular and communal politics at the base, the shifts in the ideological discourse have been painfully obvious.

The Indian state of course has been responding to what it perceives to be an assertion of Hindutva or Hindu identity at the level of society. Some scholars have described the 'Hindu resurgence' as a backlash. This notion rests on a series of questionable assumptions. First, by granting religious freedoms the Indian state is seen to have assumed responsibility for the right of minority communities to follow their laws and customs as a basic part of their personal lives. The fact that religious minorities have special

---

[3] *The Statesman*, Calcutta, 4 January 1993.

rights that cannot be challenged by the majority is a source of resentment for both secular and more communally minded Hindus. For the former because it hampers the goal of a truly secular and democratic India with equal rights of citizenship, irrespective of religion. And for the latter because it confers certain cultural privileges to minority communities which are denied to the Hindu majority on account of India's secular ethos. These sentiments have kept alive the controversy over the Indian state's decision in the fifties to adopt a Hindu code bill to reform what it considered the retrograde cultural practices of the majority community instead of a unified civil code covering all segments of society.

There are two other factors which bring into sharper focus the links between political economy and cultural politics and give an indication of the appeal ideologies drawing upon religious symbols have had on segments of India's educated middle and lower middle classes. Religious identities – those of the majority and the minority communities alike – are reinforced when there is a perception that a section of the minorities is doing better in economic terms. Based on a highly tendentious reading of social change – Hindu middle classes are doing as well if not better than the Muslim – it has been termed in political discourse as the pampering of the minorities by the Indian state. Such impressions have given new vitality to old prejudices against Muslims as belonging to an alien stock and, therefore, suspect in their loyalty to India. With their expectations soaring in inverse proportion to slumping opportunities, segments of the educated middle classes have been particularly susceptible to a reading of India's past in which all appeared glorious before the devastations wrought by foreign Muslim marauders and iconoclasts. A third factor related to the second are the growing armies of unemployed youth who have been recruited into the extremist movements of minorities and, more importantly, by the pro-Hindu political parties and their socio-cultural fronts. As the shock troops of not only the Hindutva brigades but also of Muslim fundamentalist groups, these youths have been playing a crucial role in the rising graph of communal violence in many parts of India.

Changes in the Indian political economy have certainly contributed to the new cultural politics. Yet religion and politics might not have found their current explosive mixture in the secular liberal democracy of India if the Congress party and government led by Rajiv Gandhi had not come to view Indian society through the distorting colonial spectacles which revealed large supra-local religious communities forming vote banks at the time of elections. Having whipped up Hindu fervour with his anti-Sikh posture in the 1984 elections and opened the doors of the Babri mosque in Ayodhya to Hindus in February 1986, Rajiv Gandhi sought to restore Muslim confidence in his government by introducing the Muslim women's protection or rights on divorce bill in parliament. The background to this bill is provided by the Shah Bano case which also highlights the connection between the ideological issues of community and gender.

In 1978 a resident of Indore, Madhya Pradesh, divorced his wife Shah Bano and gave her Rs.3,000 which had been her *mehr* or marriage settlement as required by Islamic law. Shah Bano sued her ex-husband for maintenance. She won her case at the lower magistrates court, the high court and the supreme court which ruled that under section 125 of the Indian penal code an Indian husband was required to pay for the maintenance of a wife without means of support. The ruling lit the fuse which sparked a major agitation. In Bombay a procession of 100,000 Muslims denounced the ruling as an infringement of Muslim personal law. At this point Shah Bano stated that she had not realized that acceptance of maintenance was against the teachings of Islam and agreed to accept the Shariat view that the obligations of a marriage contract ended with a divorce. She however added an amusing twist to her religious sentiments by going back to the court to get the current value of her marriage settlement which had risen from Rs.3,000 in 1932 to Rs.120,000 in 1986.

Matters came to a head when Rajiv Gandhi intervened on the side of the religious lobby with an eye to what he saw as the Muslim vote. According to the Muslim women's bill which was introduced by his government, Muslims were not to be made subject to the offending section 125 and instead a Muslim woman could look for support from her family and relatives or, failing that, from Muslim charitable trusts. Two hundred women, largely drawn from urban middle and upper classes, chained themselves to parliament in what they saw as an abject surrender to fundamentalist forces. For many liberal Muslims and Hindus the bill was Rajiv Gandhi's capitulation to Islamic obscurantism in the name of protecting the cultural rights of a minority. It cannot be denied that they had a point. Yet having inveighed against the Islamic bond as the main defining feature of 'Muslim interests' in order to better cultivate their secular and national ties to the state, India's liberal Muslims were reaping the whirlwind of rejection by many co-religionists who, while internally divided, look upon the men of religion for leadership in matters to do with the affairs of the community. So while an articulate cluster of liberal Muslims are understandably attached to Nehruvian secularism as a matter of right in both senses of the word, these would-be leaders of an integrated and moderate Muslim community in India have much to answer for their relative isolation and inefficacy in the maelstroms of a culturally motivated politics of difference. That their dilemma is an acute one can be seen in the marshalling of arguments by Hindu revivalists who denounced the bill as encouraging Muslims to put membership in their religious community over allegiance to the nation.

This furnished more proof that Muslims could never be trusted and it was ludicrous for the Indian state to go on pandering to their communalism in the name of secularism. Under the guise of calling for a unified civil code they have been demanding a return to the Hindu personal code which was legislated away in the early 1950s.

The sheer intensity of the Hindu movement to build a temple on the site of a mosque in Ayodhya made the Muslim campaign against the Shah Bano case look placid by comparison. Some extremist Hindu groups, notably the Vishwa Hindu Parishad, had for long been demanding that the Babri masjid be pulled down and a temple to Rama built in its place. The demand is based on the claim that Rama, the mythical hero of the great Hindu epic *Ramayana*, was born exactly on the spot where the mosque stands. Leading Indian historians have pointed out that the town of Ayodhya itself shifted from one place to another along with the political centre of gravity in the region. Moreover, there is no contemporary sixteenth-century evidence to substantiate the charge that Babur razed Ram's temple to build the mosque. One of the first historians to write about such a demolition was a Mrs A. S. Beveridge in the late nineteenth century. It is not a coincidence that a historian's discovery of the fact of a 'temple-mosque' controversy occurred about the time that the British were engaged in redefining the social and political meaning of broad religious categories in India. Anyhow those who emphasize faith over history have had no difficulty in accepting an artifact of British colonialism to make a point about a prior Muslim colonialism.

On the eve of the 1989 elections the BJP took part in the transportation of 'holy bricks' to Ayodhya and a foundation laying ceremony for a temple to Ram near the mosque. The Congress government, afraid of losing some Hindu votes, did not stop the ceremony from taking place. Less than a year after the elections V. P. Singh's decision to announce a policy of job reservations for backward castes seemed designed to divide the Hindu community by caste and thereby undermine the BJP's electoral project of mobilizing support by playing the communal card. Its leader, L. K. Advani, responded by undertaking a *ratha yatra* (a chariot journey) which critics quickly dubbed a riot *yatra*. After traversing large parts of northern India, Advani threatened to arrive in Ayodhya and start building the temple. The BJP had not only taken on its political rivals but challenged one of the main foundations of the Indian state. Those who were in charge of the state apparatus prevented the enactment of the BJP's plan. Although a government in New Delhi proved to be a casualty of this episode the Indian state managed to scotch an attempted political coup by the extreme religious right. It did, however, appear to give an ideological cover to the Bharatiya Janata Party's successful manipulation of caste and class-based interests in the state and parliamentary elections of 1991.

In an apparent concession to Hindu popular culture, however defined, the Congress government of Narasimha Rao was willing to negotiate with Hindu groups determined to carry out their plans to build a temple to Ram at the site of the Babri masjid. The readiness to countenance serious talks with the authors of a particular modern construction of Hindu culture was a measure of just how far the shrinking of the centralized Indian state's democratic base in society had led it to retreat from its much celebrated secular credentials. 'Let Muslims look upon Ram as their hero and the communal problems will be all over,' K. B. Hedgewar, the RSS's founding father and leading ideologue, had once declaimed.[4] By 1992 this communally charged exhortation seemed to have had the desired impact on the leader of a party whose grip on state power was slipping quite as rapidly as its secular and democratic moorings. The culpability of the premier nationalist party in the destruction of the mosque in December 1992, and the subsequent decision to build a temple to Ram amid the ruins, revealed in a glaring flash the full extent of the Indian state's structural atrophy and ideological bankruptcy.

Conclusion

Monolithic state ideologies in South Asia have been designed primarily to legitimize control over diverse local and regional social formations. While the non-elective institutions of the state, especially its coercive arms, impose a measure of domination over societal heterogeneities, the accompanying centralizing and homogenizing ideologies have been far less successful in achieving their hegemonic intent. The elements making up the state's monolithic ideologies are on the one hand stubbornly contested and on the other selectively appropriated by dominant social groups at the local and regional levels. A very different set of motives and meanings underlies this process of contestation and appropriation than the one informing the state's agenda. For example, socialism in so far as it promised equity and justice became widely accepted by segments of India's local and regional social formations which did not necessarily subscribe to the assumption that the central state was the ultimate instrument of redistribution. Similarly Islam forms an inextricable part of Pakistan's local and regional social structures which do not acknowledge the central state as the fount of religious virtue.

It was the deployment of ideology in the service of central authority based on the old structures of the colonial state that established the contradiction with diverse social interpretations of the dominant national discourse,

---

[4] *Organiser*, 20 June 1971, cited in Tapan Basu, Pradip Datta, Sumit Sarkar, Tanika Sarkar and Sambuddha Sen, *Khaki Shorts and Saffron Flags: a Critique of the Hindu Right*, New Delhi, 1993, p. 12.

whether of the socialist, secular or communal variety. Secularism and religious communalism in this context represented two sides of the same coin struck by the post-colonial state. As long as optimism in the nation-state ran high, India's secularism resting as it did on principles borrowed from the West retained its privileged status in the official discourse on modernization. That the secularism of the Indian state made compromises with caste and even communal ideologies prevalent at the local and regional levels was ignored as inconsequential. Pakistan's accent on Islam was deemed a trifle retrograde within the ideological paradigm of moderni-zation. But that did not bring it any closer to the social realities of its own local and regional cultures. So neither Indian secularism nor Pakistani Islam managed to bridge the gulf separating the ideology of post-colonial states and the beliefs and practices embedded in their societies and cultures.

The vacuous nature of central state ideologies became particularly trans-parent with the deepening and broadening of political processes. India's formal democracy necessitated non-secular caste and community-based political mobilization just as Pakistan's controlled elections helped perpe-tuate the significance of localized clan-based social and political networks owing little if anything to Islam. National ideologies were meant to affirm and strengthen the authoritarianisms, whether overt or covert, of the post-colonial states. Yet in practice these have been deflected by local and regional social structures and effectively neutralized the purported objec-tive of enforcing uniformity, if not national unity. Secularism, socialism and communalism all have proved to be rather fragile bases on which to build the monolithic edifices of sovereign states. After more than four and a half decades of experimenting with all these various national-isms central state authority in the South Asian subcontinent has been left facing multiple challenges framed in a variety of caste, class, religious and linguistic idioms. Structures and ideologies imposed on variegated local and regional societies and cultures from the commanding heights of only a nominally decolonized central state have achieved a degree of coercive domination in the absence of consensual hegemony. The process of decolonization in South Asia will not have been completed until social and cultural hybrids prise open contrived ideological monoliths and begin altering prevailing states of mind better versed in the unambiguous language of departed colonial masters than in the inimitable flexibilities, richness and enchanting nuances of their own historic multiplicities.

7   Conclusion

As to where Pakistan was located, the inmates knew nothing ... the mad and the partially mad were unable to decide whether they were now in India or Pakistan. If they were in India where on earth was Pakistan ... It was also possible that the entire subcontinent of India might become Pakistan. And who could say if both India and Pakistan might not entirely vanish from the map of the world one day?[1]

The idea of the modern nation-state more than any other political construct has inspired a flourish of improbable social identities. Frontiers of states have rarely matched the complex contours of multiple identities. Demanding exclusive loyalty as the price of inclusion, the nation-state's definition of citizenship has rendered impermeable the otherwise historically shifting and overlapping boundaries of identities at the social base. Assertions of identity in the era of the modern nation-state are invariably expressions of a politics of difference which in diverse societies tend to translate into a politics of intolerance. Yet nowhere have the nation-state's ineluctable rules of citizenship generated more confusion and chaos than in a subcontinent dissected by the arbitrary lines of 1947. Amidst an unprecedented orgy of communal madness, only the inmates of a mental asylum in Sadaat Hasan Manto's short story, *Toba Tek Singh*, had the courage that comes of political innocence to question the insane logic of reducing identities to fit the ideologically based territorial limits of newly proclaimed 'nation-states'. Those who rose to the helm of these post-colonial entities were equipped with the structural and ideological powers of coercion to discipline and punish anyone wavering on the issue of singular allegiance to the twin monoliths of state and 'nation'.

While the redrawing of 'national' frontiers left millions homeless and many hundreds of thousands dead, the transition from colonial subjugation to post-colonial freedom witnessed a remarkable degree of structural continuity under the rubric of apparent ideological discontinuity. Punctuated with the loaded if nebulous ideal of the 'nation', the violence embedded in

---

[1] Sadaat Hasan Manto, 'Toba Tek Singh' in *Kingdom's End and Other Short Stories*, translated from the Urdu by Khalid Hasan, Harmondsworth, 1989, p. 12.

the structures of the colonial state now turned against citizens whose right to partake of independence had to be a derivative of the officially sponsored discourse on identity. In what was a brutal irony of the coming of independence, erstwhile colonial subjects earned the trappings of citizenship by further constraining their freedom to nurture historically evolved multiple identities. It was worse than that. Liberation from the colonial yoke did not involve dismantling the structures of unitary state power. The very instruments of colonial tyranny that had so fired the nationalist ire became the lightning rods of the post-colonial order. The anti-colonial thrust of nationalist legitimizing ideologies notwithstanding, an alien concept of indivisible sovereignty was briskly adapted to delimit the acceptable parameters of political allegiance.

While the imperatives of power shaped the postures of state managers, the incomplete decolonization of the mind prevented a sustained critique of the state in post-colonial South Asia. Mindful of being labelled 'anti-state', 'traitor' and 'terrorist', many in the domain of knowledge for different reasons guarded their limited autonomy by succumbing to the dictums of the nation-state, especially its project of retroactively constructing the narrative of an inclusionary nationalism to counter colonialism's insidious legacy of dividing and ruling. The inequities rooted in the post-colonial international world system and tensions with regional neighbours justified intellectual complicity in upholding the nation-state's claims of monolithic sovereignty. Unquestioning respect for arbitrarily demarcated frontiers, partly motivated by the visceral hostility of the structural entities inhabiting them, blunted the comparative edge that might have contributed to a more incisive analysis of state–civil society relations in subcontinental South Asia.

In exploring a set of comparative themes this book has deliberately defied the border patrols and transgressed the temporal and spatial frontiers of 1947. And it has done so at the risk of incurring the displeasure of the intellectual thought police that wittingly or unwittingly have taken the inviolability of the sovereign nation-state as a main principle in defining the legitimacy of research agendas. If the scholarly community is to push forward the ongoing processes of decolonization, both structural and ideational, the wisdom of perpetuating the nationalization of knowledge on the subcontinent cannot escape systematic challenge. This attempt at smuggling ideas across the rigid barriers of sovereign states will have served its purpose if it opens the way for a free and unrestricted scholarly exchange aimed at reconceptualizing, reconstituting and rethinking the subcontinent's past, present and future.

The study has called into question some of the certitudes about post-independence states and societies in subcontinental South Asia. The simple dichotomy between democracy in India and military authoritarianism in Pakistan and Bangladesh collapses as soon as one delves below the surface phenomena of political processes. An historical interpretation in comparative light reveals more shadowy areas of difference and similarity than of flagrant contrast. Once the analytical spotlight is turned on the dialectic between state structures and political processes, post-colonial India and Pakistan appear to exhibit alternate forms of authoritarianism. The nurturing of the parliamentary form of government through the meticulous observance of the ritual of elections in India enabled a partnership between the political leadership and the non-elected institutions of the state to preside over a democratic authoritarianism. In post-1947 Pakistan and, after 1971, also in Bangladesh the suspension of political processes tilted the balance more emphatically in favour of the non-elected institutions paving the way for a military–bureaucratic authoritarianism. The recent transitions to formal democracy in Pakistan and Bangladesh have not fundamentally altered the historic institutional imbalances; they have merely permitted these countries to come a step closer to India's paradoxical achievement of a democratic authoritarianism.

The common strand of authoritarianism informing the dialectic between the state structure and political processes as well as the broader relations between the state and civil society flows from the colonial legacy of administrative centralization and the accompanying ideological idioms of monolithic and indivisible sovereignty. These structural and ideational features of colonialism in the post-colonial era from the very onset had to contend with relatively autonomous, if highly diverse and differentiated, regional and sub-regional political economies and socio-cultural formations. As long as the centre remained in British hands, the fractiousness of the subcontinent was contained and manipulated by the bureaucratic arms of the colonial state and deployed in the limited arena of electoral politics to thwart the inclusionary claims of the nationalist opposition. With the departure of the colonial rulers and the imperative of fulfilling the promise of a democratic politics unfettered by bureaucratic authoritarianism, they posed the greatest threat to the Congress and the Muslim League leadership alike.

Congress's inheritance of the British unitary centre and the chastening effects of partition facilitated accommodations with regional and subregional power brokers, many of whom had played a key role in the anticolonial struggle. Yet the pact of dominance which the Congress established in India rested as much on the formal institutions of parliamentary government as on the authoritarian legacies of colonial structures. These had sought to administer a society divided along myriad lines through an overt reliance on bureaucratic authoritarianism allayed by the periodic bending of institutional rules to preserve the colonial state's tenuous grip over the personalized networks of politics in the localities.

If the local structures of the colonial state were a flimsy matrix for rule-bound governance, the induction of democratic politics widened the scope of their manipulation for partisan or personalized ends. Under the terms of the new democratic dispensation, state bureaucrats were in principle subservient to the elected representatives. But in instances of friction and conflict between the different levels of the Congress organization, centrally appointed civil bureaucrats belonging to the IAS were not above flouting the orders of elected representatives. Of course in a context where authoritarianism inhered in local and regional structures of power and dominance, the supremacy of the elected over the non-elected arms of the state in itself offered no assurance for the democratic empowerment of the people. The Nehruvian strategy of working with rural power bosses and the policy of reformist class conciliation, while apparently consistent with the principles of a democratically constituted federalism, indefinitely postponed the more important task of deepening and broadening the Congress's social bases of support.

India's tryst with destiny brought an indigenous ruling configuration to the centre stage of state power, but not a commensurate democratization of politics at the social base. The fact of a pre-existing central apparatus together with the broad-based nature of the Congress's organizational machinery, however, allowed its high command to strike an alliance with the non-elected institutions of the state – the civil bureaucracy, the police and the military. A functioning symbiosis between the Congress and the civilian bureaucracy and, in times of civil unrest, the police mitigated the need for an overt dependence on the military. The containment of the military proved to be a critical factor in the institutionalization of India's formal democracy, albeit one resting on the well-worn authoritarian stumps of the colonial state. This becomes amply clear when one considers Pakistan's experience with representative government in the immediate aftermath of independence.

The absence of a central state apparatus in the territories constituting Pakistan gave rather a different twist to the unfolding dialectic between state construction and political processes. Needing to enforce central authority over provinces where the Muslim League's organizational machinery was virtually non-existent, Pakistan's managers approximated the example of their Indian counterparts by relying on the administrative bureaucracy. But there were important variations on the theme. In India relations between the political and administrative arms of the state beyond the confines of the centre were contentious as often as they were complicitous, depending on the balance of power within the premier political party. The

logic of consolidating central authority where none previously existed saw
Pakistan's civil bureaucrats and senior military officers stealing the march
on parties and politicians. Military hostilities with India led to the diversion
of scarce provincial resources into the defence procurement effort at a time
when neither Pakistan's territorial limits nor political processes had been
clearly defined. To further compound the dilemmas of confirming central
authority, Pakistan's economic resource base was incapable of sustaining a
viable defence establishment. Extracting resources from the provinces
strained their allegiance to the new centre, even as the invocation of threats
to the external security of the state provided a cover for political and
economic coercion. Yet it was the fact of a Bengali majority in the eastern
wing of the country which firmly set the predominantly Punjabi non-elected
institutions of the state against the social dynamics underpinning political
processes. In any representative political system, the Bengalis would dominate power at the centre. Having effectively cornered the political leadership at the centre, senior civil and military officials used their international
connections with London and, after 1954, Washington to win for themselves a strategic position within the state structure. Extinguishing the
hopes of a democratically evolved political system and state structure was an
obvious next step in the consolidation of Pakistan's military–bureaucratic
state. Taken in the autumn of 1958 it has so far proven irreversible despite
the disintegration of the country and sporadic efforts to restore a measure of
autonomy to political processes in order to correct long-standing
institutional imbalances within the Pakistani state structure.

The lack of electoral exercises in Pakistan is often cited as the main factor
ensuring the infirmity of political processes. Yet the lessons from India
serve as a warning against sanguinely interpreting periodic references to the
people as sufficient evidence of a thriving democratic pulse. An investigation of the different phases in India's political development reveals that
changes in the centre–state dialectic, frequently reduced to an examination
of Congress's organizational strengths and weaknesses, were closely mirrored by shifts in the balance within elected institutions as well as between
them and the non-elected institutions of the Indian state. A creeping if
mainly covert authoritarianism served as the principal prop of a formally
democratic political centre at the state and local levels of society. The failure
to undertake effective organizational reforms of the Congress stymied its
electoral appeal as mainly regionally based parties claimed substantial
chunks of a rapidly expanding democratic arena. The erosion of the Congress's support base in a number of regions, first registered in the 1967
elections but gathering in momentum ever since, has fostered greater
dependence by the political centre on the non-elected institutions, the civil
bureaucracy in particular.

So the institutionalization of elections in India, far from eliminating centre–state tensions, has intensified the strains of democratic authoritarianism. An opportunity to reverse this process through an alliance with populist regional leaders was squandered by Mrs Gandhi in the interests of preserving the centralized character of the Indian state. She instead opted for an overt authoritarianism in the hope of projecting the centre as the fount of all populist programmes aimed at redressing the socio-economic inequities rooted in regional and sub-regional political economies. Though short-lived, this attempt at making explicit the implicit authoritarianism of the Indian state highlighted the basic contradiction between the centralized structures of decision making and the forces of regionalism. A return to the established parameters of democratic authoritarianism did little to alleviate centre–state acrimony and, in fact, became more aggravated with the emergence of broad based coalitions of regional parties ready and able to counter Congress's hegemonic claims.

This seemingly curious result of formally democratic politics demands a more nuanced understanding of military authoritarianism in heightening provincial sentiments in Pakistan. Without doubt, the suspension of democratic processes under the auspices of a mainly Punjabi military and civil bureaucracy has encouraged feelings of provincial exclusivism in the non-Punjabi provinces. The breakaway of the eastern wing and the creation of Bangladesh was simply the most dramatic manifestation of the tussle between a centralized and undemocratic state structure and the forces of regionalism. But a comparison with India suggests that the mere existence of democratic political processes would at best have contained, not removed, the basic reasons for provincial grievances. As in India, the source of provincial disaffections in Pakistan originates in the highly centralized nature of political and economic power. Only when political processes begin altering the balance of power between centre and region and, by extension, between elected and non-elected institutions, can electoral democracy achieve its full potential in alleviating the grievances of entire regions and the various social groupings within them.

One of the major stumbling blocks in the process of democratic empowerment has been the firm refusal of political configurations at the apex of power to countenance diluting the centre's powers over the constituent units. This is not to deny the inequalities and injustices ingrained at the regional and sub-regional levels. Yet the imbalances between centre and regions have contributed in no uncertain manner to perpetuating the undemocratic and authoritarian tendencies at the social base. Social groups dominant at the regional levels have extracted a hefty premium to insure the centralized logic of the post-colonial state. Whether in compliance with or in opposition to central authority, social groupings dominant in regional political economies have been able to appropriate the structural and ideational features of the state, irrespective of the nature of the regime, to sustain their own claims to power over the subordinate strata. Without a redefinition of the centre in the post-colonial context, neither the accommodation nor forcible containment of regionalism has succeeded in undermining the local and supra-local structures of dominance and exploitation.

Here the main idioms of colonialism coupled with the grammatical innovations of the modernization paradigm and the ideologies of nationalism have stunted any sort of creative thinking about the centre's role in subcontinental societies. Borrowing the concept of monolithic sovereignty from the colonial state and the developmentalist ideals of modernization, the votaries of centralized power in post-colonial India and Pakistan imbued them with their own variants of nationalism, secular or Islamic, in efforts to sanctify the structural domain of state authority and treat challenges to it as wanton acts of sacrilege. The dominant nationalist discourse in conjunction with central power has projected ideas of indivisible and impersonal sovereignty over the historically more ingrained notions of divisible and personalized sovereignties. And they have done so by relying on bureaucratic structures which even in the colonial era showed flexibility towards the relatively autonomous social dynamics in the localities, frequently personalizing the impersonalized rules of a distant but indivisible sovereign entity.

With centrally planned economic development providing the impetus, electoral democracy in India and controlled politics in Pakistan as well as in Bangladesh have enlarged the scope of personalized transactions between state officials and dominant social groups. The politics of inclusion in formally democratic India and the politics of exclusion in military–bureaucratic Pakistan have been only marginally different in addressing the problems of economic deprivation and disparity. While the demands of electoral democracy led to a wider distribution of economic spoils, India's political economy of development has remained a grim matrix of deplorable inequalities and injustices. Neighbouring Pakistan since the initial years of independence braced itself for a political economy of defence where just the select few with direct access to the military–bureaucratic state have been able to benefit from a system based on differential patronage and selective mobilization. After an all too brief attempt at populist socialistic development, the newly independent state of Bangladesh succumbed to the conflicting interests within state and society and started approximating the Pakistani model of delimiting the field of political inclusion and economic rewards.

Entrapped in personalized idioms of rule geared to sustaining the existing structures of dominance, local as well as supra-local political arenas in India and Pakistan have been more receptive to the language of exclusionary communitarianism than to the one of inclusionary nationalism. Despite a cultural homogeneity, Bangladesh under military–bureaucratic authoritarianism could not prevent the power of Bengali regionalism from splintering along class lines. The interplay of culture as process and the structures of state and political economy may give a different accent to the processes of exclusion and inclusion. But the intimate nexus between democratic politics and authoritarian states in all three countries has militated against the institutionalization of equal citizenship rights, political, social and economic. Despite claims to the contrary, neither democratic and secular India nor military dominated and Islamic Pakistan have had significant success in constructing a common sense of unity out of a jumbled web of multiple identities. A common cultural tradition in Bangladesh has proven no more conducive to national unity. Claiming singular allegiance to the state as the passport of entry into the 'nation' is one thing, preventing legal citizens from harbouring sentiments of exclusion quite another. Feelings of denial and deprivation have been provoking potent and violent reactions against the inclusionary ideologies of nationalism deployed to legitimize post-colonial state structures and political economies. Increasingly cast in the moulds of exclusionary communitarian or even class-based identities, these expressions of disaffection have been steadily weakening the capacities of post-independence states to act coherently or effectively. Particularly true of Pakistan and Bangladesh where political processes have been suspended for extended periods under military rule, this has been no less salient in the formally democratic yet covertly authoritarian polity of India.

The creation of Bangladesh in 1971 enunciated the deficiencies of Islam as the sole basis of a Pakistani nationalism. During the two decades since the disintegration of the country, linguistic and cultural identities in Pakistan's remaining provinces have weathered state-sponsored programmes of Islamization. The politics of exclusion and the economics of differential patronage aimed at broadening the military–bureaucratic state's networks of collaboration have aggravated conflicts between the structures of governance and the aspirations of the governed. Since the mid-eighties central authority in Pakistan has been floundering in the face of a societal crisis of monumental proportions. The lower echelons of the state at the local and provincial levels have been systematically infiltrated by alienated segments in society backed by armed mafias deploying the logic of exclusion with unprecedented vengeance. Neither monolithic sovereignty nor the inclusionary ideology of nationalism seem capable of rescuing an emasculated but centralized, an interventionary but irresponsive state structure.

The linguistic reorganization of most of the Indian states in the late fifties appeared to have gone some way towards meeting regional aspirations. The ideology of secularism enshrined in the Indian constitution was designed to buttress a broad-based territorial nationalism against the forces of religious communalism. In the initial decades of independence the centralized structure of the Indian state mitigated by the Congress's federally based organizational machinery managed to counter the centrifugal pulls of a predominantly linguistic regionalism. With the expanding sphere of politics and the corresponding erosion of the Congress's social base in the different regions, the continued centralization of economic and political power has come to rest less and less on a democratic consensus reflected in electoral processes and more and more on authoritarian coercion rooted in the non-elected institutions of an inadequately decolonized state structure.

During the eighties the tenuous hold of centralized authority in India came into the foreground as movements of social dissidence at the regional and sub-regional levels acquired unprecedented intensity and simultaneity. In a chilling demonstration of their ideological bankruptcy, various political configurations at the centre since the early 1980s have been seeking to blunt the fragmentary thrust of heightened social conflict through symbolic invocations of a common Hindu cultural identity. As if to counter the processes of societal and governmental atrophy, a state-controlled media took to spinning commercial yarns based on the great Hindu epics *Ramayana* and *Mahabharata*. Images of Hindu supremacy and culture on the screen found a receptive audience among many for whom the secular ideals of the state had remained quite as far removed from the reality of everyday life as its democratic protestations. With Hindu majoritarian communalism as the latest prop of an embattled 'nation' tracing its origins in the glories of an ancient past disrupted by a stream of foreign invaders, paranoia parading as pride has found an easy prey in the religious and cultural symbols of India's minorities. If the attack on the Golden Temple in 1984 had left scope for doubt, the state's complicitous role in the destruction of the Babri mosque at Ayodhya by a mob armed with hatred shattered the aura of a democratic and secular India for a stunned international community. The blend of democratic authoritarianism and majoritarian communalism has turned poisonous, pushing India into a corner from where even the sanctimonious hypocrisy of the state's belated display of its coercive powers to uphold the ideology of secular nationalism offers no safe retreat.

Violent reactions to the destruction of the mosque in predominantly Muslim Pakistan and Bangladesh where Hindu temples were the target of rabble fury reminded the world of the inter-connectedness of developments across the artificial frontiers of nation-states in the subcontinent. The communal demon knows no limits. Far from being compartmentalized and contained by partition, it remains unbridled and undeterred more than four decades later. Scholars of South Asia for long have quibbled over the phenomenon of communalism. Although a recurring madness, it is important to avoid ahistorical assumptions which essentialize communalism by viewing it as a primordial subcontinental psychic disorder. Instead communalism or the politicization of religious identities has to be analysed in conjunction with the processes of inclusion and exclusion within a historically changing context of both intra- and inter-state relations.

Communalism's latest manifestation in the politics of the subcontinent cannot but be linked to the internal pretensions and external postures of the post-1947 nation-states. The ideologies of secularism in India and of Islam in Pakistan have proven more successful in emphasizing the distinctive identities of the two states than in furthering the respective claims of their inclusionary nationalisms. But the self-projections of states are often more revealing in what they seek to mask. Secularism in India has always co-existed with powerful strands of communalism in different regional political economies. This has given the political centre a potent weapon against the forces of regionalism. A formally secular stance has not prevented ruling parties at the centre from cynically using the communal factor to cut the losses of declining electoral support. With growing rifts in centre–state relations heightening the authoritarian features of Indian democracy, communalism has been redeployed to sustain the claims of inclusionary nationalism and monolithic sovereignty. Recourse to an inclusionary Islamic ideology in Pakistan was also designed to parry the threat of provincialism. As its democratic credentials have come under more concerted challenge, a centralized state structure dominated by the military and the bureaucracy has brushed up its Islamic identity.

Riding the religious tiger in societies undergoing rapid and uneven economic changes may well prove to be the nation-state's final fling with destiny. It is precisely because the nation-states of subcontinental South Asia as they are presently constituted have transparently failed to square their assertions of monolithic sovereignty with the expectations of equal citizenship rights that elements in civil society are seizing the initiative and directing the politics of difference to the dead end of intolerance. Exclusionary communitarianism, however ingeniously packaged, is no substitute for the inclusionary nationalism that has been the sole legitimizing factor of the modern nation-state's claims to monolithic sovereignty.

This attempt at reconceptualizing the subcontinent's recent history has revealed the inadequacies, if not the inappropriateness, of the nation-state's main structural and ideational features. The nation-state's efforts to manipulate and control the overlapping oscillations between centralism and regionalism as well as nationalism and communalism have had a direct bearing on the problem of recasting multiple social identities to fit a singular conception of citizenship in the subcontinent. Historically, multiple and shifting social identities in South Asia have found their most comfortable expression in political arrangements based on loosely layered sovereignties. It is time to abandon the dominant discourse on monolithic sovereignty and reconstitute the narrative of inclusionary nationalism. So long as it continues to be couched in the language of putative majorities and minorities, inclusionary intentions will engender exclusionary results. The more so since the democratic and bureaucratic authoritarianism of post-colonial states very early on in the day shelved the project of extending rights of equal citizenship irrespective of membership in 'majority' or 'minority' communities – whether defined along religious, linguistic, regional or even caste lines.

The history of modern South Asia has shown how the quest for a homeland to call one's own can lead to distortions and dislocations whenever and wherever there exists a lack of congruence between identity and territory. The demographic fact of as many Muslims in India as in either Pakistan or Bangladesh forty-seven years after the creation of a Muslim homeland is only the most glaring illustration of the point. A careful historical study of the politics of difference in the subcontinent makes clear that assertions of separate identity and even the territorial aspect of communitarian claims to sovereignty and nationhood tends to be more nuanced than is recognized. Demands for sovereign national status by religious or linguistic communities have generally not precluded the possibility of negotiating terms on which to associate with higher layers of sovereignty and share power within larger multinational states.

A decentring of the structural and ideational features of the nation-state may be a tall order for the hollow carcass that serves as political discourse in subcontinental South Asia. In the absence of any political will to reconstitute existing structures of states which are more lathe than steel, renegotiate societal relations which are collages of murderous passions and redefine the ideologies of dominance and resistance which are creating newer and deeper fissions out of old ones, scholars cannot afford the luxury of disengagement. Only through a concerted effort at rethinking the future can scholars of South Asia help shape the realm of political indeterminacy that is casting such a menacing shadow over the subcontinent as a whole. South Asia's historical legacy of layered sovereignties and the prospects of imaginatively fashioning innovative frameworks of decentred democracies capable of reflecting not only the multiple identities of its people but also their unfulfilled socio-economic aspirations holds out a rare glimmer of hope. If such a scholarly agenda seems like blurring the boundaries of academe and asylum it will be an exercise in madness more innocuous than the one the guardians of sanity in the subcontinent have tragically resigned themselves to go on repeating.

Bibliographical essay

Introduction

Interpretations of the transition from colonial rule in South Asia have been undergoing major revisions. Scholarly reassessments of the historical factors leading to the partition of India are helping recast many of the key analytical themes which in the past provided the basis for unravelling developments in the two states that replaced the British raj in India. The purpose of this study has been to draw the implications of these new interpretations on post-independence South Asia with special reference to the issues of democracy and authoritarianism. It has done so within a conceptual framework woven around the twin dialectics of centralism and regionalism on the one hand, and of all-India nationalism and religious communalism on the other. These themes straddle the 1947 divide, allowing for a comparative analysis of post-independence developments in India and Pakistan and, after 1971, in Bangladesh without losing sight of the common colonial legacy and history which underpinned the emergence of the modern nation-state system in post-colonial South Asia.

The changing historical canvas of South Asia's immediate pre-independence politics has yet to reflect itself in analyses of post-colonial states and societies. Most of the existing studies on India, Pakistan and Bangladesh are firmly and uncritically predicated on the analytical category of the nation-state. Disciplinary conventions have by and large deterred historians from breaching the 1947 divide. This aversion to delving into the intricacies of contemporary history has been reinforced by government policy in South Asia on the opening up of archival documents. It is extraordinarily difficult to gain access to post-1947 papers in India, Pakistan and Bangladesh. Archives in the United Kingdom and the United States of America implement a more standard thirty-year rule which has made it possible for this author to consult documents on India and Pakistan for just over a decade after independence. Even the files available in British archives, especially the Public Record Office, have undergone a highly selective policy of weeding out the more sensitive materials. They are, consequently,

258

considerably less informative compared to the voluminous records of the colonial era located in the India Office Records and Library. Research for this book has, however, taken full advantage of the available archival sources under the classifications of the Dominion Office, Foreign Office, Treasury and Defence in the Public Record Office. Papers in the National Archives of the United States of America are useful in examining the international connections of the post-colonial states of India and Pakistan. Yet it is less the quality and availability of sources and more the methodological pre-conceptions and disciplinary limitations that have prevented scholars of twentieth-century South Asia from overcoming both the temporal and spatial barriers of 1947.

With few historians ready to cross the 1947 frontier, the field of South Asia's post-independence history for the most part has been dominated by political scientists. While taking some account of the background of the nationalist movement, political scientists generally speaking have treated the decisive moment of 1947 as a critical point of departure from whence to begin tracing the separate developments in India and Pakistan. Typical and noteworthy of this genre of overviews of post-1947 politics are such works as W. H. Morris-Jones, *Government and Politics of India*, London, 1964; Rajni Kothari, *Politics in India*, Boston, 1970; Stanley A. Kochanek, *The Congress Party in India: the Dynamics of One-Party Democracy*, Princeton, 1968; Khalid Bin Sayeed, *Pakistan: the Formative Phase*, Oxford, 1968 and *The Political System of Pakistan*, Karachi, 1967; and Keith B. Callard, *Pakistan: a Political Study*, London, 1957. Among the earlier standard texts for any student of India's and Pakistan's post-independence politics, these explicitly avoid the comparative perspective. Paul R. Brass's *The Politics of India Since Independence*, Cambridge, 1990, and Lloyd and Susanne Hoeber Rudolph's *In Pursuit of Lakshmi: the Political Economy of the Indian State*, Chicago, 1987, are more recent examples of this trend.

Works which have sought to adopt a South Asian perspective are primarily compilations of separate chapters on the different states rather than decidedly comparative in approach. With the exception of the introduction where certain comparative issues are raised, Iqbal Khan (ed.), *Fresh Perspectives on India and Pakistan*, Oxford, 1985, is a collection of previously published articles on India and Pakistan. While A. Jeyaratnam Wilson and Dennis Dalton (eds.), *The States of South Asia: Problems of National Integration, essays in honour of W. H. Morris-Jones*, London, 1982, is organized around themes which lend themselves to comparative analysis, there is no attempt at a dialogue across the borders. Craig Baxter, Yogendra K. Malik, Charles H. Kennedy and Robert C. Oberst, *Government and Politics in South Asia*, Boulder, 1987, is more of an area handbook with separate chapters on all seven states in the region. For a theoretically informed and historically grounded collection of articles on common and comparable issues facing India, Pakistan, Bangladesh and Sri Lanka, see Sugata Bose and Ayesha Jalal (eds.), *Nationalism, Democracy and Development: Reappraising South Asian States and Politics* (forthcoming).

Chapter 1

This chapter aims at contextualizing the colonial period and the distinctive ways in which it impinged upon and reshaped the dialectics of centralism and regionalism as well as of all-India nationalism and communalism. Of late there has been a growing scholarly consensus that pre-colonial India was never quite the overarching centralized polity which many nineteenth-century British writers and twentieth-century South Asian historians had claimed. Irfan Habib's classic study *The Agrarian System of Mughal India, 1556–1707*, London, 1963, grounded on the notion of a highly centralized revenue extracting state has come under critical scrutiny. The portrait of Mughal India emerging from the recent historiography is that of a polity where imperial hegemony could be established only through a constant process of renegotiation with multiple layers of sovereignty at the regional and sub-regional levels. Andre Wink's *Land and Sovereignty in India: Agrarian Society and Politics under the Eighteenth-Century Maratha Swarajya*, Cambridge, 1986, makes a strong argument against the notion of a centralized Mughal state. Non-Mughal regional kingdoms in the far south are seen to have exercised a segmented and loose form of hegemony rather than one based on large surplus extracting centralized bureaucracies. This is the main thesis of Burton Stein's *Peasant State and Society in Medieval South India*, New Delhi, 1980. Susanne Hoeber Rudolph's 'Presidential Address: State Formation in Asia – Prolegomenon to a Comparative Study', *Journal of Asian Studies*, 46, 4 (1987) draws upon some of the new historiography to interpret pre-colonial land-based empires in Asia in a comparative vein.

The relatively fluid relations between centre and region in pre-colonial India suggest that the erosion of Mughal power was more in the nature of a decentralization than an outright decline. The weakening of the Mughal centre and the corresponding strength of regionally based elites is explored in Muzaffar Alam's *The Crisis of Empire in Mughal North India: Awadh and the Punjab, 1707–48*, Delhi, 1986. C. A. Bayly's *Rulers, Townsmen and Bazaars: North Indian Society in the Age of British Expansion, 1770–1870*, Cambridge, 1983, is a masterly account of how the transition to colonialism was moulded by pre-existing institutions and patterns in Indian society. Bayly underscores the collaborative role of North Indian intermediary social groups, such as merchants and bankers, in the colonial expansion. A synthesis of his main arguments, which incorporates the more recent historical monographs on this period, is to be found in the easily accessible *The New Cambridge History of India: Indian Society and the Making of the British Empire*, Vol. II.1, Cambridge, 1988.

The shifting perspectives on the transition to colonialism would appear to emphasize processes of continuity rather more than of change. Yet there can be little question of the very significant changes wrought by colonialism, especially at the level of state institutions and political economy. B. B. Misra's *The Central Administration of the East India Company*, Manchester, 1959, deals with the administrative changes during the early colonial period. His more recent work, *The Unification and Division of India*, New Delhi, 1990, is indispensable to an understanding of how the British in the nineteenth century constructed a unified and centralized institutional structure, a development which as Misra correctly notes was quite unprecedented in the history of the subcontinent. While the colonial state's centralized bureaucracy and standing army provided the institutional moorings for an impersonalized and indivisible notion of sovereignty in the directly administered territories of British India, pragmatism permitted nominal modifications with respect to the Indian princely states which were allowed to retain a measure of internal autonomy or quasi-sovereignty. Michael H. Fisher's *Indirect Rule in India: Residents and the Residency System 1764–1858*, Delhi, 1991 explores the growing sway of the central administration through the agency of political residents and the corresponding etiolation of the sovereignty of princely rulers. Yet even in the directly administered territories, it was one thing to build the institutional framework of a centralized colonial state with all its bureaucratic trappings of impersonalized and indivisible sovereignty, and quite another to translate this into everyday administrative practice. Misra (1990) and in his *Government and Bureaucracy in India: 1947–1976*, Delhi, 1986 underlines some of the contradictions between rule-bound institutions and an Indian society accustomed to a more personalized form of rule.

The inherent limitations of the colonial state in extending the logic of administrative unity to the social and political sphere has spawned engaging debates among historians. Far from being omnipotent, much less possessing a coherent agenda for 'modernizing' India, the colonial state more often than not preferred to make necessary accommodations with Indian society so long as these did not impinge upon broader imperial considerations, both economic and strategic. Acknowledging these accommodations does not, however, add up to an argument about the marginal impact of colonial rule on Indian society. David Washbrook in his seminal article 'Law, State and Agrarian Society in Colonial India', *Modern Asian Studies*, 15, 3 (1981), highlights the clash between the liberal belief in individual enterprise as essential for the operation of a free market economy and the perpetuation of communitarian principles through the codification of Hindu Brahmanical and Muslim personal law. Most historians agree that in viewing Indian society through the prism of religious communities, the British colonial state lent rigidity to categories like Hindu, Muslim and Sikh. Romila Thapar's 'Imagined Religious Communities? Ancient History and the Modern Search for a Hindu Identity', *Modern Asian Studies*, 23, 2 (1989), presents a powerful case about the fashioning of a distinctive Hindu identity based more on the high Brahmanical traditions than on the largely uncodified syncretic cults and sub-cults of popular Hinduism in nineteenth-century colonial India. Richard Fox's *Lions of the Punjab: Culture in the Making*, Berkeley, 1985 advances a comparable argument about the construction of a Sikh identity.

There has been a burgeoning of scholarly interest in the role played by the colonial state in instituting a separation between the public and private spheres on the secular pretext of keeping apart the domains of politics and religion. In 'Progress and Problems: South Asian Economic and Social History c.1720–1860', *Modern Asian Studies*, 22, 1 (1988), David Washbrook argues convincingly that the expansion of the colonial public sphere, including the paraphernalia of legal rights arbitrated in law courts, weakened but never wholly subsumed notions of rights and responsibilities embedded in communitarian structures. The notion of a separate public sphere being coeval with the development of the modern colonial state in India is helping reshape the debate on the role of religion in politics. While much more research on this issue is still underway, there have been some attempts at conceptualizing the role of the public sphere in studies of all-India nationalism and religious communalism, e.g., Sandria B. Freitag, *Collective Action and Community: Public Arenas and the Emergence of Communalism in North India*, Berkeley, 1989. The notion of indivisible sovereignty based on impersonalized and rule-bound colonial institutions together with the persistence of communitarian forms of social organization and identities had large consequences for Indian politics. This became amply evident once the colonial state sought to extend its networks of social collaboration by introducing the principle of elective representation at the local and provincial levels. By far the most decisive step in this respect was the introduction of separate electorates for Indian Muslims in 1909. Peter Hardy's *The Muslims of British India*, Cambridge, 1972, provides a general backdrop to this momentous decision. The difficulties of squaring the communal and regional interests of Muslims and the political strategy of the All-India Muslim League and Mohammed Ali Jinnah are fully explored in Ayesha Jalal, *The Sole Spokesman: Jinnah, the Muslim League and the Demand for Pakistan*, Cambridge, 1985.

Politics, society and economy in the late colonial era have been the focus of an extraordinarily rich and complex historiography. There has yet to be a synthesis of the many important research monographs and articles published over the last two decades. Able overviews and critiques of research until the late 1970s is available in Sumit Sarkar, *Modern India: 1885 to 1947*, New Delhi, 1983, and Rajat K. Ray 'Political Change in British India', *Indian Economic and Social History Review*, 14, 4 (1977). In order to gain familiarity with the more recent scholarly contributions the interested reader should refer to volumes in *The New Cambridge History of India* series and Ranajit Guha and Gayatri Spivak (eds.), *Selected Subaltern Studies*, New York, 1988.

The partition of India at the moment of independence has engaged the attention of numerous scholars, even those who have not directly studied the division of the subcontinent. A recent anthology of different approaches to the subject is Mushirul Hasan (ed.), *India's Partition: Process, Strategy and Mobilization*, Delhi, 1993. What has not been studied in as careful detail are the continuities and discontinuities that the partition of 1947 entailed. Anthony Low (ed.), *The Political Inheritance of Pakistan*, London, 1991, represents one recent attempt to weigh the colonial legacy of communal and provincial politics in the immediate post-colonial era. A few other works are rich in information on specific aspects of the features of continuity and rupture. This book has drawn on details concerning the administrative legacy furnished in B. B. Misra, *Government and Bureaucracy in India: 1947–1976*, Delhi, 1986, and the financial legacy in C. N. Vakil, *Economic Consequences of Divided India*, Bombay, 1950. Some of the statistical data has been culled directly from documents in the Public Record Office in London. In addition, an analysis of Pakistan's share of the spoils can be found in Chaudhri Mohammad Ali, *The Emergence of Pakistan*, Lahore, 1973, and Ayesha Jalal, *The State of Martial Rule: the Origins of Pakistan's Political Economy of Defence*, Cambridge, 1990. Partha Chatterjee's *Nationalist Thought and the Colonial World – A Derivative Discourse*, London, 1986, and C. M. Naim (ed.), *Iqbal, Jinnah, and Pakistan: the Vision and the Reality*, Syracuse, 1979, are of relevance to any study of the ideological legacy. This study has relied on the original writings of nationalist thinkers, and readers interested in the ideological dimension are encouraged to turn to these primary sources.

Chapter 2

The 'success' of democracy in India has led political scientists to focus their analytical lenses on the Indian National Congress rather than on the post-colonial state as a whole. Much of the work on political parties and elections in India has been confined within the liberal democratic paradigm. Notable examples are W. H. Morris-Jones, *Government and Politics of India*, London, 1964, and *Politics Mainly Indian*, Madras, 1978; Myron Weiner, *Party Building in a New Nation: the Indian National Congress*, Chicago, 1967; Stanley A. Kochanek, *The Congress Party in India: the Dynamics of One-Party Democracy*, Princeton, 1968; Rajni Kothari, *Politics in India*, Boston, 1970, and James Manor, 'Parties and the Party System' in Atul Kohli (ed.), *India's Democracy: an Analysis of Changing State–Society Relations*, Princeton, 1988. The recent work of Rajni Kothari, *State Against Democracy: in Search of Humane Governance*, New Delhi, 1988, questions some of the long held axioms of India's parliamentary democracy.

Among the better known Marxist interpretations are Hamza Alavi, 'The State in Postcolonial Societies: Pakistan and Bangladesh', in K. Gough and H. P. Sharma (eds.), *Imperialism and Revolution in South Asia*, New York, 1973; K. N. Raj, 'Politics and Economy of Intermediate Regimes, *Indian Economic and Political Weekly*, July 7, VIII, 27, 1973; E. M. S. Namboodiripad, 'On Intermediate Regimes', *Indian Economic and Political Weekly*, December 1, VIII, 48, 1973, and Randhir Singh, *Of Marxism and Indian Politics*, New Delhi, 1990. This study in particular has questioned the analytical value of Alavi's notion of the 'overdeveloped state' in explaining the reasons for the different political developments in India and Pakistan. South Asia has also provided the empirical reference for largely ahistorical approaches based on assumptions about political culture. Examples include Lucian W. Pye, *Asian Power and Politics: the Cultural Dimensions of Authority*, Cambridge, MA, 1985. More sophisticated political cultural explanations of India's authoritarianism and democracy can be found in Ashis Nandy, *At the Edge of Psychology: Essays in Politics and Culture*, New Delhi, 1980, and 'The Political Culture of the Indian State', *Daedalus*, 118, 4 (Autumn 1989), 1–25. The contrasting inheritances of India and Pakistan in terms of a central state apparatus rather than simply the relative strengths or weaknesses of political parties moulded political developments in the first two decades after independence. V. P. Menon's *The Integration of the Indian States*, Madras, 1956, remains an essential reference work on the welding of the princely domains into independent India. Granville Austin's *The Indian Constitution: Cornerstone of a Nation*, London, 1966, is a comprehensive but largely uncritical account of the constitution-making process in India. Interested readers should consult the relevant *Constituent Assembly Debates* and the five-volume set, B. Shiva Rao (ed.), *The Framing of India's Constitution: Select Documents*, New Delhi, 1966–8. For an incisive contemporary critique of the Indian constitution see Sarat Chandra Bose, 'A Constitution of Myths and Denials' in his *I Warned My Countrymen*, Calcutta, 1968.

Although most general accounts of post-independence India concentrate on parties and politics, there are a number of specialist studies on the Indian bureaucracy. These include Richard P. Taub, *Bureaucrats Under Stress: Administrators and Administration in an Indian State*, Berkeley, 1969; David C. Potter, *India's Political Administrators, 1919 to 1983*, Oxford, 1986; Stanley Heginbotham, *Cultures in Conflict: the Four Faces of Indian Bureaucracy*, New York, 1975; O. P. Dwivedi and R. B. Jain, *India's Administrative State*, New Delhi, 1985 and Dennis J. Encarnation, 'The Indian Central Bureaucracy: Responsive to Whom?', *Asian Survey*, 19, II (November 1979). Two insightful authors relate their studies of the bureaucracy to the broader context of Indian politics. They are C. P. Bhambri, *Bureaucracy and Politics in India*, New Delhi, 1971, and B. B. Misra, *Government and Bureaucracy in India, 1947–1976*, Delhi, 1986. On the Indian military see Stephen P. Cohen, *The Indian Army: its Contribution to the Development of a Nation*, Berkeley, 1971, and Lloyd I. Rudolph and Susanne Hoeber Rudolph, 'Generals and Politicians in India', *Pacific Affairs*, 37, 1 (Spring 1964). The aim of this book has been to probe the relationship between the elected and the non-elected institutions of the Indian state and place Indian politics in the context of state-civil society relations.

On the early decades of Pakistan see Chaudhri Mohammad Ali, *The Emergence of Pakistan*, Lahore, 1973; Khalid Bin Sayeed, *Pakistan: the Formative Phase*, Oxford, 1968; Keith B. Callard, *Pakistan: a Political Study*, London, 1957; Mushtaq Ahmad, *Government and Politics in Pakistan* (second edition), Karachi, 1963 and Inamur Rahman, *Public Opinion and Political Development*, Karachi, 1982. On the process of constitution-making and constitutional crisis see G. W. Choudhury, *Constitutional Development in Pakistan* (second edition), London, 1969; Ayesha Jalal, 'The Politics of a Constitutional Crisis: Pakistan, April 1953–May 1955', in Anthony Low (ed.), *Constitutional Heads and Political Crises in the Commonwealth Since World War II*, London, 1988, and the *Constituent Assembly Debates, 1947–1958*. The ways in which international, regional and domestic factors combined to pave the way for the dominance of the military and the bureaucracy within the Pakistani state structure is delineated in Ayesha Jalal, *The State of Martial Rule: the Origins of Pakistan's Political Economy of Defence*, Cambridge, 1990.

General Ayub Khan's military coup and its aftermath form the subject matter of Herbert Feldman's *Revolution in Pakistan: a Study of the Martial Law Administration*, Oxford, 1967. Another account of Pakistan's first military dictatorship is Lawrence Ziring, *The Ayub Era. Politics in Pakistan, 1958–1969*, Syracuse, 1971. Ayub's own version is *Friends Not Masters*, Oxford, 1967. A recent view by an insider is provided by Altaf Gauhar,

Ayub Khan: Pakistan's First Military Ruler, Lahore, 1993. Stephen Cohen's *The Pakistan Army*, Berkeley, 1984, gives a portrait of Pakistan's premier military institution. For a more general analysis of military rule in Pakistan see Hasan Askari Rizvi, *The Military and Politics in Pakistan: 1947–1986*, Lahore, 1986.

There are a number of studies on Pakistan's other major non-elected institution – the powerful bureaucracy. An early authoritative analysis was that of Ralph Braibanti, *Research on the Bureaucracy of Pakistan: a Critique of Sources, Conditions, and Issues with Appended Documents*, Princeton, 1963. A more focused account from a sociological perspective is Muneer Ahmad, *The Civil Service in Pakistan: a Study of the Background and Attitudes of the Public Servants in Lahore*, Karachi, 1964. Hassan Habib's *Babus, Brahmins and Bureaucrats*, Lahore, 1973 is a sharp critique of the central superior services of Pakistan. For an account of Zulfikar Ali Bhutto's reforms of the civil service see Charles Kennedy, *Bureaucracy in Pakistan*, Karachi, 1987.

Chapter 3

This chapter places the populist era and its aftermath in India, Pakistan and Bangladesh in a comparative perspective. A meticulously researched study of India's populist turn in the late 1960s is Francine R. Frankel's *India's Political Economy, 1947–1977*, Princeton, 1978. A political economy approach to Pakistani populism is taken in Omar Noman, *The Political Economy of Pakistan, 1947–1985*, London, 1988. A rigorous Marxist analysis of the shifting class basis of support of the Congress under Indira Gandhi is offered by Achin Vanaik, *The Painful Transition: Bourgeois Democracy in India*, London, 1990. The Pakistan People's Party's organization and support base are studied in Khalid Bin Sayeed, *Politics in Pakistan: the Nature and Direction of Change*, New York, 1980; Maliha Lodhi, 'The Pakistan People's Party', unpublished doctoral dissertation, London School of Economics, 1979, and Philip Edward Jones, 'The Pakistan People's Party: Social Group Response and Party Development in an Era of Mass Participation', unpublished doctoral dissertation, Fletcher School of Law and Diplomacy, April 1979. On populist mobilization in different regions of India see John Wood (ed.), *State Politics in Contemporary India*, Boulder, 1984. Henry Hart (ed.), *Indira Gandhi's India: a Political System Reappraised*, Boulder, 1976, and Shahid Javed Burki, *Pakistan Under Bhutto, 1971–77*, New York, 1980, are among the other studies of the populist era in India and Pakistan. Works focusing on the personalities of Indira Gandhi and Zulfikar Ali Bhutto include Zareer Masani, *Indira Gandhi: a Biography*, New York, 1976, and Anwar Hussain Syed, *The*

Discourse and Politics of Zulfikar Ali Bhutto, London, 1992. Stanley Wolpert's *Zulfi Bhutto of Pakistan*, Oxford, 1993, obsessively concerned with Bhutto's personality quirks, is a missed opportunity for a serious study of this important period in Pakistan's history.

A recent full-length study of the political processes and conflicts leading to the breakaway of Bangladesh is Richard Sisson and Leo O. Rose, *War and Secession: Pakistan, India and the Creation of Bangladesh*, Berkeley, 1990. General studies of the populist era and its aftermath in Bangladesh are Rounaq Jahan, *Bangladesh Politics: Problems and Issues*, Dhaka, 1980; Zillur Rahman, *Leadership in the Least Developed Nation: Bangladesh*, Syracuse, 1983, and Rehman Sobhan, *Bangladesh: Problems of Governance*, New Delhi, 1993. Lawrence Ziring's new *Bangladesh From Mujib to Ershad: an Interpretative Study*, New Delhi, 1993, suffers on account of its tendentious treatment of Mujibur Rahman's politics and personality. An incisive Marxist analysis is Kirsten Westergaard, *State and Rural Society in Bangladesh: a Study in Relationship*, London, 1985. For a revealing account of the uneasy relationship between the politicians and radical segments of the Bangladesh military see Lawrence Lifshultz, *Bangladesh: the Unfinished Revolution*, London, 1979.

Surprisingly enough, there are not many detailed studies of India's experiment with overt authoritarianism during the emergency of 1975 to 1977. But there are important sections analysing political and economic developments in this era in Lloyd and Susanne Hoeber Rudolph, *In Pursuit of Lakshmi: the Political Economy of the Indian State*, Chicago, 1987, and Henry Hart (ed.), *Indira Gandhi's India: a Political System Reappraised*, Boulder, 1976. See also Francine Frankel, 'Compulsion and Social Change: is Authoritarianism the Solution to India's Economic Development Problems?' in Atul Kohli (ed.), *The State and Development in the Third World*, Princeton, 1986.

On the dilemmas of democracy in post-1977 India see Atul Kohli (ed.), *India's Democracy: an Analysis of Changing State–Society Relations*, Princeton, 1988, and *Democracy and Discontent: India's Growing Crisis of Governability*, Cambridge, 1990, as well as Rajni Kothari, *State Against Democracy: in Search of Humane Governance*, New Delhi, 1988.

There is as yet no authoritative scholarly study of the eleven years of General Zia-ul-Haq's military rule in Pakistan. Initial attempts to analyse this watershed period in Pakistan's history are to be found in Craig Baxter and Shahid Javed Burki, *Pakistan Under the Military: Eleven Years of Zia-ul-Huq*, Boulder, 1991, and in a more journalistic vein, Mushahid Hussain's *Pakistan's Politics: the Zia years*, Lahore, 1990. Hassan Gardezi and Jamil Rashid (eds.), *Pakistan: the Roots of Dictatorship. The Political Economy of a Praetorian State*, London, 1981, and Asghar Khan (ed.),

Islam, Politics and the State: the Pakistan Experience, London, 1985, include some incisive chapters on this period. Sections of Omar Noman, *The Political Economy of Pakistan, 1947–1985*, London, 1988; Hasan Askari Rizvi, *The Military and Politics in Pakistan: 1947–1986*, Lahore, 1986, and Ayesha Jalal, *The State of Martial Rule: the Origins of Pakistan's Political Economy of Defence*, Cambridge, 1990, should be consulted for information on the Zia era. Studies of Pakistan's and Bangladesh's transition to democracy are still in their incipient stages.

Chapter 4

There is a vast literature on the political economy of development in the subcontinent. Angus Maddison, *Class Structure and Economic Growth: India and Pakistan Since the Moghuls*, New York, 1971, is an all too ambitious attempt at a comparative analysis. On policies aimed at class conciliation in India see Francine Frankel, *India's Political Economy, 1947–1977*, Princeton, 1978. Lloyd and Susanne Hoeber Rudolph, *In Pursuit of Lakshmi: the Political Economy of the Indian State*, Chicago, 1987, contains an important argument about the role of agrarian demand groups, especially 'bullock capitalists'. Amiya Kumar Bagchi, *The Political Economy of Underdevelopment*, Cambridge, 1984, shows how the statist orientation of Indian socialism paradoxically bolstered private property rights. Atul Kohli, *The State and Poverty in India: the Politics of Reform*, Cambridge, 1987, provides a general argument about Indian reformism followed by three case studies of the state governments of Uttar Pradesh, Karnataka and West Bengal between 1977 and 1980. Pranab Bardhan, *The Political Economy of Development in India*, Oxford, 1984, argues that the heterogeneity of India's dominant proprietory classes while contributing to the relative autonomy of the state has turned India's public economy into a sprawling network of patronage and subsidies. An authoritative overview of India's planning exercise is given in Sukhamoy Chakravarty, *Development Planning: the Indian Experience*, Oxford, 1987. For perceptive evaluations of the successes and failures of Indian development see Amartya Sen, 'How is India Doing', *The New York Review of Books*, 16 December 1982, and 'Indian Development: Lessons and Non-Lessons' *Daedalus*, 118, 4 (Fall 1989).

There are lively debates on Indian industrialization, alleged urban bias and efficacy of land reforms. On the problems that have bedevilled India's land reform efforts see Ronald Herring's definitive work *Land to the Tiller: the Political Economy of Agrarian Reform in South Asia*, New Haven, 1983. For two sides in the debate on urban bias see Michael Lipton, *Why Poor People Stay Poor: Urban Bias and World Development*, London, 1977, and T. J. Byres, 'Of Neo-Populist Pipe-Dreams: Daedalus in the Third World and the Myth of Urban Bias', in the *Journal of Peasant Studies*, 6, 2 (January 1979). Isher Judge Ahluwalia, *Industrial Growth in India: Stagnation Since the Mid-Sixties*, Delhi, 1985, is a carefully researched monograph on the performance of Indian industry. Bimal Jalan (ed.), *The Indian Economy: Problems and Prospects*, New Delhi, 1992, presents a collection of essays by prominent economists and planners on India's recent efforts at liberalization of the economy.

For general overviews on the early decades of Pakistan's economic development strategies see J. Russell Andrus and Azizali F. Mohammad, *The Economy of Pakistan*, Oxford, 1958, and Gustav F. Papanek, *Pakistan's Development, Social Goals and Private Incentives*, Cambridge, MA, 1967. On the nexus between class and state power see Hamza Alavi, 'Class and State' in Hassan Gardezi and Jamil Rashid (eds.), *Pakistan: the Roots of Dictatorship. The Political Economy of a Praetorian State*, London, 1981, and Richard Nations, 'The Economic Structure of Pakistan and Bangladesh', in Robin Blackburn (ed.), *Explosion in a Subcontinent: India, Pakistan, Bangladesh and Ceylon*, Harmondsworth, 1975. On industrial development in undivided Pakistan see Rashid Amjad, *Private Industrial Investment in Pakistan 1960–1970*, Cambridge, 1982, and Lawrence J. White, *Industrial Concentration and Economic Power in Pakistan*, Princeton, 1974. For useful accounts of development strategies and economic trends extending into the Zulfikar Ali Bhutto era and beyond see Shahid Kardar, *The Political Economy of Pakistan*, Lahore, 1987, and Akmal Hussain, *Strategic Issues in Pakistan's Economic Policy*, Lahore, 1988. Additional information can be gleaned from Khalid Bin Sayeed, *Politics in Pakistan: the Nature and Direction of Change*, New York, 1980, and Omar Noman, *The Political Economy of Pakistan*, London, 1988. For a recent update see William E. James and Subrato Roy (eds.), *Foundations of Pakistan's Political Economy: Towards an Agenda for the 1990s*, Karachi, 1992.

Much has been written on the failure of land reforms in Pakistan, including Ronald Herring, *Land to the Tiller: the Political Economy of Agrarian Reform in South Asia*, New Haven, 1983; M. H. Khan, *Underdevelopment and Agrarian Structure in Pakistan*, Lahore, 1981, and Akmal Hussain, 'Land Reforms in Pakistan: a Reconsideration' in Iqbal Khan (ed.), *Fresh Perspectives on India and Pakistan*, Oxford, 1985. Useful data on the first two decades can be found in Government of Pakistan, *Land Reform in West Pakistan*, Lahore, 1967. Another general overview on land reforms in South Asia containing useful data is I. J. Singh, *The Great Ascent: the Rural Poor in South Asia*, Baltimore, 1990.

A probing analysis of the interconnections between class and state power in Bangladesh is provided by Kirsten Westergaard, *State and Rural Society in Bangladesh: a Study in Relationship*, London, 1985. On the process of pauperization in rural Bangladesh see Willem Van Schendel, *Peasant Mobility: the Odds of Life in Rural Bangladesh*, Assen, 1982; Shapan Adnan and H. Zillur Rahman, 'Peasant Classes and Land Mobility: Structural Reproduction and Change in Bangladesh', *Bangladesh Historical Studies*, 3, 1978, and Willem Van Schendel and Aminul Haque Faraizi, *Rural Labourers in Bengal*, Rotterdam, 1984. On the links between governance and entreprenuership see Rehman Sobhan, *Bangladesh: Problems of Governance*, New Delhi, 1993.

Chapter 5

The abundance of material on federalism in the subcontinent is in inverse proportion to its actual practice. On constitutional aspects of India's federal relations see Asok Chanda, *Federalism in India: a Study of Union–State Relations*, London, 1965, and M. C. Setalvad, *Union and State Relations under the Indian Constitution*, Calcutta, 1974. Useful data from the reports of the finance commissions have been presented in S. N. Jain, Subhash C. Kashyap and N. Srinivasan (eds.), *The Union and the States*, New Delhi, 1972, and B. S. Grewal, *Centre–State Financial Relations in India*, Patiala, 1975. For a detailed examination of regional economic disparities see S. P. Gupta, *Planning and Development in India: a Critique*, Ahmedabad, 1989, and K. R. G. Nair (ed.), *Regional Disparities in India: Papers Presented at the All-India Conference on Regional Disparities in India at New Delhi, April 1979*, New Delhi, 1981.

For an insightful analysis of the politics of centre–region relations see Paul R. Brass, 'Pluralism, Regionalism and Decentralizing Tendencies in Contemporary Indian Politics', in A. Jeyaratnam Wilson and Denis Dalton (eds.), *The States of South Asia: Problems of National Integration, essays in honour of W. H. Morris-Jones*, London, 1982. India's federal dilemma goes back to the early demand for linguistic states. There is a large body of literature on the linguistic reorganization of state boundaries. It is worth looking at the *Report of the States Reorganization Commission*, 1955, Delhi, 1955. An early doomsday view of India's impending disintegration along linguistic lines is to be found in Selig Harrison, *India: the Most Dangerous Decades*, Princeton, 1960. For an account of the Indian centre's attitude towards regional demands see Paul R. Brass, *Language, Religion and Politics in North India*, Cambridge, 1974, and Jyotirindra Das Gupta, *Language Conflict and National Development*, Berkeley, 1970. A wide-ranging collection of essays on India's centre-state problems in the initial decades is available in Iqbal Narain (ed.), *State Politics in India*, Meerut, 1976. An analysis of the language issue in Punjab and Uttar Pradesh from the perspective of a right-wing Hindu party is given in Bruce D. Graham,

Hindu Nationalism and Indian Politics: the Origins and Development of the Bharatiya Jana Sangh, Cambridge, 1990.

A more recent collection of detailed studies of regional politics in India is Francine R. Frankel and M. S. A. Rao (eds.), *Dominance and State Power in Modern India: the Decline of a Social Order*, volumes 1 and 2, Delhi, 1989 and 1990. Some of the articles are especially worthy of attention. On the changing complexion of dominance and resistance in Uttar Pradesh see Zoya Hasan, 'Power and Mobilization: Patterns of Resilience and Change in Uttar Pradesh Politics' in volume 1. On the caste–class nexus of regional dominance in Tamil Nadu see David Washbrook, 'Caste, Class and Dominance in Modern Tamil Nadu: Non-Brahmanism, Dravidianism and Tamil Nationalism' also in volume 1. Jayant Lele's 'Caste, Class and Dominance: Political Mobilization in Maharashtra' in volume 2 analyses the class–caste moorings of political dominance in this important western Indian state. On the whole these two volumes are essential reading for an indepth account of politics in most of the key regions in India as well as of the shifting nature of their relations with the centre.

The background and nature of the regional insurgencies in Punjab, Assam and Kashmir have been attracting scholarly attention. There are a number of fine studies of India's Punjab problem. Richard G. Fox, *Lions of the Punjab: Culture in the Making*, Berkeley, 1985 is an excellent study of Sikh identity formation in the colonial period. The best short analysis of the making of the contemporary Punjab problem is Paul R. Brass, 'The Punjab Crisis and the Unity of India' in Atul Kohli (ed.), *India's Democracy: an Analysis of Changing State–Society Relations*, Princeton, 1988. A full-length study is Rajiv A. Kapur, *Sikh Separatism: the Politics of Faith*, London, 1986. See also Kuldip Nayar and Khushwant Singh, *Tragedy of Punjab: Operation Bluestar and After*, New Delhi, 1984.

A useful, if now somewhat dated, account of the problem in Assam is Myron Weiner, *Sons of the Soil: Migration and Ethnic Conflict in India*, Princeton, 1978. The question of Assam is placed in a larger context in Jyotirindra Das Gupta, 'Ethnicity, Democracy and Development in India: Assam in a General Perspective' in Atul Kohli (ed.), *India's Democracy: an Analysis of Changing State–Society Relations*, Princeton, 1988. Another important essay is Sanjib Baruah, 'Immigration, Ethnic Conflict and Political Turmoil – Assam, 1979–1985' *Asian Survey*, 26, 11 (November 1986).

The conflicting claims of India and Pakistan have had an unfortunate bearing on the quality of scholarship on Kashmir. Most of the articles and books on the subject are parti pris. For a historical account of the dispute from the point of view of India see Sisir K. Gupta, *Kashmir: a Study in India–Pakistan Relations*, Bombay, 1967, and relevant chapters in V. P. Menon, *The Integration of the Indian States*, Madras, 1985. The Pakistani perspective is elucidated in Muhammad Zafrullah Khan, *The Kashmir Dispute*, Karachi, 1950, and K. Sarwar Hasan (ed.), *The Kashmir Question*, Karachi, 1969. A more balanced account is that of Alastair Lamb, *Kashmir: a Disputed Legacy, 1846–1990*, Hertingfordbury, 1991. Among recent contributions see Raju C. Thomas (ed.), *Perspectives on Kashmir: the Roots of Conflict in South Asia*, Boulder, 1992; Balraj Puri, *Kashmir: Towards Insurgency*, New Delhi, 1993 and Ayesha Jalal, 'Kashmir Scars', *New Republic*, July 23, 1990.

For those interested in comparisons with the centre–region problem in Sri Lanka, reference may be made to Stanley J. Tambiah, *Sri Lanka: Ethnic Fatricide and the Dismantling of Democracy*, London, 1986, and Sumantra Bose, *States, Nations, Sovereignty: India, Sri Lanka and the Tamil Eelam Movement*, New Delhi, 1994.

Analyses of Pakistan's inability to accommodate the aspirations of the eastern wing include Rounaq Jahan, *Pakistan: Failure in National Integration* (second edition), Dacca, 1977, and Richard Sisson and Leo O. Rose, *War and Secession: Pakistan, India and the Creation of Bangladesh*, Berkeley, 1990. On centre–region problems in post-1971 Pakistan see Feroz Ahmed, 'Pakistan's Problems of National Integration' in Asghar Khan (ed.), *Islam, Politics and the State: the Pakistan Experience*, London, 1985, and Tahir Amin, *Ethno-National Movements in Pakistan: Domestic and International Factors*, Islamabad, 1988. The fiscal and financial dimensions of centre–province relations in Pakistan are addressed in Shahid Kardar, *The Political Economy of Pakistan*, Lahore, 1987. For a range of perspectives on the recent problems in Sind and other provinces see A. Akbar Zaidi (ed.), *Regional Imbalances and the National Question in Pakistan*, Lahore, 1992.

Chapter 6

This chapter weaves together an analysis of caste, class and community in an attempt to unravel the cultural and ideological dimensions of state-society relations in South Asia. Louis Dumont, *Homo Hierarchicus: the Caste System and its Implications*, London, 1970, is the most influential but largely ahistorical study of the role of caste in Indian society. For a critique by a leading Indian sociologist see André Beteille, 'Homo Hierarchicus, Homo Equalis', *Modern Asian Studies*, 13, 4 (1979). A more historically grounded cultural anthropological critique of Dumont emphasizing the political, and not merely the religious, aspects of caste is to be found in Nicholas B. Dirks, *The Hollow Crown: Ethnohistory in an Indian Kingdom*, Cambridge, 1987.

There is a voluminous literature on the Indian state's attempts to address the problem of social inequality. An acerbic critique of discrimination against the lower castes is B. R. Ambedkar, *Annihilation of Castes with a Reply To Mahatma Gandhi*, Bombay, 1945. Several studies by André Beteille have sought to bridge the theoretical and empirical aspects of inequality. See for example his *Equality and Inequality: Theory and Practice*, Delhi, 1983; *Studies in Agrarian Social Structure*, Delhi, 1974 and *The Backward Classes and the New Social Order*, Delhi, 1981. A major philosophical essay on the issue of inequality by a leading Indian economist and philosopher is Amartya Sen, *Inequality Reexamined*, Oxford, 1993.

For an understanding of the Indian state's policies to remove caste-based inequalities it is useful to consult reports of some major commissions of enquiry, for example, Government of India, *Report of the Backward Classes Commission* (K. Kalelkar, Chairman), 1955, in three volumes, Delhi, 1956 and the *Report of the Backward Classes Commission* (B. P. Mandal, Chairman), 1980, in seven volumes, New Delhi, 1981. On the reservation policies of the Indian government see Myron Weiner and Mary Fainsod Katzenstein with K. V. Narayana Rao, *India's Preferential Policies: Migrants, the Middle Classes and Ethnic Equality*, Chicago, 1981. A definitive work on the legal dimensions of reservations is that of Marc Galanter, *Competing Inequalities: Law and the Backward Classes in India*, Delhi, 1984.

For a general account of the role of caste in Indian politics see Rajni Kothari, *Caste in Indian Politics*, New Delhi, 1970. More updated accounts of scheduled caste and backward caste movements in the different regions of India can be found in Francine R. Frankel and M. S. A. Rao (eds.), *Dominance and State Power in Modern India: the Decline of a Social Order*, Delhi, 1989 and 1990. The struggle of the scheduled castes is treated in Barbara Joshi (ed.), *Untouchable!: Voices of the Dalit Liberation Movement*, London, 1986. Jan Breman, *Of Peasants, Migrants and Paupers: Rural Labour Circulation and Capitalist Production in West India*, Delhi, 1985, provides a graphic account of the immiseration and exploitation of scheduled castes and tribes in Gujarat.

The issues of caste and class have always been closely intertwined. For information on the communist parties see Paul R. Brass and Marcus F. Franda, *Radical Politics in South Asia*, Cambridge, MA, 1973. A good account of the Naxalite movement is Sumanta Banerjee, *India's Simmering Revolution: the Naxalite Uprising*, London, 1985. On communism in Kerala see Thomas Johnson Nossiter, *Communism in Kerala: a Study in Political Adaptation*, London, 1982. On the agrarian reforms of the Communist Party of India (Marxist) led Left Front government in West Bengal see Atul Kohli, *State and Poverty in India: the Politics of Reform*, Cambridge, 1987, and Ross Mallick, *Development Policy of a Communist Government: West Bengal since 1977*, Cambridge, 1993. For an exploration of the links between class and gender in movements of political resistance in West Bengal and

Maharashtra see Amrita Basu, *Two Faces of Protest: Contrasting Modes of Women's Activism in India*, Berkeley, 1992. An older study of women's role in rural agitations in Maharashtra is Gail Omvedt, *We Will Smash this Prison*, London, 1980. Bina Agarwal (ed.), *Structures of Patriarchy: the State, the Community and the Household*, New Delhi, 1988, contains three articles on the status of women in India and Bangladesh.

There is no single systematic work on clan-based social structures covering all the different regions of Pakistan. For an analysis of class and clan relations in Pakistani Punjab see Hamza Alavi, 'Kinship in West Punjab Villages', *Contributions to Indian Sociology*, n.s. 6 (December 1972); Saghir Ahmed, *Class and Power in a Punjabi Village*, Lahore, 1977 and Shahnaz J. Rouse, 'Systemic Injustices and Inequalities: *Maliki* and *Raiya* in a Punjab Village' in Hassan Gardezi and Jamil Rashid (eds.), *Pakistan: the Roots of Dictatorship. The Political Economy of a Praetorian State*, London, 1981. David Gilmartin's *Empire and Islam: Punjab and the Making of Pakistan*, Berkeley, 1988, has a good discussion of the ways in which the colonial state came to characterize rural Punjabi society in tribal terms. Also see Akbar S. Ahmed, *Pakistan Society: Islam, Ethnicity and Leadership in South Asia*, Karachi, 1986. Most of these works contain insights into the relation of the ties of clan and class with religious community. On the history of syncretic and reformist Islam in East Bengal society see Asim Roy, *The Islamic Syncretist Tradition in Bengal*, Princeton, 1983, and Rafiuddin Ahmed, *The Bengal Muslims, 1871–1906: a Quest for Identity*, Delhi, 1981.

The analysis on language and religion as ideology draws for information on a number of works while diverging from many of them in emphasis and interpretation. A valuable resource for the study of political culture and ideology is the microform collection entitled *Political Pamphlets from the Indian Subcontinent* in the US Library of Congress, published by the University Publications of America, 1990. Paul R. Brass, *Language, Religion and Politics in North India*, Cambridge, 1974, contains much useful information on language as ideology. Several works mentioned above under chapter 5 are also of relevance in exploring the relationship of language as culture and ideology in the different regions of India. On the adoption of secularism as an ideological pillar of the Indian state, Donald Eugene Smith's *India as a Secular State*, Princeton, 1963, is still the most comprehensive account. For a more critical analysis of the secular aspects of the Indian constitution see Ved Prakash Luthera, *The Concept of the Secular State and India*, Calcutta, 1964. Recent scholarly critiques of Indian secularism include Ashis Nandy, 'The Politics of Secularism and the Recovery of Religious Tolerance' in Veena Das (ed.), *Mirrors of Violence: Communities, Riots and Survivors in South Asia*, Delhi, 1990 and 'An Anti-Secularist Manifesto' in *Seminar*, 314 (1985). See also T. N. Madan, 'Secularism in its

Place', *Journal of Asian Studies*, 46, 4 (November 1987) and 'Whither Indian Secularism?', *Modern Asian Studies*, 27, 3 (1993). The secular position is stoutly defended in different ways in a number of recent studies on the upsurge of communalism. See for instance the collection of essays by prominent Indian scholars in K. N. Panikkar (ed.), *Communalism in India: History, Politics and Culture*, New Delhi, 1990 and Sarvepalli Gopal (ed.), *Anatomy of a Confrontation: the Babri Masjid–Ram Janmabhumi Issue*, New Delhi, 1991. See also Amartya Sen, 'The Threats to Secular India', *The New York Review of Books*, 8 April 1993. Recent studies of the political organization and ideology of the forces representing Hindu majoritarian communalism include Walter Andersen and Shridhar Damle, *The Brotherhood in Saffron: the Rashtriya Swayamsevak Sangh and Hindu Revivalism*, Delhi, 1987, and Tapan Basu, Pradip Datta, Sumit Sarkar, Tanika Sarkar and Sambuddha Sen, *Khaki Shorts and Saffron Flags: a Critique of the Hindu Right*, New Delhi, 1993.

There have been innumerable studies of the Pakistani state's search for an Islamic identity. One of the best primary sources on the ideological battles in the initial years of Pakistan is the *Report of the Court of Inquiry constituted under Punjab Act II of 1954 to Enquire into the Punjab Disturbances of 1953*, Lahore, 1954. Among the more recent studies are Anwar Hussain Syed, *Pakistan, Islam, Politics and National Solidarity*, New York, 1982; various chapters in Asghar Khan (ed.), *Islam, Politics and the State: the Pakistan Experience*, London, 1985, and Hamza Alavi, 'Pakistan and Islam: Ethnicity and Ideology' in Fred Halliday and Hamza Alavi (eds.), *State and Ideology in the Middle East and Pakistan*, New York, 1988. General Zia-ul-Haq's Islamization programme elicited strong opposition in different quarters and not least from women who were the primary target of these policies. On women's resistance see Khawar Mumtaz and Farida Shaheed (eds.), *Women of Pakistan: One Step Forward Two Steps Back*, London, 1987. The relationship of women with Islam and the state in India, Pakistan and Bangladesh has been analysed in three articles by Amrita Chhachhi, 'Forced Identities: the State, Communalism, Fundamentalism and Women in India'; Ayesha Jalal, 'The Convenience of Subservience: Women and the State of Pakistan' and Naila Kabeer, 'The Quest for National Identity: Women, Islam and the State in Bangladesh' in Deniz Kandiyoti (ed.), *Women, Islam and the State*, Basingstoke, 1991.

Index

sovereignty (*cont.*)
  of India, 21, 161, 233
  layered, 158, 257
  monolithic notions of, 5, 15, 28, 122, 158,
    161–2, 225, 229, 248–9, 253–4, 256–7,
    261–2
  of Pakistan, 15, 54, 59
  of pre-colonial empires, 12, 260
Soviet Union, 103, 129, 157, 192
Sri Lanka, 96, 125, 158, 161, 181–2
Sriramalu, Potti, 165, 226
state (*see also* Bangladesh, Indian state and
    Pakistani state),
  central authority in India, 21, 42, 64, 72,
    76, 91, 95–6, 161, 165, 226–7, 237, 240,
    252
  central authority in Pakistan, 18, 22, 36–7,
    49–50, 52, 55, 90, 101, 188, 191, 226,
    250–1, 254
  central authority in South Asia, 2, 157–8,
    160, 245, 246
  centralism and regionalism 2, 12, 16, 75,
    157, 256
  centralism and regionalism in India, 94,
    99, 161, 165, 252–3
  and class power, 144, 156, 269
  coercive power of, 2, 108, 123, 245, 247, 255
  coercive powers in India, 99, 134, 139,
    167, 214, 228
  coercive powers in Pakistan, 49, 55, 81,
    184, 251
  construction and political processes, 2, 4,
    6, 22, 31
  construction and political processes in
    India, 6, 22, 32, 36
  construction and political processes in
    Pakistan, 6, 22, 28 36–7, 50, 53, 55, 184,
    250
  in Bangladesh, 86, 90–1, 116, 140, 154,
    269
  in South Asia, 1, 14, 28, 246, 248
  legacies of colonial, 12, 29–30, 126, 191,
    249
  patronage in Bangladesh, 87, 116–18, 121,
    143–4, 149, 156
  patronage in India, 18, 39, 42, 48, 97–8,
    142–3, 156, 180, 209, 214, 268
  patronage in Pakistan, 6, 56–7, 78, 82–3,
    102–3, 106–13, 121, 142–4, 146, 153,
    156, 184, 188, 195–6, 199, 253–4
  and political processes, 7–8, 67, 122, 143,
    201
  and political processes in Bangladesh, 117,
    119, 121, 249
  and political processes in India, 6–7, 28–9,
    92, 121, 236, 249

  and political processes in Pakistan, 28–9,
    112–14, 121, 236, 249, 251
  and populism, 70, 77, 79–80, 89–91, 121
  power in Bangladesh, 101, 116
  power in India, 4, 45, 97, 100, 123–4, 127,
    227, 245, 250
  power in Pakistan, 4, 84, 104, 106–7, 109,
    111, 148, 153, 229, 232
  and regional dissidence, 2, 8, 157–8, 223
  and regional dissidence in India, 157–8,
    170–83, 199–200, 228
  and regional dissidence in Pakistan, 158,
    183–200, 229–32
  relative autonomy of, 123
  relative autonomy of Bangladeshi, 140,
    156
  relative autonomy of Indian, 124, 127,
    145, 268
  relative autonomy of Pakistani, 140, 145,
    156
  role in development, 122–3, 144
  unitary nature of colonial, 12–14, 18, 31,
    39, 48, 63, 248–9
  unitary nature of Indian, 34, 39, 43–4, 48,
    53, 63, 94, 161–4, 208, 249
  see also civil society; colonial state;
    culture; economy; ideology; Indian
    state; legitimacy; Pakistani state;
    political culture; post-colonial state
states' reorganization commission, 46, 166,
    227
students,
  in Bangladesh, 86, 119–20
  in India, 174, 213
  in Pakistan, 60–1, 186, 196, 221–2, 229
substantive democracy, *see* democracy
Sunni–Shia divide, 239
supreme court,
  Indian, 165, 178, 243, 212–13
  Pakistan, 53
Swatantra, 71
Syed, G.M., 197

Taher, Colonel, 116
Tamil, 42, 46, 92, 158, 167, 181–2, 224,
    226–7
Tamil Nadu, 46, 92, 167, 224, 227
Tandon, Purushottamdas, 39
Tashkent peace accord, 59, 78
Telugu, 46, 95, 165–6, 171, 226–7
Telugu Desam, 95, 170
Tilak, B.G., 26
Toba Tek Singh, 247
tribes, 26
  in India, 166, 175, 213–14
  in Pakistan, 190–1, 193, 216–19, 222